Mississippi Law

Justice, Power, and Politics

Heather Ann Thompson and Rhonda Y. Williams, *editors*

EDITORIAL ADVISORY BOARD

Dan Berger
Peniel E. Joseph
Daryl Maeda
Barbara Ransby
Vicki L. Ruiz
Marc Stein

The Justice, Power, and Politics series publishes new works in history that explore the myriad struggles for justice, battles for power, and shifts in politics that have shaped the United States over time. Through the lenses of justice, power, and politics, the series seeks to broaden scholarly debates about America's past as well as to inform public discussions about its future.

A complete list of books published in Justice, Power, and Politics is available at https://uncpress.org/series/justice-power-politics.

Mississippi Law
Policing and Reform in America's
Jim Crow Countryside

....

JUSTIN RANDOLPH

The University of North Carolina Press Chapel Hill

© 2025 Justin Randolph
All rights reserved
Set in Charis by Westchester Publishing Services
Manufactured in the United States of America

Library of Congress Cataloging-in-Publication Data
Names: Randolph, Justin (Justin Mark), author
Title: Mississippi law : policing and reform in America's Jim Crow countryside / Justin Randolph.
Other titles: Justice, power, and politics
Description: Chapel Hill : The University of North Carolina Press, [2025] | Series: Justice, power, and politics | Includes bibliographical references and index.
Identifiers: LCCN 2025015420 | ISBN 9781469689470 cloth | ISBN 9781469689487 paperback | ISBN 9781469686691 epub | ISBN 9781469689494 pdf
Subjects: LCSH: Law enforcement—Southern States—History | Discrimination in law enforcement—Southern States—History | Police reform—Southern States—History | Racism against Black people—Southern States—History | BISAC: SOCIAL SCIENCE / Ethnic Studies / American / African American & Black Studies | SOCIAL SCIENCE / Sociology / Rural
Classification: LCC HV8145.S88 R36 2025 | DDC 364.975—dc23/eng/20250613
LC record available at https://lccn.loc.gov/2025015420

Cover art: A Mississippi Highway Patrol officer. Danny Lyons. Used with permission from Magnum Photos, Inc.

Chapter 1 includes material from "The Jim Crow Militia: Paramilitary Police Reform and Law-and-Order Liberalism in Mississippi," *Journal of Southern History* 90, no. 2 (2024): 285–324.

For product safety concerns under the European Union's General Product Safety Regulation (EU GPSR), please contact gpsr@mare-nostrum.co.uk or write to the University of North Carolina Press and Mare Nostrum Group B.V., Mauritskade 21D, 1091 GC Amsterdam, The Netherlands.

Contents

List of Illustrations, vii

Author's Note, ix

Introduction, 1
Policing's Ungovernable Hinterland

**Part I
Force**

1 The New South Militia, 19

2 From State Troops to State Troopers, 38

**Part II
Land**

3 Fighting Police in the Rural, 57

4 Cotton Belt and Cattle Prod, 75

5 The Cattleman's Massive Resistance, 94

**Part III
Revolt**

6 States' Rights, State Troopers, 115

7 On Patrol with B. Cowart, 133

8 Mississippi Burning and the New Abolition, 149

Part IV
Public Safety

9 Cattle Pens and Federal Dollars, 173

10 Policing's Futures, 192

Conclusion, 211
Between Mississippi Law and American Law

Acknowledgments, 225

Notes, 229

Bibliography, 277

Index, 301

Illustrations

Figures

"Coat of Arms of Mississippi," 1904, 30

T. B. Birdsong at the Texas-Mexico Border, ca. 1917, 34

Hugh White invests T. B. Birdsong Jr. as commissioner of public safety, 1938, 51

Buford and Bessie Johnson, ca. 1955, 63

Beef cows and incarcerated laborers at Parchman Penitentiary, ca. 1960, 80

Walter Swoope poses with laborers and Angus beef cattle, ca. 1950s, 82

T. B. Birdsong Jr. pins Tom Scarbrough as new commissioner of public safety, 1956, 107

Paul B. Johnson Jr. confronts James Meredith at the University of Mississippi, 1962, 121

SNCC poster of a state trooper and the question, "Is he protecting you?," 1962–64, 123

Stokely Carmichael arrested by state troopers during Freedom Summer, 1964, 136

Fannie Lee Chaney speaks over ruins of Mt. Zion Methodist Church, 1964, 159

T. B. Birdsong Jr. stands with J. Edgar Hoover, ca. 1966, 163

State trooper wrenches an American flag from five-year-old Anthony Quin, 1965, 180

Students protest the killing of Phillip Lafayette Gibbs and James Earl Green, 1970, 195

Elijah Pierce, *Elijah Escapes the Mob*, ca. 1950s, 212

Map

Mississippi with selected counties, cities, towns, and farm communities, xii

Author's Note

I silently standardize grammar and spelling in quoted historical sources when I judge the original to impede understanding. For instance, the verbatim sentence that gives the book's title reads, "you no that Negro ant got no chance in Mississippi Law."

Mississippi Law

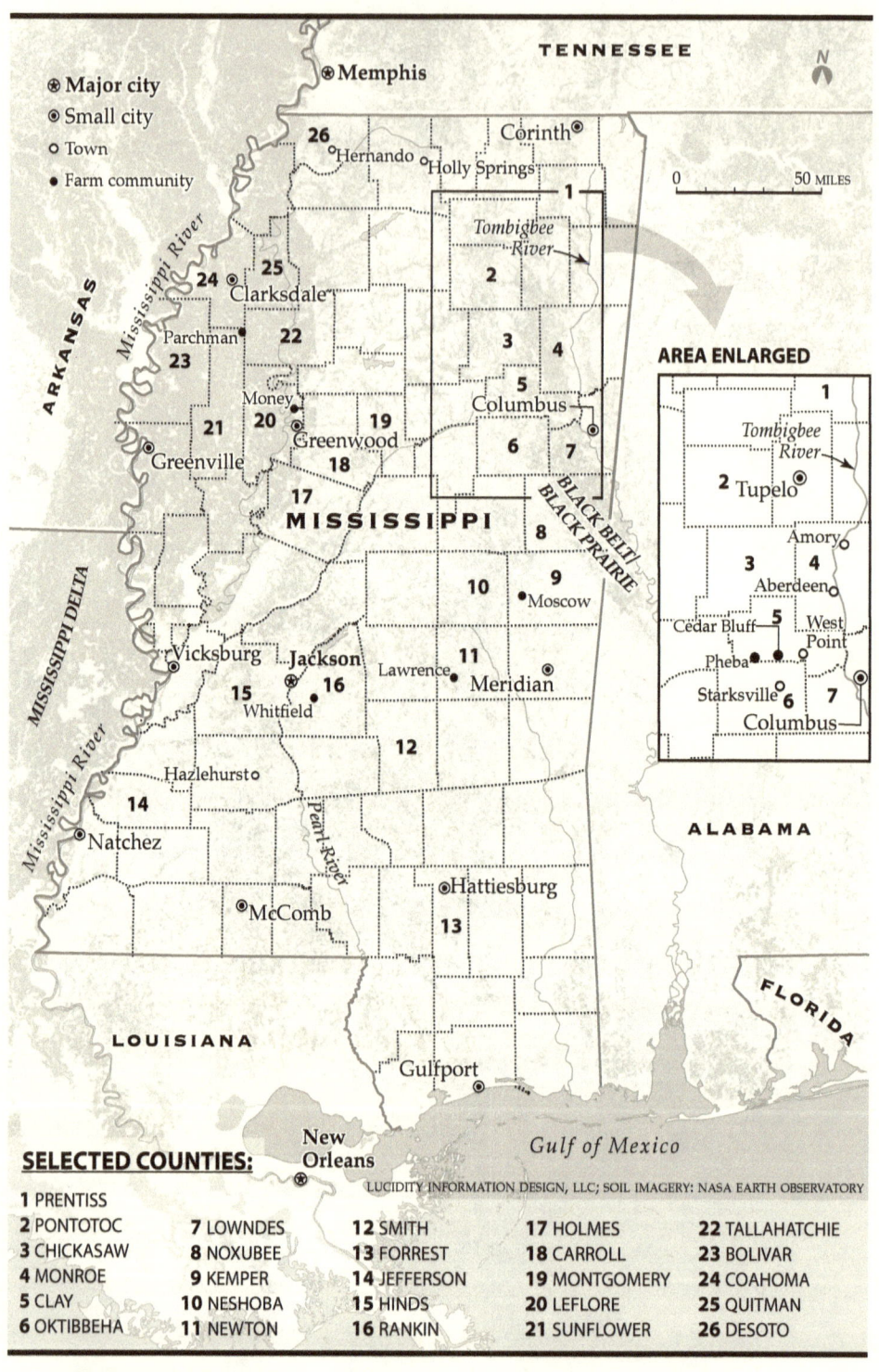

Mississippi with selected counties, cities, towns, and farm communities. Robert Cronan, Lucidity Information Design, LLC; Soil Imagery: NASA Earth Observatory.

Introduction
Policing's Ungovernable Hinterland

In March 1947, the National Association for the Advancement of Colored People (NAACP) received an unsigned letter about policing in Amory, Mississippi. The anonymous author or coauthors urgently relayed the story of Leroy Miller, a twenty-two-year-old African American man whom local police arrested after he asked to borrow a white neighbor's car to search for work. During interrogation, local policemen searched Miller's wallet. They found a photograph of the Black actress Lena Horne, whom they said was a white woman. "They beat him," the Amory author wrote. During this torture, Miller confessed falsely to burglary with the intent to rape a white Amory woman. This false confession instantly raised the threat of lynching, the extralegal mob violence where private citizens often joined local police to murder Black prisoners before they stood trial.[1]

Miller's life was saved from a possible mob, but his rescue came from a peculiar place. State troopers with the Mississippi Highway Safety Patrol took Miller into protective custody and rushed him two hundred miles away. He lived to stand trial, but by the time of the Amory author's letter, Miller sat in the county jail facing twenty years at the state's notorious prison farm, the Mississippi State Penitentiary at Parchman.

The Amory author ended their plea for NAACP intervention fearing Miller's doom: "You know that Negro ain't got no chance in Mississippi Law. So I look to hear from you soon."[2]

Whether written by Miller's mother, a cellmate, or a collective of concerned neighbors, the letter condemned more than a single act of police brutality within an otherwise fair legal structure. The Amory author's indictment of "Mississippi Law" named an entire system of white supremacist law enforcement that took hold in the 1890s and extended well into the 1970s. These lawmen and courts represented the legal guns and chains of what observers came to call the American South's Jim Crow social order, an authoritarian government that depended on manufactured racial and gender difference in pursuit of elite white male power.[3]

Mississippi Law acquitted Emmett Till's murderers in 1955, and it sent Black men and women to work on the chain gang immortalized by Sam Cooke's 1960 song. In June 1964 it killed three civil rights workers in Neshoba County, and in August 1964 a sharecropper named Fannie Lou Hamer told the world about it on live television from Atlantic City, New Jersey. It's the high sheriff in William Faulkner's novels and the judge in Bukka White's "Parchman Farm Blues." Yet the roots of Mississippi Law are deep and tangled; its branches extend far beyond these famous stories and indeed beyond the borders of Mississippi during Jim Crow.[4]

・・・・・・

Mississippi Law: Policing and Reform in America's Jim Crow Countryside explores the historical development of Jim Crow policing from the Gilded Age to the Age of Mass Incarceration. It tracks the ascendance of a particular vision of police improvement that emerged from Jim Crow. This reform, which I have called *paramilitary police reform*, can be seen in the story of Leroy Miller.[5] State troopers saved Miller from lynching but guaranteed his delivery to the penitentiary. Such reform aspired to fix law enforcement by expanding militarized police power and influence over civil society.[6] It grew from an elite white belief that the centralized expansion of policing secured the fundamental conditions for continued economic growth and human prosperity in a society built on racial capitalism: That is to say, in a social order based on white patriarchy and private property, race became real in the pursuit of profit.[7]

At stake in this study is the common sense around whether policing in the South's apartheid regime contradicted or resembled policing across modern American history. *Mississippi Law* disrupts easy assumptions of timelessness, with straight lines from slave patrols to warrior cops. It also unsettles narratives of American redemption, where the law and order of Lyndon B. Johnson's Great Society liberalism might have fixed policing in the South if not for the conservative southernization of American federal power. Instead, this book tracks a crooked path to American liberal democracy in Jim Crow's most notorious racial state. It critically explores the Americanization of Mississippi law enforcement.[8]

The rhetorically race-blind regime of law enforcement that replaced Jim Crow's race-conscious discrimination was under construction for generations. It, like other forms of American policing, enjoyed design support from architects of Anglo-American dominance in North America and around the globe.[9] Within Jim Crow policing there existed one channel of nonpartisan, professional, and bureaucratic law enforcement, with roots in both the US military and the Federal Bureau of Investigation (FBI).[10] This police reform's ascendance in Mississippi was the fulfillment of one vision of American progress that enjoyed nationwide support but fell short of even modest visions of Black freedom proposed by victims of the Southern legal system.

Only a rural history can examine the mix of plans and accidents that yielded modern paramilitary policing in Mississippi. By focusing on the Southern countryside, the rural spaces and processes outside of American cities and urban development, I follow the rise of Jim Crow's elite white police reformers, whom I call *police expansionists*.[11] For these thinkers, societal progress hinged on the economic success of an agrarian ruling class in search of the riches offered by an industrial world. That wealth accumulation depended on the state's reputation, especially as a place to do business. That reputation in turn depended on the state's ability to monopolize legitimate violence and contain a fluid definition of disorder, which might include a white mob of civilians and sheriff's deputies intent on lynching a Black neighbor, Black communities arming themselves in self-defense against white supremacist terror, or the nonviolent civil disobedience of sit-ins, marches, and mass meetings in search of democracy.[12] Police expansionists' work at state-building eventually yielded a state police force, whose state troopers' new jurisdiction overlapped the cop's city limits and the sheriff's county lines.

This state police force protected the segregationist ruling class through America's civil rights movement. The putatively race-blind social order that followed the Jim Crow order was premised on the police expansionists' politics of law-and-order police supremacy.[13] Civil society increasingly lacked basic democratic recourse to investigate or control law enforcement officers and institutions. Moreover, between 1954 and 1980, the inflation-adjusted annual state police budget alone grew 470 percent. Such growth in police capacity and police authority laid an important piece of the groundwork for Mississippi's age of mass incarceration, measured by the state's 550 percent increase in imprisonment between 1980 and 2002. The state's criminal legal system joined a national campaign to arrest and cage human beings at a scale unknown in global history. Incarceration soared because of police wars on drugs and prison-based answers to everyday and societal-scale problems, from interpersonal violence to the massive dislocations associated with deindustrialization and welfare state retrenchment. At the period's peak, the state's Department of Corrections incarcerated Black Mississippians at twice the rate of white Mississippians.[14] To understand the roots of a police power sufficient to criminalize and arrest these detainees in the first place, we must look to historical change in the countryside.

Policing's Hinterland

Mississippi Law tracks the development of policing in a historical context often framed as exceptional in American history. To be sure, the Amory author wrote from a particular time and place. White policemen had attacked a Black man living in the rural American South during Jim Crow apartheid. Under the Jim Crow system of racial hierarchy, only white men could claim the police officer's social power. Mississippi had a higher proportion of Black residents than any US state, 49 percent in 1940. Its economy and lifeway remained tied to the land and farming later than any other Deep South state. And the criminal justice system there was undeniably biased against Black residents. State prison authorities identified more than 80 percent of the 1,900 men and women incarcerated at the Mississippi State Penitentiary as African American in 1947. At Parchman Farm, prisoners grew cotton and tended livestock under armed guard for no pay. Policemen, sheriffs, and state troopers were the front line of an infamous criminal legal system, a carceral state that produced incalculable value for a planter class that held sway through single-party politics.[15] It would be easy to explain this historic period of racist inequality in terms of individual pathology or systems that begin and end at either the Mississippi border or the Mason-Dixon Line.

Mississippi's history of backwater brutality can only be fully understood when it is examined as a landscape of America's history of structural racism. When Nina Simone sang in March 1964 that "everybody knows about Mississippi, goddam," she didn't imply that Mississippi was exceptional in the South or America. Rather, the state's infamy belonged to a "whole country . . . full of lies."[16] In a nation hostile to Black life, Mississippi represented the starkest example of how a common knowledge of racist injustice did not guarantee immediate or even gradual improvement. This history uses rural policing in a Deep South state to reveal something more universal about police improvement in twentieth-century American history.

A rural history of Jim Crow in Mississippi shows the tendency for police reform to veil rather than repair the harms of policing. Urban and industrial spaces like Chicago, New York, Los Angeles, and New Orleans inspire most studies of policing. There, historians have learned important paradigms about policing's role in enforcing residential segregation and gentrification while managing sexual morality, women's bodily autonomy, and economic inequality in the American city.[17] But few studies focus on policing in African American contexts of rural life, such as landownership or agricultural tenancy, like sharecropping.[18] Rural Black Mississippians struggled for recognition and redress when police violence struck America's nonurban countryside. Activists fought against the obscurity commonly associated with a rural hinterland, a frontier, a forgotten place obscured by something more prominent.

Those who fought rural police violence fought to illuminate what I think of as *policing's hinterland*, the secrecy and hiding in which the everyday lawlessness of policing wreaked havoc in pursuit of white supremacy.[19]

More than a literal space or place, this figurative hinterland or hiding place existed anywhere the police wrote their own history. As early as Ida B. Wells's 1892 lecture tour that sought to "turn the light of truth" on "Southern Mob Rule," Black organizing against police lawlessness during the Jim Crow period sought to raise awareness. Martin Luther King Jr. gave voice to this dilemma in *The Nation* magazine in March 1964. "When the glare of a thousand spotlights illuminates the misdeeds of Southern police, their guns and clubs are temporarily muzzled," he wrote. "When a deed can be cloaked in night, the depravity of conduct is bottomless." Fannie Lou Hamer's August 1964 televised testimony about her abuse at the hands of a Mississippi state trooper in the Montgomery County jail was but the best example of an activist successfully spotlighting policing's hinterland, despite President Lyndon Johnson preempting the live broadcast.[20] These civil rights icons and the many more anonymous people who follow hoped to expose and end racist police violence that either avoided the headlines or went unaddressed by people in power.

Mississippi Law often hoped to terrorize or dispose of disorderly people quietly and without spectacle. Instances of Southern police violence could be horrific. In 1970, white state troopers fired military-grade weaponry into a crowd of Black men and women at Jackson State College for thirty seconds, killing two unarmed Black men and wounding a dozen more men and women. Yet policing's violence exceeded the common frame of *police brutality*. These cases that never made the national news were also horrific—the theft of generationally owned Black land, the harassment of constitutionally protected Black activism, income and wealth taken through fines and fees, the time and opportunity stolen with incarceration. Famous as Mississippi was for racial violence, law enforcement prevented many cases of policing from reaching the level of spectacle. Because these cases were numerous and destructive, activists worked to shrink policing's hidden hinterlands, where policing was brutality.

Thought of this way, Jim Crow police reform sought to conceal policing's violence rather than guarantee equal justice. Whether on the city street or the dirt road, policing's hinterland of legal and historical secrecy shielded the unaccountable discretion of individual officers and the political and economic issues that drive criminalization, the process by which the criminal is made in a given time and place. Jim Crow policing constantly had to overcome the crises created by its disposal of loved ones, neighbors, and strangers. Very often, life moved on, even as people disappeared. At other times, as in the case of Leroy Miller or in Fannie Lee Chaney's fight for justice after Neshoba County's Freedom Summer murders of 1964, activist struggles surged. In those moments when people organized to spotlight policing's hinterland, to call into question Mississippi Law's legal legitimacy, police expansionists had to change policing in order to save it.

......

By focusing on Mississippi, the space-made-territory where I was born and where I return to study the past, I hope to appreciate better how state police power so successfully penetrated the rural South during and after the civil rights movement. Mississippi's state police began with fifty-three troopers in 1938 and expanded to 375 by 1970, the year of the Jackson State shooting. Yet, in the wake of this tragedy, police power only grew. By 1974, the number of state policemen grew to 425, all armed with even more state and national funding for training and weapons of war. This change came instead of other imaginable outcomes: squads of deputized Ku Klux Klansmen or privatized, for-profit militias. Instead of the Black freedom struggle's demands for investment in healthcare, food security, public education, housing, a job guarantee, and safe drinking water for all rural Southerners, the South got police.[21]

Pointing down this path are many named and anonymous Black actors who fought against Jim Crow's police power and left traces in the historical record. *Mississippi Law* assembles an archive of materials created by people who experienced Jim Crow policing, their advocates, and the state's all-white criminal legal system—the policed and the police. Newspaper coverage, court filings, military records, oral history interviews, and the work of other historians supplement the book's investigation. Such an archive is necessary because most police records from the period are either lost to time or remain intentionally classified by state officials. The sources that survive show law enforcement in Mississippi to have operated through a more familiar criminal legal system, one always already reformed from a less civilized arrangement.

The Mississippi Highway Safety Patrol, a central subject of this book, came to epitomize paramilitary police reform in the rural state. This standing state police force emerged from infrastructure development. The state's investment in automobility provided the opportunity for police expansionists to institutionalize a durable, everyday paramilitary force with deeper roots in slavery and empire. Mississippi's age of wagon and rail gave way to its age of car, truck, and bus through a program of state-subsidized highways that began in the 1930s. In the realm of the everyday, troopers controlled driver licensure and wrote legally binding reports on traffic accidents. They also profiled Black motorists for fines through traffic stops, assaulted drivers on the roadside, surveilled civil rights activists, and tortured successful Black organizers in the rural jails that often served as police stations. In this mode, highway patrolmen helped to segregate the experience of participatory politics, life, and commerce through their spatial control of mobility across rural space.[22]

Yet the state police also played a peculiar role in limiting mob violence in Mississippi. Rather than the organization's sense of racial justice, this owes to its roots in counterinsurgent police practices that policed enemies of elite-defined progress.

America's state police forces grew from America's quest for an orderly overseas empire. The first state police force, the Pennsylvania State Constabulary, was modeled on a colonial force created in the Philippines during the US occupation that followed the Spanish-American War of 1898. In Pennsylvania's coal fields, these new state troopers helped to break strikes. During the nation's Gilded Age labor disputes, troopers sometimes policed and sometimes aided the private police forces employed by businessowners to brutalize working people, like Pinkerton and Baldwin-Felts agents. As the historian Matthew Guariglia has argued, the architects of early twentieth-century police reform, men like Berkeley, California's August Vollmer, slotted hopes for colonialism's centralized police power into state police forces at home.[23] Projecting the legitimacy of a professional, scientific, yet brutal policing was a paramount concern at home as it was on America's imperial frontiers.

In 1947, the Highway Patrol simultaneously provided Leroy Miller protection from a lynching and facilitated his disposal through the courts. Patrol administrators knew that municipal cops or county sheriffs were as likely to participate in a lynch mob as to stop one. Yet they sought similar ends through legal means. A grassroots lynching equated with lawlessness, but a state-led execution was order.[24] To interrogate this dynamic, the temporary, selective, or public valuing of Black life in service to longer-range racist domination, is to explore Jim Crow police reform in America.

The term *police reform* may conjure contemporary ideas of perfecting urban police practice, but reform is as old as policing in Mississippi. Michel Foucault's study of the prison offers a historical paradigm that applies. "Prison 'reform' is virtually contemporary with the prison itself," he wrote in 1975. "From the outset, the prison was caught up in a series of accompanying mechanisms, whose purpose was apparently to correct it, but which seem to form part of its very functioning."[25]

As an arm of the South's prison regime, lawless police violence coexisted with and thrived on paramilitary police reform to expand racist control in Southern society. When I write of Jim Crow *policing* or *police power*, I think less about crime fighting or the idealized drive to investigate crime and punish offenders to protect the vulnerable. Instead, I hope to shed light on the state's legal, political, and social power to enforce a given political economic vision through law enforcement tactics, what Jim Crow's police reformers called "public safety." They did so first in 1890, when they rewrote the state constitution to exclude most Black citizens along with many unruly white citizens, and again in 1938, when they created a Department of Public Safety to house the state police. The tools of public safety included guns, handcuffs, nightsticks, tear gas, polygraphs, and other weapons used to protect the reigning public and private interests of the state's white elite. To be sure, lawmen did more than racial control in their police work, inflicting one vision of safety on society. But as this book shows repeatedly, activists challenged the definition of safety that accompanied Jim Crow law enforcement in their hope to protect Black life and property.[26]

Elite white Mississippians struggled to control various levels of law enforcement in rapidly changing political and economic environments. They also frequently disagreed. As C. Vann Woodward wrote in the 1950s, and Barbara Fields reinforced in 2001, the central question of the Jim Crow racial order was less white supremacy than *"which whites* should be supreme."[27] In Mississippi's system of law enforcement, rivalry most often erupted between sheriffs and state policemen. Sheriffs and deputies often ruled their county's rural environs absolutely, using their office's prerogative to profit personally and to structure local economies to benefit their clients.[28] State police boosters, on the other hand, were more likely to have connections to the US government, whether through the military or the judiciary. Whereas sheriffs often sought to conserve the power granted to them under the aristocratic model of antebellum society, expansionist state police reformers often believed most fervently in enabling and governing free trade and mobility across county and state lines. As business progressives, expansionists commonly justified their program of centralized police power with race-blind rhetoric about equal enforcement of the law.

This book thus reads Jim Crow policing as a laboratory for the coexistence of racial authoritarianism and liberal law and order. A strand of paramilitary police reform emerged with the Gilded Age New South creed of the 1870s and evolved rapidly alongside the post–World War II transformation of rural economies and the Black freedom struggle.[29] It might be difficult to imagine a liberal creed thriving in Jim Crow Mississippi, given the state's long-standing role as a signifier of either the illiberal American radicalism sometimes confused with conservatism or the mere passive vestiges of empire, feudalism, and chattel slavery.[30] Yet the scholar Naomi Murakawa's definition of "law-and-order liberalism" shows how expansive this common ground could be: "Liberal lawmakers . . . confronted racial violence [in the criminal justice system] as an administrative deficiency. In the ideology of liberal law-and-order, police brutality was the unsanctioned use of force, but more procedures and professionalization could define acceptable use of force. Lynching was lawless mob violence, but capital punishment could be fair. . . . The more carceral machinery was rights-based and rule-bound, the more racial disparity was isolatable to 'real' black criminality."[31] Despite their peculiar historical context, Jim Crow's police reformers aligned with some liberals on the buildup of policing and a prison state. They often did so within larger Right-wing movements to enforce their understandings of welfare state retrenchment, traditional values, and natural hierarchy.

Leroy Miller faced modern enslavement on Parchman farm, but he fought a system far greater than the residual or repackaged force of a secessionist antebellum Southern aristocracy and its slave patrol. He also, importantly, fought the onslaught of a forward-looking and Washington-looking elite. These white supremacists strategically rejected mob rule and embraced policing as a force for color-blind equal rights so long as the right to white progress on white land went fundamentally unchallenged for themselves and their children. In their actions, police expansionists looked less toward Jefferson Davis than a Southern Democrat like Woodrow Wilson, who called the lyncher "no true son of democracy, but its betrayer" and warned of tarnishing America's "global reputation."[32] Mississippi Law balanced investments in futurity and reaction.

The age of massive white resistance to desegregation brought a new class of white race moderates who finally succeeded in expanding the state police. In exploring policing as another facet of "Jim Crow liberalism," where white reconciliation upheld local and national systems of racial caste through most of the twentieth century despite diverse African American activism, I join the historian N. D. B. Connolly, who warns "not to take at face value the presumed divides between classical liberalism, growth liberalism, civil rights liberalism, and neoliberalism."[33] Paramilitary policing and its reform was one category where traditional partisan divides could fall away. Self-pronounced liberals and conservatives united to yield an elite order and rule that denied any fundamental interrogation of the armed force and ways of knowing that maintained a social system premised on inequality.

Through the state troops and then state troopers, a reformist elite strove over decades to install an American military ethic of discreet barbarism in Mississippi law enforcement. Such state police power echoed the armed violence that propelled the nation to the world stage through Native dispossession and removal, the enslavement of peoples of African descent, overseas wars of imperial aggression, and the militarization of borders.[34] In fact, the white man who founded Mississippi's state police force, Thomas Butler Birdsong Jr., came from a family of settler militiamen and Confederate officers. He policed ethnic Mexicans at the US-Mexican border during World War I and aided anti-Communist Chiang Kai-shek in China after World War II. At times he worked closely with J. Edgar Hoover and the Federal Bureau of Investigation. Ultimately, he guided Jim Crow policing toward the federal funding of the Law Enforcement Assistance Administration (LEAA), created by Lyndon B. Johnson in 1965. In thought and legacy, Mississippi's Jim Crow police reformers reached for a canonical handbook of law and order, a governing strategy they linked directly to myths of the justified Anglo domination of North America.[35] This book singles out one strain of white supremacist thought that strove not toward unfettered mob rule, but toward a deliberate future of guaranteed, exclusive economic growth in a world imagined to be beset by enemies and occupied territories.[36]

Policing's Autocracy

The architects of Jim Crow's police power enjoyed neither perfect rationality nor absolute agency in molding the world to their vision. They did not usually intend to protect all Black people from white supremacist violence—physical, economic, or otherwise. Nor did they always mean for policing to harm people they considered innocent. Rather than an obsessive drive to micromanage racial disorder, the ruling-class design for maintaining white power relied on deputizing lawmen as agents of what we might call *policing's autocracy*: the discretionary, racist lawlessness that survived beneath claims of civilized, sincere law enforcement by virtuous or well-trained individuals.

As a framework to name the way lawlessness functioned at the core of Jim Crow law enforcement, policing's autocracy builds on studies of law-based orders under slavery, colonialism, and empire. I deploy *autocracy* in a way similar to W. E. B. Du Bois's use of *anarchy* in his 1911 poem "A Hymn to the Peoples": "We see the nakedness of Toil, the poverty of Wealth, / We know the Anarchy of Empire, and doleful Death of Life!"[37] For many Black Mississippians, only disorder followed police reform's promises of orderly progress. Police officers could not be ruled, and that was the point.

My use of policing's autocracy means to reappropriate the idea of disorder from the class that continually used the specter of "anarchy" to legitimize rule through disorder. In 1894, Stephen D. Lee, one of the men who pioneered the Jim Crow National Guard, decried "the spasmodic disorders and anarchy such as we have seen too often of late."[38] In September 1967, just months after white lawmen killed an unarmed Black man named Benjamin Brown on the streets of Jackson, Governor Paul B. Johnson Jr. said, "There is no place in America for anarchy. Our structure must continue to be a government of law and not of men—nor of mobs."[39] By 1970, Bob Howie, a Jackson-based cartoonist, responded to the Jackson State shootings with a sketch showing a Black hand attempting to throw a brick labeled "anarchy." A white hand labeled "law and order" interceded. This book shows that the real riot was the slow, simmering police riot at the core of Jim Crow authority.[40]

Policing's autocracy allowed Jim Crow lawmen to maintain diverse relationships to lawfulness and decency. Some openly worked with mobs while others fought them. Highly trained state troopers investigated the Ku Klux Klan *and* participated in brutality, torture, and the slayings of Black people. By simply enforcing the law Jim Crow policemen could hasten the departure of Black agrarians from the land. They racially profiled motorists for traffic stops and wrote predatory tickets that extracted Black wealth to benefit the separate and unequal Jim Crow state. Police neglect was rampant. Officers often refused to investigate crimes against Black Mississippians, especially but not exclusively those involving white people. As formal policing outgrew lynch law, the harmful actions of individual police officers totaled a destructive racial structure that fed on a culture of impunity, whether it made the headlines or survived in the shadows.

Federal courts routinely affirmed policing's autocracy, even as they struck down other pieces of the South's Jim Crow racial order. In the case of Leroy Miller, the US Supreme Court refused to hear Leroy Miller's case on appeal from Mississippi's Supreme Court, despite the inspired efforts of Thurgood Marshall and the NAACP's Legal Defense Fund. The Supreme Court tacitly affirmed the state court's ruling, which described Miller's treatment as "reasonable and time-tried police methods . . . to protect the peace and safety of law-abiding people against anti-social characters."[41] Tossed between crises, Jim Crow's reformers injected more of policing's ungovernability into various contexts that promised lawfulness but frequently delivered brutality and violence. The Amory author named this dynamic "Mississippi Law."

At times, Jim Crow lawmen admitted this lawlessness. When Winona, Mississippi's chief of police arrested Southern Christian Leadership Conference activist Annell Ponder in June 1963, Ponder reminded the chief about the legality of desegregated interstate bus facilities. He snapped, "Ain't no damn law," and took the group that included Fannie Lou Hamer to days of torture in the Montgomery County Jail.[42] The Winona chief signaled the reality of policing in America's Jim Crow countryside. Local police, jailers, and state troopers combined to produce the power that existed in the terror of the county jail and policing's other hinterlands.

Black Mississippians regularly argued that policing was itself a primary force for disorder in rural life. And this book joins the work of academic historians who have sought to comprehend the structural violence inflicted on rural Black Southerners over the twentieth century, to explore law enforcement's role in the loss of 800,000 acres of Black-owned real property in Mississippi between 1950 and 1964, as well as to better appreciate the fight of so many Black farmers—renters and owners—to stay on the land or near family and community.[43]

The promise of policing's autocracy convinced crucial white constituencies of the benefits of state police centralization during key moments of contingency. Between the Highway Patrol's creation in 1938 and 1964, proponents of local law enforcement and mob rule remained skeptical about the state police's relationship to their self-interests. For example, in 1941, troopers asked for general police powers to patrol everywhere sheriffs and cops did, and white newspapers in turn compared the state police to Nazis. After World War II, the state legislature defunded and scaled back the patrol's jurisdiction. However, during the rural upheaval that accompanied mechanization and reallocation of farmland, popular opinion shifted. Many who had previously rejected state police power embraced a new Livestock Theft Bureau (established 1950) that carried general police powers for the first time in state history. The true breakthrough came during the civil rights movement, when the Highway Patrol tripled in size. Troopers received conditional statewide jurisdiction and a training academy through which to influence law enforcement across the state.

Cows played an important role in the history of police reform in Mississippi. In the state's rural hinterland, white capitalists selectively joined police reformers to control the agricultural innovation that brought an end to cotton monoculture. After World War II, beef cattle ranching joined other land-intensive agriculture like dairy, soy, timber, and catfish to replace labor-intensive cotton. But only beef got its own state police force. Jim Crow police power helped shape the rural world that accompanied the creation of beef cattle pastures from the cotton lands once home to Black tenants and landowners. In 1890, when this book begins, any acre of land in Mississippi had a one-in-ten chance of being planted in cotton. By 1980, when it ends, any acre had a one-in-ten chance of being a pasture.[44] Mississippi's white cattlemen became a new class of rural power brokers after the global crisis in meat production that accompanied World War II. Cattlemen summoned and participated in particular forms of policing, such as the Livestock Theft Bureau, to police African American farm communities that threatened white visions of profit and progress. During massive white resistance to desegregation in the 1950s, Mississippi's land use began to look much more like the rest of the continental United States, where, as of 2018, an estimated 41 percent of total land was dedicated to livestock production. Many of Mississippi's pastures had earlier been cotton fields tended by Black sharecroppers.[45]

· · · · · ·

The Amory author could not save Leroy Miller from Mississippi Law. The NAACP brought his case to the US Supreme Court, and still Miller spent fourteen years at Parchman. However, in asking for help, the author signaled belief in a social arrangement where Black people might yet have a chance in the rural South. True, the writer could already name a system where, more so than the mob, the police, the courts, and the prison were salient threats to Black life. But he or she was not so pessimistic as to believe a meaningful truth could not be told through "investigation" of Miller's case. Accordingly, this book at times explores the alternatives to Jim Crow police supremacy proposed by activists and organizers across Mississippi's Black freedom struggle, between the end of the convict lease and the onset of mass incarceration. It follows the political and intellectual labors of a diverse cast of players, from Black mothers drawn into organizing by police violence to middle-class movement leaders active in the Black church to white volunteers and movement lawyers who saw their lives fundamentally tied to Black America's. These activists and thinkers fought to shine a light on policing's chaotic hinterland.

After World War II, Mississippi's disparate Black freedom movements at times cohered around resistance to the carceral state's enforcement of racial hierarchy. For many whose actions landed in the historical record, this activism involved summoning a strong federal government to police the police. Many put forward their own ideas of police reform to protect Black life and property through the courts or to enable Black people to join Mississippi's law enforcement agencies. The NAACP's intrepid activist-scholars dedicated significant energy to cases of Jim Crow policing like Miller's, sweeping such cases into files marked "police brutality," a frame that broadcast their hope that America's policing of Black life might one day be governable.

Some activists who confronted Mississippi Law grappled with the limits of expansionist police reform and proposed police reorganization. Some people fought back, even taking up arms against state troopers in defense of life or land. Some imagined desegregated or all-Black police forces to keep their communities safe.[46] Others sampled all alternatives and built coalitions in hopes of abolishing Jim Crow and, with it, Jim Crow policing, the way a previous generation had abolished chattel slavery. In so doing, activists raised enduring questions about the future of policing's hinterland.

· · · · · ·

As a history from the ground up, this book's most detailed examples come from northeast Mississippi's Black Prairie region, the state's non-Delta Black Belt that borders Alabama and is drained by the Tombigbee River. I conducted my first oral history interviews with Black farm owners there in 2012. Those interviews launched this yearslong study of rural policing and resistance that blends the macro- and microhistorical, focusing on long-term processes and ephemeral events.

The book views the evolution of policing and reform in four distinct chronological phases. In part I, "Force," Jim Crow apartheid emerges alongside paramilitary police reform. Chapter 1, "The New South Militia," shows how white supremacist Redeemers centralized police power after 1876 as a means to bring modern capitalist order to the countryside after Reconstruction's biracial democracy. Activist intellectuals like Ida B. Wells struggled for safety as white militia families like the Birdsongs haltingly monopolized paramilitary state power. In the new Mississippi National Guard, Thomas B. Birdsong Jr. carried that ethos to the Texas borderlands during World War I and returned with new perspectives gleaned from the US Army and Texas Rangers. In chapter 2, "From State Troops to State Troopers," Birdsong guards public executions at home in the 1920s and '30s. Here, the segregated state police force matures alongside other forms of early Sun Belt infrastructure: state highways and state-subsidized industrial relocation.

Part II, "Land," begins with World War II, when everyday Black Mississippians began to organize against racist policing through national civil rights organizations. In chapter 3, "Fighting Police in the Rural," activists like the mother and sister of Leroy Miller repurpose the NAACP to fight against the displacement of policemen, sheriffs, and troopers in the courts. In chapter 4, "Cotton Belt and Cattle Prod," state policemen find friends in cattle farmers, agribusinessmen who desired the control of pastureland more than the coerced manual labor of cotton farming. Chapter 5, "The Cattleman's Massive Resistance," shows how white supremacist reformers, many of whom had connections to the white Citizens' Council movement and the beef cattle economy, empowered police to punish more people, especially people perceived to be activists, during crises surrounding the US Supreme Court's decision in *Brown v. Board of Education* (1954) and the murder of Emmett Till (1955). A new generation of segregationists leveraged histories of beef cattle raising and policing to fight the budding civil rights movement.

Part III, "Revolt," marks a climax in the struggle around policing. In chapter 6, "States' Rights, State Troopers," Mississippi's Highway Patrol grows in size and authority as a result of the Black freedom movement's nonviolent direct action campaigns for civil and voting rights. Troopers deploy against the Congress of Racial Equality's Freedom Rides (1961), the organizing work of Fannie Lou Hamer (1963), and the Student Nonviolent Coordinating Committee's Freedom Summer (1964). Chapter 7, "On Patrol with B. Cowart," shows the impact of a single state policeman on grassroot organization in one northeast Mississippi farm community through surveillance, harassment, the investigation of racial terror, and ultimately, his death. The same highway patrolmen who police the Black freedom movement also selectively police the Ku Klux Klan in order to position the state police as the paramilitary answer to Jim Crow's extralegal contradictions. In chapter 8, "Mississippi Burning and the New Abolition," the freedom movement poses an alternative to expansionist police reform traditions following June 1964's Freedom Summer murders. Around a federal lawsuit, *COFO v. Rainey*, activists collect affidavits about police lawlessness and propose federal judicial oversight instead of state police supremacy. Seen alongside new experiments in mutual aid organizing, such truth-telling and reform constituted a modest alternative disparaged by white racial liberals and defeated by racial authoritarians.

In part IV, "Public Safety," police expansionists join a new cast of federal allies to remake policing for the post–Jim Crow world. Police desegregation brings significant change to Mississippi Law but leaves unanswered important questions about militarization and the police secrecy on which a new regime of police supremacy is built. Chapter 9, "Cattle Pens and Federal Dollars," shows the bellicose response of local and state policing after Freedom Summer. Policemen use the cattlemen's tools and infrastructure to reassert order and punish political enemies. Segregationists join a War on Crime that ignores their own lawlessness. In chapter 10, "Policing's Futures," movement lawyers desegregate the state police after the Jackson State killings. And as the direct action movement fades into memory, local activists with the American Civil Liberties Union fight for government transparency around past policing of civil rights activism. Though they attempt to open historical records of the state police, activists only succeed in opening the archives of the abolished Mississippi State Sovereignty Commission.

Mississippi Law does not chronicle the innumerable acts of police violence in Jim Crow Mississippi. Rather, it traces the historical forces that produced an ever-growing litany of victims and survivors of policing. It shows that the ascendance of police supremacy was far from an inevitable outcome, explores the specific conjunctures through which police power was consolidated, and studies alternatives posed. It directs our gaze toward the history of police expansion through reform. If Jim Crow policing created crises, paramilitary police reform proved to be a crisis of its own.[47]

Part I Force

1 The New South Militia

> Public sentiment by its representatives has encouraged Lynch Law, and upon the revolution of this sentiment we must depend for its abolition.
> —Ida B. Wells-Barnett, *The Red Record* (1895)

Writing in 1877, a former US congressman and Confederate general named Winfield Scott Featherston grieved Mississippi's reputation in the world. "The impression prevailing abroad," he feared, was "that our people look with too much leniency upon those who violate the law & slay their fellow men, that ours is a land of bloodshed & violence." In an unpublished treatise titled "But Much Yet Remains to Be Done," Featherston called for state laws to be "faithfully administered," to ensure that "life, liberty & property are well protected without regard to race, color or previous condition." If lawlessness continued, he feared for Mississippi's future: "The assurance must be given to immigrants from every land & country, that ours is a community of peace, where law & order are properly respected & enforced before they will seek a home in our midst. Desperados and bad men may voluntarily locate in a state where turmoil and strife, violence & bloodshed exist, but good citizens never will."[1]

Until his death in 1891, Featherston pursued state police power to curb violent disorder, including instances of racial violence with which he disagreed. Rather than turning to county sheriffs or local policemen, he hoped to professionalize Mississippi's volunteer paramilitary police force, at times called the state militia, the state troops, or the Mississippi National Guard.

Featherston focused on law enforcement in the aftermath of a yearslong coup that overthrew biracial Reconstruction government in Mississippi. A Democrat, lawyer, and state legislator from Holly Springs, he showed no remorse for the Black and white residents brutalized and killed in campaigns that "rescued the state government from the grasp of our political adversaries."[2] The so-called Mississippi Plan of 1875 had depended on the unpoliced violence of armed white men who called themselves White Liners or Red Shirts. Through murderous extralegal violence, mobs intimidated Republican voters and stole local elections. The fraudulent election of

November 1875 swept in a state legislature controlled by the Democratic Party that then impeached the Republican governor and lieutenant governor in 1876.³

By 1877, Featherston worried not about democracy but about press coverage surrounding ongoing extralegal racial violence. "Such violations of law here," he wrote, "are made to appear as immense mobs of almost daily occurrence." To his mind, this bad publicity explained the state's inability to modernize, to attract "men of families" who might bring capital, labor, expertise, and an industrial economy. "The sure & speedy enforcement of all laws for the prevention & suppression of crime," Featherston wrote, "will be the most effective means of . . . drawing immigrants & capitalists to us."⁴

The Black truth-seeker, teacher, and journalist Ida B. Wells shared a common landscape with Winfield Scott Featherston, but she had other hopes for the New South militia. Born into chattel slavery in 1862, Wells grew up just blocks from the Featherston family home in Holly Springs. Her parents died in the same 1878 yellow fever epidemic that killed Featherston's wife. Both Wells's mother and Featherston's wife went by Lizzy. Yet by 1892 Wells lived as a refugee intellectual, in exile from the postwar racial order that Featherston helped to create.⁵

In the 1880s Wells began reporting on extrajudicial mob violence—lynching. A mob destroyed her Memphis newspaper, *Free Speech*, and threatened her life after she wrote anti-lynching exposés in 1892. That year she wrote her first widespread pamphlet, *Southern Horrors: Lynch Law in All Its Phases*, from her home in New York. *The Red Record: Tabulated Statistics and Alleged Causes of Lynching in the United States* (1895) followed. In Chicago, Illinois, Wells married Ferdinand Lee Barnett and began raising four children. Across the South, victims of lynching numbered as high as four thousand between 1882 and 1930; in Mississippi, the number surpassed 550 between 1881 and 1940. Until her death in 1931 Wells wrote and organized to stop what she called "lynch law," the South's legal regime of chaos.⁶

Early on, the state militia loomed large in Ida B. Wells's prescribed remedy for lynch law. In *Southern Horrors*, she wrote that lynch mobs persisted because white terrorists knew "that neither the law nor militia would be employed against them."⁷ Her hope in the militia as a paramilitary police force of last resort grew from the Black experience of Reconstruction. In Holly Springs and then in Memphis, Wells saw armed Black militiamen in the streets. Often integrated and supported by white Republicans, Black militias claimed space in an environment of competing armed force during

Reconstruction. Black militias checked the racial totalitarianism of white supremacist militias.[8]

As Wells watched armed white men overthrow the multiracial democracy established during Reconstruction, her hope in the militia waned. In 1892, she closed *Southern Horrors* counseling that "a Winchester rifle should have a place of honor in every black home, and it should be used for that protection which the law refuses to give." By 1895, Wells believed that only a "revolution" of "public sentiment" could overthrow the new racial regime. This complex system of inequality required "abolition," as had the South's earlier regime of chattel slavery.[9] In 1917, she wrote that "the police were either indifferent or encouraged the barbarities" of East St. Louis, Illinois's white riot. "The major part of the National Guard was indifferent or inactive. No organized effort was made to protect the Negroes or disperse the murdering groups."[10]

This first chapter explores the evolution of paramilitary state police power in Mississippi, from its roots in Native removal and slave patrols. It pauses to consider the place of formal law enforcement as imagined during Mississippi's constitutional convention of 1890, where lawmakers formulated the race-blind blueprint of legal segregation and voter disfranchisement. Then it turns to one of the militia's first inheritors, Thomas Butler Birdsong Jr.—a man who used his National Guard service at the US-Mexico border during World War I to create Mississippi's modern state police force.

Rangers and Slave Patrols

On the day Ida B. Wells was born in Holly Springs, Mississippi, in July 1862, Winfield Scott Featherston was recovering from a combat wound somewhere in Virginia. A brigadier general in the Confederate army until its surrender in April 1865, he spent the next twenty-five years centralizing Mississippi's state militia.[11]

Featherston dedicated much of his life to defending white male supremacy and elite dominion. Born in 1820 near Nashville, Tennessee, Featherston volunteered at age sixteen to fight as a militiaman in Georgia's Second Creek War (1836). The war ended in the forced dispossession and removal of thousands of Muscogee Creek people at the behest of white real estate speculators and would-be cotton farmers, a common path for white settlers to enforce President Andrew Jackson's national policy of Indian Removal.[12] Featherston became a lawyer in 1840 and moved to the ancestral lands of the recently removed Chickasaw people in north Mississippi. In Holly

Springs, Featherston entered proslavery politics. He enslaved twelve Black people in 1860, aged three to thirty-five.[13] Featherston even served as one of Mississippi's secession commissioners before the Civil War. In late 1860 he traveled to Kentucky to convince that state's lawmakers to align with the emerging slaveholders' republic, only to be spurned by unionists there.[14]

Featherston's fight for Native dispossession and racial slavery was the fight of the American militia. As scholars of Native North America have shown, squatter settlers organized armed bands to push the boundaries of territorial possession before, during, and after the American Revolution. West of the Appalachian Mountains, militias harassed, killed, and otherwise displaced Native populations during bids to achieve US territorial status and statehood. Territorial and state militias often adopted the names used by earlier, irregular fighting forces, like *rangers* and *rifles*, which remained synonymous with genocidal violence on the frontiers of white dominion.[15]

In 1799, Mississippi's territorial governor Winthrop Sargent signed a law creating a permanent reserve militia consisting of "all free male inhabitants between the age of sixteen and fifty." Settlers were to equip themselves with weapons and drill on the second Saturday of every month in anticipation of "invasion . . . or domestic disturbances, actually existing or apprehended."[16] The militia-fueled drive toward Native removal—though never complete—only intensified with the cotton boom and the ascendance of Andrew Jackson to the presidency on the promise of wholesale dispossession of Native nations and deportation of Native peoples to lands west of the Mississippi River.[17]

By the time Featherston joined his first militia in 1836, lawmakers had expanded the duties of Mississippi's militia to include that of a slave patrol. The Mississippi territory achieved statehood in 1817, and white settlers established a cotton economy based on the perpetual chattel enslavement of people of African descent.[18] In 1822, lawmakers moved the state capital from Natchez to Jackson. That year, legislators consolidated slave patrol laws so that "every owner of slaves, and all other persons . . . liable to perform militia duty" were also "liable to perform patrol duty." So synonymous was the word *patrol* with *slave patrol*, that the two words never appeared together in the legislation. The militia's discretion to surveil and intervene in Black life was extensive. They could "visit all negro quarters, or places suspected of containing unlawful assemblies of slaves, or other disorderly persons unlawfully assembled." Patrolmen could also administer corporal punishment at their discretion, up to fifteen lashes to any enslaved person thought to be off-plantation without permission from an enslaver.[19] Historians argue that such race-based surveillance and arrest powers formed the foundation of all American policing and did not fundamentally change with the abolition of chattel slavery in 1865. Vagrancy laws criminalizing a Black person's inability or refusal to work followed emancipation. And states established systems to lease state prisoners to private contractors with no meaningful intervention from federal authorities.[20]

But the slave patrol's work of racialized policing found a particular home in the state-sponsored militia after Reconstruction. After the fraudulent elections of 1875, Republican Governor Adelbert Ames disbanded the state's five Black militia companies under pressure from Democratic officials who would eventually force him to resign under threat of impeachment. By 1877, the last US troops returned to their garrisons, and Mississippi lawmakers recognized fourteen white militia units with names like the Dixie Guards, the Oktibbeha Rescues, and the Senatobia Invincibles. In 1880, at age sixty, Featherston commissioned his own Featherston Guards in Holly Springs.[21]

It was one thing for the state legislature to centralize its white militias legally; material support was another matter. The eighteenth-century ideal of self-funding remained the norm despite the force's increasing shift to a voluntary model. In 1876, the legislature promised five cents per day to militiamen if called upon by the governor.[22]

Even by 1888, when legislators approved the official centralization of state militias into the Mississippi National Guard, the designation came with a new name and organizational flowchart—not state funding. The state's senior military officer, the adjutant general, hoped the legislature would appropriate $10,000 for a 1,700-man militia and "keep abreast of her sister States in progressive movements."[23] He encouraged the state to take advantage of a recent federal appropriation to fund each state's National Guard, counseling that "eminent writers say [guardsmen] make the best and cheapest police force in the world."[24] The adjutant general reported that the state's arsenal of guns and ammunition could be found "in quite an unsafe condition" under the stairs of the capitol's Senate chamber. Tents and knapsacks lay scattered in spare rooms across Jackson. Hundreds of thousands of rounds of ammunition sat in a railroad depot. Because the appropriation for his salary had lapsed, the adjutant general himself was in fact volunteering, not working for pay.[25] Watching from his high perch in state politics, Featherston took his concerns and hopes for reform to the state constitutional convention that met in August 1890.

Jim Crow's Constitution

"We came here to exclude the negro. Nothing short of this will answer." Solomon Saladin Calhoon, a white judge from Hinds County, thus described the purpose of Mississippi's 1890 constitutional convention.[26] Calhoon presided over the convention to overturn the state constitution of 1868, which had guaranteed Black male suffrage in a state where over 50 percent of the population was Black. The 1890 state constitution signaled a formalization of the extralegal system of antiblack discrimination, disfranchisement, and terror that began to take hold in Mississippi towns and farm communities as early as 1871, despite the continued use of US troops as a pro-Republican police force. Waves of election-centered violence followed, as in 1875, when Democrats organized armed bands to police Black neighborhoods and polling stations in what came to be called the Mississippi Plan.[27] The presidential election of 1876 dealt Black Southern voters another blow. Despite a clear victory for the Republican candidate Rutherford B. Hayes, Democrats in South Carolina, Florida, and Louisiana sent competing electoral votes to Washington, DC, throwing the election into chaos. Amid a constitutional crisis, Democrats negotiated a compromise: They would recognize Hayes as the rightful president with the understanding that he would remove US soldiers as a police force from Southern states.[28]

However, the withdrawal of US Army troops in 1877 foreclosed neither the elective franchise nor judicial participation to Black Mississippians. Black candidates were elected to local and state office with frequency. Black men also served on petit and grand juries. In 1881, Winfield Scott Featherston kept a running list of all members of the Holly Springs grand jury by race and party affiliation. Four Black Republicans and four white members of the local Greenback movement sat alongside eleven white Democrats to sign bills of indictment for the state court.[29] Featherston's obsession was not misplaced. As poor and downwardly mobile farmers, Black and white, organized against the planter-dominated Democratic Party, political solidarity and violence once again flared in the late 1880s.[30] Featherston viewed the threat of interracial fusion voting as an attempt to reinstall Reconstruction government, "a restoration of the reign of terror from 1868 to 1876."[31] Generations of historians have shown that Jim Crow's architects believed the exclusion of Black neighbors from civic life would create a one-party state and settle fundamental questions raised by the threat of cross-racial political mobilization and social equality among poor men and women.[32]

By 1890, an elite white political coalition assembled in Jackson to cement the place of Black Mississippians outside of the body politic. Following a brief electoral victory by a biracial fusion of Republicans and agrarians in 1887, conservative Democrats sought to reinstall order and reassert their rule of law.[33] Over months, they drafted a new constitution that provided the legal foundation for local policies of racial segregation. The men also enshrined a system of legal voter suppression based on local discretion. Adopted later by other Southern states, this so-called Second Mississippi Plan depended on literacy tests to determine those "legally competent to vote," and poll taxes to disqualify cash-poor voters.[34] These tools in the hands of local voter registrars disfranchised Black voters for decades.

Such forthright determination to discriminate against Black Mississippians has marked the convention and its legal strategy as reactionary and unsophisticated, a blatant attempt to restore the status quo antebellum. But delegates conceived of their work differently.

In their own minds, they were reformers. One delegate hoped the new constitution might "show to the world that Mississippi . . . stands in the fore front of reform for the attainment of justice and right under all circumstances."[35] With this belief, delegates sought to stamp their ideas of progress onto foundational notions of representative government. They thought an all-white body politic would help prove the expedience of what they simultaneously called *white supremacy* and *good government*.[36] Delegates also debated the intersection of race and public safety in the context of drug use. For those interested in prohibiting the sale and consumption of alcoholic beverages, a single issue could bridge antiblack racism, classism, and xenophobia toward recent European immigrants. "There are seventy-five counties in Mississippi," wrote a group of prohibitionists to the constitutional convention. "The thirty-five wet counties are in the blackbelt and are kept wet by the negro vote." Prohibitionists asked the convention to disfranchise Black Mississippians in order to generalize county prohibition laws. They delivered one of the most frequently quoted clarifications of the convention's intent, asking "what are you here for, if not to maintain white supremacy, especially when a majority of whites stand for a great principle of public morals and public safety? We especially appeal to the delegates from the black counties. . . . How long is it to be expected that white solidarity can be maintained, if the negro is to be brought forward to arbitrate this great question in the interest of a minority of the whites, and they mostly foreign born, and not in sympathy with our institutions?"[37] "Public safety," "white supremacy," "white solidarity"—these were largely synonymous for those troubled by moral degeneration, vice, and democracy. In Mississippi, as was the case nationally, these principles collided to spawn a racial ideology built on assumptions of inherent Black criminality and bloc voting tendencies.[38] Public safety became the reformers' euphemistic watchword for centralized police power, culminating in the creation of a Department of Public Safety in 1938.

Enacting their sense of progress, reform, and justice, delegates forcefully condemned notorious pieces of the state's criminal legal system. For example, the constitution banned the practice of leasing incarcerated men and women to private citizens or corporations after five years, beginning January 1895.[39] Instead of the convict lease system, delegates embraced a state monopoly on forced labor tied to vital infrastructure development, such as road construction, levee maintenance, and agricultural production at a state-owned prison farm.[40] Importantly, the convict lease continued under other names until 1906, when the state government centralized its forced labor regime at the Mississippi State Penitentiary, located at Parchman in Sunflower County. Parchman would be the state's only prison until the 1970s. And yet, Mississippi's statutory abolition of the convict lease predated all other former Confederate states. Its practical abolition predated some Southern states by two decades.[41]

In Jackson, Winfield Scott Featherston approached state law enforcement reform with equal zeal. Featherston chaired the 1890 convention's Committee on Militia, composed of other prominent Confederate veterans, and decried the "circumstances by which we are now surrounded." At age seventy, he and other committee members foresaw growing disorder, writing that the "great disparity in some localities between the two races which now occupy our territory; the occasional outbreaks between them which result in acts of violence and loss of life, and the occasional resistance made by both races to the enforcement of the law through the courts of the country, render it necessary to have a military force ready at all times to respond to the call of the State." Featherston's committee recommended that the state pay to maintain a force of a thousand professional militiamen "to enforce the laws, to suppress riots and unlawful assemblies, and to preserve peace and good order." Importantly, he also called for an annual appropriation of $10,000.[42]

At age seventy, Featherston was still an Indian fighter in *occupied territory*. He had seen different disorderly populations threaten the ambitions of his class. Perhaps for that reason he brought a more race-blind understanding of counterinsurgency to the constitutional convention. Black residents, the committee implied, held no monopoly on the lawlessness that threatened the ruling white elite. The disorder, more than the disorderly, was the obsession of Mississippi's Jim Crow reformers. The state needed trained, non-volunteer troops at the ready because the land was once again inhabited by a desperate class of people who might foil elite plans for development.[43]

Featherston's emphasis on "disparity" drew on an economic understanding of the roots of disorder. Earlier in his career, Featherston had spoken like an anti-capitalist in his fight to reassert white government and cut Republican taxes. "The wealth of the nation is being concentrated in the hands of the capitalists & corporations," he once said in a speech around 1876. "The laboring, toiling masses must be oppressed when this is the status of affairs. The millions are drawn from the hard earnings of the masses by unjust legislation & poured into the coffers of the millionaires." Featherston was unsurprised by the militant response to rising inequality. "Strikes, secret societies, communists, nihilists, & anarchists"—these were "the legitimate result of this state of affairs."[44] By 1890, he argued that any systemic project to disfranchise Mississippi's majority Black population had to prepare for this racialized economic disparity. Framers of Mississippi's Jim Crow constitution thought that their white supremacist revolution would require armed soldiers to subdue a more intensely subjugated Black population. Featherston no doubt had recent high-profile cases in mind.

. . . . . .

The past year had seen the militia deployed against the insurgent Colored Farmers' Alliance. In 1889, Black Alliancemen who organized around the living and working conditions of farmers began to turn political capacity into concrete demands. They developed a cooperative store, gave public speeches, and marched in armed military formation when threatened by white elites. In August 1889, Sheriff L. T. Baskett summoned three companies of white militiamen to Minter City in Leflore County. On August 31, a white messenger warned the sheriff that "the negroes in that section were in arms to the number of about 500 . . . and threatened to burn and slay as they advanced to the county seat." More pressingly, Black leaders George Allen, Oliver Cromwell, and Dolph Horton "had 2,000 alliance men (colored) who would stand by them." This threat by armed agrarian revolutionaries, thought to wield Winchester repeating rifles, moved the sheriff to summon the militia.[45]

Black survivors of the military action reported a pogrom. As the historian William F. Holmes rediscovered in the 1970s, Black observers labeled this military action the "Leflore massacre" and viewed it as a death blow to the Colored Farmers' Alliance in the Mississippi Delta.[46] When the white state troops arrived in Leflore County on the night of September 1, 1889, they took a steamboat to Minter City and immediately arrested forty Black people. Though the sheriff dismissed the militia soon after they arrived, armed white bands continued to roam the countryside for Black Alliancemen. "The negroes had broken up into small squads and had taken to the cane-brakes," the sheriff wrote. "Some of them were overtaken, and resisting arrest, were killed." Other survivors reported that Black deaths numbered one hundred, that white mobs had invaded homes and murdered noncombatant Black women and children.

Elite proponents of militia centralization blamed such turmoil on the excesses of lawless white men who also threatened the legitimacy of the Jim Crow social order. By 1894, still begging for the appropriation suggested by Featherston, the adjutant general reminded the legislature that the militia "has on several occasions saved the State from a disgraceful blot upon the pages of her history."[47] In Pascagoula, an artillery unit thwarted the lynching of two white robbers. In Lincoln and Marion Counties, militiamen reported to halt "whitecap sympathizers" from liberating white men arrested for whitecapping—armed extralegal violence organized by white agrarians to drive Black farm families from land believed to have been stolen from white farm families through foreclosure.[48] Such lawlessness would continue, the adjutant general reported. Reliance on a sheriff and his posse meant "meeting a mob *with a mob*, under no restrictions, under no commander, and unorganized; the direct results of which have not been, cannot be and will never be anything but disgraceful and detrimental to the best interest of society and the public good."[49] The militia, he dreamed, could be more than a mob.

Winfield Scott Featherston died in 1891, not living to see the legislature act seriously on his request for state funding. However, the national government stood ready to fund some aspects of the Jim Crow National Guard. In early 1892, the adjutant general reported that federal legislation had appropriated almost $8,500 for "arms, ammunition, equipments, camp outfit, and uniforms."[50] The state only had to organize and assign officers to a given number of guardsmen to qualify for the funds. In March 1892, the state legislature appropriated $5,000 to help make the Mississippi National Guard eligible for its federal dispensation. By 1895, the governor and adjutant general found it necessary to remind National Guardsmen that the clothes and weapons dispensed by the US government were meant to be used only during military service to the state.[51]

Featherston's Militia Committee made perhaps the first systematic argument for centralized, paramilitary state police power in Mississippi. Like him, those with military experience led this movement for the next seventy years. And while unique contexts differed between 1890, 1938, and 1964, the basic race-blind logic described by Featherston at the state constitutional convention stalked later debates of state police power over local law enforcement. White elites meant for Mississippi to exist in a state of "disparity"—legal, economic, human. Jim Crow's framers harbored little doubt that their new white supremacist democracy would require a militarized police force of last resort.

The Jim Crow government enshrined this spirit when it chose a new set of symbols. In 1894, a special legislative committee chose a new state flag. It featured a Confederate battle flag and likely meant to signify that they believed the Confederacy's ideals had triumphed one generation after secession. These Redeemers, or Bourbons, as Southern Democrats were sometimes called, had reversed the losses suffered during the Rebellion and Reconstruction, like the Bourbon monarchs who had regained power between the French Revolutions of 1789 and 1848. A reminder of their victory over enemies, Black and white, would fly over every court in the state. For decades to come, the myth of a Confederate Lost Cause, or the honorable fight for states' rights against an invincible foe, swept the region's white supremacist public culture, with Confederate monuments and flags as totems of the historical amnesia surrounding a war to save and expand slavery as well as an oligarchic plantation economy.[52]

Jim Crow's founders symbolized more than white freedom from federal power. The Confederate project had been about more than white Southern men fighting to preserve slavery in Holly Springs, Mississippi. It had also been about the right to expand and export Holly Springs's system of authority and wealth accumulation based on racial domination to the rest of the world.[53] This had been an American mission of Native removal, imperial instigation, and annexation (e.g., Alabama, Texas, California) before it became a hallmark of Southern nationalism.

Crucially, the same 1894 legislative committee that produced a neo-Confederate state flag also designed Mississippi's coat of arms. Below an eagle and cotton stalk, a red scroll unfurls reading "Virtute et Armis," Latin, the lawmakers said, for "by valor and arms." With this act of heraldry,

"Coat of Arms of Mississippi," in *The Official and Statistical Register of the State of Mississippi* (Brandon Printing Co., 1904), opposite p. 330. Mississippi Department of Archives and History.

Mississippi's Jim Crow lawmakers announced their new regime's guiding sentiment. The invention looked backward and forward, casting about for what they thought the State of Mississippi had been about and what it should be about in the future. For their announcement of heredity, they chose the settler state's ideal of legitimate violence wrapped in manly virtue.[54]

T. B. Birdsong, the Texas Rangers, and the US-Mexico Borderlands

On December 15, 1908, thirty years before he created Mississippi's state police, Thomas Butler Birdsong Jr. sat in a courtroom in Hazlehurst,

Mississippi. He was only fourteen years old but probably recognized the moment's gravity. His father, a militia officer with the same name, sat at the defense table—sobbing. Tom Sr. was on trial for his life. It was not the first time this south Mississippi family sat in court.[55]

The Birdsongs had been embroiled in scandal for three years. On November 25, 1905, nineteen-year-old Angeline Fox Birdsong—Tom Jr.'s aunt—shot and killed Dr. T. H. Butler in Monticello, Mississippi. Newspaper reports and court testimony conflicted. Some believed that Mrs. Birdsong attempted suicide and then shot Dr. Butler five times because he had bragged to others about "intimate" liaisons with her, a married woman.[56] When indicted for murder, Birdsong pleaded self-defense, implying that Butler had attempted to rape her before she shot him.[57] Both parties had elite family ties to governors, US senators, and railroad commissioners; the sensational case made national as well as regional news.

Angie Fox's crime thrust her husband's family into the spotlight. Dr. James Stapleton Birdsong was a dentist, the grandson of a slaving Georgia militiaman, and the son of a Confederate Army officer in the US Civil War.[58] Birdsong had married Fox when he was thirty-two; she was just thirteen years old.[59] Ignoring her claims of self-defense, a jury convicted Angie Birdsong of manslaughter and sentenced her to five years in Parchman Penitentiary on December 11, 1906. She would have been the first white woman at Parchman Farm, but Governor James K. Vardaman pardoned her before the start of her sentence in July 1907.[60]

The Birdsongs reappeared in headlines eighteen months later. On December 10, 1908, James Birdsong's older brother, Thomas Butler Birdsong Sr., also a dentist, shot and killed yet another physician, Albert B. Pitts, whose medical practice sat across the hall from Birdsong's dental practice in Hazlehurst. Pitts had complained about Tom Birdsong Sr. hosting whiskey-soaked parties during business hours. Upon learning of the physician's criticism, a visibly inebriated Birdsong burst into Pitts's office while he was examining a Black patient named William Sumrall. The dentist stepped past Sumrall and shot Pitts point-blank in the chest and "groin." After a brief standoff with law enforcement, Birdsong surrendered. He reportedly said, "Well, I intended to do it, and I've done it." Despite this admission of malice aforethought, Birdsong claimed drunkenness in court, unable to recall the incident.[61]

Like his grandfather, Tom Birdsong Sr. was a militiaman. Before murdering Albert Pitts, Birdsong led the National Guard to suppress white mob violence against Black Mississippians in the whitecapping crisis of 1893.[62] In 1898, he commanded a company of men who trained for (but saw no action in) the Spanish-American War.[63] All the while he also led the state troops' social scene in Hazlehurst. At banquets, balls, and parades, he attended festivities that projected Old South military gallantry and celebrated the sacredness of white womanhood.[64]

Nonetheless, this second murder turned white neighbors against the Birdsongs. According to newspaper accounts, the prospect of Birdsong himself being lynched was not out of the question. Birdsong's legal team recognized the popular outrage and convinced their client to plead guilty in hopes of avoiding the death penalty. In an extraordinary turn of events, members of the Birdsong family even signed an oath to the Pitts family. They promised that if Tom Sr.'s life were spared, they would never petition for a pardon or parole. The judge agreed, sentencing Birdsong to life in prison.[65] Apparently the Pitts family and Hazlehurst moved on. Governor Earl Brewer quietly pardoned Birdsong in 1915 after only seven years of incarceration on the Rankin County penal farm—not the state penitentiary at Parchman.[66]

The contradictions of American law enforcement could hardly be clearer than in Tom Birdsong Jr.'s family history. Monied white lawlessness and impunity defined generations of life that might have otherwise been marked by banishment, incarceration, and forced labor.

It's hard to know how this history of lethal violence impacted young Tom Jr. But evidence suggests he sought escape. In 1910, less than two years after his father's conviction, Birdsong left home. Just sixteen, he dropped out of high school, moved to the Delta town of Clarksdale, and joined the state militia of his father and Winfield Scott Featherston. In fact, Birdsong lied about his age in order to join the militia two years earlier than the law allowed.[67]

Outside of militia life, Tom Jr. survived in a modernizing Southern economy that reserved its best opportunities for white men. He worked as foreman of a railyard before joining his brother in a small electrician business. In 1914 he even traveled to Schenectady, New York, to attend a three-month course on electric generators offered by General Electric. This might have been Birdsong's middle-class, workaday existence.[68]

But Birdsong's hopes turned to the military. He earned his first promotion to officer in 1913, having served just three years in the militia. By 1915, at age twenty-one, he had risen to the command of his entire National Guard company. As the Texas borderlands began to interest the US government as a frontier of World War I, Birdsong saw an opportunity to transform part-time militia service into full-time military duty.

......

As trench warfare raged in Western Europe, the 1911 Mexican Revolution against president and dictator Porfirio Díaz continued in the US-Mexico borderlands. On March 9, 1916, Mexican revolutionaries affiliated with Pancho Villa's movement against Venustiano Carranza's US-supported constitutional government raided Columbus, New Mexico. In order to militarize the southern border, President Woodrow Wilson's order of June 18, 1916, called for an entire "war-strength" unit of National Guardsmen from each of the forty-eight states. On October 17, 1916, 1,819 militiamen left Jackson by train for San Antonio, Texas. From there, Mississippi's all-white guardsmen trained on long marches through rugged chapparal. They practiced shooting rifles and machine guns. They dug and defended trenches.[69]

Young Tom Birdsong probably imagined a glorious military career. At the border, Birdsong sought a commission in the regular US Army. After the US declaration of war on Germany in April 1917, he attended an Officer Training Corps camp at Ft. Logan H. Roots in Little Rock, Arkansas. He also solicited letters of recommendation from lawyers, professionals, and elected officials in Clarksdale to support his application for a commission. "Since I have known him, I have found him to be a gentleman of the highest sense of honor and integrity," wrote a US district court official.[70] Another assured Birdsong's examiners that "he has never touched a drop of intoxicating drinks"—hedging against Tom Sr.'s infamy. At the end of this first attempt, however, Birdsong failed his final exam and was forced to return to the border, where he headed an artillery unit.

At the end of the National Guard's border service, Birdsong remained in Texas, where he received a provisional appointment in the US Army. From November 1917 to October 1919, he served as second lieutenant in the Third Infantry, which remained at the border near Eagle Pass, Texas, and Piedras Negras, Coahuila. There, he observed the military-cum-police paradigm of the Texas state police force, the Texas Rangers. He also witnessed the Lone Star State's unique relationship between police power and cattle farming.

As Mississippi's militiamen arrived in San Antonio in the fall of 1916, the Texas state police was growing in scale, form, and jurisdiction. In the aftermath of Mexican-led raids on key sites of Anglo colonization (such as the million-acre King Ranch near Corpus Christi), Governor James E. Ferguson

Texas, ca. 1917. Thomas Butler Birdsong Jr. poses with rifle at the US-Mexico border during World War I. Courtesy of James Birdsong.

ordered the Ranger force doubled to twenty-six by April 1915. Many of the new lawmen were so-called Special Rangers, leading Anglo citizens—especially cattlemen—who lacked any tie to formal law enforcement and worked without pay. Instead of money, Special Rangers desired legal sanction to make war on ethnic Mexicans they accused of cattle rustling. Many Special Rangers belonged to the Texas Cattle Raisers Association who became deputized vigilantes and rode alongside veteran rangers and US soldiers dispatched to the borderlands. By 1919, 400 Special Rangers reinforced 150 payrolled rangers.[71]

In short, the rangers pioneered policing's autocracy. They frequently remade the rule of law in order to realize local systems of elite rule through white supremacy against Native, Black, and Mexican people. Most of the time, rangers contributed to a climate of terror for racialized enemies. One ranger named Napoleon Jennings described this law enforcement mandate along the border in the 1870s: "We went [to Matamoros] for two reasons: to have fun, and to carry out a set policy of terrorizing the Mexicans at every opportunity."[72] At other times rangers escalated their work to meet the removalist or genocidal impulse associated with America's westward expansion. Historians William Carrigan and Clive Webb estimate that mob violence claimed the lives of at least 550 ethnic Mexicans in Texas between 1848 and 1928.[73] During the Mexican Revolution, rangers manipulated the documentary record to avoid publicity or accountability for anti-Mexican violence. For Birdsong, perhaps, rangers were the apogee of unapologetic white male rule. For historians, the rangers epitomize armed force in the United States' continued settler conquest of North America.[74]

During the Mexican Revolution and World War I, a ranger was still somewhere between a police officer and a soldier. Though the ranger force fell under the authority of the Texas adjutant general, politicians frequently exploited the rangers' legal designation as law enforcement officers to their advantage. In February 1914, after the death of a prominent cattle rancher near Laredo, Texas, Governor Oscar Branch Colquitt telegrammed Woodrow Wilson's secretary of state, William Jennings Bryan. "I do not want to invade Mexico with a military force," the governor reassured Bryan. "I asked your consent to allow me to send Texas Rangers, who are peace officers, in pursuit of those who are constantly transgressing our laws."[75] As agents of the state, Colquitt reasoned, rangers might supersede international law. Often, a governor's threat was enough to elicit the support of federal troops. Indeed, as Birdsong's tenure with the Third Infantry attests, thousands of regular Army troops remained at the border after militiamen returned home or deployed to Europe.

· · · · · ·

No direct correspondence survives between Birdsong and rangers from the 1910s or '20s. However, by 1938 Birdsong invited Texas state police to train Mississippi's state police—as we'll see in the next chapter. And in 1952, Birdsong posed for a photo alongside leaders of the Texas Highway Patrol during a trip back to the Lone Star State.[76] Birdsong may have developed his first ties to Texas law enforcement while assigned to the border. He clearly maintained connections with Texas police for decades.

Birdsong also knew that rangers trampled basic human rights in their policing of ethnic Mexicans. For instance, he likely heard of the ranger massacre at nearby Porvenir while he was stationed at Eagle Pass in January 1918.

Cross-border raids for beef cattle and supplies intensified as one of the coldest winters on record swept the Southwest. Mexican revolutionaries sought provisions in the Big Bend region of west Texas, where the Rio Grande curves south before bending back north on its course to the Gulf. On December 25, 1917, forty-five Mexican raiders attacked a cattle ranch owned by Lucas Charles Brite, an executive board member of the Texas Cattlemen's Association. Thought to represent Pancho Villa, the group killed several civilians, including a postman, while robbing the Brite Ranch general store. An armed posse pursued the group to the border, and a unit of US cavalry followed into Mexico, killing many in the raiding party.[77] Four days after the Brite Ranch raid, rangers pursued cattle rustlers into Mexico from El Indio Ranch near Eagle Pass. Though not ultimately deployed, Birdsong likely readied to cross into Mexico when officers placed the Third Infantry on alert.

Rangers escalated their everyday harassment of ethnic Mexicans in the Big Bend after Brite Ranch. Ranger leadership mobilized for weeks to terrorize Hispanic residents they accused of being in league with revolutionaries. Word of the pending retaliation had likely spread to W. L. Wright, a sheriff from Wilson County who organized a new ranger company for Laredo.[78] "I see that they are haveing some fun in the big bend," he wrote the Texas adjutant general ominously on December 28, 1917. "I wish I was out there."[79]

Under the leadership of James Monroe Fox, ranger Company B began to harass residents of Porvenir, a small border community of ethnic Mexican farmers and ranchers. On January 24, 1918, rangers roused the village in the middle of the night, illegally searched their homes, and abducted three men at gunpoint. The rangers released their captives but returned in the wee hours of January 28 with four prominent ranchers and the Eighth US Cavalry. Convinced that residents of the village were aiding and abetting Mexican raiders, the rangers and ranchers detained fifteen unarmed men and boys while cavalrymen looked on. The rangers then summarily executed the group and fled into the night. Residents of Porvenir publicized the murder of their loved ones; Company B included no mention of Porvenir in their official report for January 1918.[80]

Tom Birdsong remained at Eagle Pass, Texas, while a year of legislative investigation into ranger violence unfolded. An inquiry led by a Brownsville legislator named José Tomás Canales demonstrated how rather than an exception, the Porvenir massacre had been but the least deniable instance of police murder against ethnic Mexican noncombatants in recent memory. For two weeks in January 1919, witnesses appeared before a joint session of the Texas state legislature. The hearings produced some 1,500 pages of typed testimony and led to several reforms that guaranteed the rangers' survival for the next round of frontier defense. Importantly, the ranger force professionalized, with higher training standards and higher pay for a smaller force.[81]

These reforms took hold as Birdsong finished his time at the border. With no prospects to continue in the regular Army, he perhaps pondered how to leave civilian life behind. Maybe he hoped to become a law enforcement officer after serving full-time at the border.

His opportunity came quickly. Birdsong's police work began the day he returned home from the border, in October 1919. Having stepped off the train in Clarksdale, Mississippi, Birdsong identified the actions of a Black man as an attempt to steal a car. Convinced of his duty to intervene, the twenty-five-year-old performed a citizen's arrest. Mimicking a Special Ranger, the vigilante brought his prisoner to jail, and the Coahoma County sheriff immediately offered Birdsong a job as deputy. He rose to Clarksdale's chief of police by 1928. And, as we will see in the next chapter, as the age of rail gave way to the age of the automobile, all of Mississippi's rural highways fell under his jurisdiction. Though he remained in the Mississippi National Guard, it was in the field of paramilitary law enforcement that Tom Birdsong fought disorderly enemies every day.[82] That martial ethic would have been impossible without his experience at the southern border.

2 From State Troops to State Troopers

> If mobs and mob methods must be, it would be better that their existence and their methods shall be kept wholly separate from the courts.
>
> —Virgil Alexis Griffith, dissent, *Brown v. Mississippi* (1935)

"A snarling wolf pack disguised in human clothing cried out for blood as three black boys went to their doom on the gallows." Glen Norse, a correspondent for Pennsylvania's Black-owned *Pittsburgh Courier*, saw not fellow humans but monsters in the predawn glow of March 16, 1934. He was in Hernando, Mississippi, as a crowd assembled to view the public execution of three Black men, Ernest McGhee, Johnny Jones, and Isaac Howard, aged twenty-three to twenty-five. The journalist's report was grisly, sparing no detail of the young men's final moments. Norse worked so the three men died in less obscurity than they might have otherwise. In this depiction of capital punishment, Norse captured fundamental changes in Mississippi's performance of the rule of law and racial justice.[1]

According to Norse, lawmen refused to cultivate a mass terroristic spectacle. Instead, the county sheriff and state troops discouraged public attendance of the state-sponsored execution. DeSoto County announced and newspapers published that the execution would occur hours later than it did. Instead of mid-morning on Friday, the sheriff executed the three men at four a.m.—before sunrise. A crowd of some fifty onlookers learned of the change and attended nonetheless. Some were intoxicated; others sang. Adults arranged for twelve young white girls to attend, Norse reasoned, because an all-white jury had convicted the three men of raping a seventeen-year-old white woman, Mildred Collins.[2]

Twice as many armed and uniformed men stood between the crowd and the condemned. Under the command of Thomas Butler Birdsong Jr., some one hundred Mississippi National Guardsmen drove McGhee, Jones, and Howard between protective custody in Jackson's Hinds County jail and the courthouse in Hernando, almost two hundred miles each way. Troops protected the hanging from any civilians or local law enforcement who might have participated in the extrajudicial mob violence that defined Jim Crow Mississippi and would recur sporadically for twenty-five more years.[3]

To Norse, the National Guardsmen were simply the new lynch mob. At times, he wrote, the all-white state troops desired to "participate in 'THE FUN,' as they called it." Some condescendingly chided the local sheriff as unprofessional. "Damn poor arrangements," one soldier scoffed when the gallows malfunctioned. Another guardsman brought a portable video camera to capture the execution on film. Norse pushed readers to consider what white supremacist inhumanity might look like after mob violence. The transition to legal lynching required a state police presence.[4]

This chapter explores how, as lynch law declined over the 1920s, '30s, and '40s, Mississippi's domestic state police power increased. It seeks to redirect our gaze onto the individuals and systems that reformed spectacle lynching into legal lynching in the Jim Crow order.[5] It begins by documenting the role of state troops in reforming extrajudicial mob violence into capital punishment. Next, it follows Tom Birdsong from policing Black vice and entertainment economies with the National Guard to creating the Highway Patrol. It concludes by showing the threat of centralized police power to Mississippi's local systems of white clientelism and inequality, especially the county sheriff.

Reforming Lynching

The prevalence of attempted extrajudicial murder fluctuated between the world wars. White Mississippi, like white America, unleashed a torrent of racial violence in the years after World War I. Historian Terence Finnegan estimates that between 1919 and 1924, when the cycle of mob violence peaked in Mississippi, the five-year moving average of documented lynching incidents in the state doubled from five to ten. After 1924, the average number of attempted extrajudicial murders fell until the 1930s, when white Mississippians again averaged four attempted lynchings per year. By 1940, the five-year moving average fell below two attempted lynchings.[6] The threat and practice of extrajudicially murdering Black Mississippians was a cornerstone on which all other social discipline relied. The threat extended to Black professionals, property owners, day laborers, domestic workers, and children alike.[7]

Meanwhile, the number of state-controlled executions in Mississippi grew steadily after 1919. Though there was no universal increase, the five-year moving average for sheriff-administered hangings surpassed the same metric for lynchings in the 1930s. Mississippi's eighty-two counties executed on average seven people per year in the mid-1930s, as many as the previous high in the 1900s. Of the fifty-three men and women legally executed in Mississippi between 1930 and 1939, newspapers identified only four as white men. The overtaking of lynching by legal execution was a product, in part, of paramilitary state police power.[8]

As early as 1890, Mississippi governors deployed the Jim Crow National Guard to protect criminal proceedings against Black defendants. In the spring of that year, Anthony Thomas stood accused of murdering Leila Lofton, a thirteen-year-old white girl. The Smith County sheriff, R. J. Harding, immediately sent Thomas to Jackson for safekeeping in the Hinds County jail. With bayonets drawn, state troops escorted Thomas back to the justice of the peace for arraignment. He returned for trial in Smith County Circuit Court on April 29, 1890, where he pleaded guilty and was sentenced to die one month later. Outside the courthouse that day, a mob took Thomas from the sheriff and prepared to hang him. The circuit court judge and a future governor, Anselm J. McLaurin, convinced the mob to release the prisoner to local law enforcement. The state hanged Thomas on May 28, in front of a crowd estimated at between two and three thousand spectators. One white newspaper speculated that Thomas's was the first legal execution in Smith County's fifty-seven-year history.[9]

This pattern repeated infrequently through the Jim Crow period, though lynch mobs sometimes challenged state troops and swayed state politics. In June 1927, hysteria swept Mississippi as law enforcement and mobs sought a perpetrator accused of the rape and murder of two white women on a Jackson dairy farm. A newspaper editor named Dennis Murphree had become governor just three months earlier, following the death in office of Henry Whitfield, a college president who sent an annual "Get to Know Mississippi Better" train through the United States in hopes of stimulating capital investment and immigration. The threat of a lynching in Mississippi's commercial center distressed Murphree, himself an industrial booster.[10]

Police officers and vigilantes established a racial profiling dragnet across the state, doing untold harm to Black Mississippians and Mississippi's public reputation. Murphree dispatched National Guardsmen to protect four Black suspects in the Hinds County jail on June 6. By June 7, fears of insurrection were so great that state troops escorted a Black Jackson resident named Walter Burley out of the state after he allegedly confessed while detained in the Hattiesburg jail. From Mobile, Alabama, on the Gulf Coast, Alabama National Guardsmen transported Burley to Kilby prison in

Montgomery. An elaborate prisoner transport followed on June 19, when Alabama officials transferred Burley back to Mississippi state troop custody, and a special train carried him to Jackson for trial. There, awaiting the prisoner was Tom Birdsong with 616 armed National Guardsmen. Overnight, troops had constructed a barbed-wire barricade and no fewer than six machine-gun nests to repel the mob estimated at 15,000 men and women. A jury found Burley guilty after one minute of deliberation, and the Hinds County Circuit Court set his execution for July 22. The state hanged Walter Burley under Guard protection.[11]

Dennis Murphree's bid for a full term as governor did not survive the scandal ginned up by his use of state troops against white mobs. Murphree ran an economic development campaign with taglines such as "Good Business Is Good Politics" and "Dennis Murphree Is a Good Business Man." His opponent, former governor Theodore G. Bilbo, politicized Murphree's use of the National Guard to protect Black life, however temporarily. Bilbo, who had refused to prevent lynchings in his first term (1916–20), returned to the governor's chair for another four years in 1928. Endorsements of Murphree and the National Guard from organizations like Jackson's Exchange Club, Biloxi's Chamber of Commerce, and Jackson's American Legion could not save Murphree's campaign for paramilitary business progressivism, what his supporters heralded as "law and order."[12]

Bilbo's victory for racial authoritarianism notwithstanding, some local lawmen increasingly took care to protect the lives of prisoners. In 1931, for instance, authorities indicted a white man named Paul Wexler and a Black man named Andrew Prince for a string of robberies and the murder of a Hattiesburg shopkeeper. The Forrest County sheriff drove his prisoners ninety miles to Jackson "to halt a possible outbreak of violence." Wexler and Prince shared what the *Clarion-Ledger* referred to as the "mob-proof Hinds county jail" with five other men either awaiting trial or legal execution from across the state.[13]

Local officials also called upon governors to supply state troops to assist in high-profile manhunts. In May 1931, white Mississippi bootleggers killed two federal Prohibition agents in two weeks. The second agent to die, US deputy marshal Clyde Rivers, was killed at a roadblock of revenue agents and Prentiss County sheriff's deputies. Late on the night of May 16, gunfire erupted from a carload of bootleggers led by Rouey Eaton, whom the roadblock sought. They killed the federal agent and vanished into the north Mississippi wilderness. In June, the Prentiss County sheriff located the Eaton gang's woodland hideout but dared not attempt to arrest the well-armed moonshiners. The sheriff appealed to Governor Bilbo, who dispatched Tom Birdsong with 119 guardsmen to apprehend the band and guarantee safe passage back to Jackson's Hinds County jail.[14]

This increased reliance on and normalization of centralized policing no doubt grew in intensity with the societal crisis of the Great Depression. In Mississippi, with a population calculated as 86 percent rural, where 66 percent of households farmed in 1920, farm incomes fell 80 percent between 1929 and 1932. The price of cotton fell from twenty cents per pound in 1927 to five cents per pound in 1932. Such financial crisis and its federal response disrupted local economies of rural tenancy and sharecropping. Of all farming households in the state, 70 percent were tenants or sharecroppers. Refugee camps of Black tenants formed after white landowners staged mass evictions. When the New Deal's Agricultural Adjustment Act paid landowners to reduce cotton cultivation and stimulate demand, many bought tractors and combines to industrialize their farming operation instead of paying tenants.[15]

In addition to counterinsurgent technologies like barbed wire and machine guns, Tom Birdsong pushed the Guard to adopt chemical weapons. In February 1933, he attended a demonstration by the Lake Erie Chemical Company in Jackson. Two days later, on February 25, he recommended the National Guard purchase seventy-two tear gas shells and two hundred gas-proof goggles. He also requested "a small quantity of 'KO' gas shells . . . for use in breaks in institutions, such as Parchman." This so-called *knockout gas* was an intensified version of traditional tear gas. After its use against striking dairy farmers in Waukesha, Wisconsin, in November 1933, a Madison chemistry professor explained that "tear gas will quickly wear off, but knock-out gas will probably require a doctor." Birdsong was convinced. He hoped the Guard would hold the gas guns and chemicals in four strategic locations across the state.[16]

When the investigation of the rape of seventeen-year-old Mildred Collins yielded three Black suspects in December 1933, Birdsong snapped into action. On January 9, 1934, he drafted a memo on riot duty that looked to the past and hoped for strong shows of force in the future. "In my humble opinion this is going to be the most serious and trying job that we have ever been called upon to assist," Birdsong wrote. After prejudging the guilt of Ernest McGhee, Johnny Jones, and Isaac Howard, he reminded his commanding officer of the 1927 Jackson riot. "Had we not applied and used strategy," he continued, "no doubt we would have had casualties on both sides." Birdsong credited the use of plainclothes spies who worked counterintelligence, likely reporting on mob thinking and seeding de-escalatory ideas. Counterinsurgent technologies received the most credit: "The barbwire fence in my opinion saved the day there," he wrote of 1927, "though it was like a slap in the face to the people of Jackson and defeated Murphree for Governor." The legal execution of the defendants in Hernando required the same and more.[17]

In February 1934, Tom Birdsong led a detachment of two hundred guardsmen from Jackson to Hernando for the trio's trial. White authorities in DeSoto County requested the troops, and Governor Martin Sennet Conner ordered Birdsong to prevent a lynching at all costs. The former border guard deployed four lines of perimeter defense around the county courthouse. First, troops constructed a barbed-wire barricade. Two lines of troops stood immediately behind. The first donned gas masks and wielded tear gas canisters while the other held rifles with bayonets. Perched above them, guardsmen "trained machine guns on a crowd moving restlessly," according to one reporter. Only one man in the mob attempted to charge Birdsong's barricade; troops arrested him after he fell into barbed wire. Inside, an all-white jury found McGhee, Jones, and Howard guilty of criminal assault, relying on alleged confessions. Birdsong then escorted the convicted men back to Jackson for safekeeping. On March 16, troops returned to Hernando to secure the group's public hanging and to show how an orderly display of state police power could bring about the same result as a lynch mob.[18]

The reemergence of the death penalty and state-administered execution, what activists styled "legal lynching," corresponded to a lasting reform effort in law enforcement.[19] The state troops' regulation of extralegal lynching signaled a moment of successful monopolization of lethal racial discipline and violence by the centralized Jim Crow racial state, often at the point of a bayonet or with threat of machine-gun fire. Outwardly quarantined from the civilian enforcement of white supremacy, state militiamen claimed scientific and professional expertise to establish themselves as a necessary good amid arbitrary, incompetent, and compromised local law enforcement. In the welter of the 1930s, these services of Mississippi's Military Department became the work of its new Department of Public Safety.

Reforming Policing

Just two weeks after the legal execution of McGhee, Jones, and Howard, another law enforcement crisis erupted in Kemper County, near the Alabama state line. On March 30, 1934, neighbors found a prominent white landowner named Raymond Stewart dead in his farmhouse near the town of Scooba. Deputy sheriffs from Kemper and Lauderdale Counties joined other leading white citizens to torture three Black tenant farmers, Ed Brown, Henry Shields, and Yank Ellington, until they confessed a conspiracy to rob and murder Stewart, who also operated the plantation dry goods store. Unlike other cases where such torture can only be assumed, here law enforcement officers admitted their violence in open court. Kemper County's thirty-two-year-old district attorney, John Cornelius Stennis, based his case on these coerced confessions, and by April 6, the future US senator secured death sentences for Brown, Shields, and Ellington.[20]

Over the next two years, this case and its appeals came to be known as *Brown v. Mississippi*. Its central academic question regarded the admissibility of coerced confessions. For many Mississippians, it addressed the proper investigatory conduct of policemen in a white supremacist social order. The case divided Mississippi's elite. In the end, a few white reformers aided by the National Association for the Advancement of Colored People (NAACP) steered the case to the US Supreme Court, where justices overturned the convictions in the shadow of rising totalitarian judicial practice in Europe.

In part, reformers who took up *Brown v. Mississippi* did this work from a personal sense of humanitarianism and deference to the US Constitution. However, this coalition of local white defense attorneys, state supreme court justices, and a former governor also acted *to save* Jim Crow policing, to preserve the structures of elite white rule in Mississippi by rehabilitating Mississippi's human rights record regarding the treatment of Black people in police custody.

These legal performances targeted the lack of sophistication in Kemper County's criminal legal system. For instance, Virgil Alexis Griffith, as associate justice on the Mississippi Supreme Court, rendered the most often quoted rebuke of local law enforcement when he dissented from the court's affirmation of the original verdict. "The transcript reads more like pages torn from some medieval account," he wrote, "than a record made within the confines of a modern civilization which aspires to an enlightened constitutional government." Here, Kemper County's police methods were antimodern, even pre-Enlightenment. Griffith described Brown, Shields, and Ellington as "ignorant negroes" and "helpless prisoners." He narrated their multiple-day torture in excruciating detail. At no time, however, did Griffith suggest that the white men who openly admitted to torturing the Black defendants were themselves criminally liable. Rather, the problem came with the evidence used in the "so-called trial . . . never anything but a factitious continuation of the mob which originally instituted and engaged in the admitted tortures."[21]

In a less familiar portion of his dissent, Virgil Griffith mused on the coexistence of the mob and the formal criminal legal system in Mississippi:

> It may be that in a rarely occasional case which arouses the flaming indignation of a whole community . . . we shall continue yet for a long time to have outbreaks of the mob or resorts to its methods. But if mobs and mob methods must be, it would be better that their existence and their methods shall be kept wholly separate from the courts; that there shall be no blending of the devices of the mob and of the proceedings of the courts; that what the mob has so nearly completed let them finish, and that no court shall by adoption give legitimacy to any of the works of the mob.[22]

The error, then, was not with the white mob but in its decision to seek legitimacy through aiding the administration of state violence. Griffith sought to distinguish between such artless behavior and the humane possibility of law enforcement practice.

Black advocates emerged to force reformers into this position. In Kemper County, the wives of the defendants boldly testified in open court. Irena Brown, Mary Shields, and Kate Ellington each took the stand to rebut Stennis's narrative and provide alibis for their husbands. Kate Ellington remembered her husband falling asleep with her on the night in question. He slept through the night. In the morning "he went in the woods to cut some poles to build a hog pen." She also recalled her husband's torture the next day. Irena Brown remembered sitting up with her husband and roasting sweet potatoes before going to bed on the night of the murder. Mary Shields remembered her husband playing checkers with friends before coming to blows with her at the couple's home. In the fight, they struggled for an axe, she remembered. He cut her leg in the brawl. Then he packed his clothes and left home. The mob of civilians and lawmen found him on the road the next day, accused him of fleeing the murder of Raymond Stewart, and tortured him.[23]

The national Black press also began to cover the case. The NAACP publication, *The Crisis*, featured the trio in its April 1935 cover story and began to collect funds for a defense. When the US Supreme Court announced its intention to hear the case, the *Chicago Defender* branded the case "Mississippi's Scottsboro," after the notorious case of nine Black boys and men falsely accused of rape in Alabama in 1931. The *Defender* covered the appeals of Brown, Shields, and Ellington. It even printed the full Supreme Court decision in February 1936. The paper then reprinted reports of the trio's second trial in Kemper County, which ended in plea deals ranging from six months to seven years at Parchman Farm. *Defender* readers learned that Yank Ellington would carry spinal damage from his torture for the rest of his life.[24]

As *Brown* garnered national and international attention, the case ignited a major debate over the future of Mississippi Law. This debate culminated, in part, in the creation of a state police force in 1938.[25]

• • • • • •

Hugh Lawson White, a lumber baron from south Mississippi, took the oath of office as governor in January 1936, while the US Supreme Court deliberated on *Brown v. Mississippi*. In his inaugural address he pledged to lift Mississippi from "the mud, dust, and gravel" of its rural past. "We have largely, as an agricultural people, created raw materials," White continued. "But we have not within the bounds of our State created other and further wealth in any marked degree from these raw materials." The high court's decision condemning Mississippi's criminal legal system came just one month into White's term, four years marked by campaigns to attract industrial capital.

A New Dealer, White launched his "Balance Agriculture with Industry" program in August 1936. His Mississippi Industrial Act empowered cities and counties to build factories by selling state-subsidized bonds and raising taxes, regardless of whether companies stood ready to occupy the structures. In theory, this building program would attract industries like a hosiery plant in Durant, wool makers in Pascagoula, or a tire manufacturer in Natchez. The companies then paid rent to the municipality and provided jobs for its unemployed citizens. Or, as the historian James Cobb has shown, some companies passed construction costs directly to workers through a tax on wages.[26]

Boosters usually described their work in race- and gender-blind terms, but they obsessed over the unemployment of white, Anglo men. In fact, Hugh White promised the Mississippi Press Association that Mississippi's white people were naturally incapable of labor radicalism. The state's "native Anglo Saxons," he thought, were unlike "disturbing elements so common in larger industrial centers." Tacitly referencing radical traditions of continental European immigrants and African Americans, such as those Black Southerners organizing with the Communist Party of the United States (CPUSA) in Alabama, White told capitalists they would find a pliant workforce. In fact, as historian Robert Hunt Ferguson has shown, White needed only to look to the interracial organizing of the Southern Tenant Farmers' Union (STFU) at Bolivar County's Delta Cooperative Farm or Holmes County's Providence Cooperative Farm to challenge such a notion. There, poor white and Black Mississippians together sought a communal alternative to the top-down development strategy on offer.[27]

Labor unrest also spilled over at Parchman's Mississippi State Penitentiary. On May 5, 1936, the all-white Camp 5 woke in revolt, likely meant to coincide with a visit by the governor.[28] Men refused to report for work in the fields and barricaded themselves inside their barred dormitory. Parchman's superintendent called on the governor for state troops, and Tom Birdsong soon arrived with fifteen guardsmen and tear gas. "This small force drawn up in front of the cage was enough to convince the unruly convicts," wrote the state's adjutant general in his after-action report. "They knew that behind this small force there stood twenty-one hundred men."[29] Though prison officials minimized the work stoppage to reporters as "mutton-headed prisoners acting up," they also revealed the frequency of such strikes, which had become "an annual spring affair."[30] Revolt by incarcerated labor signaled disorder at the core of Mississippi's carceral state.

In the end, a standing state police force came attached to infrastructure development. Hugh White's administration quadrupled the length of paved state highways in four years. In September 1936, most Mississippi counties lacked a single paved state road, relying instead on gravel roads as reliable as the weather. Counties like George, Jackson, Kemper, and Winston still had stretches of unimproved state highway made of red dirt. By 1940, the end of White's term, a driver could traverse the length and breadth of Mississippi on fully paved roads. This investment and mobility demanded security.[31]

The enforcement of vice law over these new roads afforded Mississippi's white reformer class the political opportunity to centralize and professionalize policing. In theory, this policing would be restricted to state highways. In practice, this new Highway Patrol sprawled into the wider society, including industrial employer–employee relations.

Alcohol was still illegal in Mississippi. Despite the Twenty-First Amendment to the US Constitution (1933), the manufacture, sale, and possession of alcohol remained forbidden in much of the Deep South. State-level prohibition remained in effect in Mississippi until 1966, though elaborate black-market economies kept libations flowing. As chief law enforcement officer, each sheriff determined the zeal with which county lawmen enforced prohibition within his jurisdiction. No sheriff could control the actions of a neighboring county's sheriff.

The border between Hinds and Rankin Counties became a flash point for vice enforcement. Home to Jackson, the state's largest city, Hinds County projected a zero-tolerance policy on liquor sales. For instance, in January 1936, Sheriff John W. Roberts Jr. ordered his deputies to raid several known whiskey providers around the county, including the Hickory Grove Tourist Camp. The sheriff fined the proprietor $100 and court costs. Sheriff Roberts even staged a public "pouring out party" to dispose of some 250 cases of confiscated spirits by dumping it in the Jackson sewers.[32]

Rankin County was another matter. Motorists from Jackson had only to cross the Pearl River, which was walking distance from downtown, to find the notorious open-air vice district known as the Gold Coast. There, on Fannin Road in East Jackson, Rankin County sheriff T. B. "Tom" Spann accepted bribes from Black business owners like Billie O. Stamps to overlook illegal activity. "They had to pay the sheriff's department to operate," Stamps remembered in an oral history interview. "It would sometimes be five hundred or a thousand *a week*," she emphasized. At its peak, the Gold Coast boasted over one hundred white and Black businesses, including restaurants, bars, brothels, gambling halls, hotels, and theaters. Like Black entertainment districts across the country, segregation also broke down in these spaces. White businesses on the Gold Coast refused Black patrons admission, yet Stamps's properties sometimes catered to Black and white clientele.[33]

The Stamps family represented the possibilities for Black business owners in Mississippi's illicit economy. Billie Stamps's husband, Clifton, co-owned the forty-room Stamps Brothers Hotel, opened in 1937, and the Rankin County Auditorium. The five-hundred-seat auditorium abutted the two-story clapboard hotel with a veranda. The hotel had a bar in what the Stampses called the "offbeat room," a dice room, and even a dance floor strewn with sand for the tap and flash dancing popular in the 1930s and '40s. As some of the few Black hoteliers in central Mississippi, the Stampses catered to Negro League baseball players like Satchel Paige and musical acts on the so-called Chitlin Circuit. Segregated acts such as Duke Ellington, the Count Basie Orchestra, Billie Holiday, Fats Domino, Ella Fitzgerald, and Cab Calloway performed on the Gold Coast. The Stampses also operated policy wheels, as the numbers game was known there, and procured marijuana from El Paso, Texas, to sell by the sack full.[34]

The refusal to enforce drug or segregation law accompanied police neglect, or a general refusal to protect Black property or life. "We didn't have no law to help us," Stamps remembered of local law enforcement. "Every Monday morning when they came to get their thousand dollars for them slot machines, they don't care who got killed [over the weekend]." Stamps's own personal liberties also evaporated as soon as she left her place of business. Once she was arrested for possessing a bottle of whiskey. "But right up the street, at the hotel, I stood behind the bar," she laughed. "They made me stay all night in jail." Nonetheless, county law enforcement refused to intervene in Stamps's brisk business.

This was not the economic development Governor Hugh White had in mind. "The National Guard!" Billie Stamps remembered. "Every year the National Guards had to come through to see if they could clean up the economy. Of course you definitely knew they were coming. And your walls and up under your window sill was where you kept your cases of whiskey those few days. And then you burn up all the marijuana that you had in one of the storage rooms." The illusion of enforcement, Billie Stamps insisted, was all that changed.

In January 1937, Governor Hugh White activated the National Guard's Riot Division and tasked Major Tom Birdsong with cleaning up the Gold Coast. When the Deltan resigned his position as Clarksdale's chief of police to move to Jackson, state newspapers joked that Birdsong had become "unofficial chief of police of Mississippi" and "a one-man standing police force."[35] In four years of raids, Birdsong "continuously" drew from a special $25,000 budget appropriation to destroy contraband alcohol, arrest proprietors, and padlock nightclub doors.[36]

The Riot Division's legitimacy hinged on the National Guard's ability to insulate local lawmen from political repercussions. Within earshot of newspaper reporters, Birdsong gave orders to padlock bars and brothels that would reopen the next day. In this production, he guaranteed that the sheriff's grift continued. Armed with axes and rifles, troops sometimes exchanged gunfire with disgruntled patrons. Largely, they made shows of cracking bottles and barrels of booze. Businesses always reopened, and the Gold Coast continued this cycle of revelry and raid until state lawmakers ended prohibition in 1966. As with vice districts elsewhere, the occasional raid was more of a performance of police capacity than an ideological shift toward enforcing vice law.[37] From their experiment in state law enforcement, however, White and Birdsong learned the power and politics a state police force could provide. After only one year of intermittent raids, the governor asked the state legislature to fund and empower a "highly mobile patrol force with statewide jurisdiction."[38]

County sheriffs were loath to relinquish power to a permanent state police force. In the legislature, proponents of local rule placed significant limitations on the patrol. They charged the new Mississippi Highway Safety Patrol with enforcing traffic laws and responding to automobile accidents. In the April 1938 legislation, senators explicitly restricted patrolmen from operating as the state's "organized militia" or as county or municipal peace officers. The Highway Safety Patrol Act further limited trooper arrest powers to state highways and their rights of way, unless local authorities requested help or granted permission. Likewise, lawmakers mandated that all fines from trooper tickets went to local government through the justice of the peace courts in each of a given county's five districts. Since the bill mandated that force size and operating budgets could only change by legislative act, operations plugged into politics. The legislature left only the selection of the force's leader to the governor. As before, Hugh White turned to Tom Birdsong, naming him the state's first commissioner of public safety.[39]

The patrol adopted its founder's paramilitary spirit. In total, 1,330 people applied for the first trooper class. Birdsong selected 685 men to complete an entry exam and invited ninety-eight applicants to five weeks of training at Camp Shelby, a US Army base south of Hattiesburg. There, veteran instructors from the Louisiana State Police, the new Texas Highway Patrol, the Federal Bureau of Investigation, and the American Red Cross led trainees through shooting, driving, and first-aid drills. The presence of the Texas Highway Patrol, a recent road force split from the Texas Rangers, clearly drew from Birdsong's ongoing connection to the borderlands. In the blistering June heat, recruits received "military instructions" from Texas troopers. After weekly cuts, half washed out. By camp's end, fifty-three recruits remained.[40]

At its inception, Mississippi's Highway Patrol exhibited a tendency toward pageantry and spectacle, resembling other global shows of authoritarianism that emerged in Europe. On June 17, 1938, the fifty-three troopers participated in a hundred-mile-long motorcade from Camp Shelby to Capitol Street in downtown Jackson. Along the way, the patrol's cars, trucks, and motorcycles stopped in population centers for parades with horns and sirens wailing. They donned matching uniforms, "cadet gray trimmed in royal blue," Birdsong reported, in the "army standard." Across their chests were diagonal "black Sam Brown belt[s]." Instead of trousers, they wore jodhpurs, accented by "black boots, and chromium plated buckles." After marching in review for the governor, troopers took their oaths and reported to twenty

Jackson, MS, June 17, 1938. Governor Hugh White invests T. B. Birdsong Jr. as commissioner of public safety at the inaugural parade for the Highway Patrol. Courtesy of James Birdsong.

new police cars and thirty-five Harley-Davidson motorcycles. They then set out for eight regional substations around the state. All troopers were, of course, white.[41]

Patrol architects sought to demonstrate how the organization intended to enforce the law without favor. At the close of the parade, Hugh White charged the force to be "courteous, considerate, and diligent." The drunk driver—"that most dangerous criminal of all"—was a primary target. He also imagined the patrolman's role in a new, accessible Magnolia State. "Remember this: Mississippi has opened her doors and is beckoning visitors from throughout the Nation. Treat them with respect. Give them what guidance, information, and assistance you can. I admonish you to be faithful and efficient in enforcing the laws of the state."[42] Certainly the governor imagined these visitors to be white tourists and potential investors. What role, then, did he imagine for Black and other non-white travelers?

From State Troops to State Troopers   51

As a branch of the state government, Birdsong's unit was a Jim Crow patrol. African Americans alleged discriminatory policing from the beginning. In the fall of 1939, Black picnickers from New Orleans traveled across the Mississippi state line on a Sunday church outing. Once across, an unknown patrolman stopped each truck to demand a temporary permit to operate in Mississippi. The charter drivers lacked such documentation, and the trooper issued stiff fines. Birdsong denied any such policy or the patrol's involvement in the scam. He leveled blame on county police and promised a grand jury investigation of whoever was impersonating an officer of the Highway Patrol.[43]

Early on, the patrol's enforcement of prohibition activity especially impacted the rural poor. Troopers closely policed public drunkenness in vehicles and on the sides of state roads. When patrolmen encountered pedestrians suspected of drinking, they often issued ten-dollar fines. Possession of intoxicants justified $100 fines *per container*. Driving while judged to be intoxicated also earned a $100 fine. Moreover, in order to pay fines, defendants reported to the respective justice of the peace court. If a defendant pleaded guilty, they paid the trooper's fine and court costs. If a defendant pleaded not guilty, they faced the additional cost of empaneling a petit jury. Acquittals proved rare. As the patrol's expanded enforcement capacity often ensnared rural white Mississippians too, public condemnation swelled over its first decade.[44]

・・・・・・

The next chapter dives deep into the responses of Black Mississippians to law enforcement; however, it is worth pausing here to consider the critiques that emerged from white Mississippians who disagreed with paramilitary reformers like Hugh White and T. B. Birdsong. Some white Mississippians at the time understood the state police power to run contrary to their self-interests.

The patrol's sudden impact in the everyday lives of motorists is hard to overstate. In its first five years, fewer than seventy troopers logged interactions with over 500,000 drivers. In that period, they wrote some 45,000 tickets and summonses, accounting for $580,000 in fines and court costs, all potential revenue for county governments. More than 1,200 people spent time in jail because of interactions with highway patrolmen during these years. Because patrol administrators did not disaggregate statistics by race, we cannot know the proportion of enforcement that fell on people identified as either white or Black. However, the extent of public complaint about patrol overreach suggests white motorists received their share of attention.[45]

Local white elites especially resented state policemen untethered from the Jim Crow sheriff. "We do not need a gestapo or a set of storm troopers," wrote H. Rey Bonney, editor of McComb's *Daily Journal*, in September 1941. He responded to a request by Highway Patrol administrators for "general police powers," the ability to enforce the law anywhere in the state. Bonney saw only creeping totalitarianism: "We do not need a set of police roaming the state, ready to pounce on our citizens for crimes or misdemeanors," he continued. "Our police and our sheriffs and their deputies are equipped to handle their end of the deal in their various localities. . . . Let's let Hitler and Himmler have exclusive right to the storm troopers." In the context of German fascism, Bonney sensed a power grab by centralized state power. This fear blocked the expansion of state police jurisdiction in 1941 and repeatedly for the next twenty years.[46]

As patrolmen wrote more traffic tickets during World War II, local white officials shrank patrol jurisdiction statutorily. Between 1939 and 1944, trooper-initiated arrests spiked from 3,000 to 15,000 per year. By 1946, sheriffs lobbied for a new state law that forbade troopers from operating on county roads. Legislators also cut Birdsong's operating budget. In following years, Birdsong lobbied for the legislature to reverse both regulations, noting the preponderance of crime and life-threatening traffic accidents outside of population centers. He professed to lead a "service" organization, touting its assistance to distressed motorists and the documentation of traffic accidents.[47]

Such sporadic white resistance to the Highway Patrol carried a particular goal: to banish law enforcement power all too common in Black communities from the lives of automotive white people. Such efforts had no intention of directing society away from police dependency. Yet the policing of Mississippi's Black citizens brought with it the increased policing of white Mississippians too.

The white effort to restrict police power highlighted a tension around one of paramilitary law enforcement's primary reasons for being: the maintenance of elite rule amid what Winfield Scott Featherston's Militia Committee called "disparity" in 1890. The origins of Jim Crow's system of racial capitalism demanded a militarized police force of last resort, the National Guard, to maintain order amid the fallout of inequality. This social system's perpetuation during the Great Depression's new context of disparity required a standing police army in the face of presumed labor revolt, mob violence, outlawry, and moral decay. The new Highway Patrol seemed to threaten the local white sheriffs' domination of local economies, from agricultural labor control to drugs and sex. The new bureaucratic state police force answered to different masters, men driven by a desire to attract outside capital to the state, a strategy premised on outcompeting other industrial labor markets for the lowest wage. Hugh White's Balance Agriculture with Industry program of the 1930s and '40s was but one point of reference in a long campaign to make more valuable the assets that White's social class dominated, especially fallow real property.

After World War II, Mississippi's economy stood at the precipice of a major change. New Deal–subsidized mechanization began to render the rural Black tenant population surplus to the cotton economy. Simultaneously, as Hugh White made clear, the ruling class imagined that new industrial jobs belonged to white men and women. This change reimagined the role of a state police force as less prison guard than security guard, less keeping in than keeping out. The tide of white ambivalence to policing turned, and once again coalitions of white workers and thinkers began to see their interests and those of the police as the same. When Hugh White said, "We must produce other forms of wealth through industry" in 1936, he predicted the agribusinessmen who filled the state's empty cotton fields with beef cattle.[48]

As a new phase of Mississippi's Black freedom struggle began after World War II, Tom Birdsong would lead the patrol intermittently for twenty-three more years, policing the social movement. But before the civil rights moment of the 1960s was imaginable, Mississippi Law made the land itself hostile to Black life.

Part II **Land**

3 Fighting Police in the Rural

....

Courts should not strain themselves into hypercritical condemnation of reasonable and time-tried police methods in discharge of their duties, by police officers, seeking to protect the peace and safety of law-abiding people against anti-social characters.

—Supreme Court of Mississippi, *Leroy Miller v. Marvin Wiggins* (1949)

In January 1948, Buford Johnson addressed the first annual meeting of the Kemper County, Mississippi, branch of the National Association for the Advancement of Colored People (NAACP). Activist farmers formed their NAACP branch in the year after Kemper County's white sheriff murdered and stole the property of another Black farm-owning family, Matt and Nettie McWilliams. "We realize that we have been hindered, buked, scorned and knocked back in the shadows," Johnson said, describing the way white power swept away its inhumanity. "Let us unite in one mind based on right for the common good for all colored people in America and elsewhere . . . and ask for better schools, transportation for our boys and girls, and all the necessities which we have been deprived of. This is ours by right."[1]

Speaking on the one-year anniversary of Matt McWilliams's murder by the sheriff, Buford Johnson's critique of Jim Crow had grown to demand "all the necessities" denied to Black people the world over. He belonged to a movement that confronted policing's function in a property regime that rejected rural Black belonging.

Across Mississippi, rural Black people organized against Jim Crow policing after World War II. Many also participated in the more familiar postwar struggles for voting rights and desegregation. But in places like Kemper, forthright police terror sparked an early public stand. Though they frequently drew on the resources and cachet of the NAACP, local people were not always beholden to national organizational politics or priorities. The case of Matt and Nettie McWilliams was a prime example: Though the NAACP headquarters labeled the case "police brutality," local activists challenged all that the Jim Crow sheriff represented. They fought the state's ability to dispose of a community's Black elders and seize their land. They fought a local manifestation of Mississippi's postwar political economy of white enclosure, the evacuation of America's Black countryside and the redistribution of Black-occupied land for white wealth creation.[2]

Activist neighbors took great risks to fight Jim Crow policing. They signed their names, paid membership dues, and knocked on doors because of racialized criminalization. Victims and activists ranged from landowners like the McWilliamses to rural renters, including cash tenants and sharecroppers who often lived on white-owned land and provided a share of their cash crop in lieu of cash rent. Police violence also extended to the many small-town migrants who left peasantry for rental homes in towns. Often local women led this work to remember husbands, brothers, and sons—becoming public activists and organizers. They faced what the scholar Ruth Wilson Gilmore has called "triple work-days—job, home, justice."[3] They also fought the accumulated common sense of Black criminalization in their shared civil rights movements. Writing in 1955, NAACP Southeastern regional secretary Ruby Hurley wrote to the NAACP's Mississippi field secretary Medgar Evers urging him to investigate cases of policing that the middle-class leadership of local branches often ignored. "Some of our people have class prejudice," she warned, "and are not always aware of the fact that the law should operate fairly for all."[4]

Though histories of the period before the classical phase of the civil rights movement have described the period as seedtime for organizing efforts of the 1960s, this chapter shows that local movements coalesced around policing as a central dilemma for Black rural life. It reconstructs three cases from postwar NAACP police brutality records. Focusing on northeast Mississippi's Tombigbee River Valley, it demonstrates how police terror drove local organizing efforts in rural Black communities after World War II and considers how activists sustained movements amid doubt and repression. First, it explores the ways Mississippi sheriffs cloaked the expropriation of Black-owned land in formal legal proceedings. Then it turns to the growing function of small-town police forces to manage under- and unemployed Black populations that migrated from the countryside. Last, the state police returns to assert color-blind order and rationalize retribution around the state's newest investment in infrastructure—the state highway system.

The Sheriff

Even as the state built a professional state police force after 1938, the absolute power of Mississippi's county sheriffs went largely unchecked. Under state law, sheriffs were the chief law enforcement officers and tax collectors of their respective counties. They sat with a county's board of supervisors at monthly meetings, served the Circuit Court's arrest warrants, and oversaw those incarcerated in the county jail. Excluding the Reconstruction Era of the 1870s, Mississippi sheriffs had all been white men, except in the case of their death while in office, in which case the sheriff's wife often finished his term. The first Black sheriff elected after the civil rights movement took office in 1979.[5]

The high sheriff's informal influence far outpaced his formal duties. When they weren't ensnaring offenders in the criminal legal system, they used their office to position themselves atop statewide socioeconomic hierarchies. This frequently poised sheriffs for maximum benefit during periods of agricultural revolution. In Lake County, Florida, for instance, Willis V. McCall maneuvered to buy vast tracts of land for orange groves ahead of the central Florida citrus boom of the 1940s and '50s. He also wielded his office against citrus workers who tried to organize for safer work and better wages.[6]

While Southern sheriffs technically enforced the law, they also dictated exactly when and by whom the law could be broken. In Russell County, Alabama, Sheriff Ralph Mathews carefully controlled the county's vice economy, such as illegal gambling, alcohol sale, and prostitution, guaranteeing he either received a cut of the proceeds or bribes to look the other way. In both cases, historians know the depth of a sheriff's criminal conspiracy because media spectacles and official investigations exploded around their malfeasance.[7]

Similar scrutiny might have exposed corruption in any sheriff's office. This was not because all Southern sheriffs fit caricatures of racist villains. Rather, the sheriff's job description placed him in direct control of a county's system of private property and, thus, racial capitalism. Even an honest sheriff was accountable to white property owners and the economic interests that aided in his election. Unlike other law enforcement officers, the sheriff was elected, meaning that he had the greatest incentive to serve and protect those whose support could affect elections. Like policemen and state troopers, rare was the sheriff notorious for his unbiased protection of Black life and property.

In the abstract, the work of Jim Crow law enforcement could be personally profitable for sheriffs. Mississippi's state legislature paid them for each day a person sat in the county jail, for each warrant served, and for each prisoner transported to the state penitentiary. But, as the example of Arnold

Harbour near Moscow, Mississippi, shows, the sheriff's work could be both personally enriching and valuable to the wider regime of white supremacy and wealth extraction. In fact, a sheriff's local influence could lead all the way to a US senator's office.

......

The act of police brutality that sparked a movement in Kemper County demonstrated the sheriff's overlapping worlds of capitalism and law enforcement. The case emerged from the same rural county as the 1934–35 *Brown v. Mississippi* case (see chapter 2). It revolved around two families, the McWilliamses and the Harbours.

Matt McWilliams was born in 1878 to a family of Black landowners who were themselves born into slavery. He married his wife, Nettie McWilliams, a cousin from another landowning family, in 1907. Sometime afterward they bought land on which to live and farm. They succeeded at their craft, eventually diversifying the family's agricultural operation to include tree farming.[8]

Mississippi Law interrupted. In 1944, Kemper County's tax assessor alleged that the McWilliamses had failed to pay the previous year's property taxes on a sixty-acre forest. The tax assessor enrolled a tax lien on McWilliams's land. In August of that year, the sheriff—as tax collector—sold the lien from the courthouse steps in the county seat of DeKalb. Steel City Lumber Company, a Birmingham, Alabama–based timber company, placed the highest bid. Regardless of McWilliams's refusal to recognize the lien or its new corporate owner, the timber company could foreclose and take possession of the McWilliams property if principal, interest, and fees remained unpaid after three years.[9]

Sheriff Arnold Harbour was no mere elected official. He was a farmer and merchant from a prominent white family in Kemper County. His father, John Lee Harbour, had been sheriff of Kemper County before him. During World War I, Arnold fought and was wounded in France, returning in 1919 to own and operate general stores across Mississippi. At least one of his customers held him in low esteem: In 1930, an anonymous correspondent mailed Harbour an envelope full of poison with instructions to mix the cure-all with sugar and water in order to remedy "a certain ailment." Harbour never knew for sure who mailed him the powder, but he took his vengeance against a Black man with whom he "had recently had trouble," according to one newspaper report. The accused, Guy Hall, "rigorously denied the charges placed against him." Nonetheless, Harbour saw that Hall was tried in federal court for sending poison through the mails.[10]

Seventeen years later, Arnold Harbour used the criminal legal system to take possession of McWilliams's matured timberland. At some point in the tax lien's three-year grace period, Harbour partnered with two other white men, including John Lloyd Shumate, the secretary of the Steel City Lumber Company, to buy the McWilliams lien. Despite the McWilliamses continuing to pay annual property taxes on the plot in 1944 and 1945, Arnold Harbour took legal title to the land in late 1946. He ordered the plot vacated by the end of the year. Rural white allies urged Matt and Nettie McWilliams to stand their ground and to protest the sheriff's obvious fraud. They did so.[11]

The McWilliamses' stand against Mississippi Law ended in tragedy. At 8:30 on the morning of Saturday, January 4, 1947, Matt and Nettie ate breakfast in their farmhouse as Sheriff Harbour approached with an arrest warrant for trespassing. Matt continued eating breakfast while the sheriff called to him from outside. Once he finished eating, McWilliams walked onto the front porch. We can't know how the meeting escalated, whether Matt reached for his shotgun, was calm and well-reasoned, or simply refused arrest. Sheriff Harbour shot the sixty-eight-year-old Matt dead while Nettie looked on.[12] Reverend Roosevelt Clark was away on military service at the time of Matt's death but was one of the McWilliamses' closest neighbors in 1940. Clark recalled how his father learned about the killing. Apparently Harbour approached his father and said, "Well, I just shot old Matt." In an oral history interview, Reverend Clark remembered the matter-of-fact heartlessness over seventy years later. Clark's father also told him that the church bell in the Blackwater farm community rang in the middle of the day that Saturday, to alert neighbors of a calamity and spread the word about Matt's deadly encounter with Harbour.[13]

Two days later, a justice of the peace court exonerated Arnold Harbour when the sheriff produced two white witnesses who swore they had seen a struggle of self-defense. Matt had always been a "bad Negro," one witness claimed. The other testified that he heard Matt tell Nettie he was *not* going to jail. The justice of the peace who exonerated Harbour, Louis Lloyd Shumate, was the third of the sheriff's original partners in buying the McWilliams lien. He was also the brother of John Lloyd Shumate, the secretary of Steel City Lumber.[14]

As word of Matt McWilliams's death spread, Black farmers in Kemper County began to organize. Nettie McWilliams doubtless sparked the movement, telling neighbors the longer story excluded from the trial—of taxes, liens, and evictions. An NAACP field secretary based in New Orleans traveled with another branch president from south Mississippi to interview Nettie and one of her nephews in Kemper County. They collected years of legal paperwork to substantiate the McWilliamses' story. Nettie died before NAACP headquarters could launch a full investigation. Those with her at the end said it was "shock" from the experience of Matt's murder.[15] In less than two months, fifty farmers, mostly male landowners, had bound together to charter an NAACP branch in Kemper County, just miles north of the McWilliams home.[16]

Through the NAACP, Buford and Bessie Johnson took up Nettie McWilliams's cause. The Johnsons, like the McWilliamses, belonged to Black farm-owning families whose parents had been born into slavery. Bessie Harper and Buford Johnson earned middle school educations before marrying and raising ten children on their farm near Bluff Springs. They may have joined the NAACP as individual members earlier in life, but they helped establish a branch in their late fifties.[17]

Branch organizers used NAACP infrastructure to build a grassroots movement. Buford Johnson was branch president. He proved fairly expert at adding members—ninety-seven within four months, 170 within one year. "You have got to remove the fear from a person before you can make a working member out of he or she," Johnson once wrote headquarters. The fear of police surveillance and intimidation must have been immense in the aftermath of the McWilliams murder, especially for Black property owners. Branch officers refused to host regular mass meetings, opting instead for underground organizing.[18]

Buford Johnson's letters revealed the political philosophy that energized his successful organizing efforts. He used metaphors to link his experience "in the Rural," as he called it, to a theory of justice for Mississippi's Black farmers. He emphasized the long game, stressing a different conception of historical time and the victory of survival. "Please remember," he once urged headquarters, evoking Ecclesiastes, "the race is not give to the swift nor either the strong, but he who endureth to the end."[19] In Kemper County, a local movement sought collective endurance in the face of the sheriff's power.

The loss of the McWilliamses likely sharpened Johnson's understanding of racism and the economic life of Black farmers. In one letter to headquarters, Buford Johnson compared the scales of justice to the scales of commerce, an analogy familiar to any farmer who had brought his produce to markets controlled by white elites. "The burden is on the scales," he wrote

Kemper County, MS, ca. 1955. NAACP organizers Buford and Bessie Johnson stand in front of a car, dressed for town. Courtesy of Beverly Carroll.

remembering the prophet Amos. "An[d] the scales are not just[ly] balanced." Though he never referenced Matt McWilliams or Arnold Harbour directly in his surviving correspondence with headquarters, Johnson captured an understanding of systemic rather than personal racism. There was no simple thumb on the scale whereby a nefarious party corrupted a transaction. Instead, the scales themselves, the tool for measuring worth, were defective. For Johnson, perhaps, the sheriff was not merely racist. The sheriff was racism. And Arnold Harbour still looms large in the memory of descendants of both Matt McWilliams and Buford Johnson.[20]

Buford Johnson's philosophy of justice emphasized such histories of fraud. Sheriff Harbour paid no price for killing Matt McWilliams, evicting Nettie McWilliams, or stealing the family's sixty acres. If anything, this act of expropriation contributed to his family's and his region's wealth and power in the American system.

Harbour promptly gave the McWilliamses' land to his daughter Mable and son-in-law, L. L. Wilkerson, for "ten dollars and other valuable considerations." Harbour was reelected sheriff of Kemper County into the 1960s. His son, Frederick Dale "Fred" Harbour, went on to raise beef cattle in Kemper County and enter local politics. Fred Harbour served as mayor of DeKalb, the county seat, for twenty-four years. The family built continued success on the McWilliams land.[21]

But Jim Crow was about more than building parochial pockets of white wealth in the Southern hinterland. In November 1947, just ten months after Arnold Harbour killed Matt McWilliams, white Mississippi voters elected another white resident of Kemper County to the US Senate. John Cornelius Stennis was the son of a wealthy farm family. Born in 1901, he had admitted coerced confessions as the local prosecutor in *Brown v. Mississippi* (see chapter 2). His youngest brother, John Howell Stennis, spent his adult life in the Mississippi Highway Safety Patrol. John C. Stennis served the next forty-two years in the Senate, where he, along with James O. Eastland, blocked any legislation that threatened white supremacy in America. Stennis also shepherded federal funding to white Mississippi and chaired the Senate Committee on Armed Services between 1969 and 1981. He and Eastland accumulated seventy-seven years of combined service in the Senate. At Stennis's funeral in 1996, Bobbie Harbour, a longtime office manager, said that statesmen like Stennis were "the best argument Mississippi has against term limits." Fred Harbour, Arnold's son, was one of Stennis's pallbearers.[22] Land power like Harbour's led to Washington, DC, and through seniority in the national government came power to shape the world.

The Local Police

In Mississippi's small towns, local police forces held increased sway after World War II. Some 150 miles north of Kemper County, in Monroe County, NAACP organizing began and escalated around an incident of local police terror in Amory, a town of around three thousand residents.

Amory's police department stole fourteen years from one Black family. On a Sunday morning in February 1947, just one month after Arnold Harbour killed Matt McWilliams, a twenty-two-year-old Black veteran named Leroy Miller Jr. stopped by the home of a former employer. There, Miller asked to borrow the white man's car in search of work. The septuagenarian declined the use of his automobile and reported the conversation to local law enforcement. An Amory police officer took Miller into custody by noon and placed him in the town jail.

Policing in Miller's case involved the entire town government. Two hours after his arrest, officers escorted Miller to Mayor Fred P. Wright's office. There, in the presence of the mayor, between five and eight officers with the Amory Police Department beat Miller with bare fists and a truncheon. After two hours of abuse, Miller confessed to burglarizing his former employer's home days before. Three hours later he also confessed to burglarizing a white woman's home the previous week, this time with the intent to rape the occupant. By ten p.m., policemen had put Miller's confessions in writing. When told to sign, he made only illegible scratches with a pen. An officer signed for him; Miller made his mark in the witness of an Amory banker.[23]

The state police quickly became involved in this local case. As was now commonplace, troopers took Miller into protective custody and drove him almost three hundred miles to the Hinds County jail in Jackson. Their prisoner stayed there for roughly forty-eight hours before policemen carried him back to Monroe County. This transfer protected Amory's ruling class from a potentially explosive vigilante situation because of the new accusation involving rape. In fact, on February 16, a mob in Greenville, South Carolina, had abducted and murdered Willie Earle, a Black man charged with murdering a white cab driver. Perhaps the mayor and banker feared that Miller's rape charge could incite a mob. Regardless, the state police transfer also gave time for Miller's visible signs of torture to heal before his first reappearance before family or friends.[24]

Once back in Monroe County, Miller's case proceeded at breakneck speed. The next week saw a swift grand jury indictment and hearing before Raymond T. Jarvis in Circuit Court at Aberdeen. The accused pleaded guilty and Jarvis summarily passed sentence: two consecutive ten-year terms at the Mississippi State Penitentiary at Parchman. The sheriff transferred him to the Delta penal farm the next week.

Though Miller never had the benefit of legal counsel, Monroe County lawmen failed to quiet him. Sometime on the day of his arrest, word of Miller's detention reached family. Initially unconcerned, his older sister Ruby stopped by the town lockup. She yelled to Leroy through a second-floor window and learned the gravity of her brother's situation. Leroy had never been in trouble. Yes, he had served a brief stint in the town jail for vagrancy—a common charge against Black men deemed underemployed. But Leroy now faced felony charges. Ruby reported back to Ammie Miller, their mother, and the two women sought help.[25]

Such cases of police terror and state violence compelled surviving loved ones into Mississippi's organized Black freedom struggle. Often working-class women, these survivors likely came to community organizing without formal organizing experience. When the time came, Ammie and Ruby Miller drew on everyday tactics of communication and community-building that sparked a popular groundswell and fearless public organizing where previously there had been only underground resistance.[26]

Ammie and Ruby Miller went directly to NAACP members in Amory. Together with a man named Roosevelt V. Amison, the Millers set out to ascertain the facts of Leroy's case. After casually interviewing witnesses, including white policemen, they found no physical or testimonial evidence linking Miller to either of his confessed crimes.

From their investigative work, a counternarrative emerged. Over the course of that Sunday in February, local police had marshaled heinous circumstantial and cultural evidence against Miller in an attempt to extract a confession. Just back from war and serving under a new mayor elected as a war hero, white lawmen reported that Leroy had boasted of dating white women while stationed in New York during the war. They further alleged that he had shown them wallet photographs from these relationships.[27]

Since Leroy had no trial, the Millers fought the police narrative in conversations across Monroe County. First, his mother and sister unequivocally denied that Leroy had ever been to New York; Ammie Miller carried his Army record to prove it. She also knew the picture he carried in his wallet to be Lena Horne, the fair-skinned Black singer, dancer, and motion picture star of *Stormy Weather* (1943). Finally, the Millers even sought an audience with Marie McKinney, the white housewife whom Leroy had allegedly intended to rape. McKinney said she had no way of knowing who, if anyone, had entered her home, and that she had reported as much when asked by law enforcement. The Millers circulated the tale of how a policeman had merely brought Leroy to McKinney's house in handcuffs and announced that he was the perpetrator.

As these facts came to light, the treatment of Leroy Miller in February 1947 struck a chord with R. V. Amison. He immediately wrote his contacts at NAACP headquarters. He even addressed a letter to Eleanor Roosevelt, having found her address with the NAACP board of directors on letterhead. "A long story goes with this case of Leroy Miller," he wrote. "And we who live here is handicapted in trying to investigate the matter." The former first lady's staff forwarded Amison's letter to Franklin H. Williams, assistant special counsel to Thurgood Marshall in the Legal Defense Fund (LDF).[28] "The whole community knows that it is a trick," Amison wrote to Williams. The backstory about Miller's desire for white women "was drawn up from the new officers, just out of the Army," Amison wrote. "And they are Negro haters."[29]

Amison was not alone in his recruiting the ascendant legal campaign. One anonymous informant penned a letter to NAACP board of directors president Arthur B. Spingarn soon after Miller's sentencing. Lamenting that the prisoner was already in the county jail, the writer implored Spingarn to launch an investigation. "You know that Negro ain't got no chance in Mississippi Law," he wrote. In *Mississippi Law*, a writer too afraid to sign their name captured the entire system of Mississippi policing. As constituted, the criminal legal system conspired to create injustice. Mississippi Law existed to dispose of people like Leroy Miller.[30]

Amory's campaign succeeded when Frank Williams paid a white lawyer from Meridian to investigate on behalf of the LDF. The appeal took time. The NAACP fought for Miller's freedom for two years, through 1949. Unable to appeal Miller's guilty plea from Circuit Court, the LDF initiated a separate civil procedure, petitioning for a writ of habeas corpus against the superintendent of Mississippi State Penitentiary. Thus, *Leroy Miller v. Marvin Wiggins* became the one hope for the Miller family and Monroe County's freedom movement. Judge Raymond Jarvis issued the writ to retrieve the prisoner from Parchman and allowed testimony from Leroy, Ammie, and Ruby Miller in open court. But the witnesses against Leroy Miller were "officers of the law," Jarvis wrote, their word undoubtable. He ordered Miller back to Parchman.[31]

Miller's recourse to justice now lay solely in the overburdened hands of Thurgood Marshall, who appealed the case to Mississippi's Supreme Court.

Word of Marshall's involvement quickly inspired Monroe County's wider NAACP movement.[32] Amison mailed scraps of notebook paper to New York each time he signed a new batch of members. Amison praised the LDF's work for Monroe County and only lamented that rain had washed out the roads between rural Black communities, thus hindering mass meetings. "As soon as we get the weather we have a movement," he wrote.[33] For Amison, Miller's day in court had signaled a revolution of hope on the ground.

But for Mississippi's white judiciary, Leroy Miller's case began and ended with his confession and guilty pleas. In his brief for the state, Assistant Attorney General George Hamilton Ethridge, from Kemper County, developed an elaborate states' rights defense to dismiss any allegation of a Fourteenth Amendment due process violation. The court concluded its judgment with special attention to the NAACP's argument that the illegal actions of law enforcement prior to grand jury indictment could render subsequent criminal proceedings null, arguing that "the courts should jealously guard the Constitutional rights of individuals, even suspected or actual criminals, but society has some Constitutional rights also. . . . Courts should not strain themselves into hypercritical condemnation of reasonable and time-tried police methods in discharge of their duties, by police officers, seeking to protect the peace and safety of law-abiding people against anti-social characters."[34] To be sure, Mississippi's justices saw the legal question at the heart of Leroy Miller's case. Were police officers capable of violating an individual's constitutional rights? They thought not.[35]

The LDF welcomed the decision's open antagonism toward federal judicial authority. Certain the US Supreme Court would now involve itself, Marshall hoped Miller's case might revolutionize criminal procedure for poor African Americans across the country. On September 9, 1949, he petitioned the Supreme Court for a writ of certiorari, whereby the Court would forcibly review Miller's case.

The Supreme Court refused. Despite Justice Hugo Black's desire to review the case, a majority of the justices harbored less interest. In a stroke of bad luck, the Court's most progressive justice, William O. Douglas, had been thrown from a horse and could not vote. Douglas's vote might have transformed *Miller v. Wiggins* into a landmark civil rights case on police conduct. Then again, Leroy Miller was a rural Black veteran from Mississippi, unemployed and accused of preferring the company of white women. And he had pleaded guilty.[36]

R. V. Amison, for one, kept Leroy's cause alive until the Supreme Court's final dismissal. He frequently wrote Broadway and the LDF for updates and traveled to Los Angeles, California, as a delegate to the NAACP's 1949 annual convention. He must have been devastated to learn of the end of Miller's appeals process. In the letter informing Amison of the Supreme Court's refusal to hear the case, Frank Williams reminded the branch president of the "substantial expense" incurred by fighting Miller's case. He asked for another round of fundraising in Monroe County.[37]

Ammie and Ruby Miller would have to travel 150 miles to Parchman to visit Leroy. He accrued good time days and left Parchman on April 12, 1961, four days before his thirty-seventh birthday. On the penal farm, Miller likely worked agriculturally from sunup to sundown for those fourteen years without pay—all for seeking work in an automotive rural world.[38]

The Highway Brutality Patrol

Leroy Miller's quest for automobility cost him fourteen years in Parchman. But the successful use of Mississippi's roads and highways also came with costs to Black life. The state's growing system of roads became sites of everyday debate over racism and policing after World War II. The Highway Patrol would arbitrate. Tensions flared across Mississippi as traffic increased. Locally, the situation could boil over in spectacular fashion. But the everyday violence of policing also ushered Black Mississippians off of the land.

For the spectacular, look no further than a single month in Chickasaw County: July 1949. First, on July 2, a young white man murdered a Black tenant farmer, Malcolm Wright Sr., for "hogging the road" in his mule-drawn wagon.[39] Then, three weeks later, four white men kidnapped and beat a white state trooper in retribution for what they considered targeted over-policing.

Local Black protest demanded an uncharacteristic effort by white prosecutors to convict Malcolm Wright's murderer; however, an all-white jury acquitted James Moore on April 5, 1950. In his final summation, the defense attorney said, "We're [not] so jittery that we would convict a white man for killing a Negro because of *this* situation," rhetorically gesturing to the segregated balcony filled with Black onlookers.[40] The Wrights became yet another family of Black tenant farmers forced from the land. Wright's son, Malcolm Wright Jr., and his wife, Ivy Wright, fled to Chicago's South Side after the trial. There, they worked alongside and knew Mamie Till-Mobley, herself a refugee from Tallahatchie County, and the mother of Emmett Till, who was murdered by white men in Money, Mississippi, just years later.[41]

In the case of the attacked highway patrolman, local white jurors returned a guilty verdict. For kidnapping, restraining, and assaulting Patrolman W. D. King with a rubber mallet, three brothers were sentenced to Parchman for six to eight years. Frank, Curtis Lee, and Sargent Derrel Bolin had frequently run afoul of the law. They likely had a representative history with Trooper King and the Highway Patrol. In 1949 alone, state troopers boasted nearly 256,000 unique interactions with Mississippi residents and visitors, assessing over $333,000 in fines. In court Frank Bolin alleged that Trooper King had targeted and threatened him unjustly. His brothers, Frank said, had only acted to prevent the officer from draping a personal vendetta in state power. In Circuit Court, however, the attorney general used the defendants' petty criminal records to impugn their characters, namely their records as bootleggers. The Bolins could not be trusted; the lawman could.[42]

・・・・・・

From such crises on the open road, the state police emerged as an essential service provider for local criminal legal systems. In particular, troopers increased surveillance in rural areas by policing the roads between small towns. More abstractly they began to manage social conflict that arose on trafficked spaces. Daily they used their state power to arbitrate disputes between white and Black motorists. But increasingly, they also policed Black motorists who used state roads to mobilize and organize against Jim Crow.

Paved roads transformed life for rural people. In 1938, Chickasaw County had paved only eight of its 102 miles of state highway. By 1950, concrete and asphalt thoroughfares crisscrossed the 500-square-mile county; only twenty-two miles of road lacked pavement. This trend continued across the state. In 1936, just 1,000 miles of Mississippi's road system were paved. By 1950, thanks to Hugh White's Balance Agriculture with Industry program, that number had grown to over 4,000 miles. The number of transport trucks registered in the state doubled to over 100,000 in the same period.

All-weather roads invited more traffic. While 700 of Chickasaw County's 3,000 farmers owned an automobile in 1950, wagoners also used the paved roads to their advantage. Indeed, over 300 of the state's automotive accidents involved animal-drawn conveyances in 1950 alone. The Highway Patrol maintained jurisdiction over these events. Their official reports created meaning from traffic accidents and carried the weight of law in state courtrooms.[43]

Even when they avoided the headlines, highway patrolmen facilitated racialized state violence through everyday investigative functions. On Saturday, July 19, 1952, seventeen-year-old Tommy Booker drove north on Mississippi 12 through rural Lowndes County in his mother's 1936 Buick. Near the Mullins Well community, he attempted to pass a slower moving car but met a fast-moving vehicle in the oncoming lane. Booker slowed and swerved back into his lane to avoid a head-on collision but clipped the car he had attempted to pass. That vehicle collided with the oncoming car, while Booker's car escaped with minor damage. The force of impact ejected one passenger from the colliding cars. A white woman from Caledonia, Rubye Robertson, died shortly after arriving at the Columbus hospital.[44]

A common if tragic traffic accident like Tommy Booker's illustrated the debates along paved state roads. Patrolman Cecil Cheek arrived on the scene shortly after undertakers had evacuated the injured. Cheek took photographs, measured skid marks, collected debris, and interviewed remaining witnesses, including Booker. When Cheek found that Booker lacked a driver's license, he placed the Black motorist under arrest and left him in the Lowndes County jail, where he stayed for the next two months without formal charge. On November 17, the grand jury indicted Booker on manslaughter and District Attorney Jesse P. Stennis, second cousin of US senator John C. Stennis, began his case two days later.[45]

On direct and cross-examination, the highway patrolman projected impartial expertise. Trooper Cecil Cheek answered questions, explained his measurements, and narrated his photographs without assigning guilt or wrongdoing. Neither did he confirm the pattern of facts that D.A. Stennis desired to establish Booker's negligence behind the wheel. In fact, the defendant appeared very little in the patrolman's testimony. Crumpled bumpers, cuts in the pavement, concave headlight glass—these were the subjects of Cheek's testimony.

The patrolman's testimony stood in stark contrast to the racist language and tone used by other witnesses and court officials. Another law enforcement officer, Deputy Sheriff Thomas Jefferson Glover, referred to Booker as a "darkey" from the witness stand and reproduced informal conversations from Booker's time in jail that amounted to an undocumented, off-the-record confession. Frances Taylor, the driver from the other direction, refused to refer to Booker by name, calling him only "the Negro" in her oral testimony. The prosecutors, judge, and even the defense counsel also called Booker "boy" throughout his trial. After minimal deliberation, the jury returned a guilty verdict for manslaughter. Booker had been "culpably negligent" in the death of Rubye Robertson, according to the judge. Tommy Booker went to Parchman Farm for his part in a tragic motor vehicle accident.[46]

How easy could it have been for Tommy Booker or any Black motorist to obtain a driver's license in Jim Crow Mississippi? The driver's license office was not the voter registrar's office. But the requirement to submit to white scrutiny was similar. It was another opportunity for white humiliation and rejection. It would be impossible to know, but one imagines a high proportion of Mississippi's Black motorists were unlicensed heading into the civil rights era. Part of that, no doubt, was the Highway Patrol's takeover of licensure from local governments. If a driver desired to take a driving test or renew their license, they reported to the local branch of the Highway Patrol.[47]

Around the time of Tommy Booker's conviction in 1952, statewide civil rights organizing took aim at the Mississippi Highway Safety Patrol. Activists knew that, despite its low budget and fewer than one hundred troopers, the Highway Patrol exacted an outsized toll on Black motorists. Meeting in Yazoo City, near Vicksburg, in November 1952, the Mississippi State Conference of NAACP Branches decried "intimidations, whether by hooded or unhooded groups." Regarding these *unhooded* terrorists, the state's Black leaders vowed to stymie what they identified as the "contagion" and "increasing tendency" of police brutality on Mississippi roadsides. Conference officers enjoined state officials including Governor Hugh White, T. B. Birdsong, and the state's eighty-two county sheriffs to prosecute law enforcement officers who abused their power.[48]

Middle-class Black boosters recognized the Highway Patrol's racial violence acutely. Leaders from the all-Black town of Mound Bayou singled out the Highway Patrol. Its Regional Council of Negro Leadership (RCNL) was a significant local organization of racial uplift that by turns competed and collaborated with the NAACP.[49] Led by Theodore Roosevelt Mason Howard, the RCNL decried "highway brutalities," likely to underscore the notorious acts of troopers with the highway *safety* patrol against Black motorists and tourists moving through and stopping in the state. By 1955, numerous Black drivers had reported beatings and even whippings on state roads within patrol jurisdiction. T. R. M. Howard and the RCNL weaponized bad local press in their campaign for accountability, and Birdsong routinely found himself on the defensive in public statements. Yet troopers continued to mete out punishment on Black motorists, usually under cover of night, after more than a decade of consciousness-raising.[50]

As Tommy Booker's case made clear, there could be no accident on Mississippi's highways. To be Black on the open road, as in open court, was to lack meaningful rights, to be outlawed in yet another way. Whether beaten by a state trooper for sport or doomed by a state trooper in dispassionate legal proceedings, rural Black residents saw Mississippi's public safety regime operate for the satisfaction of white neighbors. And as Patrolman Cecil Cheek demonstrated in his expert testimony, law enforcement officers did not have to present their evidence with obvious racial animosity to harm. Rather, a scientific Jim Crow coexisted comfortably with unsophisticated forms of racial domination. Policing's autocracy reigned on the open road.

Unlike Leroy Miller, Tommy Booker remained in the county jail until his appeal process was completed—unsuccessfully. There are no records to indicate that the NAACP or RCNL became directly involved in his case.[51] When Booker arrived at Parchman on April 27, 1954, at just eighteen years old, he listed his mother, Sally Turner, as his next of kin. Booker stood five feet, five inches tall and weighed just 115 pounds. Judge Jarvis had sentenced Booker to eight years; prison officials paroled him after two years of incarceration, on May 17, 1956. His term expired on August 31, 1958.[52]

......

Even in Booker's case, where the record of Sally Turner's work on his behalf does not survive, we can be sure that state violence upended her life. In each case, policing set the family and community members of those killed, tortured, or incarcerated on what Nissa D. Tzun has called a "forced trajectory." An artist and documentarian, Tzun cofounded the Forced Trajectory Project in 2009 to explore the common experience of those left behind to advocate and seek justice after policing and incarceration. No two survivors come to their forced trajectory from the same path, but state violence demands similar adaptations from all. After state violence, everyday people seek formal redress. That act, whether of simple defense or structural change, leaves a trace, a witness, a counternarrative in the historical record.[53]

In 1940s Mississippi, the paths of survivors into the historical record were similar. Policing interrupted diverse lives, interrupting years of small joys and human fulfillment. The families, friends, and neighbors who survived policing came to this work with varying political consciousness and commitments regarding the police and collective action. These mothers, siblings, and neighbors may have resisted oppression in small ways every day, but they did not formally collectivize their political grievance with the NAACP before police violence punctuated their day-to-day lives. In most cases the historical record goes cold after the act of policing that brought them into localized movements.

Certainly, some blame for this belonged to NAACP headquarters. As Ruby Hurley knew, the NAACP was a notoriously classist racial uplift organization. It generally refused to advocate on behalf of anyone thought to be guilty. Institutionally, it had little interest in social change that exceeded equality before the law and fervently distanced itself from the egalitarian horizons of possibility associated with leftist politics.[54] Nonetheless, local communities used the NAACP to pursue and organize around their own understandings of freedom.

More consequential in the long term was the collective memory of injustice spawned by Mississippi Law. If the slow violence of policing accrued over years, so too did the grassroots organization built around police terror. Black people knew that arbitrary state violence could befall most any community member and the criminal legal system would conspire to cover it up. As a result, Mississippi's Black communities developed the resources and knowledge to fight back in a way that couldn't be construed as armed insurrection or otherwise used to justify racial massacres. They did not immediately win, but as Buford Johnson insisted, many played a long game.

This tactic of underground NAACP organizing survived, as will be seen in chapter 6. The work it did in the 1940s and '50s around police terror also survived, and when rural Black communities revolted in the 1960s, when activists from SNCC and CORE descended on Mississippi, it was the NAACP's underground networks that kept the movement informed, fed, and, when appropriate, well-hidden. But the long white supremacist counterrevolution was also sweeping the land toward further Black removal in service to rural redevelopment. For the McWilliamses, it was timber. Elsewhere, it was beef cattle, to which we turn in the next chapter.

4   Cotton Belt and Cattle Prod

> This crime of genocide is the result of a massive conspiracy, more deadly in that it is sometimes "understood" rather than expressed, a part of the mores of the ruling class often concealed by euphemisms, but always directed to oppressing the Negro people. . . . This implementation is sufficiently expressed in decision and statute, in depressed wages, in robbing millions of the vote and millions more of the land.
>
> —Civil Rights Congress, *We Charge Genocide* (1951)

On February 20, 1952, a Black tenant farmer named Tobe Faulkner shot a white man's cow. Faulkner's farm lay just yards from Mississippi Highway 80, near Lawrence, a south Mississippi crossroads in Newton County. Born in 1888, Faulkner was a sixty-five-year-old World War I veteran who had lived in rural Newton County his entire life. He had farmed, worked for the railroad, and lived with his wife Margaret over those decades.[1] When Faulkner's landlord came to confront him about shooting his cow in 1952, Faulkner shot the white man, wounding him in the arm. A committee of six lawmen responded to Faulkner's farm. The county sheriff, three deputies, and two highway patrolmen ordered him out of his house. He refused, and a trooper began to break down Faulkner's door. The farmer shot him too. Tobe Faulkner refused to leave the land without a fight.[2]

T. B. Birdsong mobilized the Highway Patrol for an insurrection. With a cattleman and state trooper wounded, twenty-five more state policemen descended on Faulkner's farm.[3] Barricaded in his home, the farmer exchanged gunfire with troopers. Patrolmen deployed some two dozen tear gas canisters on Birdsong's order. Still Faulkner shot back. A crowd of onlookers estimated at one thousand formed along Highway 80. Some private citizens reportedly shot into Faulkner's dwelling alongside lawmen. After some three hours of shooting back, Faulkner's guns fell silent. Troopers found him dead inside his house.[4]

We may never know Tobe Faulkner's exact motivation for shooting his landlord's cow or refusing to go alive into the hands of Mississippi Law.

A Black paper, the *Jackson Advocate*, reported that the conflict stemmed from the cow's habit of eating Faulkner's flowers. The *Chicago Defender* reasoned that Faulkner refused to consent to a legal lynching.[5] White press coverage of the farmer's final act implied senility. Faulkner was of advanced age. He lived alone. He was a tenant farmer. He shot a cow. Such evidence conveyed meaning across numerous papers. An atmosphere of peculiarity hovered over the white reporting—how strange that an older Black tenant farmer would get into a shootout with the Highway Patrol over a cow.

In the story of Tobe Faulkner's self-defense on the land, we can see the ease with which white observers saw criminal insanity rather than humanity. Faulkner's battle was but a single incident in a swell of conflict between Black tenants, white landlords, and the state police in Mississippi. In fact, Faulkner was one of no fewer than six Black tenant farmers who fought gun battles with Mississippi lawmen between 1949 and 1959.[6] Prior to their last stands, these farmers were some of the survivors, those who refused to be displaced by less violent means of rural redevelopment after cotton monoculture, especially the insurgent white beef cattle industry.

This chapter tracks how white cattlemen became a major new political constituency in Mississippi after World War II. Unlike the cotton plantocracy of an earlier era, who had been primarily concerned with the promise of free or discounted labor, who soothed their collective conscience with paternalistic noblesse oblige toward "good Negroes," cattlemen developed a different relationship to Black rural people rendered surplus, in their opinion, by the downfall of the labor-intensive cotton economy. As their land-intensive enterprise of vast pastures with large herds joined soybean fields cultivated by tractors and timber stands for logging, cattlemen criminalized people they believed threatened their bovine capital. In the context of rural Jim Crow Mississippi, antiblack policing could be the slow drip of making a place unlivable or the instant removal to carceral institutions. In a period that corresponded to the first stirrings of Black revolt toward desegregation, rural Black people left farmland that had once sustained whole Black communities faster than ever before.[7]

For Black Mississippians who remained on farmland as tenants, the police-guarded beef rush disrupted systems of rural subsistence created inside the older cotton sharecropping system.[8] In Mississippi, the commons, or rural land shared for the common good, could be as simple as a water well, a garden, a flower bed, a fishing hole, or a burial ground. At times stealing a cow improved life too.[9] And though the cattle economy did not destroy sustenance for all, with the aid of law enforcement and the criminal legal system, beef helped to remake the countryside into a site of surveillance and increased interactions with Jim Crow law enforcement. This increased police presence disproportionately led to fines, jail time, and forced labor for Black people. In a new context of agricultural commodities, cattlemen and cops believed valuable cows were liable to theft and destruction by suspicious underemployed inhabitants. Cattlemen summoned a new policing that in part remade the land.

White cattlemen allied with Mississippi's state police force to further destabilize the Black countryside. As this chapter argues, policing joined a constellation of forces driving Black residents from the land. Lynching, mechanization, tourism, USDA discrimination: Historians have documented how each of these forces pushed Black people from the land, reallocating 800,000 acres of Black-owned land between 1950 and 1964 and dislocating 90,000 Black tenant households in Mississippi between 1950 and 1975. In turn, this fueled the migration of Black Southerners to Northern and Western cities as well as the greater migration to small and mid-sized Southern towns.[10] For all the attention paid to migration, many Black Mississippians hoped to improve their lives on the land. However, they had little recourse amid a real estate regime that made the cattle pasture a dominant use of the earth in Mississippi. In their bid to re-enclose the cotton belt, state police administrators mobilized around the imagined threat of cattle rustlers empowered by fast cars and paved roads. Demonstrating their ability to police the pastures, the Highway Patrol overcame the hesitance of some local elites to set a precedent for statewide jurisdiction, unfettered from state highways.

There will be no smoking gun in this story, no letter between ruling white Mississippians plotting a time and place to displace Black tenants or expropriate Black-owned land for cattle pastures. As members of the Civil Rights Congress wrote to the United Nations in 1951, the premeditation of America's racial regime was more often implicit than explicit. There was no better expression of this principle than the ownership, use, and occupancy of land during revolutions in regimes of value extraction. Similar to the cotton rush of the nineteenth century, the beef rush of the twentieth century required no manifesto, only white dominion with its assumptions of hierarchy and armed state power.[11] The market and policing's autocracy did the rest.

The Prison and the Cattle Industry

Estella's Flashy Blonde, Afterglow's Observer, and Bouncing Bet spent most of their days east of Memphis, Tennessee. The trio ate rye and alfalfa. They bathed in freshwater lakes. They rarely ventured from the 3,000-acre Shelby County Penal Farm but earned international accolades.

These were thoroughbred dairy cows, imported from the Channel Island of Jersey. A team of unfree farm attendants waited on them. Incarcerated men and women milked a herd of these Jerseys three or four times each day. They maintained the cows' feed, cleaned their barns, and processed raw milk for use in milk and cheese. Overwhelmingly Black and male, some eighty imprisoned farm laborers wore leg shackles at all times while outdoors. Hundreds more worked to construct roadways.[12]

These cows were the lifework of James Gale Carr, the Shelby County Penal Farm's agricultural supervisor. A Missouri farmer hired during the Great Depression, Gale Carr built the west Tennessee prison farm into a self-sustaining operation. Carr ordered the conversion of cotton fields into pastures, oversaw the planting of fruit trees, and expanded prisoner responsibilities to include pork and beef husbandry. By the mid-1930s, his farm provided the food for Shelby County's entire welfare apparatus, including a hospital, poorhouse, and retirement home. Underwritten by the unpaid labor of detainees, Carr experimented in areas of animal science and rural economic development on the penal farm. He published his research widely in trade journals, growing an international reputation in the small world of Jersey breeders.[13]

Carr frequently led tours of the prison farm for outsiders. He hosted planners from Western Europe as well as regional boosters from across the South. In November 1937, even Eleanor Roosevelt came during a New Deal tour of Memphis. After visiting a segregated school built with Works Progress Administration labor, Roosevelt found the county jail "a model farm." "There is work provided for everyone," she wrote in her daily newspaper column. Carr capped off the tour by introducing the first lady to a young heifer he named Afterglow's Eleanor. For the agricultural scientist, the photo opportunity was his crowning achievement. He meticulously pasted clippings of the newspaper coverage into his scrapbook.[14]

One hundred miles southeast of Memphis, George McLean, a newspaperman in Tupelo, recruited Carr to bring his expertise to Mississippi. Arriving in 1939, Carr helped transform the area's agricultural economy in an age of immense transition. Combining salesmanship with the resources of Mississippi State College in Starkville, Carr and McLean democratized and circulated the technology of artificial insemination to white farmers. Starting with dairy and expanding to beef, agricultural extension agents and scientists funded by the USDA brought world-class pedigrees and cutting-edge science to Mississippi. These pure-breeding production reforms, along with a global beef industry devastated by World War II, unleashed a gold rush on Mississippi's countryside, definitively turning it away from a century of cotton monoculture.[15]

Rurality in Mississippi remained exceptional as compared to neighboring states—especially for the state's Black population. By 1940, the rate of farms per 100,000 inhabitants in Southern states bordering Mississippi had fallen on average 25 percent from 1910. The rate in Mississippi fell by only 13 percent. Whereas the rate of non-white farms per 100,000 non-white residents in bordering states fell on average by 25 percent between 1910 and 1940, Mississippi's rate of non-white farms fell by only 10 percent. Even in the decade after 1940, Mississippi's rate of Black farms fell by only 15 percent. Simply put, Mississippi's economy and lifeway remained tied to the land later than any other Deep South state. Black life often meant farm life.[16]

Rural Black renters were the norm. This condition related to the cotton economy and Jim Crow's system of racialized labor. In Mississippi, the majority of agriculturalists lacked land and therefore lived on the property of a landlord. As late as 1945, 60 percent of the state's total farmers lived as tenants. For Black farmers, this ratio was much larger, as high as 88 percent in 1930. The proportion of non-white farmers who were tenants only dropped below 50 percent in Mississippi after 1964.

However, Black farm owners constituted an important class in the Southern countryside. And the decade after the stock market crash of 1929 saw a renaissance of Black landownership in Mississippi. Both the number of farms and number of acres owned surged between 1925 and 1945. Only *after* World War II did this remarkable trend reverse, coinciding with the consolidation of the beef cattle industry and a surge in Black protest (see chapter 6). In particular, the years between 1954 and 1959 saw a dramatic decrease in Black farmers, interrupting a slow, linear decline with a 40 percent downward lurch.[17]

Purebred beef breeding slowly changed the imagined use of the land by landlords. However, dreams of modernizing the countryside required state-subsidized technological innovation. The purchase price of one purebred stud could carry the price tag of a decent *farm* in Mississippi. The time required to transport bulls slowed the process of selective breeding. Luckily, Carr and McLean brought interest in cattle to Mississippi at the same time that the state's white land-grant university pioneered artificial insemination technology and its state government built a system of paved highways.

Parchman, MS, ca. 1960. Superintendent C. E. Breazeale and Mr. Bill Smith in pasture with beef cattle and unidentified incarcerated laborers. Paul B. Johnson Family Papers, M191, Box 166, Folder 3, Historical Manuscripts, Special Collections, The University of Southern Mississippi Libraries.

Mississippi State College housed the state extension service, as well as a significant agronomic research division. There, H. Joe Bearden first learned of a cost-effective European technique to circulate various purebred bloodlines through microunits of a given bull's semen. Thus made mobile, the world's finest breeding cows suddenly came as close as the nearest extension agent.[18]

The results were momentous for beef cattle farmers. Whereas dairies sought mainly to establish long-term, stable herds for milk production, beef operations sought to sell as many cows as possible. This system of husbandry, called the cow-calf system, emerged after World War II and established itself by the mid-1950s. Farms as far east as Mississippi and Alabama raised calves to an age of maturity before shipping them to feedlots in Western states like Texas, Nebraska, and Colorado. Only there did Mississippi's young cows fatten for slaughter.[19]

The beef industry traveled to and changed Parchman Farm. After New Deal cotton reforms, the USDA paid the Mississippi State Penitentiary to decrease cotton production—$155,000 between 1933 and 1935 alone.[20] The prison took farmland out of cotton cultivation, invited assistance from Mississippi State College, and assigned the incarcerated to tend to state-owned cattle herds. By 1949, cows supplied a quart of whole milk and 1.5 pounds of beef to all incarcerated residents of the massive prison complex. In 1949, the prison's animal husbandman requested $2,000 from state lawmakers for the improvement of Parchman's beef herd.[21] By 1961, the herd had grown to more than 1,000 cows and employed three incarcerated "cowboys" for daily management. Prison officials reserved these unpaid jobs for prisoners in "honor camps" and used the promise of animal care (as opposed to cotton labor) to stoke hierarchy among laborers.[22]

Even the state's infamous mental hospital developed a beef herd. In 1954, the Mississippi State Hospital at Whitfield housed over 4,000 patients and converted 130 acres of its forestland to pasture for beef cattle. One wing of Whitfield functioned as a hospital for the criminally insane, where administrators admitted two hundred prisoners per year. Both these and noncriminal patients endured the medical treatments of their day: "electroshock treatment, insulin shock, psychotherapy, group therapy and a consulting neurosurgeon who performs the famous prefrontal brain operation for the change of personality," the lobotomy. The prison-hospital's farm maintained a 134-acre garden, with milk cows and pigs. But administrators were proud of their new 140-cow beef operation. "We have a very promising beef herd growing," wrote one administrator. "We are all proud of this fine herd." The administrator did not remark upon the labor of hospital patients alongside its thirty-five paid farm attendants. All told for 1954, the farm at Whitfield yielded over $350,000 in produce consumed by patients and staff.[23]

The surging price of beef and the increase in surplus land no doubt played a role in Mississippi's embrace of beef cattle ranching. The US Department of Agriculture's January 1 census of beef cows showed that the estimated cattle population in Mississippi doubled to roughly 300,000 during World War II. Between 1948 and 1953, the number of cows doubled again, topping 600,000. By 1964 the estimated beef population topped 1 million in a state of only 2.3 million humans.[24] According to the statistical calculations of Alan L. Olmstead and Paul W. Rhode, the average price in American dollars for 500 pounds of beef steer rose 175 percent between 1938 and 1949. The price peaked at nearly $180 in 1951 before stabilizing around $120 for the next decade.[25] Likewise, the federal government now paid many farmers to take land traditionally reserved for maximum cash crop production, like cotton fields, out of production. This newly fallow land could be filled

Lowndes County, MS, ca. 1950s. Walter Swoope's cattle and men. Otis Noel Pruitt and Calvin Shanks Photographic Collection #05463, Image Box IB-5463/050, Sheet Film 05463/00208, Southern Historical Collection, Wilson Special Collections Library, University of North Carolina at Chapel Hill.

with cattle easily, leaving the countryside's likely inhabitants, Black tenant farmers, in a precarious new scenario. Remaining cotton land could be tended by mechanical cotton pickers.[26]

Less than ten years after the introduction of purebreeding to Mississippi, once massive cotton plantations had converted to beef cattle with the help of segregated agricultural infrastructure. Take the Swoope farm, for example. Born in 1889, Walter Ashby Swoope was the only son of a Lowndes County cotton planter. In 1910, the Swoope farm housed a widowed Black cook, Helen Wood, and as many as thirty-two Black tenant families, some 160 women, men, and children.[27] The younger Swoope used all state tools at his disposal to convert his cotton farm to a purebred Angus beef operation. He incorporated as Swoope Angus Farm on his family's 3,500 acres of prime cotton land south of Columbus. In time, Swoope became the first vice president of the Mississippi Cattlemen's Association, the producers' organization that began to lobby on behalf of the emergent industry. Unlike cotton planters, cattlemen like Swoope allied with a centralized state police that brought new surveillance power to the cattle countryside.[28]

The Mississippi Cattlemen's Association

Across the state, white cattlemen organized. In 1946, an extension agent from Pontotoc County and a Delta agribusinessman imagined a white producers' association to lobby state government in Jackson on behalf of beef farmers. On May 16, the two used the segregated space of Mississippi State College's annual Field Day to present their plan to an audience of white beef farmers. After touring the college's scientifically managed pastures, someone proposed the constitution of a Mississippi Cattlemen's Association. Over two hundred cattlemen joined on the spot, and the group elected their first officers.[29]

For the next twenty years, these cattlemen excluded Black farmers from the technologies and organizations used to democratize and subsidize purebreeding for white farmers. Racial animus aside, this exclusion stemmed from the private/public partnership in which white cattlemen operated. Black county extension services, segregated by law and funding, also demonstrated and boosted cattle to cotton farm owners and tenants of color. However, segregationist ideology dictated that white circuits of information and expertise remained closed to most Black agriculturalists. And Jim Crow etiquette policed new spaces for livestock commerce, such as sale barns. White cattlemen forced Black buyers to stand, bid, and sell from the back of the audience. As white cattle farmers sought greener pastures for their growing herds, the Black agriculturalist, and especially the tenant's way of life, came under threat like never before.[30]

The violent work of segregation and agricultural reform bolstered one another. In the decade after the association's founding in 1946, white cattlemen rode record beef prices and narrowed cotton production to increased prominence within Mississippi's Jim Crow government. In 1948, two cattlemen reported profits of $695 and $1,273 *per cow* at auction.[31] Segregationists like US senator James Eastland began his herd of Charolais cattle in this period, building it to three hundred cows by 1964.[32] That year, five senators and seventeen representatives in the state legislature identified themselves as cattlemen in their official government biographies. Between 1960 and 1968, a white cattleman served as president pro tempore of the state

Senate. Locally, cattlemen wielded power as sheriffs, judges, bankers, and lawyers. Sheriffs, as will be seen in the next chapter, used their office to build contiguous pastures from Black-owned land.[33]

Nonetheless, Black farmers defied exclusion to buy, sell, and raise livestock. Floyd Bailey Jr. was the son of farm owners and the grandson of slaves. He was one of two Black beef cattlemen listed in the inaugural Cattlemen's Association directory.[34] In 1947, he and his wife Irma raised Hereford cows in a Jefferson County farm community called Red Lick. Living just miles from Mississippi's Black land-grant college, Alcorn Agricultural and Mechanical College, they must have benefited from the infrastructure and expertise of the Black extension system. Irma Bailey graduated with a degree in education from Alcorn and taught in local schools for over forty years. The Cattlemen's Association was sure to mark Black farms as "(Colored)" for all who might consider doing business with them.[35]

In their hope of a life after the scourge of sharecropping, middle-class Black rural planners could also embrace logics of incarceration and land clearance. In March 1949, a Black school superintendent named Benjamin F. McLaurin Sr. critiqued the stultifying impact of white planter paternalism on the landless in Black Coahoma County. When a white planter came to bail out one of his Black workers from jail, McLaurin thought, the white landowner endorsed the character flaws that locked cotton tenants in penury. "Let him stay in jail," McLaurin said. "Let our land grow up in grass and put cattle on it and it will not be long until we come to ourselves and realize that this land is not here just to be here. This is a rich heritage to have, and let me encourage my boys to be tenants, if necessary, until they can get land."[36] McLaurin's rational, if punitive, dream was for an equal opportunity in the new cattle economy. His statement also, perhaps, captured a clear understanding of white-led agricultural transition. Black farms that survived, he knew, would be cattle farms.

McLaurin dedicated his life to improving Black life on the land, but his 1949 speech underestimated the white supremacist drive for wealth and domination. He spoke of "our land" in a room of white Delta cotton planters and cattlemen who had organized the state of Mississippi around the profitable idea that Black people, like Native people before them, could not be trusted as stewards of the land. Between 1950 and 1960, Black landowners like McLaurin lost 20 percent of their land in Coahoma County.[37]

For Black sharecroppers who hoped to buy their first land, cattle could offer false hope. When Fannie Lou Hamer was twelve, her mother and father were on the verge of paying rent with cash instead of a share of their cotton crop in Sunflower County when a white neighbor poisoned the family's growing livestock herd with insecticide. "We were doin' pretty well," Hamer remembered, "then our stock got poisoned. We knowed this white man had done it. . . . That poison knocked us right back down flat. We never did get back up again. That white man did it just because we were gettin' somewhere. White people never like to see Negroes get a little success. All of this stuff is no secret in the state of Mississippi."[38] Hamer dropped out of school shortly thereafter to help the family merely survive on the land.[39]

Though vulnerable to displacement and economic exploitation, tenant farming offered Black farmers a small degree of self-sufficiency and protection from market forces. For instance, those who sharecropped in Mississippi vividly recalled the value of gardens. Cornelius Toole Sr. grew up in Hushpuckena, near Mound Bayou. Born to Black sharecroppers in 1958, Toole bought his first land in the 1980s. "Even when we were sharecropping they would always allow you enough space to grow a garden, so we have always grown vegetables and raised livestock, cows, hogs and chickens. . . . My dad was a [survivor] from the Depression. . . . I think from that point he decided . . . if . . . there was a depression and you are cut off from the other parts of the world, or if money is not any good, you can still eat if you grow stuff. And so . . . we always would grow our own vegetables." For Toole, the security of gardening was multigenerational and carried into the twenty-first century. "It really helps us to feel a little more secure in knowing that we can grow vegetables and stuff and not have to depend on vegetables being trucked in," he said in 2006. He was in the process of transitioning his truck farm to non-GMO, organic agriculture.[40]

Some white cattlemen suggested that sharecropping was an obstacle to agribusiness modernity. In its first membership newsletter, the Cattlemen's Association blamed "out-moded systems of land tenure . . . for the lack of appreciation of the economic importance of the livestock enterprise in a system of modern agriculture."[41] Association architects referred, of course, to cotton tenancy, the old-fashioned system by which over 100,000 wealthless Black and white farm families survived on the land in 1950, despite the mechanization of cotton picking.[42]

Yet it would be a mistake to presume that Mississippi's white cattleman movement publicly spouted anti-Black or reactionary rhetoric. Gone were the days when, in 1875, white cattlemen in Alabama implored cotton landlords to embrace cattle "instead of being at the mercy of a lazy, thievish, demoralized and impudent set of negroes."[43] They seemed more intent on straightforward economic development.

For instance, white cattlemen welcomed the enclosure work of outside investors who promised to create wealth. "Our lands are still reasonable in price," the Cattlemen's Association celebrated in 1948.[44] Paul Thompson of Terra Haute, Indiana, agreed. He built a 10,000-acre ranch in rural Noxubee County. Thompson was a white cattleman who owned feedlots for fattening beef calves in Indiana and Kentucky before buying his fifteen square miles in East Mississippi. According to the Cattlemen's Association, this was not enclosure or colonization or carpetbagging. It was *an installation*. Thompson "installed" his "cattle program" onto the cotton belt land he purchased.[45] Between 1950 and 1960, nine hundred Black tenant farm families left the land in Noxubee County. Some 136 Black landowners lost 14,000 acres over the decade.[46]

While cattlemen avoided talk about race, they were proudly anticommunist. In 1950, the Cattlemen's Association attacked the "fallacious philosophies beguiling our country into socialism." The "growing power and expansion of wasteful government, the colossal public debt, heavy burden of taxation, and the malicious attempt to substitute artificial for natural economy" would mean "national bankruptcy."[47] This, they resolved, would be the natural outcome of an interventionist national government. Such thinking placed cattlemen in early agreement with the emerging neoliberal philosophy of the Mont Pelerin Society and economists like Friedrich Hayek and, later, Milton Friedman.[48]

The cattlemen kept mum on federal policies that redistributed American wealth to white farmers who wished to buy land or scale up. Subsidized loan programs from the Federal Housing Administration (FHA) and Farmers Home Administration (FmHA) drove white property ownership in the rural South while actively thwarting the upward mobility and stability of Black farmers. White farmers also controlled the implementation of federal programs on the ground. They monopolized USDA bureaucracies and benefits well after the civil rights era.[49] Cattlemen also embraced another government expansion—law enforcement.

The Mississippi Livestock Theft Bureau

In the spring of 1950, the Cattlemen's Association gathered to draft legislation that put the Mississippi Highway Safety Patrol to work for them. As enacted, House Bill 620 provided for two "special livestock investigators," which the Cattlemen's Association nominated directly. These men were to operate from the state's Department of Public Safety, with a $10,000 annual budget. Soon renamed the Mississippi Livestock Theft Bureau, these sleuths wore guns but not uniforms. And unlike other officially sanctioned state patrolmen, livestock investigators were the first state policemen free to roam about the countryside, on dirt roads, through fields, and across pastures in search of missing cotton, tractors, or cows. Lawmakers granted them "general police powers."[50]

The new cow police became yet another avenue for state police expansion. The patrol had existed since 1938, but state lawmakers refused to extend its funding, jurisdiction, or influence. As covered in chapter 2, white perceptions of patrol overreach translated into state laws that forbade troopers from operating on county roads. Legislators also reduced T. B. Birdsong's operating budget.[51] But cattlemen were a rising political constituency who demanded property protection across the many sheriffs' county jurisdictions.[52]

Patrol administrators wasted no time in expanding the Livestock Theft Bureau. After only one year, Commissioner T. B. Birdsong petitioned lawmakers for more livestock inspectors with more police power. The state legislature answered, hiring five additional inspectors and passing a law to entrust the bureau with registering and authenticating the designs on branding irons from across the state. Cattlemen paid a nominal fee to register the marks burned into their cows' skin, and this revenue defrayed the bureau's cost.[53]

The Livestock Theft Bureau justified its existence by concocting a crisis narrative of cattle rustling in the post-cotton countryside. Administrators never explicitly described the rustlers' appearance, but state policemen constructed an omnipresent yet race-blind criminal archetype. "Phoenix-like from infertile soil and eroded hillsides," one administrator wrote in 1955, "Mississippi farmers in recent years have fashioned a new major industry, cattle raising. But with the cow and the new prosperity came the rustler, sinister [and] evil. . . . The jurisdiction of a sheriff ends at his county line, but an investigator's jurisdiction knows no such bounds. . . . The Bureau also receives full cooperation from district attorneys, the Federal Bureau of Investigation, [and] the Mississippi Cattleman's Association."[54] Published in the same year that George W. Lee, Lamar Smith, Emmett Till, and Clinton Melton lost their lives in racial slayings that went uninvestigated by federal authorities, these words painted Mississippi's farmers and cattle rustlers without explicit attention to racial identity, even as they placed the FBI on the same footing as the Cattlemen's Association.[55]

This Highway Patrol origin myth for the beef cattle industry was telling. The beef industry emerged from useless land, from land ruined by cotton monoculture. Why would anyone live on this wasteland? Clearly, state police administrators shared the dream of a fresh start with cattlemen. By 1959, the bureau acclaimed itself the *"only"* agricultural law enforcement agency in the country, forgetting the Special Texas Rangers. It even bragged that the president of the Philippines, Carlos P. Garcia, had expressed interest in emulating the organization.[56]

From a public relations standpoint, the Livestock Theft Bureau excelled in color-blind, reformed Jim Crow policing. It chose against keeping statistics on the race of cattle rustlers and touted its equal function for Mississippi's Black farmers. In one case, a patrol photographer followed an investigator and the Newton County sheriff to the farm of Clovis Wright. A photo captured the moment when the bureau reunited the farmer of color with two missing Jersey heifers. Three years after the removal of Tobe Faulkner, a rash of cattle disappearances had struck cattle farms in Newton County. The bureau's hard work for Clovis Wright made the front page of the local newspaper.[57]

While its public face emphasized equal protection under law, and individual inspectors may have protected the property of Mississippi's Black cattle farms, the Livestock Theft Bureau brought a new layer of police surveillance to the countryside. It carried the philosophy and ambition of the Cattlemen's Association into Black farm committees across the state. All-white troopers freed to roam farm communities brought more Black people into contact with the criminal legal system, which then disproportionately punished Black Mississippians. The Highway Brutality Patrol now had a farm wing.

The Livestock Theft Bureau also policed a food-insecure rural Black population. Its investigative reports remain classified; however, the bureau's investigators busied themselves with more than just tracking down living animals. "In the hills of Carroll County there was not so much cattle rustling for the purpose of sale," remembered trooper Charles Alvin Marx, who joined the patrol in 1957. "But they would be slaughtered, in the owner's pasture, and that meat taken which could be carried away. . . . This was quite prevalent." When his oral history interviewer asked whether the perpetrators tended to belong to a particular race, Marx stated that "It would pretty well balance out." The incident that came to his mind, however, was a Black man: "A ten thousand dollar bull was taken from a man, in the Delta, by a black and it was subsequently made into meat.... It was a ten thousand dollar bull that was taken. But that was simply an ignorance of the value of an animal." Marx and his interviewer laughed about the criminal's "ignorance" demonstrated by the irrationality of eating a pedigreed stud and show cow, joking that it was a waste to grind such a cow's flesh into hamburger.[58] Much like the Mexican banditry T. B. Birdsong mobilized to stop in Texas, the existence of poverty and hunger amid abundance was lost in criminalization.

Nonetheless, the bureau's own reporting defied simple narratives of antiblack over-policing. In a period when state law restricted all other highway patrolmen to state roads, seven inspectors arrested over 1,400 individuals in the decade after 1951. State recordkeepers did not disaggregate by race, but livestock theft investigators reported to newspapers that over half of those arrested for cattle rustling in the bureau's first year were white.[59] In ten years, state courts sent over nine hundred men and women (70 percent of accused cattle rustlers) to the Mississippi State Penitentiary at Parchman. Over this period, prison administrators identified between 70 and 80 percent of all new prisoners at Parchman as Black.[60] It is safe to assume that courts convicted accused Black rustlers at higher rates than white ones. However, that state policemen arrested suspected rustlers in rough proportion to the state population (and publicized that fact) marked a change. In keeping with Winfield Scott Featherston's race-blind war on disorder, the patrol signaled that white people who interfered with the cattle industry could also be disposable in the state's ever-evolving property regime.

In light of this perceived success, state police doubters became believers. The arch-conservative *Clarion-Ledger* celebrated that eighty-five men had been sentenced to 215 years at Parchman for cattle rustling in the bureau's first year.[61] "We don't as a rule favor creation of any state agency or expansion of any state agency," wrote the paper's editor, T. M. Hederman Jr. "But we think the Mississippi House acted wisely ... in increasing ... the number of state investigators charged with ... combatting cattle thefts over the state." The rustler's ability to speed between counties on paved roads demanded a nimble and coordinated effort. Besides, thanks to brand registration fees, the bureau was "largely self-financing."[62]

By comparison to its 70 percent conviction rate, investigators successfully returned only 50 percent of cattle reported missing over its first decade. If unsuccessful at protecting the property of beef producers, the Livestock

Theft Bureau represented a wildly effective punitive arm of the state. Aside from formal arrests, the force no doubt added to an atmosphere of fear in rural districts across the state.[63]

......

The Livestock Theft Bureau alone did not account for rural Black displacement in this period. Convicted cattle rustlers never accounted for a large percentage of Parchman's population. And the number of prisoners in the state penitentiary remained remarkably stable through the 1940s and 1950s, hovering around 2,000.[64] Rather, the bureau joined a post–World War II law enforcement dragnet that harassed and extorted more frequently than it detained. As will be seen in the next chapter, the Highway Patrol took part in an unprecedented punitive turn during the 1950s.

Yet local law enforcement officers were already busy expropriating Black time and wealth from rural people and townsfolk who retained rural lifeways. The endangered archive from county justices of the peace and Circuit Courts bear this out. Fines for infractions spanned ten dollars for public drunkenness, fifty dollars for failure to yield right of way, or one hundred dollars for obscenity. If the convicted could not pay, Circuit Courts sentenced them to county prison farms. A Black Lowndes County tenant named Tom Elliott, implicated in the production of bootleg liquor, had to serve twelve months on the county farm for operating a personal distillery, or still. At the same time, legitimate alcohol procurement occurred through an elaborate system of black-market taxation that depended on the whims of local law enforcement.[65]

Local police plagued Black landowners especially. In a single rural district of Oktibbeha County, Sheriff M. C. Landrum and Justice of the Peace D. B. Jackson harassed and prosecuted Black landowners suspected of refining corn into whiskey in their jurisdiction. Between 1930 and 1945, they served numerous search warrants and confiscated the rare whiskey bottle. This offense, mere possession of alcohol, came with a $100 fine. John Brewer Davis, a Black landowner in the Chestnut Grove community, paid one such fine in January 1941. His penalty equaled one-fourth of his household's entire claimed income for 1939 and the whole value of his family's farmhouse. According to Justice Jackson's docket, Davis paid this lump sum immediately. But even accounting for undisclosed cash income from bootlegging or community lenders, such predatory policing might have sent Davis and his household of seven into bankruptcy. Sheriff

Landrum executed regular search warrants on Davis's property in the years that followed.[66]

Slowly, living off the land became criminal activity for those who moved to town. In September 1950, a Mississippi game warden charged Ollie Hunter with twelve counts of "illegal fishing." Such a vague charge could refer to the place or method of catching fish. Perhaps the officer found her fishing without a license in public waters, poaching fish from a private source, or using what he considered an unsportsmanlike trap. At any rate, Hunter was a widowed Black laundress who owned her own home and refused to go down without a fight. She appealed her conviction in justice of the peace court to the Lowndes County Circuit Court. Her appeal was unsuccessful; the judge upheld the lower court's ruling. Each charge cost Hunter between ten and twenty-five dollars. Appealing to the higher court brought additional court costs.[67]

. . . . . .

Levi Vernon "Beef" Henson, of Mississippi's white Cooperative Extension Service, was no politician. Beef Henson was a Quitman County cattleman, an educator, a US Department of Agriculture specialist in translating academic knowledge for everyday farm folk. In October 1954, when he wrote his regular letter to US senator John C. Stennis, Henson blended business with racial politics.[68]

He estimated that two-thirds of the state's cotton crop had survived a severe drought. The year's soybean crop had been a "total failure." And then there was the US Supreme Court's May 1954 decision in *Brown v. Board of Education*, which found unconstitutional any racial segregation of public education. "The Supreme Court decision on segregation was a very severe blow. . . . It will be fought to the last hedge row," Henson wrote. "I'm of the opinion that the segregation question has been given too much publicity from the State level. . . . We should be very conservative in our action. . . . We, as an agricultural area, are making changes in our farming pattern and will not have the heavy labor load (negro) as we have had in the past, which means they will be going to industry."[69] For Henson, structural shifts in agriculture promised the same defense of Jim Crow as radical segregationists. He believed that the latest agricultural revolution would shore up Jim Crow. Without need for cheapened, racialized labor, rural Black people would leave the countryside and stop fighting racial hierarchy in the hinterlands. Though he did not make explicit why Black Mississippians would have to leave, the implicit threats were joblessness, eviction, homelessness, starvation.

Henson's plan to preserve white supremacy was slower than the era's well-documented revival in extrajudicial killings and pogroms, harder to capture in a sensational headline or image than a segregationist's bluster. Rather than individuals or institutions, agribusiness itself would solve the problem posed by Black demands for racial equality. To be sure, many Black agrarians left places like Quitman County on their own terms, in search of better lives. But scattered clues remain about the push that accompanied the pull of the 1950s. They range from fines for illegal fishing to a pitched battle with the Highway Patrol after a Black sharecropper shot a cow.

The way Mississippi cattlemen like Beef Henson remembered their good fortunes in the 1930s, '40s, and '50s paved the way for easy, passive narratives of postwar agricultural transition. In *A History of the Mississippi Beef Cattle Industry* (1985), Mississippi's longtime secretary of agriculture, Jim Buck Ross, compiled vignettes from cattle-owning families in each of Mississippi's eighty-two counties. Ross featured great farms, ranchers, and corporations that rose to prominence after World War II. The book's narratives and pictures came directly from (almost exclusively) white cattlemen and -women.[70]

Buried deep inside this *History* is a photo of Leon Cicero Ellis, a Lowndes County physician and cattleman who lived from 1887 to 1957. One of hundreds of entries, Ellis's inscription reads, simply, "when the Black Prairie to the west opened up, Dr. Ellis moved from eastern Lowndes County to the prairie section. He ran a large farming operation and a big cattle herd on the grasslands of the prairie."[71] In Lowndes County, Ellis built his cattle empire, Ollie Hunter caught her fish, and 1,257 Black farm families left the land between 1940 and 1959. That averages more than one per week for twenty years. Black farmers tended to 70,000 fewer acres of land and owned 16,000 fewer acres by 1960. Meanwhile, the average farm size grew from 76 to 134 acres. This was land *opening up*.

The police aided a slow evacuation of the countryside and enabled the production of white wealth. The reformist state police, especially, extended its reach amid the movement to dispose of those rendered surplus by land-intensive rural redevelopment. The carceral power of this industry is in the very binding that holds Jim Buck Ross's *History* together. Incarcerated employees of the Mississippi Department of Corrections bound each physical copy in the state prison's book bindery. Its copyright page is stamped *Parchman*.[72]

As will be seen in the next chapter, the white families that populated *A History of the Mississippi Beef Cattle Industry* could reverse generational misfortunes to enter a middle-class or elite economic position. They were the latest settlers, requiring the violence of those who call land empty after the fact. They were also pioneers of a new political movement that, like Beef Henson, refused the flagrancy of the Ku Klux Klan. Instead, some Mississippi cattlemen and women founded the White Citizens' Council movement and once again began to reimagine Mississippi state police power toward the preservation of racial hierarchy.

5 The Cattleman's Massive Resistance

Let's everybody be nice.
—Unknown state trooper, Laurel, Mississippi (May 8, 1951)

Elton Franklin Deanes (pronounced *Dean*) was born in Cedar Bluff, Mississippi, a Clay County farm community, in 1933. He was the third generation of his family to own land there. His grandfather, Payton Deanes, had been enslaved in Alabama for some fifteen years before emancipation. After the Civil War, Payton moved to Cedar Bluff, in Mississippi's Tombigbee River Valley, and in 1874, he purchased his first land. Elton's father Seth, born in 1882, farmed his entire life in Clay County with his first wife Flora and second wife Clotha Bell. Elton Deanes remembered his parents' pride as Black property owners. Of his father, Elton said, "I never remember him doing any public work," what farmers called wage labor. In part, owning land carried insulation from the caprice and cruelty of white employers. But Black farmers were beholden to other white power brokers, especially bankers.[1]

In Elton Deanes's memory of the 1950s, credit became scarce. First, a bank declined a routine loan application. When Deanes needed $700 to build a new farmhouse for his wife Ruby Lee and six children, he went to the First National Bank of West Point. Inside, he was reminded that creditworthiness "depended on what color your skin was." "That man's name was Wilson," Deanes remembered of the loan officer. "And he asked me the history of my life. Then he told me 'No.' He couldn't let me have it. He said I didn't have enough collateral. And I had seven, eight cows myself at that time." Because his livestock far outvalued the amount of the loan, Deanes knew his rejection was not based on his ability to repay.[2]

At the bank, one of Clay County's most prominent citizens' councilors had interrogated Deanes. Across Mississippi and later the country, the White Citizens' Council was a collection of elites who weaponized their status in the finance, insurance, and real estate economy against Black people who, they believed, threatened Mississippi's racial order. Founded by a white Mississippi cattleman who was also a former military policeman, the Citizens' Council relied on economic pressure against movements experimenting in Black liberation. The Citizens' Council supported expansion of formal state police power through the Mississippi Highway Safety Patrol. They also benefited directly from the ongoing redevelopment of rural Mississippi by targeting the rural Black middle class.

Elton Deanes may or may not have realized that his loan officer was a citizens' councilor. Or, for him, it may have been a distinction without a difference. Regardless, Deanes knew that white farmers of equal means could get loans "on their signature." He eventually received money for the house from an aunt who had moved to California. But in 1954, he took on wage labor in nearby West Point to keep the family land—something his parents had never done. He described the double bind of this new age for Black landownership without capital or credit succinctly: "You was tied both hands."[3]

This chapter explores the white counteroffensive that targeted Deanes and countless other Black Mississippians in the 1950s. This so-called massive white resistance to desegregation and safety from lynching followed *Brown v. Board of Education* in 1954 and the murder of Emmett Till in 1955. Unlike previous surveys of this era, I focus on the ways segregationists mobilized the formal criminal legal system to terrorize rural and small-town activists who organized around these two crises. I argue that massive resistance was also a part of the larger reformist program of Mississippi's white business-progressive class, a forward-looking fight of police expansionists to extract Black income, wealth, and land on the way toward their latest regime of capitalist development.

In these years, segregationist police expanders like Governor James Plemon Coleman promised professional reform for the Mississippi Highway Safety Patrol and the Mississippi State Penitentiary. These two institutions were important to Coleman's vision of lawful white supremacy with propriety and economy. To achieve these changes, he placed Mississippi cattlemen at the head of both agencies.

The White Citizen

Everyone seemed to know Tut Patterson. Born Robert Boyd Patterson in 1921, and nicknamed "Tut" sometime thereafter, he was the son of a Clarksdale cotton broker, a man who facilitated the sale of raw Mississippi cotton to buyers around the world. As a child, Tut rode horses with a nephew of T. B. Birdsong. Aaron Henry, a future state president of the National Association for the Advancement of Colored People (NAACP), remembered Patterson as a red-headed childhood playmate. After high school, Patterson became a minor celebrity because he played on an undefeated football team at the all-white Mississippi State College in 1940.[4]

The world remembers Robert B. Patterson as a white supremacist. On July 11, 1954, Patterson founded the White Citizens' Council movement, fifty-five days after the US Supreme Court's unanimous decision in *Brown v. Board of Education*. *Brown* found the South's formal segregation of public schools illegal. It explicitly concerned education, but in Patterson's mind the ruling extended further. He lived in a majority African American county and town. He recognized that *Brown* overturned *Plessy v. Ferguson*, the 1896 Supreme Court decision that provided the constitutional rationale for explicit racial discrimination under the law.[5]

In *Brown*, Patterson saw the rights and privileges of his ethnostate slipping away. "*We will not be integrated!*" he wrote in a recruiting pamphlet from 1954. "We are proud of our white blood and our white heritage of sixty centuries." He understood the stakes for Mississippi's hierarchical distribution of wealth and state services. To his mind, local Black communities organizing through the NAACP hoped "that everybody in the world should be made equal by law, regardless of aptitude or heritage. The 'have nots' must share equally with the 'have gots' in this new world order."[6] Patterson's movement united segregationists across the state, nation, and Anglophone world against the promise of equal legal protection and wealth redistribution for people racialized as non-white.

Before he was a globetrotting white ideologue, Robert Patterson was a policeman and cattleman. He volunteered for World War II in January 1943, immediately after graduating from Mississippi State with a degree in animal husbandry. In Western Europe he fought as a paratrooper in the Eighty-Second Airborne Division. By the time of the Nazi surrender in May 1945, he was captain of his division's military police unit, stationed in a rural French *commune* in the Vosges Mountains. Before returning to Mississippi, he policed the American sector of Berlin, Germany, climbing to provost marshal, the highest rank among military policemen.[7]

Patterson returned to Mississippi with few prospects. Born to the cotton fortunes of a previous generation, but humbled by the Great Depression, he took jobs managing the profitable plantations of members of the white ruling class in the Mississippi River Valley. The US military refused him when he attempted to enlist in the Korean War of 1950, but his fortunes changed when he bought a beef cow in 1951. To expand his cattle operation, Patterson partnered with a family of Angus breeders in Montgomery County. This agribusiness venture was his family's escape from economic dependence on cotton. Eventually he passed the cattle business on to his two sons. From this foothold in property ownership and income, Patterson launched his movement in 1954.[8]

These previously unnoted links between military policing, cattle ranching, and the organization of the first Citizens' Councils emphasize the material stakes of fighting Mississippi's Black freedom struggles. In these years, law enforcement agencies had a virtual revolving door for cattlemen and activists in the political movement segregationists began to call *massive resistance*.

This convergence was no coincidence. From the beginning, movement leaders distanced themselves from the extralegal violence of the Ku Klux Klan and lynch law. In one of the earliest uses of the phrase by which the movement became known, US senator and cattleman James O. Eastland commanded a Citizens' Council rally "to fight racial integration with *massive resistance* but without lawlessness." He spoke these words in Montgomery, Alabama, just two months after a seamstress and NAACP organizer named Rosa Parks had refused to give up her bus seat to a white person. Martin Luther King Jr.'s Montgomery Improvement Association had begun to organize Black clergy and neighborhoods for the boycott against segregated buses and the indignity they represented. Eastland promised that only a "grass roots" campaign could "match the organizing ability and tactics of the NAACP." He also hoped state governments would subsidize this effort with public funds.[9] This was to be a professional, reformist movement of white law enforcement officers and business leaders—one mocked then and since as the *country-club, uptown,* or *white-collar* Klan.

To take such nicknames seriously means analyzing the evolving white supremacist power that accompanied the transition toward beef cattle economies explored in chapter 4. The violence of white resistance exploded anew into the lives of Black organizers after 1954. As many historians have shown, public activists were blacklisted and forced underground amid the hysteria. Citizens' councilors conspired to evict activist tenants, to cancel their insurance, to fire employees, to refuse them credit, and to call in their loans for immediate payment. In this age of farm consolidation and displacement that accompanied the countryside's beef cattle revolution, councilors threatened even the most financially secure rural Black activists. As we will see at the end of this chapter, when the nearest citizens' councilor was a cattleman and the sheriff, outright dispossession of land could result.

In the years of organizing after *Brown* and the murder of fourteen-year-old Emmett Till, Black farmers struggled to build momentum against everyday white reprisals. Many survived on the land to fight. Others lost everything and left the South altogether.[10]

The Mississippi Highway Safety Patrol took a leading role in the work of massive resistance. Creators of the state's newest white identity politics sought to refine racial violence, to distance themselves further from the spectacular racial violence encouraged during previous threats to the white supremacist order. State police expansionists offered the solution. They stood ready with deadly violence before arrest and attempted to control state violence after conviction. In fact, they almost installed Mississippi's gas chamber in state police headquarters.

Squeezing Mississippi, Caging Mississippi

For Mississippi's rural Black NAACP organizers, May 17, 1954, was a watershed. In ruling the separate but equal doctrine of *Plessy v. Ferguson* unconstitutional in *Brown v. Board of Education*, the Supreme Court naïvely hoped for white rulers to grapple with desegregation earnestly and in ways that met the unique needs of their localities. For NAACP branches, this conjuncture emanated less from federal courts than from the NAACP's Legal Defense Fund, headed by its chief counsel, Thurgood Marshall. Black communities across Mississippi had begun a new membership drive after World War II, donating money to NAACP headquarters. In the 1950s new communities moved toward organizing formal branches with public membership rolls. Nowhere was this more successful than in Lowndes County, Mississippi, and its county seat, Columbus, the home of the state NAACP president and an early epicenter of massive white resistance. There, about thirty miles east of Elton Deanes's farm in Cedar Bluff, the Citizens' Council movement experimented with economic and police pressure on Black residents thought to be fighting Jim Crow apartheid.

The 1950s was a decade of immense social change for Lowndes County. In 1954, the county was 55 percent African American, yet Black renters operated 82 percent of its 993 tenant farms. Columbus, the seat of county government, was the largest town in northeast Mississippi. Perched on bluffs above the Tombigbee River, Columbus with its antebellum townhomes became a receiving center for Black sharecroppers pushed from the land during the beef rush. Between 1950 and 1960, the town's population swelled from 17,000 to 25,000, a growth of almost 50 percent.[11]

If NAACP headquarters had a success story from Mississippi in the early 1950s, it was the Columbus branch and its charismatic president, Emmett James Stringer. Born in 1919, a native of the Delta's Mound Bayou community, E. J. Stringer met his wife, Flora Ghist, at Alcorn A&M College, the Black analog of Robert Patterson's Mississippi State College. He graduated in 1941. Stringer then enlisted in the US Army for the duration of World War II. His first job after service was in the Veterans Administration (the VA) in Chicago. He then moved to Nashville, Tennessee, to study dentistry at Meharry Medical College in 1947. There, he first joined the NAACP. He moved to Columbus in 1950 to open a dental practice, and Flora began to teach in local segregated schools. Together, they helped bring the NAACP to Lowndes County. The Stringers registered their first members in November 1952. By February 1953, Columbus applied for a branch, with seventy members, and Stringer joined the Mississippi State Conference of Branches' board of directors. The conference, impressed that the Columbus branch had grown to over a hundred members in its first year, elected Stringer state president for 1954. It was a momentous year.[12]

Stringer described Black Mississippi's second-class status boldly. He flatly urged members to "Pay your poll tax, register and vote."[13] For the December 1953 monthly meeting at Columbus's Black-owned Queen City Hotel, Stringer invited the Lowndes County sheriff, Charles Emerson Farmer, to speak on "The Purpose and Importance of the Poll Tax" and, presumably, whatever issues of police brutality members chose to raise. "As yet I do not know the exact number," Stringer wrote NAACP headquarters in his first year, "however, I am sure that more Negroes paid poll tax this year in Lowndes County than ever before." Stringer personally paid the fee for forty men and women of the county's American Legion post, and Black landowners learned to pay the poll tax when visiting the courthouse to satisfy other business.[14]

Stringer used his high office to interact directly with Mississippi's white ruling class. Before the Court ruled in *Brown*, Stringer formally wrote Governor Hugh White (reelected in 1952) to argue that the only legal recourse for the state was "to consolidate and integrate the present schools on all levels." When the state attorney general James Plemon Coleman attempted to organize a group of anti-integrationist leaders to speak for the entire Black community in May, Stringer declined to discuss anything except implementation of the Supreme Court's unanimous decision.[15]

On May 22, 1954, five days after *Brown*, the NAACP's national leadership echoed Stringer's hope. In what came to be called the "Atlanta Declaration," the organization declared that "Segregation in public education is now not only unlawful, it is un-American." The Columbus branch decided to organize around school desegregation as a means of equalizing Black education in Lowndes County, pursuant to the Atlanta Declaration. Columbus residents petitioned local school boards for immediate desegregation.

White resistance manifested swiftly. Store owners, bankers, landlords, merchants, and law enforcement officers joined Tut Patterson's Citizens' Council movement and collaborated to target Black residents and farmers who signed petitions or attended mass meetings. As the 1954 primaries and elections neared, councilors attacked the means of rural Black survival, especially lines of farm credit necessary to plant and harvest crops, so as to discourage all forms of Black political experimentation. The result was what NAACP counsel Franklin H. Williams called "the Mississippi Squeeze."[16]

Though strategies of white terrorism swept across Mississippi, the Columbus movement experienced extreme economic pressure from citizens' councilors. White landlords and employers organized to boycott Black dentists, physicians, and pharmacists associated with the NAACP. They paid only for tenant healthcare provided by non-activist medical professionals. Stringer, for one, experienced an instant credit freeze and an audit through the Internal Revenue Service. His insurance agent canceled his automotive policy, effectively revoking his car's registration. Bomb threats became regular affairs, and local police used every opportunity to subject the family to indignity through traffic stops. After this intimidation, Stringer refused to run for a second term as state NAACP president in October 1954.[17]

In the countryside, white conspirators tailored their intimidation to the precarity of Black agrarians. Traveling to Columbus in December 1954, the NAACP's national secretary of branches, Gloster Current, found that creditors refused to write or refinance mortgages for Black farmers associated with activism. Farmers also reported that citizens' councilors sold their existing debts, like long-term notes with merchants and liens against farm property, to new, aggressive investors who demanded immediate repayment. Headquarters responded with a national fundraising campaign. The NAACP executive board made a deposit in the Black-owned Tri-State Bank of Memphis, Tennessee, "to grant loans to Mississippi farmers, homeowners, business and professional men who have been refused credit by some white financial institutions." But the material help came too late. The NAACP's bankers routinely denied loans to farmers they determined to be unworthy of credit. Of the $220,000 available, Tri-State reported just over

$75,000 used by Mississippi activists. Emmett and Flora Stringer alone had required $4,000 in loans.[18]

Citizens' councilors in Columbus attacked rural Black organizers around Columbus. Caleb Lyde, of the Crawford community, had seen it all. Born in Lowndes County in 1889, he had paid rent with shares of his crops in the Delta during the agricultural depression of the 1920s. Sometime around 1930, authorities sent Lyde to Parchman Penitentiary. By 1940, he returned to his home in Crawford, bought modest farmland, and began to organize adult education classes. In the 1950s, Lyde joined the Columbus NAACP with his wife, Augusta; they then registered to vote with another Crawford farm owner. When a group of three white men scanned voter registries for Black farmers, they found the Lydes' names and went to their address. The councilors demanded the Lydes voluntarily strike their names from the voter roll. When they refused, someone mailed a simple, handwritten postcard to them on July 30, 1954. "LAST WARNING, if you are tired of living, VOTE AND DIE." They took the postcard seriously and stayed away from the polls. But Caleb and Augusta Lyde kept their names on the voter rolls and continued to organize neighbors.[19]

Rife with economic and physical terror, the midterm election campaigns of 1954 included key local races. Voters swept in a spate of rededicated white supremacists in positions from justice of the peace, who presided over traffic tickets, to circuit clerk, who registered a county's voters. Elected with energy from citizens' councils, the white political apparatus meant to crush emerging Black political power.

Citizens' councilors relied on local information networks that denied anonymity to Black activists. They conspired with white bankers, insurance brokers, employers, landlords, and merchants to terrorize public mobilizing efforts. For instance, a schoolteacher from an adjoining county lost her job after a banker reported to her superintendent that she belonged to the NAACP. As it happened, she was not a member. The banker had merely noted a personal check from the teacher to E. J. Stringer for dental work when it came through the bank. The banker assumed it was a membership fee for the NAACP. Even groundless suspicion of activist affiliation could precipitate financial ruin for Black Mississippians during the Squeeze.[20]

The NAACP's middle-class membership and leadership were particularly vulnerable to councilor intimidation. Stringer, like others, built the Columbus movement on urbane gender- and class-exclusive leadership. In

Columbus, professional Black men used their success and status as a bridge to white power brokers in hopes of attaining equal treatment within and bettering a system premised on inequality. Stringer particularly ignored his agrarian constituency. After a leading rural organizer from bordering Noxubee County wrote to the NAACP's regional secretary Ruby Hurley in hopes of chartering a new branch in October 1955, Stringer quashed the effort. "There are not very many courageous, *independent*, freedom-loving Negroes in Noxubee County at present," he wrote. Stringer could think of no one with "the responsibility and leadership necessary to successfully organize and perpetuate a branch." Whether the Columbus branch president harbored differences of opinion with Noxubee County's activists or merely felt national favor slipping away, he was not above denying self-determination to rural neighbors he viewed as a threat to his mission. The white power structure's unrelenting assault likely caused many such challenges to solidarity.[21]

Even women excluded from NAACP leadership positions experienced retaliation. Flora Ghist Stringer undoubtedly used her position teaching English at R. E. Hunt High School in Columbus to grow local membership and consensus around desegregation among teachers and students. Though her work goes unnoted in Stringer's NAACP records, she chartered one of Mississippi's first NAACP youth chapters in Columbus in 1954. But as an English teacher and organizer of young people, she posed a threat. In December 1954, the city superintendent fired her, even though she had attended Alcorn and held a graduate degree from the Teacher's College at Columbia University in New York. For the rest of her professional life, Flora Stringer worked outside Lowndes County.[22]

Amid such economic and political violence from Mississippi's white ruling class, national leadership in NAACP headquarters also criticized the Stringers. The family barreled toward insolvency, and the Tri-State Bank cut the family's line of credit. With nowhere else to turn, Stringer sent his balance sheet to national president Roy Wilkins asking the board to sponsor an emergency loan. Upon assessing the dentist's accounts, however, Wilkins lost all faith in Stringer. In an incredible exchange, Wilkins condemned Stringer's business model, moralized on his choice of automobile, and questioned the use of his mother's home as collateral for a loan. Believing he could judge Stringer's character, Wilkins began to question the extent of white economic retaliation against him. "Our Board will have to determine basically whether Dr. Stringer is a good manager caught in a series of emergency situations, or whether he is a bad manager," Wilkins wrote to the Memphis banker in charge of the Stringers' account.[23] Afterward, state NAACP leadership decidedly shifted west, to Mound Bayou, Jackson, and the more familiar state field secretary, Medgar Evers.

・・・・・・

From this focus on a single jurisdiction in a specific moment, it is difficult to overstate the degree to which Lowndes County's criminal legal system expanded its reach during the Mississippi Squeeze. Between 1950 and 1959, law enforcement officers and prosecutors brought more than 1,400 charges to the county's Circuit Court. Compared to the previous decade's 500, that amounts to a *200 percent increase*. Clerks kept court records imperfectly. Surviving data indicates that many of the decade's 1,400 charges were dismissed, rescinded, or remanded to lower justice of the peace courts for prosecution. However, the changing scale of charging was unprecedented. By comparison, the average increase in the number of Circuit Court cases between 1920 and 1950 was 50 percent decade over decade. Between 1960 and 1980, a period that saw total charges increase and then decrease decade on decade, the change in the number of prosecutions averaged only 12 percent. For Lowndes County, the 1950s brought a revolution in the system of policing, fining, and caging.[24]

This data suggests an earlier so-called *punitive turn* to *mass incarceration* than historians expect.[25] Lowndes County judges handed down at least 389 jail and prison sentences for charges within their jurisdiction over the 1950s. At least 286 of those rulings sent residents to the state's notorious Parchman prison farm, accounting for an increase of 140 percent in penitentiary sentences from the previous decade. County officials chose against collecting identifying information with individual entries, so it is impossible to say how racially balanced judges were in their assignment of prison sentences. However, in 1959, prison administrators identified 70 percent of the people incarcerated at Parchman as Black. Moreover, criminal charges known as pretexts to arrest Black people spiked over the 1950s in Lowndes County. For instance, charges of vagrancy, false pretense, resisting arrest, and disorderly conduct increased in this period, which overlapped with increased public stands against Jim Crow.[26]

Women accounted for a small but meaningful population of those impacted by Lowndes County's local criminal legal system. Based on an imperfect count of female given names in the records, prosecutors charged fewer than a hundred women with misdemeanors or felonies in the 1950s. And judges sentenced only fourteen women to Parchman Farm. But these figures more than tripled from the previous decade. Whether prosecuting women for vice, sex work, or operating a jukebox in a café without a permit, local law enforcement entangled women with increased frequency, especially those who sought economic independence and to profit from creating communal space amid rural dislocation.[27]

Police provocation clearly increased over the decade. While there are other possible explanations for the discrepancy between Circuit Court charges (1,400) and guilty verdicts that carried either fines or incarceration (726), the most obvious is that police enforcement greatly outpaced prosecutorial and judicial appetite or capacity. Without statistics disaggregated by race in this dataset, it is impossible to demonstrate empirically that the increase in criminal charges fell disproportionately on Black residents. Nonetheless, leading Black activists drew clear connections between new belligerent police tactics and renewed political organizing. In February 1955, the Lowndes County branch of the NAACP listed "Prevent police brutality" as its fifth goal for the year ahead.[28]

Grassroot organizers recognized that a new regime of local white power was hardening in the hamlets and fields of Mississippi. By 1957, the Columbus NAACP branch allowed donations to be made as "A Friend" of the organization, because it was too dangerous to register as a dues-paying member. "Quite a few of our former members live in nearby small towns and rural communities," Stringer wrote national membership secretary Lucille Black. "The workers who initially solicited their memberships now seem to be reluctant about making contacts regarding renewals. We don't feel that contact by mail would be effective or expedient."[29] Indeed, rural mail carriers had begun reporting the delivery of NAACP-stamped materials to citizens' councilors.

After his term as local NAACP president, Stringer seemed a step from banishment. When he appeared on a local television station to espouse the importance of dental hygiene, councilors alleged that he had disseminated a secret, subversive message to the local Black population. R. C. Herron, chief of Columbus's Citizens' Council, told Alabama's *Birmingham News* that he would launch a full investigation into Stringer's subliminal messaging. Others attacked the television station for allowing the NAACP president airtime in the first place. Stringer increasingly turned to organizing in the Black church. He preached Baptist revivals and worked on a book that never appeared in print, tentatively titled "A Chance to Live."[30]

Counterinsurgency after Emmett Till

The year after *Brown* and the Mississippi Squeeze brought a resurgence in racially motivated political violence to rural Mississippi. On May 7, 1955, an unknown assailant assassinated Reverend George Lee, who had helped create an NAACP branch in Humphreys County. Then, on August 13, someone shot and killed Lamar Smith on the courtyard lawn in Brookhaven, after he had brought Black neighbors to register to vote. And on August 28, 1955, two white men, Roy Bryant and J. W. Milam, kidnapped, tortured, and killed Emmett Louis Till, a fourteen-year-old African American boy who enjoyed baseball and listening to comedic acts on the radio. He was in the South to visit family from Chicago, Illinois. Though we may never know exactly what happened in Money, Mississippi, in August 1955, current theories contend that as little as a whistle directed at Roy Bryant's wife, Carolyn Bryant, cost Emmett Till's life.[31]

This murderous violence also flowed from the white political culture of massive resistance. However, unlike the Citizens' Council emphasis on weaponizing rural capitalism to harm those who threatened white supremacy, such extralegal violence contradicted the reformist impulse of business progressives and police expansionists. Governor Hugh White, the Highway Patrol's creator who was in the last year of a second term almost thirty years after his first, vowed "energetic prosecution" in a telegram to the NAACP and privately hoped for the murderers' conviction. He ordered highway patrolmen to assist in the murder investigation.[32]

Local responses to Till's murder sparked regional and national movements. Mamie Till-Mobley organized her son's funeral in Chicago so that the casket had a glass lid. "Let the people see what they did to my boy," she said. Journalists estimated that tens of thousands of mourners attended. She then returned to Mississippi, where she had been born in 1921, to attend the five-day trial of her son's murderers. Journalists and activists came too. Black-owned publications like *Jet* and the *Chicago Defender* ran cover stories about the heinous crime and Till-Mobley's fight for justice. The NAACP sent investigators who found witnesses among Black tenant farmers. T. R. M. Howard housed Mamie Till-Mobley and freedom fighters in his armed compound in Mound Bayou. National television reporters filmed each day from the Tallahatchie County courthouse lawn. International correspondents wired stories around the world.[33]

The trial of Bryant and Milam delivered no justice. Despite the fearless testimony of Till's uncle, Mose Wright, an all-white-male jury acquitted Till's murderers in just over sixty minutes. Bryant and Milam admitted to their crimes in a paid interview with *Look* magazine in the months after. In Milam's explanation, he meant to send a message to Black Mississippians who hoped to vote. They could never be allowed to vote "where I live," he said. "If they did, they'd control the government." Methodology, not ideology, separated the slow violence of citizens' councilors like Robert Patterson and the murderousness of J. W. Milam.[34]

The young Black people who came of age during this tragedy fought to dismantle Jim Crow apartheid in the next decade. Historians often refer to the many activated foot soldiers as the Emmett Till generation. And the phase of the American South's Black freedom movement defined by direct action civil disobedience began just months after the trial. On December 1, 1955, Rosa Parks refused to give up her bus seat in Montgomery, Alabama, later reportedly telling Jesse Jackson that, "I thought of Emmett Till, and I just couldn't go back."[35] How would Mississippi Law answer civil disobedience and direct action protest?

・・・・・・

Just five days before Till's murder, on August 23, 1955, James Plemon Coleman rode his record of law-and-order segregation to the governorship. Since 1950, J. P. Coleman had served as Mississippi's attorney general, the state's chief prosecutor, law enforcement officer, and attorney for the government. In five years as AG, he had overseen the capital punishment of twenty men. All but seven were Black. Those executed in the state's electric chair included John West Pulliam, a seventeen-year-old Black defendant convicted of killing a night watchman during the burglary of a Vicksburg gun shop at age sixteen.[36] Another, Murdock Hinton, was a white farmer convicted of murdering his entire family and the sheriff of George County.[37]

Coleman made a name for himself by blocking federal interference in Mississippi's legal lynchings. He fought off Willie McGee's final appeals as attorney general in 1951. An all-white jury had convicted McGee of raping a white woman in November 1945 despite a lack of physical evidence. Lawyers and activists associated with the radical Civil Rights Congress secured multiple stays of execution during five years of appeals. But Coleman ultimately defeated the activist efforts to save McGee's life. Before his execution on May 8, 1951, Willie McGee wrote his wife a letter saying in part, "Tell the people the real reason they are going to take my life is to keep the Negro down." The state murder of McGee resembled earlier spectacle lynchings. Thousands attended outside the Jones County courthouse where the

Mississippi, 1956. T. B. Birdsong Jr. pins Tom Scarbrough, a beef cattle rancher, as Governor James P. Coleman's new commissioner of public safety. Courtesy of James Birdsong.

execution occurred. Highway patrolmen escorted McGee at every step of the way to avert mob violence. One trooper was quoted as saying "Let's everybody be nice" as crowds assembled.[38]

J. P. Coleman took office as governor in January 1956 after promising professional reform for the Mississippi Highway Safety Patrol and the Mississippi State Penitentiary. These two institutions were important to Coleman's vision of lawful white supremacy with propriety and economy. To achieve these changes, he placed Mississippi cattlemen at the head of both agencies. As both cattlemen and law enforcement professionals, they likely embodied to Coleman the new, efficient agribusinessman ethos that departed from localistic sheriffs and cotton monoculture.

Coleman's plan to expand the Highway Patrol fell to Tom Scarbrough. Coleman named T. B. Birdsong to a new Probation and Parole Board for the Mississippi State Penitentiary, making Scarbrough the only peacetime commissioner of public safety to interrupt Birdsong's tenure. A former sheriff of Chickasaw County and rank-and-file highway patrolman, Scarbrough replaced Birdsong between 1956 and 1960. He raised purebred shorthorn cattle on prairie lands near the farm of Elton Deanes.[39]

The Highway Patrol became even more important over Scarbrough's four-year term as commissioner of public safety. At least four police killings of Black men received media attention. In each case, either a municipal police officer or sheriff was to blame. Coleman responded with a law that allowed white voters to recall local police officers and sheriff's deputies with 51 percent of the vote. The governor would then empanel a special court to decide whether to remove the law enforcement officer from duty. Coleman hoped to develop a mechanism for the removal of police officers who embarrassed Mississippi's emerging brand for modern economic development.[40]

Scarbrough's Highway Patrol set records for extractive policing that stood into the late 1960s. During his tenure, the number of state troopers on Mississippi's highways exceeded two hundred for the first time, growing 20 percent from the previous administration. Coleman paid for this expansion by passing the cost to motorists through increases in driver's license and vehicle registration fees. In 1956, the year after the murder of Emmett Till, some two hundred patrolmen ticketed, summoned, or arrested more than 100,000 people. Courts found over 90,000 of those people guilty. Troopers assessed more than $1 million in fines and facilitated over $400,000 in court costs. In almost every category, this cohort of troopers doubled the previous year's figures. The next three years saw decreases from these highs. But there was no mistaking the state police mandate for the period after Emmett Till's murder.[41]

Statewide, the new Highway Patrol also sent more people to prisons and jails. The people arrested by the state police and sentenced to jail or prison received a combined forty-two years of detention in 1956. This number increased every year. By 1960, at the end of Scarbrough's term, trooper arrests led to a total of forty-nine years of prison sentences. Scarbrough explicitly praised the Livestock Theft Bureau's "conviction record," which had "consistently run high" over his tenure. This use of the state penitentiary to remove troublesome people from civil society was exactly how J. P. Coleman hoped to counter the tide of disorder, epitomized by both Black activism and white violence.[42]

Once sentenced, Mississippi's prisoners found themselves on a prison farm operated by another cattleman cop. Bill Harpole raised beef cows in Oktibbeha County. Before his appointment as superintendent of the

Mississippi State Penitentiary, Harpole served as chief of the Highway Patrol's Bureau of Identification, its plainclothes investigatory division. As head of the prison farm's agricultural unit, he oversaw a significant diversification in farm production; unsurprisingly, this meant less cotton, more livestock. At every step of the way, Harpole utilized majority-Black incarcerated labor to facilitate the transition. He also oversaw the transition in Mississippi's capital punishment from the electric chair to the gas chamber, which the state employed between March 1955 and 1989.[43]

For a moment, the future of capital punishment fell somewhere between these expanding state institutions, the police and the penitentiary. In 1952, Coleman's predecessor, Governor Hugh White, scandalized Jackson's high society by ordering the gas chamber installed permanently in the state capital's Highway Patrol headquarters on Woodrow Wilson Avenue. State police administrators embraced the idea, clearly seeing an opportunity for the institution to expand its reformist influence into legal execution. Jackson's affluent white residents, however, opposed the death chamber as a hazard to residential areas. The city's mayor threatened to sue the state, citing in part his prediction that the gas chamber would depress the area's economic development. Two years later, in September 1954, the state legislature ordered the gas chamber constructed at Parchman Penitentiary, where Harpole and other penal reformers could further centralize, obscure, and sanitize the state's taking of life.[44]

The Highway Patrol's lobbying efforts to control the state's gas chamber epitomized its larger search to streamline and upscale Mississippi's life-ending institutions. Whether extracting wealth from the state's people, patrolling rural pastures, or sending people to Parchman to perform compulsory farm labor, the state police stood ready with counterinsurgent reform to reassert order amid threats to the sixty-year-old Jim Crow racial order.[45]

· · · · · ·

In part, historians know so much about the inner workings of Citizens' Councils and massive resistance in Mississippi because J. P. Coleman accidentally created an archive of state repression. As governor, Coleman created the Mississippi State Sovereignty Commission in 1956. It became a state agency that propagandized to the nation from an elite white Southern point of view and investigated those individuals and organizations thought to pose a threat to Jim Crow. For the decade of its greatest activity, the Sovereignty Commission worked across multiple law enforcement jurisdictions to preserve white power at all costs, as when investigators, some of whom were former FBI agents, conspired to plant evidence in the car of and arrest Clyde Kennard during his bid to desegregate the University of Southern Mississippi in 1961. A state court sentenced Kennard to Parchman. He died of cancer after prison officials denied Kennard rudimentary healthcare.[46]

The Sovereignty Commission was also a statewide clearinghouse for Citizens' Council gossip, speculation, and paranoia. Commissioners stored these intelligence reports in a centralized database in Jackson, indexing persons of interest. White employers, loan providers, and landlords could call on the Sovereignty Commission to vet applicants. If someone had signed an NAACP petition or a white person thought someone was threatening, they could be disqualified. Law enforcement, too, could check if outsiders to their communities had been reported to be involved in civil rights activism. In short, Coleman found a way to fund the counterintelligence and espionage behind massive resistance with state tax revenue paid by both white and Black citizens. In fact, the commission allocated $200,000 to Citizens' Councils between 1960 and 1964.[47]

In their investigations, sovereignty commissioners documented evidence of the land loss that could accompany Citizens' Council retaliation. In one instance, a citizens' councilor informant was a cattleman and the county sheriff. In Clay County, one Black farm family, the Valentines, had at times thrived and at times merely survived on land accrued between 1900 and 1930. They, like their neighbors the Deanes, managed most of the hard 1950s until nature conspired against them in 1957. Drought struck and two consecutive cotton crops failed. Like their cotton plants, the family's credit also dried up in 1958. West Point's Citizens' Council bankers refused to extend the family credit. In April 1958, when the state's segregationist Sovereignty Commission investigator interviewed citizens' councilors around Clay County, Tom Valentine and his daughter-in-law Charlotte Valentine topped the Clay County sheriff's list of "those who would possibly be trouble makers in the event of a racial crisis."[48]

The family's financial peril deepened in proportion to their public involvement with the growing civil rights movement. Faced with either selling farmland or defaulting on their mortgage to the Federal Land Bank, Tom Valentine and his wife Mary Valentine were forced to sell in January 1962. Their grandson Eddie Valentine, age fifteen, rode with them to the county courthouse in West Point. He sat outside in the pickup while Tom signed over three hundred acres of what his grandsons remembered as the family's best land. The buyer was a leading white cattleman, the same Clay County sheriff who had reported the Valentines to the Sovereignty Commission in 1958.[49]

· · · · · ·

The examples featured in part II were not the work of a few bad apples. Whether white sheriffs in Kemper and Clay County, the municipal police in Amory and Columbus, or the highway patrolmen who arrested Tommy Booker and killed Tobe Faulkner—the disorder brought by policing's autocracy functioned toward the dispossession and immiseration of rural Black Mississippians amid a period of unprecedented economic abundance. Neither design nor malicious intent mattered when white families wanted the land you lived on or thought you threatened the political system that supported their rule. Mississippi Law facilitated the desired outcome.

Black Mississippians who organized against policing in these years insisted that police brutality was not merely the cost of keeping the vast majority safe. Policing *was* brutality when it came for the people or the sanctuary you loved. Black farmers like the Valentines entered the new decade with full knowledge of the stakes of their community's freedom movement.

Part III **Revolt**

6 States' Rights, State Troopers

> If we permit a motley pack of troublemakers to prove to the people of this nation that a state . . . is unwilling or incapable . . . of protecting the lives and property of its citizens, then what is left of states' rights belongs in a museum.
>
> —Paul B. Johnson Jr. (March 3, 1964)

On November 3, 1959, a new Jim Crow police reformer won his first election to Mississippi state government. Lieutenant Governor-Elect Paul B. Johnson Jr. stood a slender six foot, two inches. Aged forty-three, he spoke in a guttural country drawl. But what he said with that growl set him apart from typical segregationists, such as the extremist elected governor alongside him—Ross Barnett. Whereas Barnett's most famous speech was fifteen words beginning with "I love Mississippi!" Johnson uttered phrases like "The proven price of racial integration is the enormous skeleton of dead empires."[1] Johnson used his four years as lieutenant governor to drastically reimagine white imperium through state police power.

A son of the state's popular World War II governor with the same name, "Little Paul" had exhaustively tried his hand at electoral politics in the decade before 1959. After graduating from a Tennessee military academy, he attended the University of Mississippi and was elected undergraduate student body president. Johnson finished with a law degree in 1939 before fighting as a marine in the Pacific. He returned to his family farm outside Hattiesburg and received an appointment from Harry Truman as the assistant US attorney for the Southern District of Mississippi. In November 1947, Johnson lost elections for both US Senate and governor. Running for governor again in 1951 and 1955, Johnson forced runoffs in the state's all-white Democratic Party primary, only to lose both times.[2]

Taciturn and cerebral, Johnson campaigned on a color-blindness that basically ignored Black Mississippians altogether. After his defeat in 1951, the Jackson press quoted Johnson as saying he would prefer to take his own life than "base my candidacy on race vs. race." He went on: "I don't want to win by making the Negro the whipping boy when he isn't even an issue in this race."[3] Such outspoken ambivalence to racial politics cost Johnson in elections against studied race baiters, but J. P. Coleman's term as governor (1956–60) proved that race-neutral legalism in service to massive white resistance could succeed politically if wrapped in bellicose police expansion.

Before taking office in 1960, Lieutenant Governor-Elect Johnson began campaigning for governor. Two days after his victory in the general election, Johnson addressed the first annual meeting of the Mississippi Safety Council in Jackson, combining state police power with economic modernization. "The complex traffic situation of today requires additional precautionary measures," he said. The state highway system needed wholesale expansion and reform. The opposite of safety—"danger"—stalked Mississippi's motorists no matter where they found themselves because of institutional neglect. "The dangers increase continually," he said vaguely. "And where we close the door in one place, we find that it opens in another."[4]

The only institution deserving of praise, according to Johnson, was law enforcement. Johnson took special care to single out T. B. Birdsong and the Highway Patrol for its commitment to saving lives. He hoped the patrol would expand its influence, even suggesting the patrol reexamine every licensed driver in the state and revoke the driver's license of anyone found lacking.[5] More basically, Johnson foretold that the roads would be a site of politics and influence in the years ahead. Indeed, no sooner did the Student Nonviolent Coordinating Committee (SNCC) begin to organize potential Black voters in the Magnolia State than the Highway Patrol began to dictate what sort of movement would be possible.[6]

Freedom Rides and White Riots

SNCC field secretary Robert Parris Moses remembered his work in Mississippi as part of an unarmed insurrection. A local Mississippian introduced him to movement strategy in 1960. "That summer," Moses wrote decades later, "Amzie Moore, head of the Cleveland [Mississippi] NAACP laid out . . . the concept of a voter registration insurgency in the Mississippi Delta." Every courthouse, every road in between, would be the site of what Moses described in hindsight as a "low-grade Mississippi guerilla war." Voter registration volunteers constantly sought to evade surveillance, relying on Mississippi's long-standing NAACP members as an underground "black network" through which to work with minimal detection while they laid the groundwork for a watershed that came four years later during 1964's Freedom Summer.[7]

In Moses's framework, local law enforcement and state police mounted a counterinsurgency. A math teacher from New York, he remembered his first arrest coming in July 1961 while building the movement around McComb, in the southwest corner of the state. He had spent the day raising awareness and soliciting donations for sustained voter registration drives in neighboring Amite County. State troopers were around, Moses remembered, but they refused to interfere while SNCC worked in town. "The highway patrol that sat all morning at the foot of the sloping lawn in front of the courthouse flagged us down as soon as we crossed the county line back into Pike [County] and I was arrested." Unlike town or county law enforcement, troopers tracked organizers across jurisdictions. They could—and did—arrest suspected civil rights activists on any grounds they chose. Much of this police work was covert.[8]

The quieter grassroots war between SNCC and the Highway Patrol continued, but the Freedom Rides posed the first spectacular challenge to white supremacist public safety on the open road. There, the Highway Patrol had its first opportunity to maintain its outwardly color-blind brand of law and order in the glare of an international media spotlight.

In the spring of 1961, the first thirteen Black and white activists affiliated with the Congress of Racial Equality (CORE) boarded a bus in Washington, DC, to challenge federal enforcement of desegregated interstate transportation. The Interstate Commerce Commission (ICC) had declared illegal any racially segregated seating or services on interstate buses in 1955.[9] Yet Southern states resisted desegregation on carriers and in bus stations within their borders. CORE's Freedom Riders meant to flout state and local ordinances and test federal enforcement by busing an integrated party through the Deep South to New Orleans, Louisiana.

The first ride nearly ended three times in Alabama. A motorist firebombed a bus near Anniston; a mob dragged many riders off a bus in Birmingham, beating them badly as Police Commissioner Theophilus Eugene "Bull" Connor looked on. In Montgomery, when Martin Luther King Jr. offered riders solidarity in Reverend Ralph Abernathy's First Baptist Church, white terrorists besieged the mass meeting, threatening to burn the church to the ground. Each time, however, activists replaced the jailed and hospitalized. On May 24, riders set out west from Montgomery on US 80, heading to Jackson, Mississippi.[10] CORE director James Farmer remembered, "I was frankly terrified . . . that the trip to Jackson might be the last trip any of us would ever take."[11]

Mississippi's state government tested a new law-and-order solution when Freedom Riders crossed the state line from Alabama. The president of Jackson's White Citizens' Council had urged his members to help thwart the Freedom Riders' skillful use of the media to highlight white lawlessness, writing, "You and I can help by letting our highway patrolmen, policemen, and other peace officers handle any situation which may arise."[12] Despite bomb threats, twelve patrol cars, loaded with four troopers each, ferried the Freedom Riders to the Jackson city limits without incident.[13]

Riders found policemen instead of Klansmen when they debarked in Jackson. Members of the Jackson Police Department arrested the integrated group for violating state segregation ordinances. The Hinds County Circuit Court sentenced riders to steep fines and months in jail. Some two hundred more riders flowed into Jackson over the next weeks, filling the city jail, county jail, and county prison farm. While organizers voiced a "fill the jails" strategy, Lieutenant Governor Paul Johnson took to the road, alongside the state's attorney general, to assure local governments that the state's strategy was sustainable, that state police and prison resources were at their disposal for the duration of the crisis.[14]

Mississippi's innovation was simple enough. Birdsong's Department of Public Safety secured safe passage for activists to go directly to jail. The state used its carceral infrastructure both to protect the Freedom Riders from extralegal white supremacists *and* to punish them for their affront to the state's racial order. As scholars Ruth Wilson Gilmore and Craig Gilmore write of this moment in Jackson, "The movement's interdependent ideologies and tactics ran up against counterrevolutionary forces that regrouped behind a blue line they could move at will. . . . The legitimacy of the badge replaced the discredited Klan hood."[15] Instead of death at the hands of Ku Klux Klansmen or "parties unknown," the State of Mississippi had a prison farm.

In June 1961, Barnett and Johnson decided to use this gravest tool at their disposal, the Mississippi State Penitentiary at Parchman. On June 15, Hinds County circuit court transferred the first male offenders to state custody, citing overcrowding at local facilities as an excuse. These political prisoners then rode a prison bus four hours north to Parchman Farm. Women followed from the Hinds County jail on June 23, as cells designed for two filled to twenty prisoners each.[16] Joan Trumpauer Mulholland, a twenty-year-old white activist from Washington, DC, remembered that sexual terror began at intake, where nurses conducted violent gynecological exams. Likewise, guards beat C. T. Vivian, a thirty-seven-year-old Black minister with the Southern Christian Leadership Conference (SCLC), for laughing at questions regarding his venereal health.[17] Corrections officers also stripped Black male Freedom Riders of Parchman's already spare amenities and privileges. When riders refused to stop singing freedom songs, guards confiscated mattresses and toothbrushes; they denied outside communication and exercise. They doused occupied cells with fire hoses and set up high-powered box fans to create refrigerated conditions. Guards routinely placed men in solitary confinement.[18]

In mid-July, a Jackson lawyer arranged bail for the riders in Parchman, contingent on a reappearance in Jackson for arraignment. It would not be the last time activists found themselves behind bars, but Barnett and Johnson had successfully mobilized the state's criminal legal system to avert a direct confrontation with either the federal government or white mobs. They would not be so lucky in 1962.[19]

Paul Johnson raised his statewide profile stumping for the use of state police and prisons against the Freedom Riders in 1961. But he made his career sixteen months later, standing alongside highway patrolmen during James Meredith's attempt to become the first Black student to attend the University of Mississippi in Oxford.

On September 20, 1962, Johnson flew from Jackson to Oxford aboard a Highway Patrol airplane. Meanwhile T. B. Birdsong and a convoy of state troopers escorted US marshals and James Meredith, a triracial Air Force veteran from Attala County, to campus for the first time.[20] Meredith arrived at the university's Center for Continuation Study to find a cordon of more than one hundred troopers guarding the site of his sham rejection by Governor Ross Barnett, who had declared himself university registrar.[21] Five days later, Barnett prevented Meredith from registering again, this time at the state's Institutions of Higher Learning office building in Jackson. In less than a week, this cast of characters returned to Oxford for the white riot that left two dead—a French journalist, Paul Leslie Guihard, and Walter Ray Gunter, a local jukebox repairman on campus to observe the commotion. Armed white rioters wounded dozens more. The number injured surpassed one hundred.[22]

In the days before the segregationist riot, the patrol obstructed the implementation of the Supreme Court order to desegregate the University of Mississippi.[23] Ross Barnett sparred with the Kennedy administration. National and international media outlets descended on Oxford. Instead of protecting

Meredith, T. B. Birdsong mobilized the state police for the dual purpose of riot control and state obstruction of federal civil rights enforcement.

On the morning of Wednesday, September 26, a wall of twenty troopers stood with Paul Johnson to block the entrance to campus. Under the impression that state forces intended to yield after a slight use of force, Chief US Marshal James McShane pushed the lieutenant governor in an attempt to move past him. Instead, Johnson held his ground, stating he had no intention of letting Meredith onto campus. Troopers closed ranks when Assistant Attorney General John Doar attempted to guide Meredith around the lieutenant governor, and Johnson eventually raised his fists, warning McShane of his resolve to "meet force with force." The two men stopped short of blows, and the marshals drove Meredith back to the Oxford airport.[24]

Unlike the violence inside Parchman, this moment went global. A photo of the confrontation landed on the front page of dailies such as the *New York Times*, the *Chicago Defender*, the *Los Angeles Times*, even making page two of Australia's *Sydney Morning Herald*. Flip Schulke, a photojournalist at the scene, captured one version. Johnson, in a fedora, blocked McShane and raised his fists. W. G. "Bud" Gray, a trooper from Hattiesburg, stood beside Johnson in the frame, while Meredith stared stoically in the direction of campus. Suggesting Johnson was in a clear position of advantage, the photograph represented what law enforcement on the scene saw and remembered. Patrolmen applauded Johnson as federal representatives drove away.[25]

This was a clear public relations victory for Johnson and Birdsong's Department of Public Safety; however, the Highway Patrol's role in the riot four days later, on the evening of September 30, proved more difficult to spin. That afternoon, in their final attempt to enroll James Meredith, US marshals escorted the twenty-nine-year-old to his dormitory, as negotiated between Ross Barnett and the Kennedys. Students, Oxford residents, and white supremacist operatives from across and outside the state responded to rumors of Meredith's enrollment by descending upon the small town and manicured campus. The Circle, a roughly three-acre plot of grass and hardwood trees ringed by administration buildings, attracted the mob and the most violence. As the day wore on, white protesters grew increasingly antagonistic toward federal authorities. Patrolmen refused to intervene when rioters began to sabotage the marshals' vehicles parked around the Circle. The patrol began to abandon the fray altogether after 7:25 p.m., on the order of Barnett's representative on the ground, cattleman and state senator George M. Yarbrough.

Oxford, MS, September 26, 1962. Backed by state troopers, Paul B. Johnson Jr. raises his fists to federal authorities and James Meredith at the University of Mississippi. © Flip Schulke. Reproduced by permission.

The few troopers who remained clearly sought an excuse to depart their position of authority over the rioters. One, who refused to aid a journalist under attack from the mob, commented that the solution was to "let them kill the n——."[26] Another responded to a marshal's use of tear gas: "If y'all hurt one of those students I am going to take this magnum . . . and kill every god damn one of you."[27] By 9 p.m., the patrol's total retreat opened campus to armed mobs and outright assaults on the marshals. Firing tear gas, Justice Department representatives endured sniper fire, broken glass, lead pipes, and acid attacks. Rioters commandeered heavy machinery, including a bulldozer and a fire engine, in attempts to extract and kill James Meredith.[28]

The Highway Patrol's original stand with Paul Johnson and its later retreat demonstrated its growing influence in fights over civil rights. Faced with few options, John Kennedy summoned both National Guard and regular military to quell the uprising on campus and in Oxford. Meanwhile, James Meredith, whom marshals had sequestered in a dorm room, remained on campus the next morning. Under constant protection of federal bodyguards, he studied political science for ten months and graduated.

· · · · · ·

Debates over the Highway Patrol's role in escalating the Oxford crisis raged among Mississippi's white pundit class. "One of the important pieces of news coming out of the riot . . . was the fact that the Justice Dept. gave one story and the Highway Patrol another," wrote the Carroll County *Conservative*.[29] Under the headline "Our People Have Right to Know All the Facts," the editor of McComb's *Enterprise-Journal* asked bluntly: "Did the Mississippi State Highway Patrol pull away from the scene at the time of trouble? . . . By whose orders?"[30] For his part, the mayor of Oxford told national press outlets that he saw a trooper watch white men firebomb Black-owned automobiles but refuse to take action. "We have orders not to interfere," he remembered a trooper saying.[31] The mayor "felt the Highway Patrol . . . let us down."[32]

The reality was no match for a politically expedient fantasy. State senator Yarbrough fed the press a new story, that the patrol never left the scene of the riot. "The highway patrol remained on duty until Monday morning when relieved at bayonet point by federal troops," he said in an interview.[33] And the Mississippi state Senate—chaired by Paul Johnson—affirmed this alternate reality when it passed a resolution on October 3 commending the Highway Patrol's conduct during the riot. "As long as the police powers of the State of Mississippi were vested in the chief executive officer . . . no such violence or untoward incident occurred. . . . During the course of events the Highway Patrol and other officers conducted themselves in an admirable manner."[34]

This fanciful account went uncontested by white elites, even those critical of patrol influence, because highway patrolmen spent far more of their time performing valuable police work behind the scenes. Troopers were busy building a reputation for the harassment of Mississippi's grassroot freedom struggles—those that didn't make the *New York Times*, or even the *Winona Times*. The benefits outweighed the risk. And Bob Moses's insurgency built from NAACP members was only growing.

SNCC activists struggled to publicize the scale and impact of police harassment on community mobilization in these early years. By 1963, SNCC headquarters had crystallized their critique of state police expansion that white supremacists touted as safety. The photographer Danny Lyon made a

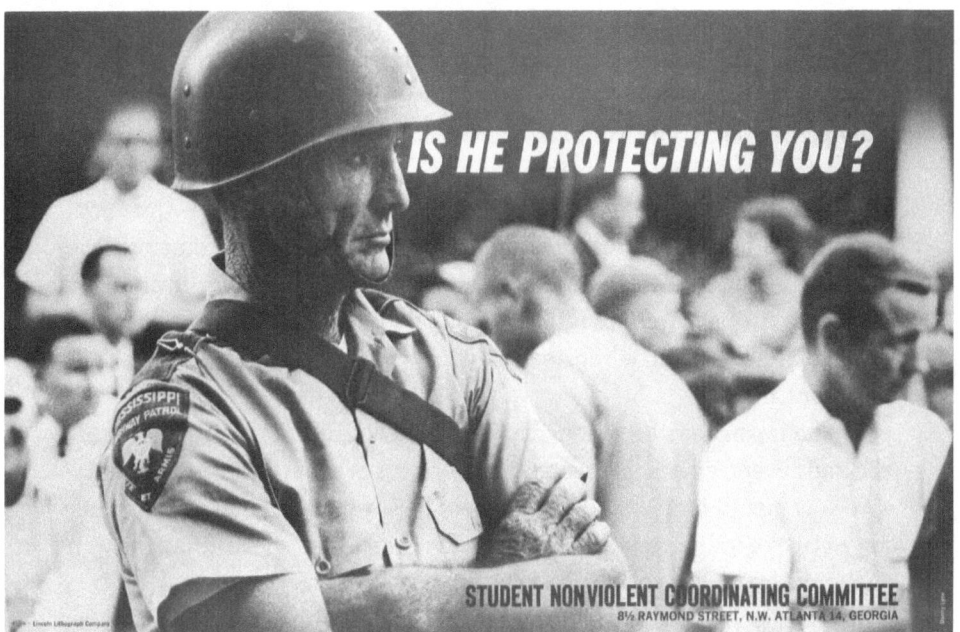

1962–1964. A SNCC poster, designed in the office and printed in the thousands. Copies were sold, mostly in the north, for $1.00. Copyright Danny Lyon/Magnum Photos.

poster out of his close-up photograph of a state trooper at the desegregation of the University of Mississippi in September 1962. With steel helmet and "Virtute et Armis" shoulder patch visible, Lyon and activists inserted white text on a dark background. The broadside asked, "Is he protecting you?" In the aftermath of summer 1963, the Highway Patrol and SNCC's question took on added meaning nationwide.[35]

The Trooper and the Montgomery County Jail

While Paul Johnson fought the Kennedy Justice Department on national television, SNCC grew to include local members like Fannie Lou Hamer. Born Fannie Lou Townsend near Tomnolen in 1917, Hamer's family sharecropped for the first two years of her life in Montgomery County. They moved to the Delta's Sunflower County in 1919. At age twelve, her mother and father were on the verge of paying rent with cash instead of a share of their cotton crop when a white neighbor poisoned the family's growing livestock herd with insecticide.[36] She dropped out of school shortly thereafter to help the family survive. Around 1944, she married Perry "Pap" Hamer and built a life combining sharecropping and wage work in Ruleville.[37]

When Hamer first encountered SNCC organizers in the summer of 1962, she had just survived two great tragedies. In February 1961, she suffered the loss of her mother, for whom she had cared for the last decade. Then, while she was under general anesthesia for a routine surgery, a white doctor hysterectomized Hamer without her consent. Informal yet commonplace at the time, the state legislature attempted to legalize such sterilizations to purge Mississippi's welfare rolls and landless Black population. "When the cutting starts," said state representative Stone Barefield in 1964, "they will head for Chicago."[38]

White lawmakers bet wrong on Fannie Lou Hamer. On August 31, 1962, she and seventeen others filed applications to register to vote in Indianola. "We was met in Indianola by policemen, highway patrolmen, and they allowed two of us in to take the literacy test at the time," she testified in 1964. "After we had taken the test and started back to Ruleville, we was held up by the city police and the state highway patrolmen and carried back to Indianola where the bus driver was charged that day with driving a bus the wrong color." She paid her fine and returned to Ruleville only to be evicted from her longtime home the same day.[39]

Experienced in so much of Jim Crow's capacity to disorder Black life, Hamer posed an incredible threat to Mississippi's ruling class. Slowly, she joined the work to register neighbors and bring others into the movement. In early June 1963, she traveled with a group of young civil rights workers on a seven-hundred-mile trip from Sunflower County to Charleston, South Carolina. A Citizenship School hosted by the SCLC and Septima Poinsette Clark was to prepare them for the summer's Mississippi Freedom Vote, a house-to-house Black primary to choose candidates for the following year's challenge to the all-white state Democratic Party. The trip united activists who organized through an umbrella civil rights organization known as the Council of Federated Organizations (COFO). Joining Hamer, SNCC activists like June Johnson, Euvester Simpson, Rosemary Freeman, and James West traveled with the SCLC's Annell Ponder to learn from one another and strategize on community mobilization.

They left their Charleston training ebullient. Having met national SCLC icons, including Martin Luther King Jr., and learned the uniting features of movement culture, they began the daylong trek to Greenwood, where they planned to report back before dispersing to various rural movements. From Tuscaloosa, Alabama, the group set off for the last leg of their long trip on

US 82. But the group's trip ended short of the Delta. When their Trailways bus pulled into the Columbus, Lowndes County, bus station around 8 a.m. on Sunday, June 9, someone called the Highway Patrol.[40]

For the group of activists, the next hours and days demonstrated the dragnet of state police powers governing political protest. When the bus reached Winona, the Montgomery County seat, at 10:50 a.m., some riders debarked at the stop, Staley's Café.[41] Winona's chief of police, Thomas Herod Jr., and highway patrolman John Lutellas Basinger waited. The patrol followed the bus from Starkville. As officers rounded up the café-goers and a group who had recorded the squad car's license plate in protest, the sheriff of Montgomery County, Earle Wayne Patridge, also arrived on the scene. As Chief Herod escorted the SCLC's Annell Ponder to his squad car, she argued that the officers had acted in violation of civil rights law. "Ain't no damn law," the chief said, and informed six of the original ten passengers that they were under arrest for disturbing the peace and resisting law enforcement. As Hamer alit from the bus, Patridge arrested her too. He kicked her as he placed her into the back of his car. As Patridge made clear, once in the custody of law enforcement the Black Mississippians entered a space that epitomized the absence of law and order.[42]

The horrors that ensued inside the Montgomery County jail are well known to historians. White lawmen heaped upon Black men and women verbal, psychological, physical, and sexual abuse that betrayed not only well-practiced sadism but also sophistication in the manipulation of criminal legal procedure. For Hamer and her activist brothers and sisters the county jail became Jim Crow in vacuo, capable of collapsing a lifetime of abuse and indignity into an hourly reminder of Mississippi's system of racist inhumanity. Party to all of this pretrial torture was Patrolman Basinger. His conduct epitomized the public safety that white Mississippians understood the Highway Patrol to deliver by 1963.

According to Hamer, Basinger orchestrated the torture. He ordered three Black men incarcerated at the time, Sol Poe, Roosevelt Knox, and Willie Kidd, to beat James West for roughly thirty minutes. The trooper rewarded their efforts with a pint of moonshine. He next turned Poe and Knox on Fannie Lou Hamer, handing them his patrol-issue blackjack. When Poe hesitated, Basinger threatened, "If you don't beat her, you don't know what we will do to you." Hamer remembered the patrolman saying, "I want you to make that bitch wish she was dead." Given the jail's open layout, prisoners heard their comrades being tortured, not knowing when their time would come.[43]

Police officers also sexually abused COFO activists. Hamer made clear that officers groped her during the bludgeoning. Likewise, June Johnson, Rosemary Freeman, Annell Ponder, and Euvester Simpson experienced physical violence with sexual overtones. Basinger, especially, demanded that volunteers use the courtesy title "sir" when addressing him. The young people almost categorically refused, and this offense spurred some of the trooper's worst violence. When SNCC's Lawrence Guyot arrived in Winona in search of the missing activists, he declined to "sir" the state trooper. Basinger punched the twenty-three-year-old organizer in the mouth on Main Street in broad daylight. He took Guyot to jail, where the trooper beat and sexually humiliated the activist before an audience of other lawmen.[44] Unmitigated white male power remained to ensure the highest cost for the politically active.

Behind jail walls, officers used legally binding paperwork and procedures to obstruct future investigations and shield localities from federal scrutiny. On Monday, June 10, the second day of incarceration, officers brought activists before a tribunal overseen by Winona's mayor. There, he found the activists guilty of disorderly conduct and sentenced each to pay a $100 fine.[45] When officers returned the group to jail, Patrolman Basinger handed Hamer paper and pencil; he told her to write down exactly what he said. "Since I [have] been in jail I have been treated well; I [have] been fed . . . nobody mistreated me . . . and I [am] writing it of my own free will." Threatened with the trooper's sidearm and a repeat of the previous night's attacks, Hamer resisted by feigning illiteracy. She scrawled his instructions illegibly. Basinger then took pictures of Hamer for evidence, using the jail's dim lighting to obscure her injuries in carefully staged photographs.[46]

Primarily remembered because of its sadism, Montgomery County's carceral state also touted sophistication and subtlety. Though no historian can venture to say with precision how often white troopers weaponized sexual assault and rape against citizens of color to solidify white supremacy, the Winona incident shows that lawmen lied in official reports and preempted future complaints through coerced or fraudulent affidavits. These juridical tactics constituted a repertoire of trained police behavior available to all law enforcement agencies.[47]

Chief Herod, Patrolman Basinger, and Sheriff Patridge could little imagine their routine actions circling the globe in the testimony of civil rights activists. Basinger must have been surprised when Assistant Attorney General Burke Marshall initiated a federal investigation into the three-day incident and then filed a criminal complaint in the US district court in Oxford, on September 9, 1963. After hearing the evidence, a jury of twelve local white men acquitted the officers despite the bold testimony of the white bus driver, the activists, and even the three Black prisoners forced to mete out their punishment. Far from facing punishment, John Lutellas Basinger eventually received a promotion.[48]

· · · · · ·

On June 12, 1963, Andrew Young, one of Martin Luther King Jr.'s top lieutenants at the SCLC, arrived in Winona to pay the group's fines and take them onward to Greenwood. The previous twenty-four hours had seen victory and defeat. One hundred forty miles east of Winona on US 82, Vivian Malone Jones and James Hood had desegregated the University of Alabama, in Tuscaloosa, Alabama, despite Governor George Wallace's stand in the schoolhouse door. But ninety miles south on US 51, Byron de la Beckwith murdered Medgar Evers, Mississippi's national NAACP field secretary, with a deer rifle while Evers's family looked on.

Now, in Winona, a crossroads he had never heard of, Young looked upon the crimes of white supremacist law enforcement. He told the battered group about Tuscaloosa and Evers. He also said that President John Kennedy had addressed the nation the previous night, from Washington.[49] Kennedy's remarks, the ideological program for the next five years of civil rights reform, labeled the question of "segregation and discrimination" a "moral issue" that transcended section and time. In his famous formulation, the question of racial equality was "as old as the scriptures and . . . as clear as the American constitution." Kennedy dreamed of an ordered civil society where neither lawmen acted violently nor the oppressed took to the streets. "We face, therefore, a moral crisis as a country and as a people," Kennedy said. "It cannot be met by repressive police action. It cannot be left to increased demonstrations in the streets. It cannot be quieted by token moves or talk. It is a time to act in the Congress, in your State and local legislative body and, above all, in all of our daily lives."[50] Kennedy suggested that individual soul searching and the rule of law made progress possible.

Neither Kennedy nor the liberal Democratic Party wanted to see Winona, a hinterland without national press coverage, where logics of order had different authors and followed different scripts. Fannie Lou Hamer called Winona "the most horrifying experience I've ever had in my life."[51] Policing subsequently moved to the center of her analysis of Jim Crow and her vision to overthrow it. The carceral state she knew lived at the spatial interstices between urban movements. In Mississippi's vast hinterland, raw and unapologetic state power operated to stymie the Black freedom struggle's gravest threat to white supremacy: the free flow of thinkers, their ideas, and their culture in rural space. To white landowners and exploitive agricultural labor regimes, this political mobilization represented more than the threat of biracial democracy. It signaled the breakdown of an entire system of social and labor hierarchy. It threatened the underpinnings of their world.

An All-Out Assault

As details about Winona trickled out, Paul Johnson made his 1963 gubernatorial campaign into a referendum on state police power. His campaign hoped that for some white voters, his stand with the Highway Patrol at the University of Mississippi in 1962 would make a difference. Featured in the Citizens' Council propaganda film, *Oxford, USA*, Johnson praised the Highway Patrol and absolved them from responsibility in the riot's outcome. He once again promoted the illusion of unbiased public safety; campaign literature promised a "positive, progressive program" for education, infrastructure, tourism, and "agribusiness." Using Flip Schulke's photograph as his advertising centerpiece, Johnson adopted the slogan "Stand Tall with Paul" against James P. Coleman in the 1963 Democratic primary. In a rematch of the 1955 election, Coleman forced a runoff, but Johnson won by a healthy margin before defeating a Republican candidate in the state's first seriously contested general election in almost half a century.[52]

What Johnson didn't say about the Highway Patrol went without saying: A vote for Paul Johnson was a vote for Trooper John Lutellas Basinger.

In January 1964, Paul Johnson used his inaugural address to crystallize his philosophy of order in a moment of growing upheaval. COFO's 1963 statewide campaign, the Freedom Vote, had laid bare the violence awaiting any effort to organize Black political power. Moreover, national mourning over the Kennedy assassination promised a new emphasis on the Democratic Party's civil rights agenda. Sharing the platform with Arkansas's Orville Faubus and Alabama's George C. Wallace, Mississippi's new governor struck a tone that sounded moderate to many listeners. "If I must fight," Johnson said, "it will not be a rearguard defense of yesterday. It will be an all-out assault for our share of tomorrow. You and I are part of this world, whether we like it or not. What happens in it, through no fault of our own, affects us too. We are Americans as well as Mississippians. . . . Hate, or prejudice, or ignorance will not lead Mississippi while I sit in the Governor's chair. . . . God bless you all, all Mississippians both black and white." The next day, Johnson shared the front page of the *New York Times* with Nikita Khrushchev and Fidel Castro, the headline echoing his "Anti-Hatred Vow."[53]

By March 3, Governor Johnson had to convince a tougher audience—a joint session of the state legislature. He spoke on "the maintenance of civil order, peace and tranquility."

> Each of us knows that law and order *will* be maintained—*ultimately.* The question—the all important question—is: By *whom?* Will we Mississippians of today exercise the rational judgment, the wisdom and the foresight to assure . . . that law and order and peace will be maintained . . . or will we, by failing to do so, invite the government of the United States to impose its brand of law and order upon us? . . . The truth is this. The predictable historical process, and the unpredictable surging of human events, has brought to our doorstep a cataclysmic issue.[54]

That looming cataclysm facing Johnson and white Mississippi was COFO's Mississippi Summer Project, or Freedom Summer, a statewide voter registration drive, building on the capacity of the previous fall's Freedom Vote and promising to bring even more federal scrutiny.

Signaling a break with the type of local violence experienced by Fannie Lou Hamer and nameless others, Johnson's rhetoric conjured the spirit of racial liberalism. Seemingly capacious enough to include the lawlessness of Klansmen *and* the organization of activists, his remarks promised a clear intention to secure Mississippi's public sphere. However, rather than intervene in the state's hundred years of white lawlessness, Johnson began a trend of publicly prioritizing the work of the state police over the vigilante work of groups like the Klan or even the State Sovereignty Commission. In part, he built consensus for empowering the Highway Patrol by framing Freedom Summer as an invasion akin to the carpetbaggers of Reconstruction. Johnson invoked the threat of federal armed intervention that had cost Mississippi's ruling class political power between 1865 and 1875.[55]

If empowered, Johnson promised to ensure peace and quiet for white Mississippians, especially property owners and employers. In preparation, Johnson asked the legislature for an unprecedented expansion of the Highway Patrol, requesting an increase in the number of patrolmen, the modernization of equipment, the creation of a law enforcement training academy for municipal and county officers, and a vast increase in the scope of the patrol's statutory police power. "If we permit a motley pack of troublemakers to prove to the people of this nation that a state . . . is unwilling or incapable . . . of protecting the lives and property of its citizens," the governor reasoned, "then what is left of states' rights belongs in a museum. . . . Let us decide now that law and order will be maintained . . . by disciplined, uniformed, duly-authorized law enforcement officials and by no one else!"[56]

The legislature met Johnson's requests in May, overcoming lawmakers' perennial and vocal concerns about ceding local law enforcement to the state capital. In accordance with House Bill 564, authored by House speaker Walter Sillers Jr., the Highway Patrol would grow by two hundred new officers. Most importantly, however, the 1964 bill lifted the quarter-century restriction on Highway Patrol jurisdiction to the enforcement of traffic laws on state highways or responding to traffic accidents when requested. Instead, the state granted Mississippi investigators in divisions like Livestock Theft, Auto Theft, and the Bureau of Identification (or Investigation) "full power to investigate, prevent, apprehend and arrest law violators anywhere in the State," along with "the power of general police officers in the performance of their duties."[57] The hiring, training, and deployment of new troopers took just three months.

・・・・・・

On August 31, 1964, Johnson celebrated the graduation of 103 new state troopers. He used the occasion to summon all patrol employees to the state coliseum in Jackson. According to the *Delta Democrat-Times*, he barred members of the press from attending. However, someone recorded the speech on reel-to-reel tape. The Mississippi Department of Archives and History digitized and transcribed the audio in the early 2000s. With a friendly audience, Johnson was uninhibited. He spoke for thirty minutes to the white men who embodied his dream of professional, bureaucratic police supremacy.[58]

Paul Johnson spoke to the guardians of a settler society in revolt. "In these turbulent and unsure and sometimes unsafe times," he began, "we are faced with a great many problems that people used to never even dream about. Things are changing and changing fast." After cynically exaggerating about there being "open season upon policemen of any type," he turned to colonial humor. "Like I told some of them [troopers] the other day, I think I'll vote for Tarzan. He's not afraid of the natives."[59] Johnson likely meant to reference the presidential election of 1964, where the Jim Crow Democrat could endorse neither Lyndon Johnson nor Barry Goldwater. The reference to Edgar Rice Burroughs's *Tarzan of the Apes* (1912) and subsequent motion pictures based on the same character was clear: Tarzan murdered native Africans "frequently," according to the scholar Gail Bederman. Tarzan embodied the primal European man, a descendant of Anglo-Saxon aristocrats who ran loose in the jungle. He answered to no one.[60]

Johnson's commencement address to the patrol included an unmistakable invitation to lawlessness when it came to civil rights activism. "If you have to kill a man, you can be certain that if it is done . . . [in] self defense that you'll have a pardon from the state penitentiary before you get there," he said. "I am not going to stand back and see any of the highway patrolmen beaten up or . . . [degraded the way] police in New York and Rochester and Philadelphia . . . have been."[61] Indeed, he would not be activating the National Guard, he vowed, because the Highway Patrol would be a force for constant surveillance and broken-windows-style counterinsurgency:

> From time to time, you will receive orders. Some of them are going to come pretty quick. We've got some visitors in our state that are not the type that have come here for outdoor camping purposes. We expect to see that they are checked, not once, but twelve and fifteen times a day. Their position should be a position that is uncomfortable. Bad brakes, bad windshield wipers, running through stop signs, topping the hills on the wrong side of the road. This is a time when people have got to use their ingenuity, their resourcefulness and their ability. And Hades is not hot compared to what we want it to be for some of these people.[62]

Perhaps remembering the Little Rock Central High School desegregation crisis of fall 1957, Johnson said, "I do not want to get in a position of the state being in open defiance with the federal government."[63] Arkansas Governor Orville Faubus had learned that the president could always federalize the National Guard. Johnson imagined a state police force immune from all national authority.

The FBI was another important topic for the new troopers' orientation. Johnson admitted being moved by FBI director J. Edgar Hoover praising the patrol as "one of the crack police outfits of America." "It made a lump come up in my throat to know that such a man looks upon this organization as he does," Johnson said. Aiding the US Department of Justice was another matter. "Neither you nor I have any obligation to enforce the Civil Rights Law," he believed. Troopers were not to aid FBI agents in civil rights investigations; only "heinous crimes" like bank robberies deserved state police assistance.[64]

Importantly, Johnson's frank vision of white manly policing was inconsistent with extralegal terror organizations like the Klan. "I have nothing whatsoever against the Ku Klux Klan," he confided. "But if you are a member of the Ku Klux Klan now or if you plan to join, the best thing for you to do is to get your hat and leave. . . . That is true of any other organization in this state that sees fit at any time to try to take the law enforcement into their own hands." Police order was to rule the day. As Johnson colloquialized, "We can't help people starting things, but we can be this first group to shut it off like you would a water hydrant."[65]

Longtime Highway Patrol leaders remembered the expansiveness of the governor's remarks to the new patrolmen. Kenneth Fairly heard his boss make a promise that he remembered Johnson repeating throughout his term: If a Mississippi court convicted a trooper of a crime in the line of duty, the convicted could expect a pardon from Johnson the same day. A Mississippi highway patrolman would not serve a day in jail.[66] Paul B. Johnson did not promise to pardon troopers without reason. A close look at the interplay of activists and patrolmen in northeast Mississippi's rural Tombigbee Valley shows policing's autocracy in fine detail.

7   On Patrol with B. Cowart

Get the equipment you might need on hand, . . . cameras, bull horns, radio equipment (mobile and portable), tear gas, night sticks, riot guns and ammunition, helmets, bolt cutters, portable lighting equipment, and recording equipment.

—T. B. Birdsong to all troopers (1964)

At noon on July 16, 1965, Black farmers, local teenagers, and white civil rights volunteers walked into a livestock sale in the Clay County seat, West Point. A fixture of the local agricultural economy after World War II, the sale barn hosted regular auctions and drew farmers from across Mississippi and Alabama. Sales also followed a careful racial script. White auctioneers and cattlemen allowed Black buyers to attend, bid, and sell from the back of the room.[1]

Lawmen also assembled at cattle sales. Sheriff Joe Ed Strickland was a leading Clay County cattleman and row-crop farmer. Trooper B. Cowart of the Highway Patrol's Livestock Theft Bureau attended regularly, checking brands and surveilling the marketplace. Tom Scarbrough, a cattleman from bordering Chickasaw County and the former head of the Highway Patrol, now worked for the Mississippi State Sovereignty Commission, Governor J. P. Coleman's civil rights watchdog organization formed after the murder of Emmett Till. Scarbrough had come to buy and sell cattle, but he and other white lawmen had to defend Jim Crow before the first cow stepped onto the auction block. Such spaces were sites of rural Black freedom struggle.

Activist farmers arrived at the market an hour early. David Tobis, one of the county's twenty volunteers with COFO's Mississippi Freedom Democratic Party (MFDP), organized in the farm community of White Station. In an oral history interview with students from Stanford University, the twenty-one-year-old white New Yorker explained that local people

> wanted to buy a pig for a barbecue to raise money. We also wanted to sit in the good seats, because the Negroes when they buy or sell animals have to sit way in the back and they can't see the scales,

and they can't see what they're getting for their animals. The auctioneer just gives them a couple of dollars and they have no idea if that's what their animal sold for. And there were good seats right in front where the white people sit. So they were going to sit in those seats. Then we went to buy the animal.

As Black farmers claimed their front-row seats, Tobis walked across the street with teenagers to a white-owned café affiliated with the auction. "A couple of guys went to the counter, and three Negroes and I sat down at a table," Tobis recalled. "And a kid come over with this big club and put it in my face and said, 'Get outta here. We're not gonna serve you and those n——s. Get outta here or I'll just smash you.'"[2]

From across the street, Tom Scarbrough and Sheriff Strickland watched as the sit-in unfolded. That "big club" was a common accessory of cattlemen, the original cattle prod. "Most all of them carry a stick or walking cane," Scarbrough reported to the Sovereignty Commission, "which, when properly applied, would change the mind of a stubborn bull." Then came the melee. "Confusion broke out," Scarbrough wrote. "Someone let out a war-whoop and yelled 'let's get them.'" Antagonized by the group's statement of resistance at the sale barn, a mob of cattlemen attacked the Black youth, hitting them in the heads as they fled down the roads and into surrounding pastures.[3]

The bloody scene inspired a walkout among Black employees. "A couple of the guys who were with us worked at the place," Tobis remembered,

> They said, "If they're not going to serve us, we're not going to work." So one guy quit his job, and he started talking to other people. . . . Eight out of the ten quit. This guy's wife who worked in the kitchen, she quit also. So spontaneous, sort of beautiful. Oh then, you know, the sheriff came and took us to jail for disturbing the peace. And, you know, as we were dragged off, taken to jail, the white guys with, God, you know, shoulders four inches wider than a normal person. Six two or three inches tall with this enormous club. Wham! Started swinging it and hit a couple of guys. One little kid, Negro kid, who was with us, very weak, grabbed him and bit him. That was kinda good.[4]

These were the stakes of local struggles out of town and out of well-known sites of civil rights struggle. For Black rural dwellers living in farm communities and small towns, such was the possibility for change that mobilized Black residents to challenge the rural power structures of the beef economy and law enforcement. Such everyday threats to segregated rural economics, one local manifestation of racial capitalism, built white consensus around state police power. Over 1964's Freedom Summer and beyond, B. Cowart, the local Highway Patrol livestock investigator, represented more than a single law enforcement officer. Rather, he represented an entire system of rural control built around white supremacist economic inequality.

Drawing on Highway Patrol records archived with Paul B. Johnson Jr.'s governorship papers, the records of civil rights activists, and oral history interviews, this chapter explores the everyday work of policing's autocracy on rural freedom movements. First, it documents how T. B. Birdsong and other Highway Patrol administrators prepared rank-and-file troopers for the crisis of Freedom Summer and the ongoing organizing work that followed. Then it turns to appreciate the particular ways movement people collectivized around improving Black farm life. Finally, it uses unredacted Highway Patrol reports to sketch state police impact on the Black freedom struggle and the meaning made of B. Cowart's death while policing a civil rights protest.

······

Officially, troopers spent little time policing civil rights activism over Freedom Summer. Between July 1963 and June 1965, highway patrolmen reported responding to two hundred "sit-ins, voter registration drives, marches, demonstrations, etc.," fifty-nine racial arsons, thirty-two racial bombings, and five racial beatings, for a total of 296 incidents. But these figures vastly undercount the numerous daily incident reports compiled at each patrol substation. In some patrol districts, troopers and investigators likely explored as many activist-related occurrences in months, not years. All patrolmen involved themselves, including an area's auto theft and cattle theft investigators. The spike in total arrests probably indicated the scale of state police encounters with civil rights workers. Statisticians recorded 200,000 total arrests and $2.4 million in fines and court costs recovered between summer 1963 and summer 1965. This amounts to a 20 percent increase from the previous two years. As an additional two hundred troopers fanned out across the state in 1964 and 1965, the patrol's capacity to intervene in local movements only expanded. Publicly identifiable leaders of the movement attracted particular attention. By June 1966, Stokely Carmichael claimed he had been arrested twenty-seven times. One arrest came from troopers in Mileston, Mississippi, early in Freedom Summer.[5]

Mileston, MS, June 1, 1964. Stokely Carmichael, SNCC field secretary for Holmes County, being arrested by Mississippi Highway Patrol near Mileston. Photograph by Matt Herron/Take Stock/TopFoto.

Rehired as commissioner of public safety in 1961, T. B. Birdsong saw the Highway Patrol's new mandate as permission to renew its legacy of militarization. On March 25, 1964, Birdsong wrote to Kenneth Phillips, director of the Mississippi Civil Defense Council, inquiring as to how the state might "better equip present personnel" with three hundred steel helmets, gas masks, riot shotguns, M-1 Garand rifles, and bayonets. Phillips, in turn, directed Birdsong to the appropriate suppliers of helmets and gas masks and referred him to the US government's Federal Center in Battle Creek, Michigan, for military surplus firearms. Birdsong further urged all patrolmen to "get the equipment you might need on hand," personally suggesting "cameras, bull horns, radio equipment (mobile and portable), tear gas, night sticks, riot guns and ammunition, helmets, bolt cutters, portable lighting equipment, and recording equipment." This was to be a patrol prepared for new scales of insurgency.[6]

Birdsong's response to Freedom Summer also revealed the patrol's dedication to surveillance and counterintelligence, as espoused by the Sovereignty Commission and White Citizens' Council, as everyday police practice.

In August, Birdsong compiled a broad set of suggestions for the surveillance of civil rights activists and local allies. He urged officers to identify local Black leaders in preparation for the arrival of "imported" demonstrators, suggesting that "background information" on all activists would "prove helpful," as would "an *intelligence network* to acquire information on the plans of the civil rights groups." He stressed the need to discern whether local movements were composed of "the criminal element or better-type people," while suggesting that municipalities begin to consider "where mass numbers of prisoners are to be held; how they will be fed; how they are to be transported; [and] how they will be processed." With such considerations, the commissioner signaled his intention to continue the use of state policemen and jails to quell localized protest.[7]

Agricultural Justice

The vast majority of Highway Patrol police work occurred not in spectacular events like the Freedom Rides or the Oxford riot but in the hinterlands of everyday Black organizing. In order to understand why law enforcement expended so much energy tracking and harassing civil rights workers, we must understand the fights that grew from local communities. Often, outside organizers found Black landownership and retention to be generational struggles.

Elton Deanes (introduced in chapter 5) was born in Clay County's Griffith community, in 1933, just as the Agricultural Adjustment Act took effect and the US Department of Agriculture (USDA) began to pay Southern farmers to take cotton land out of production in order to boost demand and prices. By the 1950s, Elton Deanes could not comfortably sustain his family with "cotton, corn, and cows" on his farm in Cedar Bluff.[8]

As was increasingly the norm, Deanes began supplementing his agricultural earnings with wage work associated with the growing beef cattle industry. In 1954, he began as a "tank cleaner" at the Bryan Brothers meatpacking plant in West Point. Relegated to menial labor, Deanes got his first glimpse of employer power when the Bryan Brothers forbade him from commuting between West Point and his farm out in the county. Instead, they compelled Deanes to rent a downtown apartment during the week, perhaps an apartment owned by an owner or friend of the Bryan Brothers. He returned to help his family farm on the weekends, where he continued to grow cotton until he lost his supply of family labor in the 1970s.[9]

In the 1960s, Deanes's success on the land hinged on the operation of the county branch of the USDA, in particular its Agricultural Stabilization and Conservation Service (ASCS) committee. Black farm owners like Deanes faced the USDA's institutional racism with little hope of escape. Deanes recalled that his interaction with the county ASCS committee usually took place in the context of the policing of cotton allotments. A USDA holdover from New Deal crop controls, each county's farmer-elected ASCS committee assigned acreage allotments to individual landowners yearly, based, in theory, on the quality of past cotton production and national production goals set by Congress. The federal government paid farmers so that they would not overplant cotton, so county committees hired federally paid fieldworkers who retained surveillance and enforcement power on cash crop production. The committee also maintained custody of certain excess and reserve acreage that it could assign to farmers at its discretion.[10]

Mississippi's movement people set out to create knowledge around the assignment of crop allotments. They found yet another pretext for rural racial discrimination and Jim Crow economics. Interpersonally, ASCS committees operated to reinforce rural white supremacy through the humiliation of Black agriculturalists. Deanes remembered that white county agents "would come by and measure your cotton after you got it planted. And if you had more than the allotment said, you'd have to plow it up." To say nothing about whether white field-workers measured Black cotton allotments impartially, their tactics added indignity to the financial sting of wasted cottonseed, fertilizer, pesticide, and human labor. White field reporters measured the Deanes farm only after the planted cotton had bloomed, or "made," thus forcing Elton Deanes himself to plow under a portion of his family's livelihood just before harvest.[11]

Spanning four generations on the same prairie land, the Deanes family's comparatively brief experience under the New Deal regime offered a representative example of the nationwide discrimination against rural and agrarian African Americans.[12] The campaign for agricultural justice spread across Mississippi with the help of COFO volunteers, mostly Northern white college students and Southern African Americans. It was simultaneous with better-known mass demonstrations for equitable public education, voter registration, and fair employment practices.

Local interest in the ASCS grew in proportion to the community's knowledge of the county USDA committee's rural power. The Valentine family of Clay County's Pheba community spread the word as much as anyone. Reflecting on the governmental programs of the ASCS and Farmers Home

Administration (FmHA), a USDA agency that extended low-interest loans to farmers in times of crisis and expansion, Tommie Valentine said, "Before the Civil Rights Act and civil rights movement . . . I never heard talk about it." The son of Charlotte and Vernon Valentine, whose family farm dated to 1910, Tommie and his brother Eddie were teenagers when their parents began organizing adjacent farmers for equal representation on the county USDA committee. Their farm drew attention when they offered to house civil rights volunteers in a shotgun shack formerly occupied by Black tenants on the Valentines' cotton land. In SNCC culture, activists called such all-purpose dwellings Freedom Houses, and Eddie Valentine laughed at a memory of Black and white activists moving onto the farm. The family's privately maintained gravel road ran past his home, the Freedom House, and the nearest church. The road became "just like a freeway" in terms of traffic volume. The scene of young white women and Black men working and living alongside one another drew onlookers from the surrounding countryside.[13]

The New Deal's agricultural bureaucracy proved complex, even for organizers from farming backgrounds. Federal statute tasked USDA committees with distributing loans to established farm owners. Coupled with information about conservation programs, these loans could be the difference between a farmer's survival and ruin. The ASCS committee controlled funding for drainage improvements on land prone to flooding. It disbursed funds for the conversion of exhausted acreage (previously used for cash crops) to trees or pastures. Yet the elaborate process of electing committee members was enough to produce a substantive hurdle to Black representation. State-level USDA administrators divided each county into a number of ASCS "communities." Clay County had six. Each community's eligible farm men and women—owners, sharecroppers, tenants—elected a chair, vice chair, and a third member. The three voting members from each community committee then convened at a county convention to appoint five farmers from among themselves to form the all-powerful county committee. Jim Crow thrived: All-white community committees meant an all-white county committee.[14]

Activists learned how white landowners had adopted and modified Jim Crow political culture to exclude non-white farm operators. Even getting Black farmers on the ballot for community-level elections proved challenging. Officially, the petition of six eligible farmers guaranteed the placement of a candidate on community ballots. Sam Carr, an MFDP state executive committeeman from Aberdeen, in Monroe County, remembered the Clay County committee's intransigence. "We worked until we was dead, going to the ACS office downtown . . . and presenting our candidates." Even after two Black farmers were successfully on the Tibbee community's ballot, Carr found that gerrymandering worked against the interests of the Black farming population. The county committee kept the southern portion of Clay County divided in a way that split the heavy Black majority and advantaged white farmers. After threats to report the electoral irregularity, the committee combined the two southern farming communities. With this victory, Carr felt certain that 1965 would see the first Black farmers elected in Clay County.[15]

Beyond committee elections, the Tombigbee Valley's MFDP organizers like Carr saw the necessity of Black representation in allotment enforcement and the opportunity of federal wages. Carr had researched the pay and benefits of county field-workers. "The government pay them [a] salary," he told a Stanford University interviewer. "Dollar-and-a-half an hour and so much per farm." Likewise, ASCS office managers received competitive wages for clerical and administrative work. When presented to farmers, Carr's numbers meant a great deal. Those who rented land or struggled to remain landowners without nonfarm work saw supplemental income safe from white employers' discriminatory pay practices. In fact, they recognized that a field-worker or office manager stood to make more from part-time work on the federal payroll than from their full-time farm production. Pay of $1.25 per hour drove Black rural folk to mobilize. That was too much for the racial regime secured by the Highway Patrol.[16]

The Backroads of Police History

In their work on and between Black farms, organizers encountered the Highway Patrol on an everyday basis. On the evening of July 31, 1964, COFO volunteers joined local Black residents for a mass meeting outside the small Monroe County river town of Aberdeen. In such meetings, activists organized upcoming marches for voter registration. Perhaps this time they debated the exigency of armed self-defense or boycotting segregated businesses and discriminatory employers. Such a rural movement would also have planned protests for equal access to education and the USDA. Activists may have discussed how to recruit children to COFO Freedom Schools.[17]

Sitting in the back row of this country church was a plainclothes white trooper named B. Cowart. An investigator with the Highway Patrol's Livestock Theft Bureau, he scribbled minutes of the proceedings for a case report filed soon afterward.[18]

State troopers like Cowart alternated between menacing and protecting Mississippi's Black freedom movement. Patrolmen spent whole days following voter registration volunteers from beat to beat. They targeted known organizers for offenses like speeding, following too closely, having loud mufflers, and parking improperly. They confiscated legally held firearms and collected biometric data from activists booked at local jails. They even collaborated with local police and sheriffs to illegally tap telephones and listen in on citizen band (CB) radio transmissions. Operating in the shadows of grassroots civil rights movements across the countryside, Mississippi's highway patrolmen surveilled and shaped local protest politics.[19]

Tracing the role of one patrolman in his jurisdiction's Black freedom movement gives a sense of how the Highway Patrol operated at scale, across deeply rooted community movements.

B. Cowart—whose given name was the letter *B*—proved one of northeast Mississippi's most enthusiastic sleuths in 1964 and 1965. Born in 1911, the second son of a country doctor, Cowart served in military intelligence during World War II. He joined the Highway Patrol in 1946 but made a costly mistake early in his career. In March 1949 he struck and killed a seventeen-year-old white pedestrian with his squad car while responding to a traffic accident near Jackson. Demonstrating the antipathy commonly held for state policemen, a local court actually tried Cowart for manslaughter but acquitted him. The incident undoubtedly impacted him personally, and it may have affected him professionally. Soon thereafter he transferred to north Mississippi and found himself working for the new Livestock Theft Bureau (see chapter 4). During Freedom Summer, policing cattle was a smaller part of his job than political surveillance.[20]

Cowart's purpose in surveilling movement activities was twofold: to glean intelligence and to inspire order among would-be white assailants of civil rights activists. In August 1964, Cowart attended another mass meeting in Aberdeen and trailed the activists to an unsuccessful attempt to desegregate a local movie theater. He also shadowed some fifty local Monroe County residents who attempted to register to vote at Aberdeen City Hall, where angry whites quickly outnumbered the group. The protest dispersed without violence, but Aberdeen's mayor thanked Cowart for "the moral support, advice, . . . and the aid that he might have obtained had the situation merited it." Cowart built a market for patrol services one mayor at a time.[21]

Patrolmen worked hard to catalog and surveil subversive subjects, often resulting in steep fines and detention for the accused. On August 6, 1964, investigator Cowart reported that he had spent most of the day trailing

Russell S. Clay, a twenty-eight-year-old Black man, across rural Monroe County. Two weeks later, Cowart pulled over Wayne David Anderson, a white seminarian from Minnesota, for speeding. The investigator wrote Anderson a ticket and claimed falsely that the Minnesotan was required to be booked at the nearest police station. Anderson acquiesced, and Cowart retained the student's fingerprints and mug shots for the patrol's Identification Bureau in Jackson. In early September, Cowart repeated his targeting of activists, writing tickets to two local Black residents for "following too close" and "improper mufflers." Later, two state police investigators arrested Edward Benjamin Ziff for "improper drivers license and improper license plate" in West Point. When it came time for booking, however, the patrolmen insisted that the other activist in Ziff's vehicle, an English national, was also subject to being fingerprinted and photographed. In this case, law enforcement created a record of the passenger for headquarters, without charging either of the men with a crime. Patrolmen continued to use the traffic stop as a tool to interfere with movements and collect biometric data such as fingerprints in sparsely populated communities.[22] Given the treatment of activists like Fannie Lou Hamer by one trooper in a local jail, such trips undoubtedly carried the threat and fear of violence.

Black and white activists often consented to the Highway Patrol's unofficial policy of collecting biometric data. However, when Cowart fined Ronald Stanley Bridgeforth in Starkville for "improper parking," the Black Los Angeles native flatly refused to be fingerprinted. He had not been arrested for a crime, he reasoned, and should not be booked. According to Cowart's report, he insisted Bridgeforth "submit to being finger printed and have pictures taken as requested by a police officer as required by State statue [sic]. He refused twice and was placed under arrest." Cowart placed Bridgeforth in the Starkville city jail, where he awaited arraignment before the local Oktibbeha County justice of the peace. Upon repeated refusal to be fingerprinted, the JP found Bridgeforth in contempt—a process repeated for three days. Finally, Bridgeforth submitted to being fingerprinted and photographed, after which he had to pay hundreds of dollars in fines and fees.[23]

Increasingly, local law enforcement joined state police in surveillance efforts. Livestock Theft Bureau investigators accompanied the West Point chief of police and his assistant to a mass meeting of COFO activists in November 1964. The patrol noted that the forty African Americans and three Northern whites in attendance participated in "no activity other than singing and speeches." In the church parking lot, however, a trooper recorded the license plates of all cars in attendance and solicited the policemen for identities and backgrounds of the visiting volunteers.[24]

Evidence suggests the Highway Patrol frequently intercepted private audio communication during and after Freedom Summer. COFO volunteers utilized CB radios to communicate with fellow organizers across the vast countryside, often separated by miles on visits to farms and ranches. The patrol learned of this medium of communication early on and kept a log of known COFO radio frequencies, listening in from radio command units across the region. Keeping a leg up on local activism, patrolmen stayed abreast of movement strategy, activist locations, and cooperating locals on a daily basis. "A new radio antenna had been installed on the COFO Headquarters at Aberdeen within the last two or three days," one investigator reported in November 1964. He went on to obtain the operation's new frequency and pushed the Aberdeen Police Department to obtain the appropriate equipment so as to continue interception of COFO communications immediately. By August 1965, even US senator John Stennis knew who was in charge of maintaining the movement's CB radio equipment in Mississippi. Such was the importance of electronic eavesdropping to the rural white counterinsurgency.[25]

Law enforcement in counties with direct action campaigns took surveillance methodology a step further, eavesdropping on telephonic communication. Likely gaining access to public phone lines through local telephone switchboards, authorities learned activist strategy before rank-and-file members of the movement did. Following a consultation with Clay County sheriff Joe Ed Strickland on the county's movement activity in August 1964, for instance, B. Cowart reported the following: "From a listen in on telephone conversation, three workers were ordered to report to COFO headquarters Jackson. No reason given over the phone. . . . For some reason there is a lot of movement going on, moving COFO workers in and out of this district." Troopers tracked nonviolent activists with zeal.[26]

At the same time, troopers like Cowart still carried the patrol's older mandate to protect against white violence that might injure Mississippi's reputation. A Livestock Theft Bureau colleague stationed in Chickasaw County, Lloyd Bean, investigated Ku Klux Klan activity and assisted the Federal Bureau of Investigation (FBI), as when Bud Wiggs, Billy Joe Wright, Don Womack, and Floyd Reese attempted to burn a cross in the front yard of Joe "Hambone" Hill Jr. Hambone Hill was apparently a well-known white bootlegger who cohabited with a Black woman, which drew local Klan attention. However, this attempted Klan intimidation did not go according to plan. The Klansmen did not realize that Hill was hosting a fish fry on the night they arrived to burn the cross. The cross was never lit, and a car chase ensued. According to the Chickasaw County sheriff and a Klansmen who accepted FBI payment to turn informant, Hill exchanged gunfire with the Klansmen at high speed on back roads. Though far less aggressive than their surveillance of civil rights activists, patrolmen like Bean and Cowart occasionally kept tabs on white terrorists during the direct action phase of the civil rights movement.[27]

Charging white men with civil rights violations was another matter. For instance, the Chickasaw County sheriff also reported to the Highway Patrol that he *knew* the Klansman Bud Wiggs had shot into a Black activist's house. Patrolmen found another Wiggs brother, Sam, working for West Point's auxiliary police department. But, as was the case when patrolmen confiscated "two shotguns and a pistol" from white men sitting outside a COFO mass meeting, local officials "would not make any charges."[28]

Notwithstanding the Highway Patrol's conditional concern with white violence, B. Cowart functioned within racist systems to injure rural Black people in his jurisdiction. Cowart's authority to investigate racial terrorism mattered deeply to a Black community's ability to claim compensation from its insurers. When night riders burned the all-Black St. Peters Baptist Church in August 1964, Cowart saw fit to investigate the church's insurance policy rather than identify suspects. Two weeks later, terrorists bombed Mt. Moriah Baptist; Cowart interviewed local bankers about the church's construction debts. Shady Grove Baptist burned next, and this time Cowart wrote to headquarters at length: "This writer believes $2500.00 is well above the actual value of the church," he wrote of the congregation's insurance coverage, "and this is the second church to be bombed or burned while under repairs, and it is also noted that the repairs are going well over the original cost estimate." He implied that Black parishioners across a hundred miles of countryside had conspired to burn their own churches for insurance payouts. Cowart's sentiments were common enough in white Mississippi, but as a state policeman his claims became the official and legally binding record of events.[29]

Patrol surveillance of the Klan continued. On a Sunday in the fall of 1965, one Klan rally outside Columbus, Lowndes County, attracted eight hundred attendees, while in August 1966, a smaller rally in Tupelo celebrated the burning of a cross, Beatles records, and wigs imitating the stereotyped "long-hair" look of white male civil rights volunteers. Beyond investigating mass gatherings, the patrol found that the Chickasaw County klavern, formed in 1962, was the most active. Only in January 1966 would law enforcement charge known Klan members with the burning of African American churches in Clay County. One convicted church arsonist was, in fact, the brother of Aberdeen's police chief.[30]

For the public, Birdsong and administrators painted a different picture of the patrol's policing of racial violence in 1964. A series of church and home burnings from Pike County, in the countryside around McComb, led to the patrol's arrest and conviction of ten arsonists. A circuit court judge sentenced each man to five years in Parchman. Signaling a new norm, the patrol was precise in its description of the assailants: "Most of these suspects," administrators reported, "were members of the Ku Klux Klan."[31] They implied the men were something different than the Citizens' Council businessmen; they were explicitly members of an increasingly condemned terrorist organization that state law enforcement now hoped to control. After conviction, however, the circuit court judge suspended each sentence to probation.[32]

· · · · · ·

No feature of B. Cowart's life held more public meaning than the events surrounding his death in August 1965. The scene unfolded as local law enforcement arrested a large group of Black and white activists on August 6 in West Point for "blocking the sidewalk" during a protest of the conditions in the county's rural Black schools. During prisoner intake at the county jail, Cowart stood at the head of a cell block, stripping demonstrators of the buttons and pins advertising their organizational affiliation: SNCC, COFO, SCLC, MFDP. As Cowart reached to rip away the button of eighteen-year-old Michael Reuss (pronounced *Royce*), the white Stanford University student spun to avoid his grasp. "I can do it myself," Reuss remembered saying, as he removed his SNCC button.[33]

Reuss recalled a shift in Cowart's complexion from red to "a deep shade of purple," but caught in the flow of other protesters, he shuffled with the group into a single, overpacked cell. Reuss couldn't know, however, that Cowart fell unconscious immediately following their brief confrontation. Colleagues quickly carried the stricken trooper from the jail, where a physician provided oxygen. It came too late. The physician pronounced Officer Cowart dead on the scene.[34]

Because of the state's successful politicization of law enforcement as a bulwark of segregation, Cowart's death from natural causes rippled through white Clay County as the murder of a public servant. To some, no doubt, he had been a voice of reason and moderation amid chaos. For others, he had died while policing the Black freedom movement.

Though the investigator had suffered from congestive heart failure for years it meant little to Cowart's colleagues in the patrol. "There's the bastard killed Cowart!" Reuss remembered a patrolman shouting later that day. He remained dumbfounded, recalling that "after knocking me down, they dragged me from the cell into the office of the Chief of Police. Seven officers . . . pinned me in a corner punching and kicking me for several minutes. . . . One of them spat, 'That's for Cowart,' as he punched me in the face. I didn't understand why I'd been singled out. It was ominous, however, that coursing through their profanity was a common theme—someone had died."[35] After his beating, Reuss remembered asking Sheriff Joe Ed Strickland, "Can you stop the troopers from killing me?" Strickland responded "I don't know, son."[36]

Charged with manslaughter, Reuss brought policing's hinterland briefly into the national spotlight. Reuss's father was US representative Henry S. Reuss, Democrat, from Wisconsin's Fifth District. The congressman's arrival in West Point convinced local officials to drop the charge of manslaughter. But the elder Reuss stayed in Clay County for a tour of the local Black freedom struggle that he eventually narrated on the floor of Congress.[37]

On the same day as the trooper's death in northeast Mississippi, Lyndon B. Johnson signed the Voting Rights Act in Washington, DC. In addition to its measures overriding state laws that suppressed Black voting, the bill ordered federal registrars into counties all over the South, including Clay County, to eliminate local chicanery, such as literacy tests. "It is difficult to fight for freedom," the president said in the Capitol rotunda. "But I also know how difficult it can be to bend long years of habit and custom to grant it. . . . There is no room for injustice in the American mansion. But there is always room for understanding toward those who see the old ways crumbling." Rather than crumbling, the seven troopers who beat Reuss participated in the construction of a new mansion. They stood in another big house, the Clay County jail.[38]

A lone player in a much broader drama, Cowart died at the high tide of the biracial civil rights movement's liberal promise. He left behind a rural white society that had come to associate his surveillance and harassment of the Black freedom movement with massive white resistance, to associate state troopers with states' rights and the defense of racial hierarchy. Some members of the white countermovement decided to terrorize the rural freedom movements that they believed had cost Cowart his life.[39]

In the predawn darkness of August 8, 1965, shotgun blasts rang out over the Vernon and Charlotte Valentine farm in Pheba. A night rider showered the front of a tenant shack housing six white and Black activists affiliated with the Clay County freedom movement, then sped down the dirt road to shoot into the Valentines' farmhouse. The shooters missed occupants, by inches in some cases, and vanished into the night before the activists had pulled themselves from the floor. The shooters had also just missed shooting at Congressman Reuss, who had left the Freedom House ten minutes before. Without a telephone, and leery of driving miles to the nearest one, the Valentines waited for daylight in the family home. At 5:30 a.m., Congressman Reuss called the FBI's Jackson field office from his hotel room in West Point. He demanded a full investigation.[40]

FBI resident agent Lynn P. Smith of nearby Columbus caught the Valentine case. A graduate of nearby Mississippi State College and a decorated veteran of World War II, Smith still worked from home for lack of a formal office. He arrived to find Sheriff Strickland, a state trooper, and Congressman Reuss already on site at the Valentine farm. Interviewed in 2008, Smith re-created the scene for an interviewer. While the liberal Midwestern congressman looked on, agents poured plaster into the shooters' tire tracks, attempting to form casts for comparison to suspect vehicles. They removed slugs of buckshot from the farmhouses, promising a full ballistics investigation, and methodically interviewed all witnesses. At one point, Reuss said to the pair, "You're all doing a wonderful, wonderful job." Safely out of earshot, however, another FBI agent joked with his fellow agent: "Lynn, you're just like a Hollywood director!"[41]

Indeed, the FBI investigation in Pheba was a production, as ordinary law enforcement investigations were across rural Mississippi during the period. Neither Agent Smith, the Highway Patrol, nor the FBI followed up with the Valentines regarding the Freedom House shooting. They merely filed a formal report and passed their conclusions to the Clay County sheriff, who in turn brought the guilty party to the Valentine home the next day. He had been shooting at a rabbit in the road, the white assailant told the African American family. Ricocheted pellets must have hit the houses. Sheriff Strickland considered the case closed with the shooter's apology, but over the next five years, arsonists would destroy Valentine family property twice in further retaliation for their role in the freedom movement and their threat to the root of white economic power. Disgruntled neighbors frequently cut the barbed wire fences that hemmed in the Valentines' cattle. In each case, the FBI formally investigated, turning their findings over to local authorities. None of the Valentines' tormentors faced legal charges. And soon Mrs. Charlotte Valentine lost her job. The local school district fired and blacklisted her. She sold Avon products to supplement the family income until she found work teaching in a neighboring county.[42]

In December 1965 US Department of Agriculture's community elections occurred under such threatening circumstances across Clay County. Vernon Valentine lost his bid to serve on the Pheba community committee. MFDP activists noted that rural renters "usually did not get ballots, or if they did, they were sent to the landlord instead of them directly." Other Black farmers received their voting slips to find the outgoing county committees had "flooded the ballot with Negroes," lacking the surprised candidates' "knowledge or consent." This split the Black vote. Across the state incumbent committeemen counted ballots behind closed doors. In a process in which incumbent white men oversaw elections, seventy-five years of functional disfranchisement would not suddenly be abandoned because cotton allotments were involved instead of presidents.[43]

With little to show for a year of unprecedented activism, the Valentines transitioned back into a county without community organizers supporting their local struggle. Pheba's Freedom House had emptied of volunteers, who returned to their college campuses or joined other protests like the growing anti-war, women's, and environmental movements, leaving the local people to continue their fight. The Black Clay County residents and Black Southerners who had played an active role in the year's racial agitation lived in a county without the son of a US representative or coverage from the *Washington Post*.

Militant whites reminded the Valentines of this early on. In the wee hours of December 5, just three days after Vernon Valentine's ASCS loss, someone set the farm's Freedom House ablaze. With no rural fire department, the family could only watch the symbol of their civil rights movement burn. The bullet holes in the façade of the Valentine home remained. Perhaps as a reminder of the family's collective risk and the ongoing lawlessness of Mississippi Law, Charlotte Valentine refused to allow her sons to repair the holes in her lifetime.[44]

Elsewhere, legal activists in Mississippi's movement began to investigate the police as a centerpiece of Jim Crow's social order. After the summer of 1964, activists, thinkers, and lawyers analyzed the activist experience of Freedom Summer to begin a decades-long conversation, imagining a world without Jim Crow policing.

8 Mississippi Burning and the New Abolition

∙∙∙

> This is not something that has just now started; it has been going on before my time and I imagine before my parents' time. It is not just now the white man is doing this; it was borne from generation to generation.
>
> —Fannie Lee Chaney, speech (October 23, 1964)

On the afternoon of Sunday, June 21, 1964, two troopers patrolled state highways in rural Neshoba County. At two p.m., they wrote some forgotten driver a ten-dollar speeding ticket near Tucker, a Choctaw farm community, and proceeded toward the county seat—Philadelphia. They chose a secluded area to wait for speeders, just east of town. There, around three p.m., they watched a deputy sheriff named Cecil Ray Price drive out of Philadelphia. Price soon called the troopers over their CB radio. "I've got a good one," the deputy said. A blue station wagon came into view and throttled down at the sight of the patrol car. Trailing at a distance was Cecil Price, who slowed enough to cast an unmistakable smile in the troopers' direction. Price, a Ku Klux Klansman, thought the troopers were on his side.

Deputy Cecil Price drove on his way to abet one of the most notorious white supremacist murders of the twentieth century. He expected the highway patrolmen to understand and support the extrajudicial violence that accompanied policing civil rights activists. But Price clearly underestimated the power that came with being legitimate law enforcement while others became illegitimate. When an FBI agent came to interview the troopers about the events of June 21, 1964, the pair incontrovertibly implicated Cecil Price in what came to be called the Freedom Summer murders. They told everything they knew. Down to the smile.[1]

In the blue station wagon were three civil rights volunteers with the Congress of Racial Equality (CORE). James Earl Chaney, a Black man from nearby Meridian, drove Andrew Goodman and Michael Schwerner, both white Jewish New Yorkers. CORE volunteers had been in Neshoba County since May 1964, going door to door to organize mass meetings for voting rights and political power. After one such meeting on June 16, white supremacists beat parishioners and burned the Mt. Zion Methodist Church in a Black community called Longdale. Chaney, Goodman, and Schwerner rushed back to Mississippi after news of the fire reached them in Oxford, Ohio, during orientation for the Council of Federated Organizations' (COFO) statewide voter registration drive known as Freedom Summer. On June 21, they took photographs of the church building's charred remains and were on their way to deliver their evidence to a COFO office in Meridian when the sheriff's deputy saw them.[2]

Once in downtown Philadelphia, Deputy Cecil Price signaled for the station wagon to pull over. Price arrested the three men, who remained behind bars while the sun set. Around ten p.m., Price released the group after alerting other Klansmen. Two carloads of white men formed a lynch mob, led by Edgar Ray Killen, a minister. The group beat James Chaney badly. James Jorden, a gas station attendant, and Alton Wayne Roberts, a truck driver, killed the three men and drove their remains to a fallow cotton farm that its owner, Olen Burrage, was converting to cattle pasture. The murderers burned the CORE station wagon in a blackberry thicket and buried the volunteers in an earthen dam built to hold back the water in Burrage's new cattle pond.[3]

・・・・・・

Known by the FBI code name *Mississippi Burning*, or *MIBURN*, the murders of June 1964 directed unprecedented public attention to Neshoba County. In the month it took investigators to find the remains of Chaney, Goodman, and Schwerner, the US Congress passed and Lyndon Johnson signed the Civil Rights Act of 1964.

From the beginning, some activists questioned the bill's remedy for state violence meted out by policemen. In advance of the previous summer's March on Washington for Jobs and Freedom, SNCC chairman John Lewis and staff drafted a fiery speech, predicting the Civil Rights Act would be "too little and too late." "There's not one thing in the bill that will protect our people from police brutality," they wrote, condemning both "the Democrats and the Republicans" as "cheap political leaders who build their careers on immoral compromises and ally themselves with open forms of political, economic and social exploitation." SNCC's draft speech ended by previewing a revolutionary attack on the whole Jim Crow racial order.

> If any radical social, political and economic changes are to take place in our society, the people, the masses, must bring them

about.... All of the forces of Eastland, Barnett, Wallace and Thurmond won't stop this revolution.... We will march through the South, through the heart of Dixie, the way Sherman did. We shall pursue our own "scorched earth" policy and burn Jim Crow to the ground—nonviolently. We shall fragment the South into a thousand pieces and put them back together in the image of democracy.[4]

This was not the speech John Lewis gave on the steps of the Lincoln Memorial. The Kennedy administration read a draft and pressured SNCC to change the message. Martin Luther King Jr. and A. Philip Randolph convinced Lewis to sanitize the speech in order to avoid allegations of communism and sustain a tenuous harmony between establishment liberals and young radicals.[5]

But SNCC's leadership meant to warn racial authoritarians and racial liberals alike that the revolutionary spirit of the 1860s and '70s lived on. They hoped for an army dedicated to voter registration and nonviolent direct action to dislodge the segregationist regime, just as a liberating army had abolished the racial order of chattel slavery during the Civil War. Just as freedpeople had struggled after slavery to "reconstruct democracy in America," in the words of W. E. B. Du Bois, Black Southerners freed from Jim Crow would remake Southern society. SNCC's uncensored analysis mirrored *Black Reconstruction* (1935), in which Du Bois described a post–Civil War program of "abolition-democracy" in the South, "based on freedom, intelligence, and power for all men," where fleetingly "a dictatorship of labor ensued, with a new democratic Constitution, new social legislation, public schools and public improvements."[6] Though clearly grappling with the contradictions and limits of nonviolence, SNCC went to Mississippi in hopes of fundamentally reordering Southern society.

Student radicals were not alone in their analogies to abolition and Reconstruction. Ida B. Wells had reapplied the word *abolition* to her hope to end lynch law in 1895 (chapter 1). And in a book published in September 1964, the historian Howard Zinn referred to SNCC voting rights volunteers as "the new abolitionists" who organized to reinvent democracy across the rural South.[7] In the aftermath of the Freedom Summer murders, people like Fannie Lee Chaney, the mother of slain James Earl Chaney, framed the movement against a racist capitalism in terms of multigenerational struggles against white power in the South. In the aftermath of a horrific tragedy, activists dreamed of a new abolition-democracy for a second Reconstruction. This time, they confronted policing head-on, proposing reform that grew from a grassroots politics. Instead of police expansion, they sought constraint and reorganization.

This chapter shows that the Mississippi Burning crisis opened a significant debate about fundamental change in Jim Crow policing. Autumn 1964 belonged to survivors of policing's autocracy. Collectively, Freedom Summer's survivors challenged America's commonsense model of expansive paramilitary police reform. And for a season, the movement's vanguard paused to imagine an off-ramp for a society based on Jim Crow police supremacy. That fall, activists gathered in federal courtrooms, churches, and on front porches. They began to think together about what it would mean to abolish Jim Crow policing.

In its fight to abolish Jim Crow's police form, COFO's strategy prefigured what came to be called *non-reformist reform*. Importantly, COFO organizers did not demand police disappearance. There is no evidence that activists imagined a South without law enforcement. Rather, activists in 1964 approached Jim Crow policing as the enforcement mechanism of white supremacy. Their larger project to abolish Jim Crow necessarily meant reimagining Southern law enforcement. They rejected key aspects of the expansionary and unaccountable, or *reformist*, model of reform that defined Jim Crow policing.[8] Instead, they sought supervision and replacement of Jim Crow lawmen by federal courts. In this moment they sought neither the integration of Black officers within existing law enforcement agencies nor a reliance on the FBI or Department of Justice. Thus, Freedom Summer's particular historical conjuncture yields a richer origin story of *non-reformist* reforms, the social and legal experiments that attack inequitable social orders. Mississippi's legal activists and community organizers fought to "reduce the power of an oppressive system while illuminating the system's inability to solve the crises it creates."[9] However incomplete or imperfect their analysis, some sought to reconstitute government authority after Jim Crow. They attempted what was in their moment the impossible.

Activist colleagues contributed to the fight for abolition-democracy through renewed experiments in Black community policing, armed self-defense, and mutual aid. The scholar Akinyele Umoja in part pinpoints this resurgence in organized self-defense to Freedom Summer, showing that COFO's grassroots campaigns for institutional change would have been practically impossible without armed Black counterpressure. White terrorists as well as local and federal government came to understand that some activists shot back.[10] The activism after Freedom Summer may help us to understand better what Robin D. G. Kelley has identified as the watershed abolitionist experiment, California's Black Panther Party for Self-Defense (established 1966). Famously the Panthers organized to police the police and to provide basic human services in cities across America. They also, Kelley writes, "proposed reorganizing the police."[11] COFO's success and failure after Mississippi Burning highlighted both the radical imagination of nonviolent activism and the necessity of revolutionary struggle to confront the American system of police supremacy. This new abolition, like the old, had Deep South roots.

In reaction to COFO's alternative visions for policing there emerged a willful misrepresentation of its efforts to expose the ubiquity of police violence and wrest basic democratic control over state violence. By the summer of 1965 Freedom Summer activists published their collective narratives of police abuse for national consumption. The response to this truth-telling, especially the response of white Southern liberals, signaled the challenge ahead for visions and collectivities that struggled to shrink the roles of policing and imprisonment in society.

COFO v. Rainey et al.

On July 10, 1964, COFO's executive committee met in Jackson. At the table were leaders from SNCC, including Bob Moses, Stokely Carmichael, James Forman, and Casey Hayden. They sat with activists from the SCLC, people like Andrew Young and Annell Ponder. The room must have been heavy with uncertainty. After nineteen days, Chaney, Goodman, and Schwerner remained missing and feared dead in Neshoba County. Nonetheless, the group built an agenda and gave the floor to COFO's legal coordinator, who reported on eighteen movement lawyers operating across Mississippi.[12]

Just hours before the meeting, lawyers filed *COFO, et al., v. Lawrence A. Rainey, et al.*, "a suit asking for an injunction to enjoin unlawful action and violence" against civil rights activists. Annell Ponder, a survivor of the Montgomery County jail, recorded in her minutes that the class action lawsuit "aimed especially at KKK, white citizens councils, and similar groups."[13] Those "similar groups" included practically every police officer in Mississippi: its eighty-two county sheriffs, their deputies, local policemen, and state highway patrolmen. Citing the Civil Rights Act of 1964, signed just eight days earlier, COFO meant to challenge the legal basis of white supremacist policing across Mississippi.[14]

In broad strokes, *COFO v. Rainey* implicated the sheriff of Neshoba County, Lawrence A. Rainey, in a conspiracy with local Ku Klux Klansmen to murder the CORE volunteers and argued that the same dynamic pervaded law enforcement agencies in Mississippi. The suit presented a strategy through which the federal judiciary opened Jim Crow law enforcement to scrutiny and legal liability. Existing lawmen would be enjoined against depriving Mississippians of civil rights, and federal peace officers would operate from each county to arrest lawmen thought to be in breach of federal civil rights law. The community organizing that accompanied *COFO v. Rainey* exposed how, to those who had experienced Jim Crow policing firsthand, such confrontational approaches to police reform were less radical than commonsensical. To make their case, jurists looked to America's first abolition and the Reconstruction-Era laws that once promised democracy after plantation slavery but before Jim Crow.

Radical lawyers such as Arthur Kinoy, who served on COFO's Legal Advisory Committee, saw the crisis as an opportunity to counteract white supremacist law enforcement in Mississippi. Kinoy had built a career defending high-profile clients and earned a reputation as "a people's lawyer" over two decades on the Left. In 1953, he defended Julius and Ethel Rosenberg in their final fight against the death penalty. In 1956, Ella Baker telephoned him to ask that he counsel Montgomery, Alabama's growing bus boycott. A year later he worked with Baker, A. Philip Randolph, and Bayard Rustin to plan the Prayer Pilgrimage for Freedom, a dress rehearsal for 1963's March on Washington. By July 1964, Kinoy had worked with Baker on movement legal strategy infrequently for eight years.[15]

Kinoy was a frequent collaborator with such movement intellectuals. In the summer of 1964 the son of Jewish immigrants created a law firm with William "Bill" Kunstler, later famous for defending the Chicago Seven, Attica prison rebels, and Assata Shakur. Kinoy regularly sat in strategy meetings with Bob Moses and Ella Baker in preparation for Freedom Summer. In legal terms, as Kinoy, Moses, and Baker discussed in one meeting, they saw *COFO v. Rainey* as a test of "the relationship of judicial action to the problem of executive intervention" posed by the Civil Rights Act of 1964. In lay terms, their class action lawsuit alleged that white sheriffs, deputies, local policemen, and highway patrolmen conspired with non-state actors to discriminate against the Black Mississippians battling Jim Crow.[16]

Activists carefully selected named plaintiffs. First was Fannie Lee Chaney, a Meridian native and mother of James Chaney. Next came Fannie Lou Hamer, who sued "individually and on behalf of all Negro citizens of the State of Mississippi," evoking her treatment by lawmen in the Montgomery County jail in June 1963. Other plaintiffs included Bob Moses, who represented over a thousand civil rights volunteers across the state; representative parents of Northern civil rights volunteers; and Reverend R. Edwin "Ed" King, who represented those white Mississippians "actively concerned with assisting . . . the Negro citizens of this state to achieve freedom." Each plaintiff embodied a facet of the civil rights movement impacted by lawless law enforcement.[17]

In its justification for court action, COFO argued that little distinction existed between Mississippi's regime of public safety and private terrorism. Lawyers wrote that "defendants acting under the color and authority of the State of Mississippi, have engaged in widespread terroristic acts including beatings, arson, torture and murder in a concerted effort to intimidate, punish and deter the Negro citizens of the State of Mississippi." Furthermore, COFO activists argued that police oppression had grown worse, not better, since the disappearance of Chaney, Goodman, and Schwerner, notwithstanding the passage of the Civil Rights Act. "This concerted, planned and organized conspiracy to utilize these terroristic acts of violence has continued *and accelerated*," they urged; summer 1964 marked an "intensification of this continuing conspiracy," not a starting point. They feared that "unless this illegal conspiracy is restrained, the Plaintiffs will imminently suffer . . . and continue to suffer immediate and irreparable injuries."[18]

In its pursuit of relief, the movement's legal arm attacked the institutions and offices responsible for policing as opposed to individual law enforcement officers. Activists sought a permanent injunction against "the use of force, violence, or any terroristic act" by a class constituting every lawman in the state. Using the recent example of Neshoba County, they sued Sheriff Lawrence A. Rainey and his deputies, "individually and as representatives of other Mississippi sheriffs and deputies." Next, they sued Highway Patrol commissioner T. B. Birdsong "individually and as representative of all members of the State Police." For good measure they even sued "John Doe and Richard Roe" as representative law enforcement personnel who intentionally hid or obscured their identity in the process of brutalizing activists. Together, activists alleged, all police officers joined codefendants like the Ku Klux Klan, the White Citizens' Council, and Americans for the Preservation of the White Race to discriminate against Black citizens, as forbidden by the Civil Rights Act.[19]

In a nod to the lawless white upheaval after the abolition of chattel slavery, lawyers turned to the federal laws passed during Reconstruction. They proposed that civil rights law be enforced and overseen by officers of federal courts, not the state or the Department of Justice. Specifically, they called for the installation of US commissioners in each of the state's eighty-two sheriffs' offices "to provide for the speedy arrest" of those who would violate or threaten to violate a citizen's civil rights.[20] Akin to present-day US magistrate judges, commissioners were judicial functionaries who worked from federal district courts as process servers empowered to issue arrest and search warrants, similar to early uses of the US marshals. But Kinoy, a keen student of American legal history, invoked the Reconstruction-Era Civil Rights Act of 1866 to justify the use of commissioners as a makeshift force of peace officers.[21]

Though its complete vision for the future of Mississippi law enforcement is lacking, *COFO v. Rainey* seemed to propose an intermediary or transitional step toward building a credible police power. The suit's legal architects mention nothing about banishing the idea of a police force altogether; however, they imagined that federal commissioners would keep peace in the absence of Jim Crow's sheriffs and other policemen. They would hold sway over Mississippi's enjoined white law enforcement officers and, ostensibly, detain Mississippi's lawmen who violated injunctions against harming civil rights activism. Unaffiliated with the preexisting regime, commissioners would in theory arrest state and non-state actors accused of breaking the law and escort them to the custody of federal courts.

Such a systemic critique of Jim Crow policing was equally notable for the legal pathways it altered and refused. Activists built on the idea of prosecuting bad cops, a past framework for dealing with police brutality pioneered by the NAACP and codified by so-called smart segregationists like James P. Coleman, and made a class action suit against the entire personnel of law enforcement agencies.[22] However, they did not argue for police desegregation, as Stokely Carmichael would just three years later when he declared "a black sheriff can end police brutality."[23] And the litigation completely ignored what had for half a century been a national police force—the FBI. Instead, the crises of Freedom Summer called for a pause to reimagine the front line of Mississippi's criminal legal system. They lacked all faith that T. B. Birdsong's state policemen could be more than the protectors of racial hierarchy.

・・・・・・

Far more important than its particular legal remedy was the grassroots organizing and collective envisioning that accompanied *COFO v. Rainey*. "The suit became one of the most effective organizing tools ever used in the state," Kinoy remembered.[24] Named plaintiffs like Fannie Lou Hamer mimeographed copies of the official complaint and sent it to COFO sites across the state, showing activist names at the very top. Hamer encouraged Kinoy to come personally to mass meetings to explain the significance of such a lawsuit. One day, after an all-day trial, he tried to beg off. "Oh Mrs. Hamer," he sighed. "I don't think I can make it." She doubled down. "You've got to understand that this kind of a meeting is more important than anything that goes on in the courtroom." Kinoy buckled. They arrived to find only three community members inside the church. "Mrs. Hamer took a look at me and she grabs a hold of me," the lawyer recalled. "Three people are better than no people," she said.[25] In time the effort to document police violence wouldn't worry about small crowds. But word of the suit had also spread among Mississippi's ruling class.

The suit was on the minds of leaders of the Highway Patrol. On July 21, just two days before the case's first scheduled hearing, the patrol celebrated the FBI naming Mississippi the "Most Law-Abiding State" on the front page of the state's most circulated newspaper. Citing J. Edgar Hoover's release of the most recent Uniform Crime Statistics, a patrol spokesperson said the Magnolia State's system of policing was "worthy of emulation, especially in Northern cities like New York." (State newspapers had salaciously covered the Harlem revolts sparked by racist policing for days.) "The popular conception of Mississippi as a crime-ridden state has been perpetuated by wildly distorted reports of scattered incidents," the trooper told a reporter. "Our problems have been blown out of proportion."[26] Such was the publicity COFO would fight in court. After a week's continuance, the two sides met on July 30, 1964.

COFO's preparatory work was extensive; its first day in court was brief. Lawyers appeared in a Hattiesburg district courtroom alongside hundreds of volunteers and local people. In the face of such popular support, Judge Sidney Mize swiftly dismissed the class action suit in an explanation from the bench: "This complaint is a scatter load, the worst I have ever seen. It brings in John Doe, Richard Roe, John Paul Jones. . . . I believe the complaint is insufficient on its face and for that reason will be dismissed." According to Mize, COFO's systemic indictment of Mississippi's criminal legal system constituted a "failure to charge overt acts, failure to charge conspiracy, where it was made, when and how it was made." The attorneys and activist plaintiffs left Hattiesburg empty-handed, but in less than a month, the US Court of Appeals for the Fifth Circuit agreed to hear COFO's appeal.[27]

Given this second wind, the lawyers and organizers hoped to prove Mississippi's emergency to a higher court in order to bypass district court judges altogether. In August, COFO called for activists from across the state to put their experiences with law enforcement in writing. In autumn 1964, some 257 survivors of Mississippi Law compiled affidavits to concretely demonstrate the conspiracy and collusion described in COFO's complaint. Arriving at the appellate courthouse one by one, the affidavits made up "a continual flow," according to Kinoy.[28] These affidavits of local residents and civil rights volunteers documented "illegal acts of Mississippi law enforcement" and "the failure of the law enforcement officers . . . to prosecute known perpetrators of violence . . . all of which is daily occurring."[29]

COFO's success in gathering evidence surprised even the affidavit campaign's organizers. After compiling the incidents of police violence in the town of Canton alone, one staffer came to a succinct conclusion: "The legally constituted authorities are themselves the lawless."[30]

The Hope of Fannie Lee Chaney

Organizing success in *COFO v. Rainey* built on the tireless work of the lawsuit's lead plaintiff, Fannie Lee Chaney. Her son's murder launched Chaney and her children on a forced trajectory into the local and national spotlight. On August 16, 1964, Chaney spoke at her son's memorial, staged over the ruins of the Mt. Zion Methodist Church in Longdale. "Well, you all know that I am Fannie Lee Chaney," she began, going on to describe her son's organizing work with CORE. "Y'all know what my son has done. He was trying for us all to make a better living." On her own motivations to participate in the movement, Mrs. Chaney was clear. "I just don't want those children's work to be in vain. . . . They're dead. Are we gonna let all of it die? I can't let it die. . . . I want to know if somebody is gonna help me. . . . If we're going to do something, we had better try to do it now. I want help. I want help. And I need all of you all. . . . Please don't let those children's work go in vain. They're dead. Don't let their work die. That's when freedom started." Harnessing unspeakable pain, Chaney placed her hope in collective action.[31]

Other speakers at the memorial service made clear connections to *COFO v. Rainey*. Mrs. Chaney's younger son, Ben Chaney Jr., said "Most of you know about those three missing boys. Well, we've got to finish what they've started. And the only way we'll be able to do that is by stopping Sheriff Rainey and his deputies. . . . Sheriff Rainey is the cause of this and all of

Philadelphia, MS, Neshoba County, August 1964. James Chaney funeral. Mrs. Chaney, mother of James Chaney, gives funeral oration in the burned ruins of the Mt. Zion Methodist Church. It was this fire the three murdered civil rights workers were investigating when they were arrested. Photograph by Dave Prince/Take Stock/TopFoto.

his other deputies and the Klan." The memorial's preacher even mentioned the police:

> These fellas have laid down their lives here in Neshoba County. They have laid down their lives in Mississippi. They have laid down their lives in America, that we may have life more abundant. . . . Though they were destroyed, the cause that they stood for is not dead. This cause will be here. (The cause that Christ died for on the cross is still here with us.) . . . All the cops in Philadelphia and Neshoba County, all the cops in the United States of America, all the cops around the world will not be able to kill this cause.[32]

The police could not stop the Black freedom movement's fight for "life more abundant" in Mississippi.

COFO's success in gathering affidavits for *COFO v. Rainey* accompanied a speaking tour featuring Fannie Lee Chaney. She spoke at New Orleans's

New Zion Baptist Church on August 27 and Harlem's Metropolitan AME Church on October 23, 1964.[33] In Harlem, having known her son's tragic fate at the hands of Cecil Price and the Ku Klux Klan for more than a month, she took to the pulpit for a short but epic speech. "I am here to tell you about Meridian, Mississippi," she began. "That's my home. I have been there all my days. I know the white man; I know the black man. The white man is not for the black man—we are just there."[34] Born Fannie Lee Roberts sometime around 1923, she grew up on a farm in Lauderdale County. One of her grandfathers had met a fate similar to her son's when he refused to sell property to a white man. His body was never found. As an adult, she became a well-known baker in Meridian, a town of around 50,000, where she lived with James, whom she called *J.E.*[35]

Apparently someone recorded and transcribed Chaney's speech. Under the direction of Black radical thinker Jack O'Dell, the journal *Freedomways* published it in full in 1965. By 1977, Ruby Dee, a later *Freedomways* contributor, performed Chaney's speech on vinyl alongside the thought of Ida B. Wells, Coretta Scott King, and Angela Davis.[36]

In her Harlem speech, Chaney took the opportunity to eulogize her son and the organizing work he had done to register voters in Black communities.

> A lot of our people are scared, afraid. . . . "I will lose my job; I won't have any job," [they say]. . . . My son, James, when he went out with the civil rights workers around the first of '64 . . . he stayed in Canton . . . working on voter registration. . . . When he came home he told me how he worked and lived those few weeks he was there; he said, "Mother, one half of the time I was out behind houses or churches, waiting to get the opportunity to talk to people about what they needed and what they ought to do." He said, "Sometime they shunned me off and some would say 'I want you all to stay away from here and leave me alone.'" But he would pick his chance and go back again.[37]

Chaney chose to emphasize the challenges rather than the successes of her son's organizing work. Neighbors did not automatically join the freedom movement. It was instead something to be worked toward.

In Harlem, Chaney painted the picture of a family dedicated to the movement. "Mississippi right now," she sighed. "There is one more test I want to do there"—perhaps speaking of the COFO lawsuit. "I am working with the civil rights movement; my whole family is. And my son Ben, here, he is going to take his big brother's place." Ben had been arrested for participating in demonstrations twice before age twelve. "He is not afraid; he would go to jail again." she said. "We've got to go to jail and we've got to go where the white man is. The white man has got Mississippi and we're just there working for the white man. He is the one getting rich. And when he gets rich, we can be outdoors or in old houses and he is going to knock on the door and get his rent money."[38] Her vision of Mississippi's carceral state was inextricable from its system of racialized economic inequality.

Chaney left her Northern audience with a genealogy of her family's struggle in Mississippi. "This is not something that has just now started," she said. "It has been going on before my time and I imagine before my parents' time. It is not just *now* the white man is doing this; it was borne from generation to generation."[39] For Chaney, her family's work survived in a continuum that stretched to emancipation. She spoke broadly about a Black freedom struggle against what is now recognizable as racial capitalism, epitomized by the white rentier and the jail. But as she spoke, she was also the lead plaintiff in a class action lawsuit against the lawless police who put some Black Mississippians in jail and sent others to Parchman Farm. If Fannie Lee Chaney's name was forever attached to the loss of her son, it was also attached to an effort to rethink policing in her home state.

For the next month, three appeals court judges pored over the affidavits from *COFO v. Rainey*. Despite such evidence of systemic police discrimination, the judges refused to grant relief on December 22, 1964. Instead of enjoining Mississippi's white law enforcement establishment or appointing US commissioners, the court only ordered a rehearing in the lower court. COFO's records lack court filings to suggest that the Legal Advisory Committee resumed litigation in district court. But the case's precedent remained, driving county-level litigation against lawless police conspiracy and by attempting to "remove" state cases against civil rights workers to federal court.[40] COFO's legal strategy had hoped to aid, as Arthur Kinoy put it, the Black Mississippian, the "virtual outlaw" who sought "the fulfillment of his status as a citizen and a human being."[41] The group of Black Mississippi residents filling the courthouses affirmed the common hope for an end to a key feature of Jim Crow policing.

COFO v. Rainey was a long shot, not a delusion. It grew from a moment in which the experiences of those harmed by lawless law enforcement formalized into a unified complaint that imagined redress. Movement thinkers had proposed a new system through which to interrogate public safety more fully. A far more lasting model took hold ten months later, when

Lyndon B. Johnson declared the first, liberal War on Crime. Like COFO, Johnson also acted with Mississippi's crisis of law enforcement officers and Klansmen in mind. With additional legislation like the Law Enforcement Assistance Act (1965) and the Omnibus Crime Control and Safe Streets Act (1968), the national liberal focus pivoted to reforming the police by growing police forces across the Jim Crow South with high hopes placed on training and technology. As Mississippi law enforcement came into public compliance with liberal expectations of policing, federal funding began to flow into local and state police departments, settling the problem of state parsimony that dated to the creation of the Mississippi National Guard.[42]

This intervention by expansion assumed that police officers, properly trained and funded, would cease to function like clandestine terrorist organizations under color of law. COFO's attempt to empower the judiciary as peacekeepers had anticipated and rejected this premise. "At this moment," Kinoy wrote in his final appeal in November 1964, "there is *no* remedy at law in Mississippi through the normal enforcement of the criminal law."[43] The nationwide fervor to remedy police violence or inaction with *more*, *better*, or *desegregated* policing drowned out the movement's call to scrutinize policing's more fundamental relationship to the Jim Crow order.

Preserving Policing

The opportunity for systemic police reform created by the Mississippi Burning crisis met serious obstacles. In addition to a hostile Southern judiciary, the attempt to politicize Mississippi Law as more than the work of a few rabid individuals tied to a segregationist regime came crashing down with the high tide of American liberalism. Federal law enforcement interested in enforcing civil rights protections pursued individual policemen rather than exploring or indicting the deep-rooted systems that produced violent police officers like Cecil Ray Price or John Lutellas Basinger. And for their part, liberal white Southerners with a national audience minimized the contentions of Fannie Lee Chaney and others that Mississippi's system of policing existed in a longer continuum of racialized labor extraction, land theft, and jailing.

The Highway Patrol played a leading role in containing the crisis and renewing the State of Mississippi's public commitment to enforce the law through its Department of Public Safety. In its investigation of the Freedom Summer murders, the patrol continued its decades-long mission to monopolize legitimate violence without sacrificing political power.

"Highway Patrol commissioner Col. T. B. Birdsong Jr. (*left*) and unidentified gentleman [J. Edgar Hoover] standing next to American flag, ca. 1966." Paul B. Johnson Family Papers, M191, Box 178, Folder 8, Historical Manuscripts, Special Collections, The University of Southern Mississippi Libraries.

The Highway Patrol's ascendance during the Mississippi Burning crisis accompanied a public show of unity between T. B. Birdsong and J. Edgar Hoover. On July 10, 1964, the same day COFO met to discuss *COFO v. Rainey*, Hoover flew to Mississippi on Lyndon Johnson's orders to reopen an FBI field office in Jackson. The commissioner of public safety met Hoover at the airport. According to one journalist, Hoover greeted Birdsong by saying "Good to see you, Colonel. You and I have more or less been partners in crime for a long time."[44] At a press conference later in the day, Hoover praised Jackson and Mississippi's state government more generally, joking that he wanted to move FBI headquarters from Washington, DC, to Jackson, where he admired the city's "vital new industry." Governor Paul B. Johnson Jr. reiterated his state police reforms, and Hoover congratulated the governor "for a philosophy of government that . . . would be well to be adopted in all areas of our country." Hoover also flattered Birdsong's assistance in federal investigations. "I don't know of any state police organization that has been more cooperative, more dedicated, or more helpful in their duties than has been the Mississippi highway patrol under Colonel Birdsong," Hoover said. Birdsong in turn praised Hoover, saying "I myself have held you in highest esteem for many years—and I do mean many years."[45]

Away from the cameras, patrolmen foiled the murder cover-up orchestrated by the Neshoba County sheriff's office. Inspector Maynard King, known until 2005 by the FBI's alias *Mr. X*, most likely provided the anonymous tip that revealed the location of the victims' grave on August 4, 1964.[46] At the time, the FBI claimed all credit for closing the investigation. But J. Edgar Hoover wrote Governor Paul B. Johnson Jr., thanking him for "the excellent cooperation [of] law enforcement agencies in Mississippi" just six days after agents recovered the bodies of Chaney, Goodman, and Schwerner.[47] The FBI showed little interest in how exactly King came upon the knowledge that closed the case.

Just as the two rank-and-file patrolmen reported the actions of Cecil Price to the FBI, Inspector Maynard King collaborated with the bureau to further the Highway Patrol's agenda of state police supremacy. Special Agent Joseph Sullivan was in charge of the MIBURN investigation. Decades later he remembered the Highway Patrol as "a traffic outfit." "They weren't pushing their people to investigate this case at all," he told a reporter.[48] But the FBI agent viewed Maynard King differently, even affectionately. The first time they met, King produced a bottle of moonshine for the two men to share, in a scene similar to John Lutellas Basinger's use of confiscated spirits to reward assault in the Montgomery County jail.[49] In Special Agent Sullivan's memory, King was "a good police officer, an up-front legitimate police officer." Why would Mr. X break with the Klan and local law enforcement over the murders of Chaney, Goodman, and Schwerner? "He didn't think it was good for Mississippi," Sullivan said.[50] Maynard King's vision of order and progress differed from that of Cecil Price.

While the Freedom Summer murders convulsed the nation, the Highway Patrol sought out a middle ground on which most white Mississippians could agree. Statewide papers like Jackson's *Clarion-Ledger* praised troopers who "spent long hours keeping tabs on civil rights organizations."[51] Readers shocked that the Klan burned a cross on the front lawn of the white mayor of Ruleville because of his perceived moderation could find that both the FBI *and* Highway Patrol investigated.[52] Small-town newspapers began to report when T. B. Birdsong accepted local men into new, larger police academy classes.[53] Even the Klan-adjacent Americans for the Preservation of the White Race "pledged full support and cooperation to Governor Paul Johnson, the highway patrol, and to all state and local law enforcement officers" in August 1964.[54]

・・・・・・

As *COFO v. Rainey*'s bid to suspend law enforcement fell to the Highway Patrol's reassertion of order, activists turned away from the courts and toward the reading public. Sometime after the appeals court decision in December 1964, activists aided the publication of some of the case affidavits for a wide audience. Appearing on newsstands and in bookstores in April 1965, that publication was *Mississippi Black Paper: Fifty-Seven Negro and White Citizens' Testimony of Police Brutality, the Breakdown of Law and Order and the Corruption of Justice in Mississippi*. At ninety-two pages, it was the size of a magazine. The cover looked as though blood had dripped on it. It sold for $1.95.[55]

Little has been written about how COFO participated in the publication of *Mississippi Black Paper*. Its title was likely a play on *white paper*, a governmental or expert report on a given subject. The National Welfare Rights Organization's funding arm, the Misseduc Foundation, Inc., paid for its copyright. And Random House, a major New York publisher, printed the book with substantial help from SNCC's Bob Moses. Random House arranged for the seminarian Reinhold Niebuhr to write a foreword and for the white moderate Mississippian William Hodding Carter III to write an introduction. The rest of the book's material came directly from affidavits submitted in *COFO v. Rainey*.

Readers opened the *Black Paper* to find stories of police violence from across Mississippi's geographic and activist landscape. NAACP veterans like Aaron Henry and Vera Mae Pigee wrote that law enforcement in Clarksdale had refused to investigate white racist violence directed at them. A Freedom Rider from Jackson reported multiple instances of police abuse and his treatment from guards when sentenced to the county chain gang in 1961. Fannie Lou Hamer, Annell Ponder, and June Johnson recounted their time in the Montgomery County jail in the summer of 1963. Michael Schwerner's activist partner and widow, Rita Schwerner, spoke to the police harassment that accompanied the couple's work in the months before his disappearance in Neshoba County. COFO volunteers from across the state and nation wrote in New York, Connecticut, Chicago, Ann Arbor, Los Angeles.[56] Each had their own story of police harassment to report. Collectively, they exploded the notion that the Civil Rights Act alone could meaningfully combat the police violence that met any attempt of Black community mobilization.

A. C. Whitaker, who remained anonymous in the publication, singled out the violence that attended the Highway Safety Patrol's most basic work: highway safety. "I am a citizen of the United States of America and am a Negro," Whitaker began. His story was innocuous. His car broke down in rural Sharkey County. It was late; he didn't have the tools to fix a tire. So Whitaker left his vehicle on the roadside and hitchhiked to the nearest town. Upon returning to the roadside, he searched for hours. His car had vanished without a trace. The next day a garage owner told the activist to check with the Highway Patrol, who might have towed the disabled car. When the civil rights worker found a trooper on a highway, the patrolman told him where to find the car. The activist asked why his car had been towed and the trooper exploded. "The best thing for you to do is go up there and pay . . . for the damn car," the trooper roared. "And get your black ass out of Sharkey County."[57]

On this note Whitaker turned to depart, but the trooper called him back. "The patrolman got in his car and told me to come on to the garage where the car was," he recalled. "We got to the garage and he asked me to come inside." Once in the garage owner's office, the trooper bolted the door. "He asked me why I locked the car 'in his territory.'" Then the trooper began to beat the volunteer with his truncheon until the victim grabbed it in mid-air. "He said to turn the blackjack loose. . . . I told him that he could kill me before I'd turn it loose." The lawman decided against killing the COFO activist. He told Whitaker to return to his native Greenville. "When you get there tell the police department which is y'all's good friends, that we whip n———s' ass in Sharkey County. . . . Don't be caught here no more." Boldly, the writer listed the trooper's name and badge number on his affidavit. He had made it out of Highway Patrol territory alive.[58]

Despite broad evidence of systematic police oppression, white liberal reviewers of the *Black Paper* overwhelmingly missed the original lawsuit's deeper critique of Jim Crow policing, if they acknowledged the attached lawsuit at all. Instead, they focused on individual acts of police violence as discrete events rather than recent manifestations of a historical pattern.

The trooper's suggestion that Greenville was a more racially progressive place had much to do with Hodding Carter III, who wrote an introduction for the *Black Paper*. Carter edited Greenville's *Delta Democrat-Times*, a paper founded by his father, who had himself aligned with the national Democratic Party and openly criticized the White Citizens' Council. The younger

Carter had been outspoken in his support of Freedom Summer and the MFDP's challenge to the all-white state Democratic Party. When the archconservative *Clarion-Ledger* reviewed *Mississippi Black Paper*, it called Carter "a wheel for the Great Society" and accused him of being in league with Black revolutionaries. Generally, however, the Jackson paper was restrained in its handling of Carter's role in the *Black Paper*'s "anti-Mississippi smear and slander by assorted pinks, punks, and pundits." It called his introduction "favorable."[59]

Perhaps Hodding Carter drew praise from segregationists because by 1965 white elites shared a common politics of policing, regardless of their emotions toward Black neighbors. "What can a white Mississippian say in the face of these affidavits?" Carter began. "He can point out some of the possible exaggerations, cry foul because allegations are presented with no attempt to balance them with rebuttals, or he can claim the incidents cited were exceptions rather than the general rule in Mississippi last year. He can point to such communities as my home town of Greenville which never experienced such events."[60] Bad apples all.

When he wasn't playing devil's advocate, Carter parroted the empirical language of law enforcement professionals. He ended sentences with parentheticals such as "whether all the charges in the following pages are completely correct or not." Like the Highway Patrol's public relations department, he noted that "the FBI's records indicate that, on the whole, Mississippi is one of the most crime-free states in the nation." He lamented the "black racists," "extreme leftists," and "perhaps Communists" who had infiltrated COFO. His hope for the book? To be "a vivid reminder to all Americans that . . . all that is necessary for the triumph of evil is for good men to do nothing."[61] Carter articulated his liberal milieu's hope in law enforcement reform and skepticism of victims who named police abuse.

For its part, Random House was concerned about Hodding Carter's contribution to the *Black Paper*. A senior editor read an early draft of his introduction, thought it was worth printing, but predicted that "most of the people who signed these affidavits . . . will blow a fuse when they read these pages." "It would be extremely hard to ask Carter to censor himself," the publishers conceded. But there was no denying it: "SNCC, COFO, et al. are going to feel betrayed after all that they have done to help us get this book published." The editor proposed allowing Bob Moses to write a rebuttal, but it never materialized. Random House printed Carter's backhanded introduction with minimal editing. In the end, marketing concerns outweighed betrayal.[62]

Carter wasn't alone among the white Southern literati. Walker Percy, a prize-winning novelist raised in an aristocratic Greenville family, reviewed COFO's *Black Paper* in the *New York Review of Books*. "There is not really a great deal to be said about Mississippi now," Percy wrote. "There is . . . a sameness about violence, especially Mississippi violence." In a move similar to Hodding Carter, Percy recommended metropolitan readers look to their own benighted downtowns for evidence of similar racialized oppression, naming Chicago's South Side, Los Angeles, and New York. Yet he quoted two *COFO v. Rainey* affidavits at length. First, Bessie Turner's testimony of being sexually abused by lawmen in the Coahoma County jail. His analysis of her account amounted to "There is not much to say now, except to issue progress reports." Percy ended with Vera Mae Pigee's account of being beaten by a white gas station owner and then arrested for reporting her attacker. "It is somewhere along here that it comes over you that there is not really much to say," Percy concluded. For him, thinking people were trapped in an intellectual bind, never mind what *COFO v. Rainey* had tried to do about such police violence.[63]

In their attempts to implicate white Northern racism in a national racial project, Carter and Percy predicted public interest in civil unrest in Northern Black communities. But such Southern white intellectuals helped establish a liberal paradigm of airing and then promptly forgetting exceptional racial violence in the South that survives to the present day. Carter, the reformer, pinned his hopes on the FBI. Percy, the artist, had little hope at all. *COFO v. Rainey*, the litigation that so boldly proposed a solution to the racial order, was naïve, hysterical, or worse—uninteresting.

Lost in reviews full of unqualified praise and horror was the radical proposition at the heart of *COFO v. Rainey*. Most reviews failed to note that the affidavits had emerged from a political campaign attached to a lawsuit to interrogate racist police power in light of the Civil Rights Act. That legal solution to Mississippi Law had not occurred in a vacuum. It grew from the collective demands of community members and advocates who dared to mobilize.

· · · · · ·

If, as Dan Berger has argued, the Southern Black freedom movement's interrogation of the prison regime expressed "a tactical continuity . . . between Fannie Lou Hamer and Angela Davis, between Martin Luther King Jr. and George Jackson," surely the speculative work of *COFO v. Rainey* was a link in the chain between past and future struggles that imagined an off-ramp for lawless policing and the fight for a new safety. The success and failure of the grassroots campaign for judicial intervention sheds light on what scholars recognize as *abolitionist* or *non-reformist* reform, which emerged in the late 1960s and early 1970s as an answer to policing's continued racist ungovernability.[64]

The movement's lawsuit refused to suggest a police reform that equated expansion as the answer to Mississippi Law. Rather, a radical legal mind like Arthur Kinoy and a grassroots Black feminist organizer like Ella Baker anticipated facets of abolitionist police reform in an age before it had been named. Building from an impulse to "fragment the South into a thousand pieces and put them back together in the image of democracy," the social movement around *COFO v. Rainey* sought to abolish Jim Crow. As the geographer Ruth Wilson Gilmore has argued, after Du Bois, "Abolition isn't just absence. . . . Abolition is a fleshly and material presence of social life lived differently."[65]

During and after the court battle for *COFO v. Rainey*, the Chaney family also worked to sustain Black life in Mississippi. In October 1964, Fannie Lee Chaney worked with the Meridian Community Center, her hometown's conduit for the freedom struggle's philanthropic and mutual aid networks. From 1964, COFO Community Centers were spaces constructed by local people and volunteer organizers to meet the needs of poor and working-class Black people, places to imagine different ways of living while movement lawyers fought against Jim Crow in the courts. Organizers designed centers to host childcare, adult education, libraries, and a rudimentary healthcare space. Activists meant for the Meridian Community Center, which Chaney codirected with Eric and Elaine Weinberger, to distribute food, vitamins, and clothing donations. Something like the opposite of the jail Chaney described in her Harlem speech, the Community Center was to be a site for care and repair.[66]

Across Mississippi, rural Black communities thought together and organized toward the society they wanted. Movement families like the Chaneys fought to curtail the racist carceral state's function through policing and jails, but they also battled to meet the basic needs of neighbors and neighborhoods. When asked about her mother's mutual aid work in an interview, Julia Chaney-Moss said, "My mother's activism was really just her ability and capacity to care. She loved her people, her family, her relatives. . . . Everyone came together to protect each other. The sharing, the living in community in that way: That was just a lifestyle." Fannie Lee Chaney joined others, in the words of her daughter, "to build a new life, a new world: peace, prosperity, growth of their children, opportunity for work, growth, education."⁶⁷ In short, as local people joined a new cast of white allies to fight the public safety regime of Jim Crow police expansion, they also continued to imagine a fuller meaning of safety in a world that might follow the extremes of legal apartheid.⁶⁸

One interpretation of COFO's call for federal intervention became mainstream in the years after Freedom Summer. This included Department of Justice and FBI investigations of police abuse, eventually leading to court-ordered consent decrees for local police departments. However, COFO's larger interrogation of policing would not win the day. As the last two chapters of *Mississippi Law* demonstrate, the years after 1964 saw police violence with a new scale of bestiality and unaccountability fueled by expansionist police reform. On June 21, 1965, when Fannie Lee Chaney and others returned to Neshoba County for a one-year anniversary march to commemorate the abduction of Chaney, Goodman, and Schwerner, Deputy Cecil Price directed traffic. Mississippi highway patrolmen lined the twelve-mile parade route and escorted the Chaneys from Philadelphia to the ruins of Mt. Zion Methodist Church. Meanwhile, in Jackson, troopers locked activists in cattle pens.⁶⁹

Part IV **Public Safety**

9 Cattle Pens and Federal Dollars

> Our founding fathers came to these bleak shores. They were met with a wilderness. They encountered insects, pestilence, hunger, disease, cold and starvation, with Indians shooting at them from several directions.
> —Mississippi Crime Commission (1968)

"These cops were terrible." Thus Mrs. Lucinda Rancher closed her report on state and local police at the Mississippi State Fairgrounds in June 1965.[1] Officers arrested Rancher and 471 others near the Mississippi capitol on June 14, during a silent march against a special session of the state legislature designed to shield Mississippi from the Voting Rights Act being debated in the US Congress. Protesters like Rancher marched with the Mississippi Freedom Democratic Party (MFDP) to dramatize the illegitimacy of the state's all-white Democratic Party and its attempt to block federal intervention in civil and voting rights. While federal law enforcement looked on, police loaded Rancher and others onto a caged garbage truck and drove to a part of the fairgrounds complex used as covered cattle pens, now encircled with chicken wire but still reeking with the scent of livestock.[2]

Reporters and some detainees mocked the shabby accommodations as the "Fairgrounds Motel." MFDP officials called it the "Fairgrounds stockade," evoking a makeshift confines for livestock and prisoners of war. Weeks of secluded brutality in Mississippi's capital city coincided with the Highway Patrol publicly guarding Neshoba County's Mississippi Burning anniversary march on June 21, 1965.

The MFDP *Newsletter* reprinted Lucinda Rancher's description of the fairgrounds camp verbatim. "Childrens were struck and punch with black jacks," she wrote. They "were being beat so badly that I decided to help." When she came to the defense of the brutalized, officers beat Rancher to the point of hospitalization. "Another woman," she remembered, "was beaten in the stomach and had to be taken to the doctor."[3] Jackson police and state troopers detained more than a thousand people at the state fairgrounds over weeks of marches.

Yet if brutality thrived in policing's urban hinterland, so too did self-defense. Another detainee, Robert W. Park, may have recorded the attack of Lucinda Rancher and the second, unnamed woman in his log of the brutal chaos at the fairgrounds. A white student from the University of Wisconsin, Park wrote that during breakfast on Wednesday, June 16, at 7:10 a.m., a "Negro woman is hustled away being hit [from] behind with a club; another is led away." Afterward, word came back that the first woman "refused to stop singing and kicked the cop in __."[4]

Nonviolent direct action campaigns for Black political rights and fistfights for riotous dignity against policing's autocracy continued in Mississippi's movements. Freedom Summer's voter registration and the autumn's radical debate around police reform were only peaks in a sustained struggle against Jim Crow that lasted well into the 1970s. Thousands of local Black Mississippians, like Rancher, and civil rights volunteers, like Park, continued to put their bodies on the line in hopes of making Mississippi—and America—a democracy. Some worked with the Deacons for Defense and the Black United Front, organizations that supported using force of arms to fight for survival against white terrorists and cops. A growing number of local communities organized to make local meaning of the federal War on Poverty, participating in experiments that reimagined government as serving society's most vulnerable and historically excluded from decision making.[5] Such everyday and extraordinary people fought back against Mississippi Law. Some hit cops where it hurt.

・・・・・・

This last part of *Mississippi Law* explores the emergence of a public safety regime based on allegedly race-blind police supremacy. In Mississippi, policing's enhanced position in society developed alongside a renewed investment in police reform that coincided with the cresting tide of Great Society liberalism and an unsatisfied Black freedom movement.

This chapter focuses on a transitional period in Mississippi history, 1965 to 1969, with a focus on how the infrastructure and ideas of rural policing flowed back and forth between the countryside, small towns, and Mississippi's capital city—Jackson. Its two sections unite two distinct venues of policing's violence, the street and the statehouse. "Cattle Pens and Federal Dollars" recasts these years as a time of bellicose police violence rewarded with unprecedented empowerment. First it looks at the use of the cattlemen's state-subsidized infrastructure as tools for immobilization and mass imprisonment. Then it turns to the Mississippi Crime Commission (1966 to

1968), where Paul B. Johnson convened token representatives of Mississippi's Black middle class with white cattlemen cops, massive resisters, and the FBI to reimagine criminalization for a desegregated future. Importantly, the commission laid the groundwork for state and local police funding from the federal Office of Law Enforcement Assistance (OLEA), forerunner to the Law Enforcement Assistance Administration (LEAA, pronounced *Leah*).

Cattle and Counterinsurgency

Throughout the 1960s, Southern law enforcement officers used agricultural technologies to terrorize and detain civil rights workers. They repurposed readily available tools such as the electric cattle prod, cattle pens, and cattle trucks to serve a brutal purpose. Officers attacked organizing efforts meant to disrupt business as usual. Cops immobilized nonviolent direct action protesters, the vast majority of whom were Black, often inflicting torturous pain that marked activists as outside of both the human family and a self-governing society. Local and national activists publicized this mistreatment with agricultural tools as bestial.

Media spectacle drove police reformers toward new expansionist police reform. As will be seen in the next chapter, federal dollars eventually supplied Jim Crow policing with more militarized tools for their counterinsurgency against continued revolts for Black freedom and whatever else was labeled as crime—especially drug use.[6]

Activists reported law enforcement officers using electric cattle prods across the Southern civil rights movement.[7] In Mississippi, the electric cattle prod traveled from the prison farm to the free world as revolt intensified. In 1961, nineteen-year-old Stokely Carmichael (later Kwame Ture) discovered the cattle prod while incarcerated with Freedom Riders at the Mississippi State Penitentiary. "Parchman was a farm," Ture remembered in his memoirs. "I guess it had cattle. Guards carried what I at first thought were long nightsticks. But these seemed to be [made] of metal with three sharp points. . . . The three little points were terminals emitting a strong electric charge. . . . When those points touched your skin, the pain was sharp and excruciating, at once a jolting shock and burn. You could actually see . . . and smell . . . your skin burning."[8] Ture no doubt remembered this pain when he came to the defense of a Greenwood woman whom police officers shocked on Freedom Day, July 16, 1964.[9]

As the scale of direct action protest grew over the early '60s, officials used state-owned cattle pens against the civil rights insurgency. The fall

Mississippi State Fair dated to the nineteenth century, and state newspapers mention the fairgrounds' Agriculture and Industry (A&I) buildings as early as 1907.[10] Hugh White, the same governor who gave Mississippi a modern highway-building program, a Highway Patrol, and promised to Balance Agriculture with Industry (chapter 2), modernized the fairgrounds complex in the mid-twentieth century. In September 1955, as the beef industry boomed during White's second term as governor, McComb's *Enterprise-Journal* reported "the complete reconditioning" of the A&I buildings.[11] In 1957, Governor James P. Coleman, with his preference for cattlemen in law enforcement (see chapter 6), oversaw the construction of two open-ended airplane hangar-like buildings at the fairgrounds. These were the A&I buildings encountered by civil rights workers in the 1960s. As historian John Dittmer put it, "the arrested were literally herded into cattle barns."[12]

In using livestock pens to quash Black revolt, Mississippi's law enforcers joined an American tradition of carving out authoritarian spaces to contain crises. Observers and survivors drew connections to the racialized concentration camps of Nazi Germany. But the use of animal pens to incarcerate Americans would also have been familiar to survivors of World War I mine wars in places like Bisbee, Arizona, or the West Coast Japanese internment during World War II. In 1942, the US military forcibly relocated these suspected enemies of the state to temporary shelters, including the racehorse stables at California's Santa Anita racetrack. The phenomenon grew. The US and Canadian governments temporarily housed people of Japanese descent in animal pens at fairgrounds and livestock exposition centers from Vancouver, British Columbia, to Pomona, California. Though such incarceration seemed uniquely Southern in the 1960s, Jackson's fairgrounds stockade was unexceptional in societies without the means for mass imprisonment.[13]

The City of Jackson first experimented with using the fairgrounds as a stockade in June 1963 to detain protesters from the area's Black high schools and colleges who participated in sit-ins, boycotts, and marches. Mayor Allen Thompson and T. B. Birdsong no doubt learned from the Birmingham, Alabama, campaign of spring 1963, where state and local police also detained protesters at the state fairgrounds.[14]

Nighttime brought opportunities for police officers to terrorize detainees with chemical aerosol. Ed King, the white chaplain at Tougaloo College, remembered city policemen and state troopers pretending that thick clouds of anti-mosquito insecticide were poison gas in June 1963. "We're gonna finish this in Jackson, tonight," King reported one cop saying: "We got gas for you n——s!"[15] Such treatment led NAACP president Roy Wilkins to think of Mississippi policing as existing in "the Nazi spirit." At a mass meeting in Jackson, Myrlie Evers recalled, Wilkins described "the setting up of hog-wired concentration camps" as "pure Nazism and Hitlerism." Alluding to death camp crematoria, he said, "The only thing missing is an oven."[16] Police arrested Wilkins with Medgar Evers on June 1, 1963. And shortly after, Jackson's mayor announced that he would meet some demands of Black protesters, including the hiring of the Jackson Police Department's first Black officers, who later detained activists in 1965.[17]

Protesters in June that year saw much the same terroristic treatment by Jackson police and highway patrolmen when they marched with the MFDP. A twenty-one-year-old white Jewish man from Brooklyn named Ira Grupper remembered Jackson's state fairgrounds as a hell. "We were put in a place where cattle had been kept," Grupper remembered in an oral history interview. "They were moved and it was hosed down." On June 14, Grupper was one of many activists forced to run a gauntlet of highway patrolmen swinging batons. "I remember being hit in the lower part of my back," Grupper tearfully remembered in an oral history interview. "And I reeled back in pain, and I was hit again. And I don't remember what happened. I remember the next scene: I was in another building. . . . I must have become unconscious or passed out."[18] Robert W. Park, another white volunteer, smuggled a letter out of the fairgrounds that reported humiliations in detail. "A guy had his head bloodied when he told a cop the place stunk," Park wrote of the animal pens. One officer forced a Black man to chew on his SNCC button. Others reportedly deprived detainees of sleep by cracking a bullwhip, striking metal trash cans, and playing music into bullhorns at night.[19]

Black women endured and fought back against misogynistic police violence at the fairgrounds. Some detainees reported sexual harassment, including white officers' quid pro quos: sex for early release.[20] For Mrs. Annie Mae King, a forty-five-year-old woman from Sunflower County, the fairgrounds stockade was a "stock barn." "When we got inside the barn there were about 100 or more cops and patrolmen, and they began to push us," she remembered. Two unnamed pregnant women were detained, King said in a statement to SNCC. She recalled that "they beat one of them so she had a miscarriage." A nurse with the Medical Committee for Human Rights reported that by June 21, two protesters had miscarried after their time in the stockade. King also saw Mrs. Maggie Lee Gordon, from Holmes County, attacked by officers.[21]

Maggie Gordon drew the fury of the police when she refused to rise for breakfast before clothing herself. Gordon was a thirty-two-year-old woman from Holmes County who washed and dried her underclothes overnight on June 15, 1965. When she attempted to retrieve them at 6:30 a.m. on June 16, officers attacked her. Policemen dragged her across the floor. "It was four of them," she reported to SNCC. "They grabbed me, and just pulled my legs apart and they kicked me in the privates." Gordon defended herself. "I caught one of the policemen by the leg. . . . He fell over. . . . The one that had kicked me, I caught him on his shoulder and I hit him with my fist." At this, more officers attacked Gordon. "Excuse this expression," she told her SNCC interviewer, "I said to all of them, I said, 'I am not afraid of none of you motherfuckers.'" She paid dearly for her counterattack. Policemen beat her throughout her transfer to the Jackson jail, where authorities kept Gordon in solitary confinement for twelve hours without food, clothing, or toilet.[22]

Maggie Gordon's case joined others to draw national attention to police torture in Jackson's cattle pens. Eventually police transported Gordon to the hospital for treatment, and she spoke to two FBI agents. The Jackson Police Department, however, took to the newspapers with their side of events. "Negro Woman Attacks Jackson Police Officers," read one headline in the *Clarion-Ledger*. The article stated that Gordon sent patrolman E. L. Eldridge to the hospital.[23] Mississippi congressman John Bell Williams also defended Mississippi's police response in Washington, DC. Narratives of police brutality were, he said, "carefully rehearsed fictions" in service to the "defamation of police authority everywhere." Maggie Gordon was merely "a paid professional agitator, . . . a giant of a woman" who had brutalized law enforcement officers.[24] Yet Gordon carried the scars of her fight for Black life in Mississippi. She reported to SNCC that she was still bleeding internally from injuries to her urinary tract. "It's getting better," she said hopefully. "I got medicine for it." Yet police harassment continued when she returned to Holmes County, where terrorists also attempted to burn her home.[25]

Condemnation of the fairgrounds stockade slowly filtered through a busy news cycle. On June 21, Howard Zinn, Noam Chomsky, and Charles Smith, all college professors from Boston, arrived in Jackson to observe. They avoided arrest but interviewed several survivors of the stockade.[26] On June 22, representatives of the National Council of Churches joined thirteen sympathetic congressmen and two survivors of the fairgrounds in Washington, DC, to publicly condemn the open-air stockade as a "concentration camp . . . operated with full support of one of our state governments and apparently with full knowledge of the government of the United States."

San Francisco's *Examiner* called the fairgrounds a "torture camp."[27] One week later, on June 30, 1965, US district court judge W. Harold Cox ruled on a lawsuit brought by the MFDP: Mississippi lawmen could not peremptorily arrest marchers without a permit or activists passing out leaflets. And so the fairgrounds stood empty by July 8.[28] No more substantive federal intervention from the Department of Justice was forthcoming.

· · · · · ·

To add insult to protesters' many injuries, Lyndon Johnson announced the appointment of former segregationist governor James P. Coleman to the US Court of Appeals for the Fifth Circuit during the fairgrounds ordeal. As governor, Coleman had epitomized "smart" segregation. He was a chief proponent of shrouding policing's autocracy through sanitized and centralized law enforcement.

On June 19, 1965, the *New York Times* ran news of Coleman's nomination opposite the photo of highway patrolman Huey Krohn wrenching an American flag from five-year-old Anthony Quin on the steps of the Mississippi governor's mansion. Police had arrived to find Quin's mother, Aylene Quin, holding a sign that read "NO MORE POLICE BRUTALITY/WE WANT THE RIGHT TO REGISTER TO VOTE." It now curled in another trooper's hand. Activists knew Coleman's history as a segregationist. They also knew him to be a current lawyer and researcher for the state government's fight against the MFDP's legal challenge to Mississippi's all-white congressional delegation. In fact, another activist had sat among the Quins holding a sign demanding "UNSEAT 5 ILLEGALLY ELECTED MISSISSIPPI CONGRESSMEN."[29]

Activists sat in the fairgrounds stockade because the MFDP was in a multipronged offensive against Mississippi's white lawmakers elected in the absence of African American suffrage. Following the MFDP's failed attempt to be seated at the August 1964 Democratic National Convention, a team of MFDP lawyers led by Arthur Kinoy challenged the seating of Mississippi's five white congressmen elected in 1964 to the US House of Representatives. Mississippi's white power structure mounted a massive legal defense against the prospect of being unseated. When the Eighty-Ninth Congress convened on January 4, 1965, the sergeant-at-arms barred Hamer and others from the House chamber, while a member of the American Nazi Party in blackface snuck onto the House floor. The House ultimately seated Mississippi's five white congressmen.[30]

Activists were skeptical of Lyndon Johnson's commitment to Mississippi's Black grassroots insurgency. His nomination of J. P. Coleman to the federal

Jackson, MS, June 17, 1965. "No More Police Brutality." Mississippi highway patrolman arrests Anthony Quin, 5, son of Mrs. Aylene Quin, during voting rights protest. When Quin refused to give up his small American flag, the patrolman went berserk, wrenching it out of his hands. WINNER, WORLD PRESS PHOTO CONTEST. Photograph by Matt Herron/Take Stock/TopFoto.

judiciary came as an "unbelieving and indescribable shock" to Mrs. Victoria J. Gray, a congressional candidate on the MFDP ticket.[31] On July 2, 1965, Gray appeared with SNCC chairman John Lewis at Coleman's hearing before the US Senate's Judiciary Committee, chaired by the Mississippi planter and cattleman James O. Eastland. The nominee himself called in sick. "Just having been released a few days ago after ten days in the Jackson, Mississippi, jail, it is with a troubled mind that I come before this committee," Lewis began. The SNCC chairman urged senators to reflect on the importance of federal courts since the Supreme Court's 1954 decision in *Brown v. Board of Education,* to consider how Coleman would have judicial authority over a region home to many Black Americans. "This appointment is an affront and an insult to the Negro people of the South and to all Americans of good will," Lewis said. "If this body wishes to ignore the years of suffering, of death, and of dingy prison cells that the Negro has had to face, then let it confirm the appointment of J. P. Coleman." Lewis knew the mainstream liberal apologies: Democratic Party patronage for loyalty in the face of Southern Republican Party inroads, Coleman's reputation as a racial moderate. "When is it that justice is based on the lesser of two evils?" Lewis asked.[32]

Yet in his own statement to the Judiciary Committee, US attorney general Nicholas Katzenbach painted the freedom movement's objections as exaggerated and politically immature. After himself establishing Coleman's segregationist bona fides, including Coleman's role in incarcerating Clennon King and Clyde Kennard when they attempted to desegregate Mississippi colleges, Katzenbach found that "these statements are not the whole story or even its most significant aspect." Coleman's litany of offenses, less than a decade old, had to be "considered in the context of the society and the times in which they were made." Detailing Coleman's opposition to the White Citizens' Council movement alongside support of the FBI investigation of lynching, Katzenbach believed that "when the full picture is considered, we see not the caricature of an unyielding white supremacist but a man who was frequently willing to take great political risks to support moderation and respect for law and order." Offering tokenized Black praise for Coleman from NAACP national secretary Roy Wilkins and explaining how Coleman's support of John F. Kennedy as Democratic Party presidential candidate cost him in the gubernatorial election of 1963, the attorney general was certain: "Some say that Mr. Coleman is a racial extremist. In the context of Mississippi politics, he could not be so classified in any sense of that term." Katzenbach knew that for "detached observers," "what is even more relevant to his nomination to a Federal judgeship is his consistent stand for law and order."[33] Coleman, in other words, was the sort of oppressor that the liberal Department of Justice could do business with.

For Katzenbach, neither Coleman's record nor the firsthand testimony of his victims were relevant in the debate over Coleman's lifetime appointment to the federal bench. The system of racial terror that Lewis summarized as Mississippi's "dingy prison cells" was acceptable, the attorney general implied, in the slow progression toward a new ideal of social order. And the man who defeated Coleman in 1963, Paul B. Johnson Jr., who mirrored Coleman's approach to law enforcement, sought to cement the aspirations of Lyndon Johnson over the democratic vision of the MFDP.

Mississippi Crime

By September 7, 1967, three and a half years had passed since Governor Paul B. Johnson Jr. stood before the state legislature asking for emergency expansion of the state police force. On a rainy morning in Jackson, he again stood in the Mississippi House chamber, this time before an assembled group of state and national experts in law enforcement and corrections. The occasion was the organizational meeting of the Mississippi Crime Commission, summoned one year earlier, amid a storm of local protests and national anxiety over insurrections in American cities.

As his four-year term came to an end, Paul Johnson joined his desire for the police to stifle the Black freedom movement with the nationwide politics of urban disorder and street crime. Johnson invited the first African Americans to serve on the Crime Commission, the first to serve on any state commission since Reconstruction. He hoped to make permanent the centralization and supremacy of police power extended by lawmakers on a temporary basis in 1964.

In the installation of Mississippi's first desegregated commission, Johnson found new race-blind language for criminalization in a moment of increasingly impatient Black activism. He jettisoned his earlier focus on nonviolent civil rights protest as criminal, instead focusing on the outbreak of urban uprisings in Black neighborhoods across the nation since the summer of 1965.

These expressions of spontaneous discontent often grew from police violence and white terror, yet they drew widespread misrepresentation from media and politicians. A *Los Angeles Times* headline from the Watts rebellion of August 1965 read "'Get Whitey!' Scream Blood-Hungry Mobs." By

July 1967, President Lyndon Johnson explicitly decoupled riots from civil rights protest but referred to uprisings as "pillage" and "plunder."[34] In October 1967, just a month after Mississippi convened its Crime Commission, Richard Nixon launched his 1968 presidential campaign in one of the new conservatism's nationwide organs, *Reader's Digest*:

> Some will argue that dispatching thousands of police into the slums will not solve the problems of jobs and housing and schools or alleviate the conditions that breed crime and violence. No, it will not; but the first requisite of progress is peace and the purpose of these police is to ensure that peace. . . . Some see the answer as simply more money. . . . Certainly money will be needed; but the extremists who threaten riots or "long hot summers in the streets" to get it are gravely mistaken to think that the threat of pillage is the way to sell Americans on social justice.[35]

In Mississippi, Paul Johnson likewise rebuked the freedom struggle's demands for a government to serve poor Black Mississippians with anything but riot batons and cattle prods. He connected ongoing direct action protest movements and to a lesser extent white terrorism with the alleged savagery of America's urban rebellions.

The governor stoked fear that the rebellious spirit of Watts, Cincinnati, or Cambridge, Maryland, might descend upon Mississippi at any moment. When calling on the state legislature to create the Crime Commission in January 1966, he boasted of "more than a quarter of a billion dollars of new capital" brought to Mississippi by outside investors in 1965, but warned of "violent and unrestrained action in other parts of the Nation." He warned lawmakers of Mississippi's own extremists, "the lawless men, Negro and white, who don't believe hell is hot," and promised to protect "the lives and property of all of Mississippi's citizens . . . from the ravages of civil disorder." In the wake of the 1966 riots in Chicago and Cleveland, Paul Johnson preached expanded police power as necessary for further economic development. He hoped that law enforcement would be the answer for Mississippi's modernity amid ongoing uncertainties.[36]

In fact, paramilitary state police had mobilized to protect Black life under Johnson's watch. In September 1965, the patrol joined the National Guard and FBI to suppress Klan violence in Natchez. In the curiously named "Operation Wet Blanket," highway patrolmen responded to Black and white residents arming themselves in response to weeks of unrest. Klan car bombings of local NAACP leaders had spurred Black rioting in downtown Natchez along with public shows of armed Black self-defense by NAACP members and Deacons for Defense. Paul Johnson cast blame on "radical Negroes and radical whites" for the need of a state police takeover. The coalition disarmed and arrested a convoy of Klansmen with machine guns. FBI agents held three conferences for local and state police that fall.[37]

As rain pattered the Jackson sidewalks in September 1967, the governor addressed leaders who had watched rebellions in stretches of Newark, Detroit, and Buffalo over the span of a month. "Our system is undergoing a severe test at this time," Johnson told Crime Commissioners. "We are witnesses to a wave of defiance of the law which has produced death and destruction in some of our great cities. . . . There is no place in America for anarchy. Our structure must continue to be a government of law and not of men—nor of mobs." Ignoring the violence perpetrated by lawmen against Black Mississippians, Johnson reassured his audience that, according to the FBI, Mississippi did not have a crime problem. "Mississippi enjoys the second lowest crime rate in our nation." But he wanted "maximum training opportunities" for law enforcement, as well as "excellent equipment" and "proper pay scales." Having set the commissioners' goal, Johnson ended his speech with a homespun peroration on progress and reaction. "My faith is unshakable but not stationary; it is and must be a moving faith, shown by valiant and intelligent effort to save our precious heritage of 'praise the Lord and pass the ammunition.'"[38]

Johnson reframed a much older idea about the necessity of righteous martial force to ensure orderly progress in a world of occupied territories. "Praise the Lord and pass the ammunition," went the 1942 tune by Frank Loesser, "And we'll all stay free."[39] The "heritage" Johnson claimed for the room had never existed in a states' rights vacuum. Instead, the firepower necessary to establish and uphold the Jim Crow racial order came in a state and federal partnership that guaranteed elite control. As had been the case with the Jim Crow militia, there was a ready source of "ammunition" for securing inequality in the Southern landscape: the US government.

To that end, Johnson chose a former assistant director of the FBI to chair his Crime Commission: Hugh H. Clegg. Born in Mathiston, Mississippi, in 1898, Clegg graduated from Mathiston's all-white high school, finished at Jackson's private Millsaps College in 1920, and secured a job at the Library of Congress through his local congressman. In Washington, DC, he worked the night shift at the library's circulation desk and enrolled at the segregated George Washington University law school, where he overlapped with James P. Coleman. There, he boarded for free at the chapter of his undergraduate fraternity, Kappa Alpha, known for its romanticization of plantation slavery and embrace of the cult of the Lost Cause during Jim Crow. The highlight of any KA member's college calendar was an "Old South" ball, held annually. Through Kappa Alpha, Clegg met FBI director J. Edgar Hoover and related to Paul B. Johnson Jr., both fellow KAs.[40]

Hugh Clegg began work under Hoover in 1926 and stayed for twenty-eight years. In the 1930s, Clegg laid the foundation for the bureau's National Training Academy at Quantico, Virginia. He recruited academics and members of local law enforcement to ally with the national fight against communism and bank robbers. Under Clegg's watch, the National Academy became a training site for law enforcement personnel from across the country selected for advanced training, especially Southern cops. Clegg retired in 1954 and joined the administration of the University of Mississippi in Oxford, where he oversaw James Meredith's desegregation in 1962.[41] Johnson's choice of Clegg and two other FBI agents signaled the governor's desire to cement Mississippi's system of white supremacist inequality with Washington ideals of well-funded, professional, and impartial law enforcement.

In this context, desegregation occurred within the Mississippi Crime Commission. Clegg and Johnson selected three African American leaders to serve alongside some thirty white commissioners. These first African Americans to serve on a state commission since Reconstruction were N. R. Burger, a grammar school principal from Johnson's hometown, Hattiesburg; Walter Washington, a junior college president and later the first Black man to receive a doctorate from a historically white Mississippi university; and John A. Peoples Jr., a mathematician and the new president of Jackson State College. Of the group, observers credited Peoples with the most progressive reputation because he believed direct action protest was legitimate. N. R. Burger, meanwhile, had worked strategically with the state Sovereignty Commission, including in its early attempts to dissuade Clyde Kennard from attempting to desegregate the University of Southern Mississippi. And Walter Washington had publicly argued against school desegregation in his role as president of the all-Black Mississippi Teachers Association.[42] These men became commissioners just months before Robert G. Clark Jr., the first Black Mississippian elected to the state legislature after 1965, arrived in Jackson.[43]

Burger, Washington, and Peoples sat alongside Mississippians who ran the gamut of late Jim Crow white male supremacist politics. The group included the likes of Tom P. Brady, a judge on Mississippi's Supreme Court and a race-scientist father of massive white resistance. Ten years earlier, in *Black Monday*, his book-length response to *Brown v. Board of Education*, Brady stated his belief that Black people were evolutionarily primitive compared to Europeans and inherently criminal.[44] In 1967, Brady joined men who selectively persecuted the Ku Klux Klan in hopes of preserving orderly home rule amid Black revolt, men like Birdsong; Roy K. Moore, special agent in charge of the Jackson FBI field office; and state attorney general Joe T. Patterson. Cattleman sheriff Bill Harpole, who had worked for the Highway Patrol and helped to modernize Parchman Penitentiary in the 1950s, was present, as was William C. Burnley, the chief of police in Greenville. Faith leaders, lawyers, prosecutors, judges, mayors, and academics convened with law enforcement officers, corrections personnel, and representatives of police fraternal organizations around the crisis of crime.[45]

Central to the Crime Commission's vision of ordered society was a better-trained, professionalized police force. In 1967 commissioners hoped to attract Mississippians to law enforcement as a respectable, middle-class vocation. Officials established the Mississippi Law Enforcement Officers' Training Academy in preparation for Freedom Summer in the spring of 1964. The academy began operation in 1966; seven hundred local and county law enforcement officers were expected to graduate in 1967. By the time of its report, the commission believed additionally that "law enforcement personnel must be trained to cope with new situations resulting from riots and civil disorders."[46] Such emphases mirrored national models of riot training, such as the so-called Riotsville, established to train counterinsurgents on numerous US military bases.[47]

Commissioners also took on the long-standing tension between sheriffs and state police power. Clegg involved a cattleman sheriff who had risen to prominence during J. P. Coleman's lawful massive resistance of the mid-1950s: Sheriff Bill Harpole of Oktibbeha County. A ranking member of the Mississippi Sheriff's Association, Harpole commended state lawmakers for their empowerment of the state police to assist local policing in the aftermath of Freedom Summer. One of Harpole's resolutions thanked J. Edgar Hoover for "his efforts toward elevating law enforcement to its proper perspective as a proud and honorable profession" and pledged Hoover "our cooperation and assistance." Another resolution praised Johnson's "zeal to preserve law and order" and announced the association's appreciation for Highway Patrol aid to rural law enforcement.[48]

On this score the Crime Commission was adamant: The body's *first* recommendation was the continued extension of general police powers to

Highway Patrol investigators after June 1968, when the 1964 law was set to expire. The state legislature gladly conceded, extending the patrol's new police powers every four years before finally amending the state code permanently. Far from the enemies they had been in the 1940s and '50s, county sheriffs and state law enforcement had come together around the coordinated surveillance demanded by the civil rights revolt.[49]

・・・・・・

Lacking statutory power, the Mississippi Crime Commission waxed philosophical in its report. Commissioners linked the necessity for discipline and punishment to the history of Anglo-American conquest in North America. In a chapter titled "Personal Responsibility," they lamented "the readiness to excuse unlawful acts as the responsibility of society or environment." Sure, they believed the state should "seek in every reasonable way to improve society and environmental conditions" and study the causes of crime. "But each person of accountability," they insisted, "must be held responsible for his acts." To be merciful would be to teach an offender to be unrealistic, they thought: "Although we may not be responsible for our environment, we are responsible in our environment." Their understanding of Mississippi history as American history proved this view of society: "Our founding fathers came to these bleak shores. They were met with a wilderness. They encountered insects, pestilence, hunger, disease, cold and starvation, with Indians shooting at them from several directions. This was their reality—their environment. . . . They pulled themselves up by their own bootstraps and helped to carve the beginnings of a great nation." This vision of American history ignored the presence of African American people altogether and forgot slavery. The commission clearly analogized un-raced criminals to Native people, considered by colonists to be enemies of civilization. The arsonist, car thief, cop killer, burglar, and bank robber betrayed their American heritage when they participated in these activities and had to be corrected.[50]

Commissioners also argued that adherence to Judeo-Christian faith traditions assuaged crime. The men wrapped "civilization's concept of law and order" into Jewish and Christian religious practice. They excluded Eastern faith traditions from this model of "purity of heart and moral conduct," though Roman Catholicism seemed appropriate. People of "God-changed and directed lives" would embrace the status quo "instead of lending their influence to demonstrations, pressures, defiance of authority, contempt of courts, and general rebellion against constituted authority. . . . The Church, the Cathedral, and the Synagogue should concern themselves with man's . . . acceptance of and obedience to the majesty and mandate of the law."[51] Submission to Mississippi Law was the straight and narrow path to salvation.

The commission sought to generate popular consent for their ideas through education programs. Newspapers across the state began to publish articles on the public's obligation in crime prevention. The commission distributed over 2,500 memoranda to "civic clubs, youth organizations, education groups, church organizations, and women's groups" with suggestions for talking points and consciousness-raising programs.[52]

Here, the commission imagined Black commissioners playing an important role. Jackson State's president Peoples and the two primary and secondary educators, Burger and Washington, either volunteered or were volunteered to bring tough-on-crime speakers to religious, fraternal, educational, and professional assemblages of "our Negro citizens."[53]

The topics for public discussion likely mirrored the commission's problem and solution approach. Clegg formed five committees regarding "The Crime Problem," "Police and Public Safety," "Administration of Criminal Justice," "Corrections," and "Science and Technology."[54] Crime Commissioners imagined a society with an expanded role for scientifically trained law enforcement and modern prisons. They built this future in part with funding from the national government.

Paul Johnson's Crime Commission took inspiration from federal bodies and initiatives. At Lyndon Johnson's command, the Department of Justice created an Office of Law Enforcement Assistance (OLEA) in 1965 as part of the president's newly announced War on Crime. The president also inaugurated the Commission on Law Enforcement and Administration of Justice to study organized crime, drugs, and gun control. The federal commission found a stark disparity between areas of affluence and the urban and rural poor in its report, *The Challenge of Crime in a Free Society*. US attorney general Ramsey Clark mailed a copy to Mississippi commissioners in February 1968, as the National Advisory Commission on Civil Disorders, led by Illinois Governor Otto Kerner, published yet another report, predicting further rebellion without significant attention to Black and Brown integration into white America's economic system. Memorably, it argued that white America created and profited from the immiseration of urban ghettos. But it also recommended federal funding for recruiting Black policemen, increased training for law enforcement officers, the advent of non-police "community service officers," and "nonlethal weapons development." The Omnibus Crime Control and Safe Streets Act of June 1968 allocated

$100 million in block grants to the states through the OLEA's successor, the Law Enforcement Assistance Administration.[55]

Beyond inspiration, the US Department of Justice also *funded* the Mississippi Crime Commission and several of its initiatives. At the very time federal legislation like the Civil Rights Act of 1964 used federal funding as a cudgel to compel states to protect Black Mississippians' civil and voting rights, national crime-fighting initiatives like the OLEA gave money directly to Mississippi's notoriously racist police state to expand its military and surveillance capabilities. A $25,000 grant allowed the commission to hire a secretarial staff to compile and circulate committee reports and literature, as well as an editor to polish the committee's report for presentation to the governor and state legislature.[56]

Crime Commissioners hoped this federal funding would continue to flow. By the fall of 1966, OLEA began to fund the University of Mississippi's development of the bachelor of police administration degree and a study of the American sheriff, research approved by the National Sheriff's Association, to which Bill Harpole belonged.[57] In their report submitted February 1968, commissioners wanted this access to vocational training extended to more Mississippians through the state's two-year junior college system. In December 1968, with a new governor and a different kind of law-and-order president-elect in Richard Nixon, they got their wish: James O. Eastland, chairman of the US Senate's Judiciary Committee, who campaigned on having shaped the LEAA and the 1968 crime bill, boasted grants totaling $44,000 for junior colleges across the state to entice new students and current officers to study law enforcement in college with student loans and grants.[58] This direct benefit from the Crime Commission began small, but it was a fit ending for the governorship of Paul B. Johnson Jr.

......

As the Mississippi Crime Commission printed its report in January 1968, T. B. Birdsong resigned as commissioner of public safety, ending his fifty-year career in policing. On April 4, James Earl Ray assassinated Martin Luther King Jr. in Memphis, Tennessee. Both nonviolent protests and riots again gripped America. State troopers responded to civil unrest across Mississippi, from Jackson to Itta Bena to Meridian. Some protesters marched peacefully, while others expressed their discontent by throwing stones, looting, and burning. In the words of historian Elizabeth Hinton, the 137 national uprisings that followed the King assassination were "rebellions—political acts carried out in response to an unjust and repressive society."[59]

At his April 30 retirement celebration, Birdsong's granddaughters unveiled an oil portrait to be hung in state police headquarters. His replacement as head of the patrol, Giles Crisler, read Birdsong's biography aloud, beginning with his 1919 Clarksdale citizen's arrest. The room's uniformed Highway Patrol personnel remained all white.[60]

The retirement was brief. In March 1969, Governor John Bell Williams appointed Birdsong, age seventy-four, to chair the Mississippi Commission on Law Enforcement, which shared many members in common with the 1967 Crime Commission. White lawmen like Sheriff Bill Harpole and FBI agent in charge Roy K. Moore joined some thirty others, including at least one Black Mississippian, the former and more conservative president of Jackson State College, Jacob L. Reddix.[61] This new commission's statutory purpose was to advise a new state agency, the Division of Law Enforcement Assistance (DLEA). Answering to the governor, the division grew from Lyndon Johnson's 1968 crime bill to administer LEAA block grants for Mississippi policing, jails, and prisons.[62]

Between 1969 and 1971, Mississippi DLEA administrators reported receiving $8 million. That figure paled in comparison to the $317 million in total federal grants to Mississippi in fiscal year 1968–69 alone. But as Elizabeth Hinton has argued, "LEAA became the fastest-growing federal agency in the 1970s," with a budget of $850 million in 1973.[63] In Mississippi, this federal funding contributed to a dramatic increase in funding for law enforcement.

The state budget for the Highway Patrol's Department of Public Safety was set at $12 million for the two years between July 1968 and July 1970, a 250 percent increase from 1958. Between 1969 and 1971, the Highway Patrol received some $800,000 in additional federal funds from LEAA. With the DLEA's advice, the LEAA also allotted money to municipal and county law enforcement and corrections agencies across the state.[64] By 1975, statewide payouts climbed to $7.5 million *annually*.[65] No blank check, LEAA nonetheless helped to resolve the contradiction between the white ruling class's promise of welfare retrenchment and expanded police power. State government provided a small amount of matching funds and the federal government paid the rest. "In simplest terms," state DLEA executive director Wayland Clifton Jr. wrote, "the Division receives $100 in federal funds for every $6.25 appropriated by the Mississippi State government." Spending was good, so long as it prioritized elite white power over the vision of society offered by the Black freedom movement.[66]

This federal funding arrived despite nationwide knowledge of Mississippi's draconian police regime. From Jackson's cattle pens to the everyday jail or prison—white lawmen often ruthlessly policed, tortured, and incarcerated people they criminalized. Though at times law enforcement officers now protected Black Mississippians from spectacular racial violence, lawless law enforcement still thrived in policing's hinterland.

National funders accepted the collateral damage that came with endorsing Mississippi Law. On May 11, 1967, before LEAA sent its first funding to the state, troopers and Jackson policemen shot into a crowd of 1,000 students protesting the wrongful arrest of a Jackson State student for speeding. One student, twenty-two-year-old Benjamin Brown, was a well-known organizer, but he was not protesting that night. Officers shot Brown as he exited the Kon-Tiki Café with takeout food for his wife. He died the next morning.[67] The next week, state officials refused to take action against the two leading suspects in Brown's death. In 2009, an FBI cold case investigation concluded that Trooper Lloyd Silas Jones was "likely" Brown's killer, given forensic evidence and a hearsay confession reported in 2000, five years after Jones's death while serving as sheriff of Simpson County. Lloyd Jones was a World War II veteran and lineman for Bell Telephone when he joined the state police in 1956, the same year Governor James P. Coleman tasked cattleman Tom Scarbrough with expanding the Highway Patrol.[68]

Like other instances of life-stealing police work, the murder of Benjamin Brown galvanized activists against the latest iteration of Mississippi Law. Of the Black students who marched for Benjamin Brown, one was Bennie G. Thompson, a future US congressman. Another protester was Constance Iona Slaughter, just months from entering the University of Mississippi law school as the first Black woman student in its history. In May 1967, Slaughter hid under cars as state troopers unleashed tear gas and riot batons on protesters in Jackson. In May 1970, after yet another federally subsidized police killing at Jackson State College, Slaughter would sue to desegregate Mississippi's state police.

10 Policing's Futures

> Even if our agents worked 24-hours a day, it is doubtful that they could obliterate the infested sores of drug abuse . . . and its accompanying vermin.
>
> —Kenneth W. Fairly, Mississippi Bureau of Narcotics (1973)

Jerome Mangum saw rural Rankin County, Mississippi, transform over his lifetime. Born in Brandon, the county seat, in January 1950, he grew up in farm communities. He picked his first cotton on a white-owned plantation at age four, alongside his grandmother, Elnora. "We just stayed in an old wooden shack," he said in an oral history interview. "You didn't have to pay no rent. You just stayed to work on their plantation, in their fields." After his grandmother married a landowning farmer near Puckett, he plowed his family's seventy-two acres with mules. His house was almost a mile from the nearest road because the county refused to build a road to the family farm. Mangum remembered the first electric lights installed in his house around 1960.[1]

One of Mangum's memories of the Highway Patrol from the late 1960s mapped the past and present of rural power onto the Rankin County geography he knew so well. One Friday night in 1968 or '69, he rode with his grandfather to pick up his grandmother at the end of her shift. His grandfather was behind the wheel. "My grandmother worked at the state hospital—Whitfield," he said, the state asylum and sanitorium.

> They had a roadblock set up. . . . In fact, they were beside the Mississippi highway patrol training academy where the prison is now. . . . This white state trooper walked up: "Let me see your license." . . .
>
> "Captain, I don't have any," [his grandfather said].
>
> He said, "*Well boy, pull right over to the side I'm gonna get you some license.*"
>
> "*Yes, sir! Thank you, captain!*" So he pulls over to the side. And I'm educated enough by now to know. . . . He's about to give you a ticket.
>
> He was real nice. And he gave him some driving license, just like he said. He gave him . . . a driving license with a picture on it, had a

hole punched in it, dead in the middle. It was a white gentleman's picture on that driver's license. He gave it to him. And he gave him a ticket. And he laughed. And he said, *"Go ahead and drive on these."* ... God knows I remember that like it was a few minutes ago.[2]

Cotton fields and the psychiatric hospital's beef cattle herd joined the land's more modern features, such as the Mississippi Law Enforcement Officers Training Academy (1966) and the Central Mississippi Correctional Facility (1986) as backdrops to one of Mississippi Law's cruel and routine jokes. The story helps Mangum make sense of his life in the years after. Because by the summer of 1970, Jerome Mangum joined a lawsuit to desegregate the Mississippi state police.[3]

This final chapter of *Mississippi Law* explores various features of post–Jim Crow law enforcement seeded in the 1970s. Policing had many possible futures in Mississippi as the Jim Crow racial order gave way. Reformers advocating for Black life had high hopes about both the future safety work of police officers and the future secrecy of police archives. Yet "Policing's Futures" historicizes the desegregation of law enforcement in Mississippi alongside its renewed militarization and political supremacy. In tracking the legal movement to create a representative state police force for a state that was 37 percent Black, it covers the Jackson State shootings of May 1970 and the lawsuits led by Constance Iona Slaughter against the Mississippi Department of Public Safety. It also excavates local archives to show how rural white leaders accessed federal funding from LEAA to realize their dreams of police expansion. The chapter ends by focusing on the fight over the Highway Patrol's archive and the subsequent normalization of secrecy around police records. These "futures" of police power, its simultaneous desegregation, militarization, and rededication to secrecy, epitomize the long negotiation for accountability and basic humanity in the face of policing's autocracy.

Desegregation

Late on May 14, 1970, Phillip Lafayette Gibbs stood in a dormitory at Jackson State College. It wasn't his; a friend lived there. Gibbs had taken two years of classes at the state capital's all-Black public college but sat out the spring semester because his wife, Dale Adams, had given birth to their first child. The twenty-one-year-old Gibbs caught work where he could and sent money home. By all accounts, he was at a crossroads: Should he, a civil rights activist from Tippah County, finish his degree at Jackson State and go to law school? Or should he drop out and join the US military? Gibbs never came to a decision on his future.[4]

Shortly after midnight on May 15, he stepped out of Alexander Hall and into gunfire from forty-three Mississippi highway patrolmen and members of the Jackson Police Department. Police had come to punish days of dynamic protest against the draft and American war-making in Southeast Asia. Throughout the protests the police presence grew. In the words of Jackson State president John Peoples, offenses of a "faceless, mindless mob of students and non-students" included throwing stones at white motorists who often sped through campus to terrorize Black students and lobbing failed Molotov cocktails at the campus Reserve Officers' Training Corps building. By May 15, troopers spoiled for a fight. In response to a thrown glass bottle, officers fired into a crowd of some two hundred people for twenty-nine seconds. Police wounded at least eleven, killed Gibbs, and killed a Black high school student named James Earl Green. Nearly four hundred bullet holes marked the façade of Alexander Hall.[5]

The meeting of Phillip Gibbs and white state troopers was years in the making, but its culmination was unmistakable. White policemen had murdered two unarmed Black men and attempted to murder many more men and women in a firing squad fusillade of "buckshot, rifle slugs, a submachine gun, carbines with military ammunition, and two .30-06 rifles loaded with armor-piercing bullets," according to President Richard Nixon's Commission on Campus Unrest.[6] Answering a scenario they classified as disorder, the state police unleashed war.

・・・・・・

Constance Iona Slaughter began a lifetime seeking justice for Mississippians by suing the Highway Patrol over the Jackson State killings. In fact she sued them twice. After protesting the state police killing of Benjamin Brown near the Jackson State campus in May 1967, Slaughter had entered the University of Mississippi law school. The daughter of a Black man who paid his poll tax, Slaughter was the third generation of Black women in her family to attend Tougaloo College. She completed her legal training in the fall of 1969 and joined a group of movement jurists based in Jackson, the Lawyers' Committee for Civil Rights under Law. With the Lawyers' Committee, Slaughter first oversaw a civil suit against the Highway Patrol on behalf of Myrtle Green Burton, the mother of James Earl Green, the Black high

Jackson, MS, 1970. Students protest the murder of two students by Jackson police. Photograph by Matt Herron/Take Stock/TopFoto.

schooler killed on May 15. The patrol refused to admit responsibility, and Myrtle Green Burton lost her suit in court. The patrol never apologized for its actions at Jackson State. Instead, it doubled down on its unsubstantiated defense, that troopers had responded legitimately to fire from a Black sniper. With her hope for restitution and accountability for individual victims dashed, Slaughter turned to forcing change on the patrol, an institution she viewed as "an extension of the Klan."[7]

Connie Slaughter undertook a second lawsuit with the Lawyers' Committee, targeting the Highway Patrol for race-based employment discrimination outlawed by Title VII of the Civil Rights Act of 1964. As of the Jackson State shootings, the patrol lacked a single Black trooper. On June 1, 1970, Willie L. "Huckie" Morrow, a Black Vietnam War veteran and military policeman, traveled to the Department of Public Safety's headquarters in Jackson to apply to be a trooper. A personnel officer refused to give the Black man an application, saying that the patrol wasn't hiring. Morrow informed a friend, James "Jimmy" Harvey, a paralegal at the Lawyers' Committee and well-known Jackson activist who later married Connie Slaughter. Together, they convinced a high school friend of Morrow's who attended Jackson State, Jerome Mangum, from Rankin County, to attempt to join the Highway Patrol also. In a test case, they hoped to catch the patrol in incontrovertible racial discrimination.[8]

With levity, Jerome Mangum remembered being tricked into joining the lawsuit in an oral history. Huckie Morrow convinced Mangum that the patrol allowed Morrow to apply in a ruse. If Mangum applied now, Morrow promised, he would have a job waiting for him after graduation. "I said, 'What!? Man are you losing your mind? A highway patrol job? No way. *No way!* Man, them folks gonna kill you." Jimmy Harvey convinced Mangum to give it a try by talking about the potential salary. But Mangum was afraid as he entered state police headquarters in north Jackson. "I walked in the front lobby like I owned the place," Mangum laughed ironically. "The only thing I saw Black was the black chair I sat in to wait for these guys to come and get me." "You're Black and twenty years old," he remembered of his mindset at the time. "And you know what the situation was with the highway patrol. I go out there, and this dude—he must have been 6-6, 295-, 300-pounds, and I had to follow him. . . . And I realized I had messed up. I walked behind this guy and he closed the door—just like closing a jail cell. . . . And I got scared. He had a gun on. And I had already heard about the highway patrol beating Black folks with their gun, flashlight, blackjack. And I knew I couldn't beat this big guy." A baseball star on a college scholarship, Mangum developed an exit strategy as he moved deeper into patrol headquarters. "I walked in[to his office]. And there was a big stapler on his desk." If the trooper had attacked Mangum, he was resolved to hit the white man in the head with the stapler and escape through the window. It didn't come to that. Instead, the personnel officer simply said that the patrol wasn't hiring. It didn't have an appropriation for the year. If Mangum tried again in a year or two, then he'd be happy to give him an application. Mangum made it out of headquarters unscathed. Only years later was Mangum able to ask Huckie Morrow why he had felt the need to trick him into participating. Laughing, he recalled Morrow's response: "We couldn't find anyone else crazy enough to go."[9] Such was the reputation of the Highway Patrol in 1970.

The case that attorney Connie Slaughter brought, *Willie L. Morrow and Jerome Mangum, et al., v. Giles Crisler, et al.*, charged that the patrol had discriminated against Morrow and Mangum. Filed on July 30, 1970, it sued the new commissioner of public safety, Giles Crisler. It grew from the fact that after the patrol refused to give application materials to both Morrow and Mangum, two white friends of Slaughter's received applications from state police headquarters easily.[10]

Morrow v. Crisler also sought to end state police massacres of Black Mississippians. Early on, the patrol petitioned for a summary dismissal of the suit, and the Lawyers' Committee submitted a long brief on the merits of their case. The lawyers quoted the report of President Richard Nixon's Commission on Campus Unrest (1970), also known as the Scranton Commission, named after Pennsylvania congressman William Scranton. Sparked by the National Guard killing of four students at Kent State University, in Ohio, and the Jackson State killings, the commission wrote of Jackson State: "Of the 65 law enforcement officers in front of Alexander Hall, two were black." The Lawyers' Committee emphasized that *"they did not shoot."*[11] Those two Black officers of the Jackson Police Department represented the committee's hope for a turn away from deadly white supremacist policing. When it mattered, they believed, Black highway patrolmen would save Black lives.

During the pretrial discovery phase, the Lawyers' Committee accessed Highway Patrol records and deposed administrators. *Morrow v. Crisler* grew from a simple employment discrimination suit into a larger fight for state police accountability. Slaughter learned that as of spring 1971, the patrol stood at 370 uniformed officers. In the last three years alone, the defendants had hired 107 new patrolmen, all of them white. Though the patrol was a demonstrably segregated institution, the federal Law Enforcement Assistance Administration (LEAA) had disbursed nearly $20,000 to fund its training of all-white recruits. One administrator even admitted in a sworn deposition that "he would like to see the Highway Patrol remain all-white."[12]

Stunned by the patrol's continued growth while in open defiance of civil rights law, Slaughter and her colleagues sought a court-ordered hiring freeze. On May 24, 1971, the Lawyers' Committee requested "an order restraining the defendants from hiring or training white applicants for patrolman positions unless and until the defendants offered employment and training to all Black applicants who had applied." Asking for such a pause in police expansion was a secondary outcome of their attempt to desegregate the patrol, but it was the first time since 1950 that state residents challenged the growth of the Highway Patrol.[13]

The Lawyers' Committee saw the patrol desegregation suit as an emergency solution to everyday police terror. Aaron E. Henry, the president of the Mississippi State Conference of the NAACP, testified to matters less extraordinary than the Jackson State shooting. "The Highway Patrol has a state-wide reputation in the black community for refusing to hire blacks and for harassing black people," he said. During discovery, Slaughter found that administrators knew of their organization's disparate impact in Black communities. An external study invited by patrol administrators and completed by the International Association of Chiefs of Police found that the patrol "represents in the Negro mind another repressive force of the white community. . . . There is differential treatment of Negroes in the manner of enforcement of traffic laws." Investigators added that "this appears to be particularly acute in the rural areas of the state." In fact, as Jerome Mangum drove to the courthouse for the first hearing of his lawsuit on June 27, 1971, a highway patrolman initiated a traffic stop and called the car's Black male driver "boy" while citing him for exceeding the speed limit.[14]

The evidence of discrimination proved overwhelming for the US district court. On September 29, 1971, Judge Walter J. Nixon Jr., himself an appointee of Lyndon Johnson who was later impeached for perjury, found that "racial discrimination in hiring by the Department and the Patrol was . . . a pattern and practice of long-standing, as old as the Patrol itself."[15] He ordered the agency to desegregate but answered none of the case's larger concerns about policing's racist brutality. In response to the court's finding, patrol administrators disqualified Huckie Morrow and Jerome Mangum on technical grounds but admitted the first Black recruits to the state's training academy: Walter C. Crosby, Richard O. Williams, and Lewis T. Younger Jr. The Lawyers' Committee appealed the district court's passive order to desegregate to the US Fifth Circuit Court of Appeals, in hopes the higher court would grant affirmative hiring relief or freeze white hiring.[16]

After four years of back-and-forth appeals, on May 15, 1974, a federal court ordered the Highway Patrol to freeze *all* hiring. Until patrol administrators could sufficiently prove the absence of racial discrimination in its employment practices, they lost control of personnel decisions. The US Department of Justice had joined the Jackson lawyers' appeal by submitting an amicus brief in support of affirmative action desegregation. Federal courts set affirmative action guidelines and retained the right to approve the patrol's hiring decisions for the next five years. One order even mandated the hiring of *any* qualified Black candidate before the hiring of a white candidate. Such interference in the Highway Patrol's day-to-day administration was unprecedented and signaled a major victory for Connie Slaughter's fight against the Highway Patrol. But throughout her life, Slaughter remembered the case's success in balance with larger failures, especially the lack of redress for Myrtle Green Burton and the continued violence of state police officers against Black Mississippians.[17]

The web of federal judicial oversight over state police employment practices signaled a major rapprochement between Mississippi Law and American law. Connie Slaughter and the Lawyers' Committee had hoped to change everything for which the Highway Patrol stood in the lives of Black Mississippians. Regardless of its success in creating less violent policing or revolutionizing public safety, *Morrow v. Crisler* dealt a momentary blow to an institution built on secrecy and white supremacy. Relative transparency and representation mattered to the ongoing movement against carceral state violence in Mississippi's climate of white supremacist police violence. To the Lawyers' Committee's credit, the Highway Patrol has perpetrated no known shootout-style massacres against protesters since 1970.

But rather than existentially threaten Mississippi's state police power, desegregation in the hands of career police expansionists effectively multiplied it. Even as the desegregation suit made its way through federal court, the US Department of Justice lent significant support to grow Mississippi's state police power.

LEAA grants played a crucial role in state-level law enforcement modernization and militarization for the growing drug war. On April 16, 1971, Mississippi's state legislature created a Bureau of Drug Enforcement, situated within the State Board of Health. The state's Uniform Controlled Substances Act largely mirrored federal statute, establishing "schedules" for drugs and hiring twenty-four "agents" to watch for the production and distribution of such substances—both licit and illicit. These agents liaised with law enforcement, but lawmakers did not originally understand drug control to be a matter for police action. Rather, as its association with the Board of Health indicates, the Bureau of Drug Enforcement oversaw a rising issue of public health.[18]

This medicalized understanding of drug enforcement, itself far from restorative, proved fleeting. Just one year later, on May 19, 1972, the legislature transferred the bureau's authority from the Board of Health to the Department of Public Safety. Specifically, the bill renamed the *Bureau of Drug Enforcement* as the *Bureau of Narcotics*—the newest branch of the Mississippi Highway Safety Patrol. As the patrol faced a federal lawsuit to hire its first African American troopers, state law empowered the commissioner of public safety to hire fifty drug enforcement agents. As soon as its transfer to law enforcement was complete, the bureau received an LEAA grant of $300,000. In its first seven months alone, these troopers brought over five hundred cases involving seven hundred defendants to criminal court. In Jackson, the Delta, and the Black Prairie—those urban and rural areas with the highest density of Black residents—LEAA sent an additional $200,000 for local and regional narcotics units. In his speech to the legislature in 1972, the trooper-turned-chief of the Bureau of Narcotics warned, "Even if our agents worked 24-hours a day, it is doubtful that they could obliterate the infested sores of drug abuse . . . and its accompanying vermin." So far, he counted 593 arrests linked to marijuana, twenty-one linked to heroin, three arrests for sniffing glue, and many more. With federal funding and state disbursement, the Highway Patrol once again led criminalization in Mississippi.[19]

• • • • • •

Elsewhere in Mississippi, the numbers of Black policemen, deputies, and sheriffs grew slowly. The Mississippi Committee for Human Relations (MCHR), an offshoot of Atlanta's Southern Regional Council, undertook a count of all Black law enforcement officers statewide in 1972. MCHR hired political science students as interns at Jackson State College to survey county and municipal administrators. Only sixty of 320 law enforcement agencies deigned to respond, but interns found an expected disparity. They identified eighty Black local and county officers of the 431 reported—representing just under 20 percent of reporting police forces.[20]

An emphasis on Black police employment muted voices critical of policing as structurally racist. In the run-up to a report on police violence in Clay

County and West Point from March 1971, a local organizer with MCHR interviewed three Black women from Clay County: Ruby Smith, a schoolteacher; Earline Coleman; and Dora Adams. In the course of their discussion about undocumented police brutality, the interviewer wrote in her notes that "Black policemen brutalize black citizens." This admission appeared nowhere in MCHR's final report, but the dilemma was voiced in that room and others across the state as law enforcement agencies desegregated.[21]

In Clay County, three Black women troubled the common sense of police reform through desegregation. Dora Adams was a longtime community organizer and employee of West Point's Bryan Brothers meatpacking plant. Adams had grown up a sharecropper and moved to town as beef cattle interests reconfigured the Black Prairie's cotton lands. In 1964, Adams had invited COFO activists into her home at great risk to her life and well-being. In the early '70s, she nurtured the struggle still. Perhaps, if given the chance, the three women would have indicted West Point's few Black officers as merely bad apples in a world that required reasonable police violence. But the ideal size and scope of policing imagined by lifelong activists in this period of transition awaits deeper research and study. Regardless, they recognized that racial parity on the police force did not necessarily cleanse their rural world of a culture of police violence. Such doubt in policing shows itself only rarely in the archive, but it was clearly in the room with some activists.[22]

In a landscape that began to feature African American police officers, some activists argued that blue at times mattered more than Black or white. In Hattiesburg, the NAACP called for the dismissal of two local Black police officers as early as 1967.[23] More radical leaders in Holly Springs' United League threatened a town-wide boycott in 1978 if a Black officer named Lannie Cummings wasn't fired.[24] In 1979, the Simpson County Welfare Rights Organization hosted a rally at Mendenhall because they alleged brutality from a Black officer named R. T. Walker. That same year, Jackson's NAACP branch asked for a Black narcotics officer in the Jackson Police Department to be dismissed after years of complaints and his recent undertaking of a warrantless search that ended in a shootout.[25] This was only one portion of the continued movement against police violence.

In a rejection of expansionist reforms, some activists sought to defund unacceptable police activity. Holly Springs' United League also attempted to defund the Marshall County Sheriff's Department of federal law enforcement monies. In January 1978, the United League arranged for nine victims of police violence to testify before the Marshall County Board of

Supervisors. The League successfully persuaded the Board to "terminate the sheriff's federal funds" at the hearing. The Marshall County sheriff sued in federal court to restore federal funding but lost.[26] One month later League followers boycotted to demand the firing of two white Tupelo policemen who beat a Black man in the county jail. League leaders also mailed LEAA about the incident, demanding federal funds be withheld if a court proved the charges.[27] The United League developed an analysis of police improvement where federal carceral funding was one of the only levers of power available to communities. We turn next to the full context of that federal funding.

Militarization

In September 1970, as Connie Slaughter's case made its way through court, the sheriff of Winston County wrote to his county board of supervisors. In Louisville, Mississippi, Sheriff Charles Fred Sloan listed twenty items that he and his single deputy sheriff needed for the coming year. Trousers and winter hats. Four new guns—one shotgun and one pistol each. The only big-ticket items were new patrol cars. All told, he estimated the cost to be $9,000. When the Winston County board set the next year's budget, it fell well short of the sheriff's expectations. It appropriated only $6,500 to be divided among the sheriff's office *and* county courts.[28]

The following spring, however, Sheriff Sloan received a lifeline from B. A. "Buff" Hammond, the police commissioner of Greenwood. Hammond, a founding member of the White Citizens' Council in 1954, wrote Sloan on June 3, 1971, in his new capacity as the regional program specialist of Law Enforcement Assistance Regional Council No. 2. "This is an important communication requiring immediate action," he began. Mississippi's Division of Law Enforcement Assistance (DLEA) had allotted Winston County $9,000, "which means," Hammond clarified, "if you buy $12,000.00 worth of equipment, D.L.E.A. will pay $9,000.00, or 75% of that amount. . . . Send me a list immediately of exactly what you wish to buy for the Sheriff's office." Hammond even thought to include a "list of anticipated basic equipment."[29]

Five days later, on June 8, the board of supervisors met to consider Hammond's offer. "It is in the best interest of Winston County and all the citizens of Winston County to participate in the Law Enforcement Assistance Program," the board decreed. Sheriff Sloan's original wish list followed, with significant additions: enough firearms, riot batons, nylon handcuffs, and body armor for *three officers*. And, strikingly, the board now requested large amounts of Mace and tear gas. They even ordered eighteen hand grenades, including six "baseball" grenades, which violently explode instead of simply spewing noxious gas from a canister. Roper Supply Company, in Picayune, Mississippi, delivered the supplies to Sheriff Sloan in early 1972.[30]

Across rural Mississippi in the spring of 1971, county governments ordered exactly the same firepower. For instance, in north Mississippi, where Akinyele Umoja has shown that radical Black politics squared off against a resurgent Ku Klux Klan movement allied with racist policemen, law enforcement officers sought similar weapons of war.[31] In Tupelo's Lee County, officers attended regular meetings of Law Enforcement Assistance Regional Council No. 1, where lawmen standardized such wish lists and coordinated across county lines. On the Tennessee border, in Corinth, Alcorn County's board approved its LEAA wish list and began seeking federal funding to build a new, larger county jail. And in New Albany's Union County, the board of supervisors now wrote its annual budgets expecting income from the LEAA.[32]

In Mississippi, the Division of Law Enforcement Assistance used federal funding to build a police economy in rural areas. In 1972, subgrants to county and municipal governments for "basic and sophisticated police equipment" totaled $520,000. State administrators boasted that it had "been one of Mississippi's more popular law enforcement assistance programs. Sheriffs' departments in all 82 counties and practically all incorporated municipalities have received funding from this program." LEAA grants even subsidized the employment of college student interns in county law enforcement agencies. In the summer of 1972 alone, fifty-two undergraduates majoring in law enforcement—the major requested by Paul B. Johnson's Crime Commission in 1968—interned in local sheriff and police departments. Here, administrators reported, they "gain[ed] first hand 'street' experience" and saved local taxpayers 75 percent of the cost of full-time employees.[33]

This disproportionate redistribution of federal resources to rural law enforcement was a national phenomenon. "Specifically," writes LEAA historian Elizabeth Hinton, "White House officials and LEAA administrators soon struggled to address the mismatch between where reported crime was rising (usually in American cities) and where law enforcement block grants actually ended up (usually in rural towns)."[34] But the funding and the weapons kept coming.

In rural counties with low expenditures for social services, the federal subsidy of law enforcement was stark. In Kemper County, the board of supervisors doubled its annual public safety budget between fiscal years 1971 and 1976. Over the same period the county's spending on welfare services increased by only a third. In fiscal year 1974, Kemper County spent slightly more on law enforcement than welfare services. The next year it budgeted a full $10,000 more for public safety.[35]

Secrecy

As a decade of pitched battles against state-funded racial apartheid melted into memory and history, new battles over policing's secrecy emerged. Ironically, the downfall of Mississippi's State Sovereignty Commission (MSSC), the state's segregationist watchdog that lacked police powers, forced a larger reckoning with the state police.[36] Were law enforcement's investigative reports classified as state secrets? What about internal communications or policies? What did the public have a right to know about the conduct of policing? In the aftermath of segregation, the 1970s were a flashpoint in the future of policing's secrecy, a moment where some veterans of the Mississippi struggle and new activists called into question the public accessibility of police conduct and intelligence gathering. In a moment that demanded truth and reconciliation for the Black freedom struggle, activists received half measures of both.

James P. Coleman had created the Sovereignty Commission in 1956, as governor, in the aftermath of desegregation decisions and the trial of Emmett Till's murderers. Throughout the 1960s it practically served two purposes: to surveil suspected civil rights activism and to provide legal and public relations expertise to local white governments.[37]

The MSSC collected information on many people and organizations remotely connected with policing and its reform. To take but one example, investigators collected intelligence on Fannie Lee Chaney's family as late as 1973, the year of the Sovereignty Commission's defunding. In that document, Muhammad Ahmad, cofounder of the Black radical Revolutionary Action Movement listed Chaney's younger son, Ben Chaney, as a political prisoner incarcerated in West Palm Beach, Florida.[38] The Mississippi Department of Archives and History preserves the organization's casefiles online. As of this writing, anyone with uncensored internet access can navigate to the MDAH website, search for Ben Chaney, and read the four-page mailer from the African Prisoners of War Solidarity Day Committee. There, activists called on people to show up to commemorate the injustice of an August 1971 raid by FBI agents and local police officers on the Jackson headquarters of the Republic of New Afrika. Sovereignty Commission employees indexed proper nouns in such documents, filing everything from newspaper clippings and photographs to formal investigative reports under the names of individuals and organizations worthy of surveillance.[39] The MSSC's public accessibility remains an incredible example of state transparency. That success hinged on historical contingency; people fought for that archive.

While the legal saga of the Sovereignty Commission's archive has inspired writers, this was exactly half of the story. Lost in previous writing on Mississippi's bizarre spy agency was the accompanying attempt of activists to open the records of the state police. The demand to open the historic archives of the Mississippi Highway Safety Patrol came in the same lawsuit that eventually declassified Sovereignty Commission records, but the Highway Patrol fell out of the lawsuit. Thus, the successful movement to open the Sovereignty Commission's archive was also the failed movement to open the patrol's archive.[40] At stake in telling the full story of the fight for police archives in Mississippi is a better understanding of state repression in the civil rights struggle and the archive-based histories that are possible as long as state police archives remain classified.

······

As early as 1964, Governor Paul B. Johnson Jr. began to obstruct the Sovereignty Commission's work while he built up the Highway Patrol. At various times during his tenure, he refused to name commissioners and starved the commission of funding. He worked to establish the Highway Patrol as the legitimate surveillance force in rural Black communities and activist circles.[41] While Johnson recognized the commission's utility in coaching all-white governments through federal litigation, in just four years he built the competing state police force into an organization that could simultaneously snuff out extralegal white terror, impede Black activist organizing, and attract federal funding.

Johnson's successor, Governor John Bell Williams, renewed interest in the Sovereignty Commission, but the outpouring of journalistic exposes of abuse of governmental power in the early 1970s made it difficult to defend a secret police force.[42] In the summer of 1971, government transparency became an everyday conversation across the nation when the *New York Times* began publishing Daniel Ellsberg's Pentagon Papers, which exposed the Vietnam War to be a conflict that America's war-making class never expected to win.[43] Then, the next summer's Watergate break-in brought a flood of scrutiny of the Nixon administration that came to a head in the spring of 1973. A parade of witnesses sat before the Senate Select Committee on Presidential Campaign Activities, composed of four bipartisan Southern senators, and described a vast White House coverup.[44] William "Bill" Waller, elected governor of Mississippi in 1972, saw the resonance between Nixon's henchmen and the Magnolia State's segregationist watchdog clearly enough. On April 17, 1973, Waller vetoed the legislature's bill to fund further snooping on the part of the Sovereignty Commission. He declared to lawmakers that the commission's "investigative work can and should be done by either the Department of Public Safety or the Attorney General's Office." To Waller, method rather than outcome was the problem.[45]

Longtime Mississippi journalist Bill Minor celebrated the governor's decision to defund the Sovereignty Commission and began to speculate about the agency's spy files if the commission were to be closed. In his weekly column for the New Orleans *Times-Picayune*, "Eyes on Mississippi," Minor had frequently written about how the commission surveilled and blackmailed white reporters, but Minor hesitated to guess what commission records might unveil if rumors of the organization's widespread espionage proved true. "What about files?" Minor asked in his headline. "Who knows how many magnolia-scented Watergates have been conducted over the years?"[46] Minor's formulation captured a growing consensus on executive overreach and government transparency.

The battle over the Sovereignty Commission's surveillance files began when the state legislature voted to abolish the organization in January 1977. Originally, lawmakers proposed a direct transfer of its files to the Department of Public Safety, which housed the Highway Patrol. However, an extreme faction of white state legislators countered that the archive should be destroyed.[47] At least one lawmaker hoped the libricide might "get this sorry bit of history behind us."[48] A resolution for archival destruction had almost made it to the floor for a vote when the legislature's three Black members, all from Hinds County, protested and publicized the proposed legislation.

One Black opponent of archival destruction, Representative Horace L. Buckley, famously compared the proposed action to a "book burning," evoking Nazi attempts at censorship. Another, Fred L. Banks Jr., said, "The Sovereignty Commission and these records are a part of the history of this state. . . . I don't think we should be about the business of destroying any of the history."[49] Journalist Bill Minor once again entered the fray. He advocated open access for the surveilled and lambasted the Sovereignty Commission as the "Redneck Gestapo."[50]

While lawmakers debated, on February 18, 1977, activists sued. Both Greenville's Delta Ministry, the National Council of Churches' civil rights outpost, and the American Friends Service Committee, the Quaker peace and justice organization, joined lawyers with the American Civil Liberties Union (ACLU) of Mississippi to sue the state for immediate access to Sovereignty Commission files. An emergency US district court order prohibited elected officials from destroying any records, and with renewed media attention, lawmakers compromised.[51] They passed a law transferring the commission archive to the Mississippi Department of Archives and History instead of Public Safety and sealed the records for fifty years—until 2027.[52]

In addition to the records of the Sovereignty Commission, activists also sued for access to the records of the Highway Patrol. In *ACLU et al., v. Cliff Finch et al.*, veteran activists saw their moment to expose decades of illegal political surveillance by the state police in hopes of ending ongoing surveillance.

At the heart of *ACLU v. Finch* was an understanding of police abuse that linked the well-known wrongdoing of the Sovereignty Commission with that of the state police. Named plaintiffs included Cliff Finch, Mississippi's governor; Commissioner of Public Safety James Finch, who headed the Highway Patrol; W. Webb Burke, the last director of the State Sovereignty Commission; and the state's attorney general, Albioun Fernando Summer. The lawsuit alleged that the organizations participated in "unlawful government intrusions," including the clandestine infiltration of civil rights organizations, surveillance, data collection, intentional disruption of activist activities, and fraudulent concealment of such activities by state actors. Activists asked the court to open agency records for discovery and enjoin the agencies from further intrusion.[53]

In Judge W. Harold Cox the litigants had a normally unsympathetic judge. He might have dismissed the case early on, but Cox ordered pretrial discovery on May 21, 1977. An elated ACLU attorney told the press, "We have literally thousands of documents we want to review." Civil liberties activists like Ken Lawrence with the American Friends Service Committee came to call their larger fight the Mississippi Surveillance Project, which slotted into a nationwide campaign against police spying.[54]

Such movement veterans faced a dilemma: How could they request documents that the state refused to either confirm or deny existed? Activists cast a broad net in June 1977. First, they sought "all indexes, card files and procedural manuals regarding Highway Patrol surveillance techniques, use of informers and dissemination of intelligence data"; second, "all information gathered about groups which the Highway Patrol considers to be militant or subversive." Finally, they demanded from Governor Cliff Finch "any documents authorizing an extension of the investigatory powers of the Highway Patrol."[55]

The precision of their requests demonstrated both the activists' experience of Highway Patrol surveillance and a keen strategy for opening law enforcement records more broadly. An index or card catalog might reveal the scope of state police surveillance to the court without jeopardizing specific investigative details, which might be protected. Likewise, they hoped that a demonstration of the Highway Patrol's expansive definition of subversiveness might trigger broader discovery. If they could show that the governor had directed the state police to surveil or harass civil rights activists, they could charge abuse of executive authority that resonated with Watergate. However, the state promptly asserted executive privilege over patrol files, causing Bill Minor to ask rhetorically in the week's column, "Shades of Richard Nixon?"[56]

The state's attorney general, A. F. Summer, who was simultaneously advocating for statewide prison construction, formed a defense in line with the 1967 Freedom of Information Act's exemptions for law enforcement. In July 1977, Summer alleged that the requested documents included "intelligence or investigatory files compiled for law enforcement related purposes, some of which contain intra-agency communications. . . . In other words," he wrote, "these are criminal intelligence files which relate directly to knowledge about individuals and organizations involved in or contemplating involvement in criminal activities." Summer went further to state that opening Highway Patrol files endangered the lives of existing confidential informants as well as the patrol's ability to secure informants in the future.[57] Judge Cox sustained the state's objection and ordered the Highway Patrol's archive sealed from discovery altogether. Only the Sovereignty Commission's documents remained in the lawsuit, making it a fight over the archive of a defunct organization, an institutional relic of the segregationist order.

Over the next twenty years, federal courts rejected every state argument against opening the Sovereignty Commission's records. Whether for discovery in the ACLU's political surveillance lawsuit, or eventually for open access to the public, district and appellate courts consistently chose transparency. Under court order, all Sovereignty Commission files officially opened to the public in 1997, thirty years before the original release date.[58]

But activists had also fought for basic transparency around law enforcement surveillance records. In that imagined archive, highway patrolmen like the ones who tortured Fannie Lou Hamer in 1963 stood equal alongside Sovereignty Commission sleuths. Writing in *The Police Threat to Political Liberty* (1979), a book that placed the Mississippi Surveillance Project in context with similar projects across the country, the American Friends Services Committee repeated what they had learned through *ACLU v. Finch*. Though the Sovereignty Commission was abolished, "statewide political surveillance has continued under the jurisdiction of the highway patrol . . . while municipal police and county sheriffs have expanded their intelligence-gathering abilities, largely through LEAA grants."[59] Movement veterans imagined a more complete archive to study, publicize, and hold to account the everyday apparatus of law enforcement that had asserted itself against the Black freedom struggle in Mississippi and marginalized populations across the country. Their imagined archive would have unlocked the records of Mississippi's state police, a type of law enforcement agency that, unlike the Sovereignty Commission, maintained legitimacy in every state of the nation.

・・・・・・

The historical records of American law enforcement agencies remain largely off-limits to the public and researchers. In Mississippi, only the records of a defunded and abolished instrument of state violence, the Sovereignty Commission, are open to the public. There is no schedule to declassify historical police records. My early attempts at state police freedom of information requests for this book yielded a total of three useless pages.

Over the decades that saw the rise of mass incarceration, law enforcement solidified its exceptional place in American government, one backed by tight controls over what the public can know about its actions. What is the truth of the Jackson State killings? Officially, the Highway Patrol believed there was a Black sniper when it opened fire on Alexander Hall in May 1970, and this assertion protected it from so much as paying restitution for the lives it stole. Researchers have found that troopers like Lloyd Jones, who likely killed Benjamin Brown on Jackson State's campus in 1967, arrived at Alexander Hall in 1970 to "scatter them n——s," according to patrol radio transcripts recovered by a federal inquiry. Troopers continued to use racist language over the radio as they summoned medical care for the Black students they killed and injured.[60] The patrol's greatest penalty—perhaps its only penalty—was its desegregation.

In the 1970s, veterans of Mississippi's freedom struggle demanded an accounting of the police-led counterrevolution they overcame to solidify civil and voting rights. The desegregation of the Mississippi Highway Safety Patrol was far from inevitable. The institution's limited progress came through terror, courage, and happenstance. The very same police expansionists who once fought any federal attempt to overturn the state's system of racial apartheid now allied with federal funders to subsidize a system of militarized policing. Such militarization often came instead of basic welfare functions of government. Locally, LEAA set Mississippi's law-and-order police power on a path to access personnel, technologies, and weapons of war. Through a parallel series of events, Mississippi's ruling class could not resist the opening of Sovereignty Commission archives but found a friend in the federal judiciary, which shielded the archives of formal police agencies like the Highway Patrol from posterity's judgment.

Facing a fight over the future of policing in a post–Jim Crow world, the secrecy required to seclude policing's hinterland flowed backward and forward. Anyone can read the Sovereignty Commission background check on Jerome Mangum, instigated upon his lawsuit in 1970. But one is at a loss to study quantitatively or qualitatively the pattern of Highway Patrol roadblock activity that swept up Black drivers like Mangum's grandfather and countless others in these years.[61] For now, Mississippi's state police records remain closed because of previous legal decisions that distinguish between the policing of political enemies and the policing of "criminal activities," in the words of Attorney General Summer. After 1977, political surveillance was abusive and unlawful even as policing crime was legitimate and legal.

We should perhaps understand policing's post-Watergate reinforcement of archival secrecy as a product of the legitimacy reproduced through expansionist police reform. More than sixty years after Freedom Summer, the regular activities of Mississippi's modern, bureaucratic police state during the civil rights movement remain hidden from the public because of the assumption that legitimate police work occurred alongside the unlawful police action alleged by activists at the time and since.

Perhaps a new judge in a new case will someday grant discovery or academic research in Mississippi's state police records. Something similar occurred in the 2010s, when the historian Johanna Fernández successfully sued the New York Police Department for surveillance files from the civil rights era.[62] Mere access to police archives might not lead to justice, but it would surely start a fuller debate about the meanings of safety, repair, and the institutions capable of delivering either.

Conclusion
Between Mississippi Law and American Law

Elijah Pierce was born on a farm near Baldwyn, Mississippi, in 1892. The son of formerly enslaved parents, he grew up sharecropping. His family lived in a log cabin in the middle of a cotton field. "Never dreamed that I'd be in a city," he told an interviewer in 1974.[1] Rural life for Pierce meant plowing fields with a mule and escaping farm work when he could. "Seemed like there was something out in the woods I enjoyed better than most anything," he said.[2] Sometimes he trekked through nearby Twentymile Bottom, where trees and canebrakes "were so tall and so thick until you couldn't see the sun till noon." Nature inspired much of Pierce's art as a whittler and wood carver. He learned that trees like beech, box elder, or hawthorn made for easy carving. Over his ninety-two years, he carved animals, athletes, scenes from the Bible, even dinosaurs. He also carved the politics he lived and observed.[3]

In *Elijah Escapes the Mob* (ca. 1950s), Pierce carved part of his autobiography. "Back in them days, whites in Mississippi were just unbearable," Pierce told an interviewer in 1980. One day around 1913 he was arrested while playing baseball in Tupelo. "The detective walked up to me and told me to stick 'em up. . . . I didn't know what it was all about. I asked him, I said, 'What is wrong?' He just kinda cussed and said, 'You'll find out,' and marched me down to the jail." Unbeknownst to the baseball team, a white mob was rampaging through the county in search of a Black man believed to have killed a white man. The detective thought Pierce fit the assailant's description. In the Tupelo jail, a white witness cleared Pierce's name, but the lawful authorities ordered the Black man to leave Tupelo lest he be misidentified and murdered. "At that time I knew what the life of a colored man in Mississippi was," he recalled. "I didn't try to linger round there. It was no more to kill a Negro than killing a rabbit." He walked backroads for eighteen miles to his family's farm and left Mississippi on a freight train sometime later. Eventually he made a life as a barber and artist in Columbus, Ohio. But he spoke of his experience in Mississippi often, believing that

Elijah Pierce's *Elijah Escapes the Mob*, carved and painted wood relief, 1950s. Reproduced by permission of the Columbus Museum of Art, Ohio.

God had acted through "that little detective" who may have saved Pierce's life by arresting him by mistake.[4]

Elijah Escapes the Mob depicts the impossible position of Black life under Jim Crow in Mississippi. On the left of his woodcut, a mob rages. On the right stand the police and the jail. Elijah is caught in the middle, arms raised in surrender. Above Elijah, two pale hands unite in a handshake, appearing to unite the mob and the police. Below, Elijah joins the rabbits, escaping through the deep woods.

America is conspicuously present in Elijah Pierce's woodcuts. His carvings show histories of slavery and emancipation, *Slavery Time* (1965–70), as well as the chain gang, *Presidents and Convicts* (1941). Uncle Sam appears in both, within sight of the lash and shackle.[5] In the 1970s, Pierce was moved by the Jackson State killings to depict the chaos of a new age of violence and reconfigured empire. "There's more killing and slaughtering and hatred in the human heart than there ever was in history," Pierce said in one grim assessment. "These nations now, they're just sayin' peace, but going back and making ammunition and missiles and every other device."[6] In *Watergate* (ca. 1975), the artist depicts the Mississippi Highway Patrol's victims, Phillip Lafayette Gibbs and James Earl Green, alongside those killed by the Ohio National Guard at Kent State University. Vietnam-era warships ply the waves; warplanes fill the sky. The American flag presides over all, with only an all-seeing eye above.[7]

Never offering a singular message or revealing a pure meaning, the art of Elijah Pierce, a survivor of Mississippi Law, suggests that racial injustice long occurred under the American flag. It's a long story that never guarantees progress for all. Death-dealing at home blends with violence abroad. The artist's political commentary joins his desire to capture beauty, humor, and hope.

・・・・・・

Mississippi Law has told a deep history of white supremacist policing, change, continuity, and the fight for things to be otherwise. It has sought the tangled roots of a police power that could at once rescue Black Mississippians like Leroy Miller from the mob and then ferry them toward the inhumanity of Parchman Farm. To be sure, Southern policing changed significantly in response to the civil rights movement. Yet law enforcement departed the civil rights era and entered the age of mass incarceration with a new scale of resources and authority in civil society. So-called smart segregationists, the ones who fought against both the radical democracy of local Black freedom struggles and the racial authoritarianism of local policemen affiliated with the Ku Klux Klan, did so in hopes of continued home rule by a small white elite. With federal support, these rulers elevated the police to their position of privilege on the promise of race-blind impartiality despite ample evidence to the contrary.

This history has also interrogated a notion of police reform that simply expanded policing's role in society. Mississippi's inflation-adjusted annual state police budget grew 470 percent between 1954 and 1980: more state revenue for more lawmen, weapons, cars, and training.[8] Never preordained, this expansionist reform succeeded in different moments of possibility—moments where some critics called for policing's fundamental rethinking or shrinking.

Mississippi Law has considered the ways that Black Mississippians named and confronted policing's autocracy, a state project under which peace officers routinely unleashed chaos under color of law. Mississippi's ungovernable regime of public safety disordered individual lives, families, and whole communities. This professionalized state violence benefited a particular government's plans for rural economic development that required secrecy and hiding for the disposal of racialized enemies of progress. Such expanded police power increased everyday interactions between rural Black residents, activists, and law enforcement, which could bring fines, dispossession, incarceration, and death. The inhumanity of Jim Crow policing far exceeded physical violence associated with police brutality. More policemen contributed to the violence and discrimination that drove rural Black populations from the countryside in the years after World War II.

From 1890, with the hardening of Jim Crow, one subset of white elites reformulated the antebellum period's militia ideal of paramilitary policing. Lawmakers summoned unprecedented state and federal resources for New South militias while defunding Reconstruction's welfare state. Activists such as Mississippi-born Ida B. Wells stood against the consolidation of the Jim Crow regime and recognized that the state troops would be an important arbiter of Black life and death. In *Southern Horrors* (1892), Wells hoped that the militia might be called on to halt extrajudicial murder but also called for Black self-defense. By 1895, Wells could only hope for a "revolution" in white "sentiment," away from "Lynch Law" and toward the "abolition" of this new legal order that reconciled lawlessness with legal authority. Meanwhile, Mississippi's Jim Crow National Guard offered a new pathway to soldiering for white Americans. At the southern border with Mexico, militiamen like Thomas Butler Birdsong learned from the US Army and Texas Rangers while racializing ethnic Mexicans. In a world of occupied territories and cattle pastures, Birdsong led the fight for centralized state police power for the next fifty years.

State investments in automobility and highway infrastructure led to a merger of military and civil authority in the Southern countryside. In the National Guard's riot squad and the Mississippi Highway Safety Patrol (established 1938), police expansionists and industrial modernizers found a way to overcome boundaries between county jurisdictions to govern disorder across the state. State troops and then state troopers guarded the legal execution of Black men, attacked illicit Black businesses, and fanned out to regulate Jim Crow roadways.

Post–World War II police power reshaped rural Black life in Mississippi. In the case of Matt McWilliams, a sheriff used his authority to steal Black land for post-cotton agricultural futures. In Amory, local police stole fourteen years of Leroy Miller's life to appease anti-Black paranoia toward a new underemployed urban Black population. He merely needed to borrow a car to find work. On the road with Tommy Booker, state troopers wielded state violence to satisfy white demands for vengeance in the face of tragic automobile accidents. Communities organized for justice, whether in the courts or going door to door to refute police lies. Such everyday police attacks on Black life and fights against "Mississippi Law" spurred organizing through the NAACP that set the groundwork for the nonviolent direct action campaigns of the 1960s.

Rural police power also grew in relation to a major postwar economic sector, the beef cattle industry. Though one of many redeployments of Mississippi's post-cotton countryside, only land- and water-intensive beef cattle brought its own police formation, the Highway Patrol's Livestock Theft Bureau, designed by the Mississippi Cattlemen's Association. Unlike paternalistic or labor-hungry cotton planters, cattlemen embraced a new relationship to centralized police power and incarceration that welcomed the removal of rural residents who stood athwart the development of larger herds. When occupants of would-be cattle pastures refused to leave quietly, the patrol could make life difficult with surveillance and fines. If a Black tenant farmer like Toby Faulkner defended his garden or himself, troopers unleashed war.

White cattlemen also overtook key parts of the state government in the age of massive resistance to desegregation. From the Department of Public Safety to the penitentiary at Parchman, agribusinessmen assumed places in an expanding state bureaucracy. Governor James P. Coleman expanded the Highway Patrol in both scale and influence as activism increased around the US Supreme Court's *Brown* decision, the murder of Emmett Till, and the rise of Martin Luther King's bus boycott movement in Montgomery, Alabama. As the movement's direct action phase wore on, police and corrections officers used the cattleman's tools of torture, including cattle prods, whips, and trucks.

Local and outside activists did battle with Mississippi's state police as the civil rights movement evolved from a series of local struggles to a region-wide assault on Jim Crow. State troopers ferried Freedom Riders away from the mob but toward Parchman's cells. Birdsong's Highway Patrol guarded the integration of the University of Mississippi alongside federal US marshals but then left the campus to the mob. Activists like Fannie Lou Hamer built networks and circulated the freedom movement's philosophy. They faced arrest, torture, and confinement in spaces such as the Montgomery County jail. Such police terror was well practiced by 1963, and Governor Paul B. Johnson Jr. convinced lawmakers to triple the number of state troopers and expand the police powers for investigative units like Livestock Theft and Identification.

On the civil rights movement's rural byways, troopers like B. Cowart, a Livestock Theft investigator, shaped the possibility of rural organizing. Troopers selectively policed white terrorists alongside the FBI and used statutory authority to thwart insurance claims from burned Black churches. In this negotiated climate of state repression, activist farm families like the Valentines of Clay County found themselves caught in the balance, usually protected from non-state actors but far from safe. B. Cowart's heart attack launched near murderous violence from night-riding white neighbors. And not even the presence of a US congressman could ensure a serious investigation from state and federal law enforcement on the Valentine farm. Black landowning farmers paid a high price for supporting civil and voting rights volunteers with COFO and the MFDP, those whom historian Howard Zinn called "the new abolitionists."

Neshoba County's Freedom Summer murders generated an expansive reimagination of policing for a future beyond Jim Crow apartheid. Radical lawyers joined gifted organizers to craft a multilayered campaign against Mississippi's system of legal lawlessness. They convened small community meetings, met in the US court of appeals, and published a trade press paperback book. The family of Fannie Lee Chaney joined a movement to recast the Mississippi Burning case as more than a simple Klan lynching. In *COFO v. Rainey*, the freedom movement put Mississippi Law on trial, suing to suspend Jim Crow policing of freedom fighters and appoint federal peacekeepers in the place of all-white troopers, sheriffs, and cops. Invoking the Reconstruction-Era Civil Rights Act of 1866, activists sought an off-ramp for the conspiracy of lawful and lawless white power, the only policing most had ever known. The movement imagined a new abolition-democracy of COFO Freedom Houses for a second Reconstruction. Federal judges rejected the legal challenge to Mississippi Law, and white liberal responses to the reporting of policing's violence presaged a world where fundamental solutions posed by the policed would be dismissed as radical and unsophisticated. Mississippi's state police force took credit for exposing Neshoba County's Klan conspiracy and deepened its relationship with the FBI.

Police violence between 1965 and 1970 only intensified in its gall and lethality. State troopers joined local police and corrections officers to implement some of rural Mississippi's most bestial police methods to punish unsatisfied Black activists in cities and towns. The cattleman's tool, the electric cattle prod, drove activists to despair. The police detained protesters marching for voting rights and against police brutality in cattle pens at the state capital's fairgrounds. President Lyndon Johnson appointed segregationist James P. Coleman as a justice on the Deep South's US court of appeals and began a program that would funnel money, guns, and Cold War expertise into Mississippi's still-segregated criminal justice system. Governors Paul B. Johnson and John Bell Williams joined law-and-order liberalism's War on Crime. The outcome was police war on any social movement for democracy.

Troopers fired federally subsidized submachine guns and armor-piercing rifles into a crowd of unarmed Jackson State students for thirty seconds on May 15, 1970. Activists like Constance Iona Slaughter and Jerome Mangum transformed these Jackson State killings into a campaign to desegregate the patrol. By 1972, law enforcement in Mississippi no longer bore the mark "white only." Desegregation came slowly and despite bad-faith efforts from the state. Some local movements began to confront the limits of desegregation as a panacea for police violence against Black Mississippians.

As it did across the country, the US Department of Justice Law Enforcement Assistance Administration (LEAA) funneled resources for increasingly militarized tools of counterinsurgency into Mississippi's crossroads and hamlets. Local welfare spending shrank. Over the 1970s, reformers debated what the future of policing should be. State and federal governments continued to fund a carceral state over a welfare state, and officials made clear that policy decisions would be made with neither transparency nor public participation. Institutions entered policing's future with neither truth nor reconciliation over policing's past.

In Mississippi, hope for an accountable, scrutable criminal legal system waned as the State of Mississippi embarked on paths to investigate, arrest, and incarcerate more people for longer sentences than ever before. The Vera Institute of Justice estimates that by 1980 Mississippi imprisoned over 3,500 people and for the first time surpassed the national rate of imprisonment per 100,000 residents. After 1980, Mississippi's rate of imprisonment decreased only once before 2002, the year state prison populations peaked at 22,705. That amounted to a 550 percent increase from 1980, 60 percent more than the national rate of imprisonment for the same year.

In 2002, 48 percent of men and women incarcerated in state prisons were Black. The criminal legal system imprisoned African Americans at twice the rate of white Mississippians.[9]

......

Despite federal court refusals to open Mississippi's police archives to the public, critical records of policing survive across the state and nation. Victims of police violence strove to document their treatment at the hands of already-reformed troopers, sheriffs, and cops. Sometimes with an eye to the future and sometimes by accident, Mississippi's policed people created an oral and documentary record. The persistent fight against a life-destroying police power in Mississippi has made this book's historical narrative possible.

But this history of Jim Crow policing does not belong to the dead past. In hauntingly resonant ways, renewed fights over the nature of police reform exploded during this book's research and composition. Immigration enforcement launched Mississippi into national news in 2019. Protest and revolt over the murder of George Floyd and Breonna Taylor in 2020 swelled the movement against racist policing into perhaps the largest social protest in American history. New explorations of non-reformist and abolitionist police reform went mainstream with ongoing demands to defund the police, remake civilian oversight, and reconstruct society away from the prison regime's paramilitary policing and toward what geographer Ruth Wilson Gilmore calls "life-affirming institutions." Yet even as the video-recorded police murder of Floyd brought American life to a halt and police reform to the center of politics, less well-known incidents of policing's autocracy have flourished in policing's hinterland.

In January 2023, two survivors of racist police power in Rankin County, Mississippi, exposed a band of white sheriff's deputies who unleashed lawless terror onto countless victims. Michael Corey Jenkins and Eddie Terrell Parker, both Black, encountered the police during a warrantless drug raid in the mostly white Braxton community. During the hours of abuse that followed at Parker's house, officers called the men racial slurs and alleged that they dated white women. The police beat, tased, and waterboarded their victims, threatening to rape the men with a sex toy. Such unspeakable horrors may never have been investigated or believed if one officer had not accidentally shot Jenkins in the mouth while attempting to intimidate him with a pistol the policeman believed to be unloaded. The crime could not as easily be concealed.[10]

We now know that officers terrorized some of the most vulnerable residents of this rural and exurban area around Jackson for decades. Suspected involvement in criminal activity was always legal pretext for the officers' extralegal methods. But their brutality fell especially on drug users of all backgrounds—the "accompanying vermin" referred to by the Mississippi Bureau of Narcotics chief in 1972. Armed with police torture tactics much older than the Jim Crow era and much newer technologies, these deputies called themselves the "Goon Squad," a nickname for lawless cops that hearkens to the civil rights era. Robert Park, who was brutalized in the Fairgrounds Motel in the summer of 1965, wrote that the Jackson and state police contained "many individuals who can only be described as goons with an especially vicious streak." Watchdog journalists at *Mississippi Today* found that Rankin County's twenty-first-century Goon Squad embraced this appellation, even creating a commemorative coin that depicted them as mafioso caricatures. When reporters asked to see the years of complaints against the Goon Squad, sheriff's department lawyers refused,stating that such documents were protected by state law. Text messages obtained by journalists show how policemen still pursue inhumanity for sport.[11]

Because their lawless policing came to light, six white deputies resigned and pleaded guilty to both federal civil rights abuses and state crimes. They now face more than a decade in prison. Images of the former deputies in court show them being secured by Black state troopers.[12] The possibility of such police officers being removed from duty and prosecuted would have been unthinkable in 1965. And yet, journalists found complaints against the same officers as early as 2009. The Rankin County deputies tortured victims in hopes of cultivating a climate of fear and extracting intelligence for their prosecution of the drug trade. In the 1980s, Tasers replaced cattle prods as the police weapon of choice. Each time an officer used a Taser it registered on a computer in the Rankin County sheriff's office. This register, intended for police accountability, showed that three deputies fired their Tasers fourteen times in one two-hour torture raid against a man named Jerry Manning in 2008. Manning's abuse was not public knowledge until the case of Jenkins and Parker spurred journalists to investigate.[13]

Even as I write these lines, the unspeakable horrors and lessons of policing in Rankin County fade from public consciousness despite continued reporting. They are likely unfamiliar to even a specialist reader, just like the next case from Holmes County that broke in September 2024.[14] Policing's hinterlands have a habit of swallowing the efforts at sustained investigation and news-making. Some cases make the national papers of record. They stay for a season and fall from the headlines into obscurity as promises of reform arrive and depart.

In the post-2020 era, historic contingency aligned once again to send the federal government into policing's hinterland. The US Department of Justice serving under President Joseph R. Biden placed the Goon Squad squarely within a paradigm referred to as "unconstitutional policing," perhaps just the newest euphemism for the lawless legal system at the heart of what an anonymous author in Amory called "Mississippi Law."[15]

Debates around fixing unconstitutional policing are familiar. In his 2022 state of the union address, Biden said, "We should all agree the answer is not to defund the police. It's to fund the police. Fund them. Fund them. Fund them with the resources and training . . . they need to protect our communities."[16] In a bipartisan strategy applauded by many contemporary liberals and conservatives, public and private partnerships propose to build high-tech, high-dollar training facilities such as Atlanta, Georgia's Public Safety Training Center. There, the theory goes, police officers interested in joining a respectable middle-class profession would receive the very best training and finally enforce the law virtuously to keep us all safe. Known as Cop City to its enemies, Atlanta's Training Center is a $90 million answer to lawless policing. If built, Cop City would be erected on the ruins of a Jim Crow prison farm that chained and exploited earlier people deemed disorderly by ruling classes and their supporters. Thoughtful observers believe that better training and equipping law enforcement officers is a winning political position. They overlook more than a century of defining police reform as police expansion in the American South at society's peril.[17]

The historical record shows that Mississippi built its own Cop City in 1964. Men like T. B. Birdsong modeled the Mississippi Law Enforcement Training Academy on Hugh Clegg's FBI Academy at Quantico, Virginia. Sheriff Bryan Bailey, whose Goon Squad deputies terrorized the backroads and trailer parks of Rankin County for decades, is a graduate of the Mississippi Law Enforcement Training Academy.[18] In 2006, the sheriff's department paid for Deputy Hunter Elward, who shot Michael Corey Jenkins in the mouth, to attend the Mechanical and Ballistic Breaching Instructor Course so that he could teach other deputies how to effectively blow the doors off buildings to be raided. Goon Squad deputy Christian Dedmon's skills in drug enforcement were so desirable that the Highway Patrol's Bureau of Narcotics hired him in 2022 as a "Special Contract Investigator to detect and apprehend violators of the criminal statutes pertaining to the possession, sale or use of narcotics or other dangerous drugs."[19] The police have been funded. They have been trained.

Perhaps the best-trained law enforcement officers in the state are the troopers that some leaders want to assume even more duties. For instance, the state police may seize the jurisdiction of Jackson, Mississippi's local police department. As of this writing, leaders propose to deploy the state police to the Capitol Complex Improvement District, an amoeboid map of Jackson's most affluent neighborhoods and the business districts where leaders hope to attract commerce, revenue, and wealth. State leaders in effect invite a particular form of police-led gentrification.[20]

Once again Mississippi's reputation for disorder and dreams of economic development drive state police politics. This time, the specter is violent crime in downtown Jackson. Flanked by state troopers (a Black man and white woman), Governor Tate Reeves cited "a never-ending cycle of violent crime" in a summer 2021 press conference about public safety in the state capital.[21] That year, the Highway Patrol's Department of Public Safety took over the Capitol Police, tasked with security duties around state buildings, received authority to police traffic on Jackson's interstate highways, and received $24 million in funding for a new headquarters. The state police now have legal authority to patrol downtown Jackson's Improvement District, and the state is creating a separate court system to attend to this new colony within America's Blackest city.[22]

When Reeves promised in the summer of 2021 to keep all residents of Jackson safe, he couldn't have been clearer about his larger dreams for a state police takeover. "To our residents and those looking to relocate and those looking to invest in our capital city . . . ," Reeves said, "my administration will do whatever it takes to help keep downtown Jackson safe. . . . In Mississippi, we don't want to defund the police, we want to refund the police." The commissioner of public safety, Sean Tindell, said that he hoped for a total staff of 900 state police officers stationed across Mississippi: 600 troopers on the roads, 150 Capitol Police officers in Jackson, and 150 Bureau of Narcotics officers. "As we increase the presence of state law enforcement, we feel we can make our community safer."[23]

History takes on strange shapes in calumnies against non-expansionist police reform. Can Mississippi's police be *refunded*? Many things have been defunded in Mississippi since 1980, public welfare, education, and health among them, but the police have only absorbed more funding over time. By 2020, the Department of Public Safety's budget surpassed $222 million.

In the throes of a global public health crisis around the novel coronavirus pandemic, the department claimed emergency CARES Act funding from the US Congress.[24] This is the care delivered by expansionist police reform. In the woods south of Atlanta and on the streets of Jackson, the latest police expansionists promise to deliver safety in the spotlight while policing's autocracy thrives in the shadows.

Mississippi's recent history shows the perils of defining police improvement as police expansion anywhere. As I write, a Right-wing national government is deploying the police expansion cosigned by some American liberals in the decades after the civil rights movement against enemy others.[25] New racialized criminalities and federal law enforcement collaboration have yielded a new era of policing that coexists with its destructive traditions. In August 2019, the US Department of Homeland Security's force for Immigration and Customs Enforcement (ICE) conducted deportation raids on poultry processing plants in rural Mississippi. The detention of nearly seven hundred Latinx and Indigenous migrant workers marked the largest single-state raid in American history. ICE tactics were ruthless, advocates reason, because chicken workers had successfully sued employers for sexual harassment and discrimination one year earlier. Children came home from their first day of school to find caregivers vanished. The raids left a climate of fear that has only intensified under a second Donald Trump administration bent on dismantling due process rights, especially for working-class migrants.[26]

Such enforcement will only expand with the collaboration of state and local law enforcement. As early as 2007, future governor Phil Bryant recommended that Mississippi cooperate with ICE by participating in the 287(g) Program "that trains and authorizes local and state law enforcement officials to enforce federal immigration laws." In particular Bryant desired more ICE officers and more technology for state law enforcement to identify deportable people who encounter law enforcement for any reason.[27] In March 2025, Mississippi Attorney General Lynn Fitch announced her office had signed a 287(g) memorandum of agreement with ICE, with roughly eighty certified law enforcement officers.[28] Some Mississippi lawmakers want to empower private citizens to enforce immigration under the guise of bounty hunting. Others want the state police to take over this newest enforcement terrain as well. Though defeated in 2025, Mississippi lawmakers proposed creating a state-level immigration police force to be housed under the highway patrol's Department of Public Safety.[29] Mississippians have thus far resisted this growth of autocracy and secrecy in law enforcement.

Across the country new collectivities study, organize, and fight to end the destructive potential of policing and the prison regime it serves. Some educate and organize. Some occupy forests. Some file lawsuits. Some burn police stations.[30] They fight in the traditions of those who put their lives on the line to halt business as usual and overturn Jim Crow. They fight for their own visions of a healed world. Perhaps they show us that a better future relies on those who fight the enduring logics of Mississippi Law, and in the words of Fannie Lee Chaney, "for us all to make a better living."

Acknowledgments

I thank the interviewees and interlocutors who gave time, stories, and wisdom. Without them I could neither have begun nor sustained this study. And though I alone bear responsibility for this book's faults, many of its virtues owe to the community built around it.

I thank Elton Dean Jr. and his late father Elton Deanes Sr., who believed in recording oral history in western Clay County and invited me onto their land to do so; Brenda and Tommie Valentine for leading me to their family's rural struggle "for humanity," the story of B. Cowart, the Livestock Theft Bureau, and the state police; Michael Reuss for the perspective brought by decades of reflection on activism and its price; Faye Washington and Reverend Roosevelt Clark for shedding light on the world of Matt and Nettie McWilliams; Carmel Baldwin, Beverly Carroll, Elvira Johnson, Lindy Johnson, Thurmond Johnson, Elaine Perryman, and Melinda Windham for helping me place Buford and Bessie Johnson's activism into the context of an extended family; Obbie Riley for guiding my tour of Neshoba County; Rita and Bill Bender for going back to autumn 1964 and sharing all that their study of the law has yielded since; Connie Slaughter-Harvey for candor and unceasing hope for better; Jim Birdsong for photographs of T. B. Birdsong; and Julia Chaney-Moss for the memories of her family's extraordinary vision for a better world.

Numerous teachers and mentors trained me to research and draft this history as I grew and changed my mind over a decade. Adrienne Petty and Mark Roman Schultz introduced me to the methodological and ethical practices of oral, rural, and African American history as an interviewer in the Breaking New Ground Project. At the University of North Carolina at Chapel Hill, W. Fitzhugh Brundage, Robert Hunt Ferguson, and James L. Leloudis encouraged me to conduct original research in Southern history as an undergraduate. Their patience with and advocacy for a first-generation, community college transfer student was immense. They modeled a richer life based on critical engagement with the South and its past, including racial capitalism. I'm grateful.

While a doctoral student at Yale University, I benefited from an intellectual community of scholars, labor organizers, and political theorists. I thank my four closest interlocutors, Glenda Elizabeth Gilmore, Beverly Gage, Jonathan Holloway, and Matthew Frye Jacobson for translating me and guiding me toward an intellectual practice of lifelong learning and revision.

Likewise, the thinkers with whom I struggled to build workplace democracy in higher education around UNITE HERE Local 33 shaped my hopes for researching and writing history. I thank Tiraana Bains, Salonee Bhaman, Camille Cole, Lena Eckert-Erdheim, Emilie Egger, Monique Flores Ulysses, Christopher Forney, Puya Gerami,

Kelly Goodman, Sarah Ifft Decker, Emmanuel Lachaud, Zaib un Nisa Aziz, Mireille Pardon, Nick Rogers, Taylor Rose, Zhenya Sakal, Alex Schweinsberg, Paul Seltzer, Hannah Srajer, Thuto Thipe, Beans Velocci, Adam Waters, Gabriel Winant, Lindsay Zafir, and Holden Zimmerman for thinking and fighting with me. Union yes!

I also thank my colleagues and students in the History Department at Texas State University, who helped me start a life as a junior faculty member and offered comments on this work at various stages. I have come to believe that Jessica Pliley keeps the historical profession afloat with both a critical sense of justice and abiding belief in the possibility of teaching and mentorship. Likewise, Anadelia Romo's analysis of the university as a workplace and space for genuine friendship and humor is unmatched. Additionally, I thank Tom Alter, Ron Brown, Sarah Coleman, Sara Damiano, Peter Dedek, Paul Hart, Kenneth and Patricia Margerison, Jimmy McWilliams, Jason Mellard, Rebecca Montgomery, Angela Murphy, Casey Nichols, Ruby Oram, Josh Paddison, Louis and Liz Porter, José Carlos de la Puente Luna, Caroline Ritter, Joaquin Rivaya-Martinez, and Dwight Watson. I learned from many exceptional students at Texas State, but I'm especially thankful for the research assistance of CM Marihugh and Rachel Lopez, as well as the public history work of Avery Armstrong, Patrick Bassett, Emma Beard, Regan Davis, Allison Hopson, Mary Kahle, and Emma Long. For being the best chair I could have hoped for, thanks, Jeff Helgeson.

My approach to writing a rural history of policing in the American South developed through feedback from interdisciplinary scholars of the American South, the carceral state, Black politics, and public history. For providing critical feedback on drafts and presentations of this work, I thank Luther Adams—Free Man of Color, Kemi Adeyemi, Mal Ahern, Teal Arcadi, Jordanna Bailkin, Simon Balto, Evan Bennett, Stephen A. Berrey, Dan Berger, Jane Dailey, Pete Daniel, Purnima Dhavan, Garrett Felber, Max Felker-Kantor, James Gregory, Matthew Guariglia, Cindy Hahamovitch, Françoise Hamlin, Walter Johnson, Andrew Kahrl, Matthew Mancini, Katherine Mellen Charron, Adrienne Petty, Loretta Pierre, Peter Pihos, Chandan Reddy, Zachary Sell, David Silkenat, Maya Angela Smith, William Sturkey, Kerry Taylor, Emma Teitleman, and Madeline Yue Dong. Additionally, several collectives invited me to think with them, including Yale's Racial Capitalism and the Carceral State Working Group, the University of Edinburgh's American History Seminar, the University of Texas at San Antonio's John L. Nau III Conference on Texas History, Brown University's Ruth J. Simmons Center for the Study of Slavery and Justice, and Queen's University Belfast's Centre for the Americas. The University of Washington's Walter Chapin Simpson Center for the Humanities earned my boundless gratitude when it invited me to be ACLS-CHCI Visiting Fellow and participate in its 2023 Society of Scholars. Rachel Arteaga, Caitlin Palo, Julie Stoverink, Kalia Walker, and Kathleen Woodward created a home for some of my best living.

Some friends deserve special thanks. It's hard to imagine my life without Lucia Ruth Hulsether. She's the sort of critic and community builder the world needs more of. Also irreplaceable as sounding boards and sages were Bench Ansfield, Lucy Caplan, Ian Foss Hathaway, Daniel Judt, Micah Khater, Tyler Kynn, Anne Lessy,

Nichole Nelson, Kate Redburn, James Shinn, Emily Snyder, Scott Stern, and Alex Zhang. I owe a special debt to Amanda Joyce Hall, who joined me in creating a writing group that became much more. Bianca Dang, Anna Duensing, Alycia Hall, Micah Jones, Naomi Sussman, Viet Trinh, and Teona Williams have read most of this book. More importantly, we've tried to build a collective that never stops seeking to define constructive critique, justice-directed scholarship, and dialogue. Thanks, HQH.

Though we rarely spoke about this book, my central Texas neighbors were invaluable in shaping the everyday life from which this work grew. Gina Alba-Rogers, Jonafa and Alex Banbury, Sam Benavides, Evan Bookman, Jordan Buckley, Anita Collins, Elle Cross, Tammy Gonzales, Cyrus Gray, Lisa Haegele, Joe Laycock, Kate McIntyre, Mark Menjivar, Natasha Mikles, Karen Muñoz Treviño, Mariah Partida, Nathan Pino, Rosalie Ray, Idris Robinson, Juania Sueños, and Rick Treviño made life imaginable in my new home. If you've made it this far, google Mano Amiga and the *Caldwell/Hays Examiner*.

This study has enjoyed the trust of many patrons. They include the University of North Carolina at Chapel Hill's Department of History; Yale University's Graduate School of Arts and Sciences, Department of History, and John Morton Blum Fellowship for Graduate Research in American History and Culture; the Beinecke Rare Book and Manuscript Library; the Gilder Lehrman Center for the Study of Slavery, Resistance, and Abolition; the Southern Historical Association; the Agricultural History Society; Texas State University's Office of the Provost, Research Enhancement Program, Department of History, and College of Liberal Arts; and Texas A&M University's Department of History. Texas State University provided a generous publication subvention. The American Council of Learned Societies (ACLS) Fellowship allowed me to complete the first draft of my manuscript and granted me the time to think about the way my life fit within my work as a scholar.

I have also benefited from the knowledge and time of many archivists, records specialists, and journalists. At Mississippi State University's Archives and Special Collections, I thank Nikita Gandy, Jennifer McGillian, Jessica Perkins-Smith, and Fred Smith; at the Mississippi Department of Archives and History, Clinton Bagley, Jeff Giambrone, De'Niecechsi Layton, and William Thompson; at the University of Southern Mississippi's McCain Library and Archives, Jessica Clark, Joshua Jenkins, and Andrew Rhodes; at the University of Mississippi's Department of Archives and Special Collections, Jennifer Ford, Greg Johnson Leigh McWhite, and Lauren Rogers. Thanks to Constance Slaughter-Harvey for granting me access to her private archives around the Jackson State killings and the Highway Patrol's desegregation, and to Jerry Mitchell at the Mississippi Center for Investigative Reporting for sharing expertise and contact information on interlocutors.

At UNC Press I enjoyed fantastic editorial assistance. Brandon Proia helped shape this study long before and after his obligation. Dawn Durante guided the manuscript through review and production with clarity and precision. Carol Seigler provided invaluable help with production. I thank the Justice, Power, and Politics Series editors, Heather Ann Thompson and Rhonda Y. Williams, as well as the Editorial Advisory Board, for their decade-long contribution to the histories of policing, the prison regime, and defiance. I likewise thank the press's anonymous readers, who made this a much better book through the peer review process, and Robert Cronan of Lucidity Information Design, LLC for his map of Mississippi.

I thank my family: here, gone, right, wrong, of origin, of choice. Ovella, Junior, Mavis, Fred, Phyllis, Mark, Stephanie, Adam, R, R, R, Colette, Zack, Lena, Rae, Gabriel, Esta, Ann, Paul, and Adam. And to Miranda Sachs, my thanks for introducing me to a wider, less desperate world. You nourished this work and the mountains of work that go into professing and organizing. We're not promised tomorrow, but I'm glad so many yesterdays have included you. I'm grateful for our evolving mode of care, companionship, entertainment, movement, and rest.

Notes

Abbreviations

C-L	*Jackson Clarion-Ledger*
COFO	Council of Federated Organizations
CORE	Congress of Racial Equality
JDN	*Jackson Daily News*
MDAH	Mississippi Department of Archives and History, Jackson
MFDP	Mississippi Freedom Democratic Party
MHSP	Mississippi Highway Safety Patrol
MSP	Mississippi State Penitentiary at Parchman
MSSC	Mississippi State Sovereignty Commission Files, MDAH, Jackson
NAACP/LOC	Records of the National Association for the Advancement of Colored People, Manuscript Division, Library of Congress, Washington, DC
NAACP/PQ	Records of the National Association for the Advancement of Colored People, as digitized by ProQuest History Vault
NARA	US National Archives and Records Administration
NYT	*New York Times*
OMPF	Official Military Personnel File, Thomas B. Birdsong Jr., NARA, National Personnel Records Center, Spanish Lake, MO
PBJ	Johnson (Paul B.) Family Papers, Special Collections, McCain Library and Archives, University of Southern Mississippi, Hattiesburg
WHS	Wisconsin Historical Society

Introduction

1. Unsigned letter to Arthur B. Spingarn, ca. March 17, 1947, 1, NAACP/LOC, Box II:B125, folder: Miller v. Wiggins, Correspondence. See chapter 3 for more details and sources on the Miller case. Silvan Niedermeier, "Forced Confessions: Police Torture and the African American Struggle for Civil Rights in the 1930s and 1940s South," in Wood and Ring, eds., *Crime and Punishment*.

2. Unsigned to Spingarn, 2.

3. Historians call the American South's legal and social system of white supremacist apartheid that followed Reconstruction and Redemption "Jim Crow." Historical actors only referred to it as Jim Crow later. See Foner, *Reconstruction*, 372; Woodward, *The Strange Career of Jim Crow*.

4. For histories of Jim Crow and the Mississippi freedom movement, see Carson, *In Struggle*; McMillen, *Dark Journey*; Payne, *I've Got the Light*; Dittmer, *Local People*; Ransby, *Ella Baker*; Ownby, ed., *The Civil Rights Movement*; Hamlin, *Crossroads at Clarksdale*; Sanders, *A Chance for Change*.

5. Randolph, "Jim Crow Militia." I use the term *paramilitary* advisedly, to stress the domestic war-making aspirations that Jim Crow reformers masked in terms of public safety: that is, not state troops but state troopers. I also mean to emphasize how the ethos of legally unauthorized paramilitaries infiltrated legally authorized law enforcement. For a prudent call to dispense with the term *paramilitary* in analyses of police militarization, see Seigel, "On the Critique of Paramilitarism."

6. For histories that emphasize reform over the life of the Jim Crow racial order, see Link, *The Paradox of Southern Progressivism*; Johnson, *Reforming Jim Crow*; Kato, *Liberalizing Lynching*; Schoenfeld, *Building the Prison State*; Smith, *Managing White Supremacy*; Ward, *Defending White Democracy*; Crespino, *In Search of Another Country*; Sturkey, *Hattiesburg*; Luckett, *Joe T. Patterson*. For snippets of Mississippi's Jim Crow elite at this work, see Alexander, *The New Jim Crow*, chapter 1; Ruth Wilson Gilmore and Craig Gilmore, "Beyond Bratton," in Camp and Heatherton, eds., *Policing the Planet*.

7. For discourse on racial capitalism, see Robinson, *Black Marxism*; Hudson, "Racial Capitalism and the Dark Proletariat"; Burden-Stelly, "Modern U.S. Racial Capitalism"; Jenkins, "Ghosts of the Past"; Kelley, "Insecure." For the prerogatives of gender and sexual domination under Jim Crow's white male supremacy, see Gilmore, *Gender and Jim Crow*; Haley, *No Mercy Here*; Dailey, *White Fright*.

8. I build from the work of Egerton, *The Americanization of Dixie*; Carter, *The Politics of Rage*; Lassiter and Crespino, *The Myth of Southern Exceptionalism*; Cowie, *Freedom's Dominion*; Murakawa, *The First Civil Right*; Hinton, *From the War on Poverty*; Haley, *No Mercy Here*. For examinations of Jim Crow that stress its nationwide reach, see Muhammad, *The Condemnation of Blackness*; Purnell, *Fighting Jim Crow*; Purnell and Theoharis, eds., *The Strange Careers of the Jim Crow North*; Connolly, "The Strange Career of American Liberalism"; King, "Reckoning with Regionalism"; King, *The Politics of Safety*; Hill, *Strike the Hammer*.

9. Seigel, "Always Already Military"; Go, "Imperial Origins of American Policing."

10. Pliley, *Policing Sexuality*; Gage, *G-Man*.

11. My thinking here builds from Crespino's "strategic accommodation"; Weaver, "Frontlash"; and Whitlock and Heitzeg, *Carceral Con*.

12. The famous framing of the modern state as a "human community that (successfully) claims the monopoly of the legitimate use of physical force within a given territory" comes from Weber, "Politics as a Vocation."

13. Arsiniega and Guariglia, "Police as Supercitizens"; Schwartz, *Shielded*.

14. Laws of the State of Mississippi, 1954, 105–6; Laws of the State of Mississippi, 1980, 349, 310–12, 508–12, 63–64, 292–94; Vera Institute of Justice, "Incarceration Trends," https://trends.vera.org/state/MS. For nationwide histories of mass incarceration, see Thompson, "Why Mass Incarceration Matters"; Gilmore, *Golden Gulag*; Alexander, *The New Jim Crow*; Bardes, *The Carceral City*; Perkinson, *Texas Tough*; Chase, *We Are Not Slaves*; Newport, *This Is My Jail*; Pelot-Hobbs, *Prison Capital*.

15. MSP report, 1947–49, 25–26; Oshinsky, *Worse Than Slavery*; Key, *Southern Politics*. Writing of this value production in an earlier period of the incarceration of Black women in Georgia, Haley named "the ideological value of the continued relegation of black people to things and, inextricably, carceral value for southern racial capital through the use of such objects for labor." See Haley, *No Mercy Here*, 87.

16. Claudia Roth Pierpont, "A Raised Voice," *New Yorker*, August 3, 2014.

17. Muhammad, *The Condemnation of Blackness*; Felker-Kantor, *Policing Los Angeles*; Balto, *Occupied Territory*; Adler, *Murder in New Orleans*; Prince, *The Ballad of Robert Charles*; Baker, *To Poison a Nation*; Jett, *Race, Crime, and Policing in the Jim Crow South*; Murphy, *Jim Crow Capital*, chapter 3; Self, *American Babylon*; Gray Fischer, *The Streets Belong to Us*; Stewart-Winter, "Queer Law and Order"; Winston and BondGraham, *The Riders Come Out*; Brooks, *Gotham's War*; Guariglia, *Police and the Empire City*; King, *The Politics of Safety*; Williams, "For 'Peace, Quiet, and Respect.'"

18. Early Black scholars drew attention to rural African American life. See, for example, Woodson, *The Rural Negro*; Hurston, *Of Mules and Men*; Padmore, *Life and Struggles*. More recently, scholars have focused on contemporary rural Black life: Schultz, *The Rural Face of White Supremacy*; Hersey, *My Work Is That of Conservation*; de Jong, *A Different Day*; Daniel, *Dispossession*; Kahrl, *The Land Was Ours*; Berrey, *The Jim Crow Routine*; Reid and Bennett, *Beyond Forty Acres and a Mule*; Hosbey and Roane, "A Totally Different Form of Living"; Petty and Schultz, *Breaking New Ground*.

19. My formulation of policing's hinterland is informed by scholars of transnational rural and carceral history, those scholars who tell the histories of conquest and interrogate the construction of lacunae. See, for example, Trouillot, *Silencing the Past*; Khalili, *Time in the Shadows*; Nixon, *Slow Violence*; Paik, *Rightslessness*; De Leon, *Bundok*; Gilmore, "Forgotten Places and the Seeds of Grassroots Planning," in *Abolition Geography*.

20. "A Lecture," *Washington Bee*, October 22, 1892, 3; Martin Luther King Jr., "Hammer of Civil Rights," *The Nation*, March 9, 1964, 232–33; Brooks, *Fannie Lou Hamer*, 2.

21. Woods, *Development Arrested*; Eason, *Big House on the Prairie*; Prifogle, "Cows, Cars, and Criminals"; Stoll, *Ramp Hollow*; Catte, *What You Are Getting Wrong about Appalachia*; Kang-Brown and Subramanian, "Out of Sight"; Stein, "Why Coretta Scott King Fought for a Job Guarantee." Mississippi's expenditure on armed force to maintain social order while preaching retrenchment (as opposed to allocating tax revenue to promote collective well-being) aligns with what Ruth Wilson Gilmore has theorized as the bipartisan "antistate state." See Gilmore, "In the Shadow of the Shadow State," 43; Gilmore and Gilmore, "Restating the Obvious," 140–43.

22. General studies of the state police in America include Bechtel, *State Police in United States*; Ray, "From Cossack to Trooper"; Musgrave, "Bringing the State Police In." For the importance of roads and road disorder in American history, see Seiler, *Republic of Drivers*; Sorin, *Driving While Black*; Seo, *Policing the Open Road*.

23. Mayo, *Justice to All*; Vollmer and Parker, *Crime and the State Police*, chapter 4 and 140; Guariglia, "On August Vollmer's 1935 *Crime and State Police*"; Immerwahr,

How to Hide an Empire; Schrader, *Badges without Borders*; Go, "Imperial Origins of American Policing."

24. Burnham, *By Hands Now Known*.

25. Foucault, *Discipline and Punish*, 234; Berger, Kaba, and Stein, "What Abolitionists Do." My thinking also borrows from the Annales School's distinction between histories of the event, *événement*, and the *longue durée* as seen in Clyde Woods's and William Sturkey's application to Mississippi; Derrick Bell's "interest convergence" thesis, as previewed in Bell, "*Brown v. Board of Education*"; and Hulsether, *Capitalist Humanitarianism*.

26. Seigel, *Violence Work*; Neocleus, *The Fabrication of Social Order*; Singh, "The Whiteness of Police"; Gilmore, *Golden Gulag*; Mills, *The Racial Contract*; Spade, *Normal Life*, 7. For the interconnection of policing and the prison, see Felber, *Those Who Know*, 194n6; Foucault, *Discipline and Punish*, 282; Berger, *Captive Nation*.

27. Woodward, *Origins of the New South*, 328; Fields, "'Origins of the New South,'" 815.

28. Recent studies of the American sheriff abound. See Hahamovitch, "The 'Profane Margins' of the State"; Hale, *In the Pines*; Pishko, *Highest Law*.

29. For studies of New South liberalism, see Dailey, *Before Jim Crow*; O'Brien, "C. Vann Woodward and the Burden"; O'Brien, *The Idea of the American South*; Dabney, *Liberalism in the South*; Henry Steele Commager, "Why Call It Liberalism?" *New Republic*, April 5, 1933, 221–22; Woodward, *Origins of the New South*, 74, 163–64.

30. Hahn, *Illiberal America*; Cowie, "Defend Liberalism?" Julian Go has demanded and given more concrete histories of the empire's afterlives, with necessary historical contingency. See Go, "Reverberations of Empire"; Go, *Policing Empires*. For studies of law-and-order liberalism of the postwar era, see Flamm, *Law and Order*; Murakawa, *The First Civil Right*; Hinton, *From the War on Poverty*; Forman, *Locking Up Our Own*. For the classic analysis of right-wing and liberal convergence into a single "party of Order" when confronted with revolt, see Marx, "The Eighteenth Brumaire," sec. 1. For the application to America's prison regime, see Jackson, *Blood in My Eye*, 118; Davis, "Political Prisoners, Prisons and Black Liberation." Alberto Toscano analyzes the critique of prison authoritarianism made by George Jackson and Angela Davis to write that American "racial fascism" is more "a process of seepage . . . [into] actually existing liberalism" than "an unwanted return from the other place of colonial violence." See Toscano, "The Long Shadow of Racial Fascism"; Toscano, *Late Fascism*, 41.

31. Murakawa, *The First Civil Right*, 18.

32. Wilson, proclamation, July 26, 1918, quoted in Martinez, *Injustice Never Leaves You*, 172.

33. Woodward, *Origins of the New South*, chapter 12; Crespino, "Mississippi as Metaphor." In 1964, James Silver wrote that "the time is fast running out when the country will longer tolerate this enclave of feudalism within the United States." See "Mississippi Must Choose," *New York Times Magazine*, July 19, 1964, 8. Louis Hartz described Old South ideology as a liberal tradition of slavery, where some thinkers claimed timeless, conservative roots in order to hide self-interested advocacy toward property-in-man. See Hartz, *The Liberal Tradition in America*, chapter 6.

34. Seigel, "Always Already Military"; Singh, *Race and America's Long War*; Mann, *The Dark Side of Democracy*, chapter 4; Schrader, *Badges without Borders*; Kuzmarov, *Modernizing Repression*; McCoy, *Policing America's Empire*; Edgerton, *American Datu*; Hernández, *Migra!*; Martinez, *Injustice Never Leaves You*; Hernández, *City of Inmates*, chapter 1.

35. Seigel, "On the Critique of Paramilitarism," 171; Dunbar-Ortiz, *An Indigenous Peoples' History*, chapters 4 and 5; Richter, *Facing East from Indian Country*; Grenier, *The First Way of War*; Miles, *Ties That Bind*; Saunt, *Black, White, and Indian*; Yarbrough, *Choctaw Confederates*; Dimock, *Empire for Liberty*, 8–10, 24; Gilmore, "Race, Prisons, and War," 78.

36. We might call agents of police reform like Featherston and Birdsong "imperial importers." See Go, *Policing Empires*, 24.

37. W. E. B. Du Bois, "A Hymn to the Peoples," in *Darkwater*, chapter 10; Kaplan, *The Anarchy of Empire*; Derrida, *Archive Fever*, 79. Jacques Derrida theorizes "the anarchive" as the opposite of the archive, a place for forgetting. Historians of colonialism, like Elizabeth Kolsky, refer to a "legal regime of exception" in British India, after the philosopher Giorgio Agamben's analysis of the "state of exception." See Kolsky, "The Colonial Rule of Law," 1223n24; Dalrymple, *The Anarchy*; Stoler, *Duress*; Dubber, *The Police Power*, chapter 5; Woodruff, *American Congo*; Singh, "The Whiteness of Police," 1096. See also Marx, *Capital*, part 8, on primitive accumulation; Melamed, "Racial Capitalism," 76, 80–82; Harvey, *The New Imperialism*, chapter 4.

38. Biennial Report of the Adjutant General of the State of Mississippi, 1896, 6.

39. Address of Paul B. Johnson, Organizational Meeting—State Crime Commission, September 7, 1967, PBJ, Box 100, Folder 18.

40. Bob Howie, "Must Be Stopped," *JDN*, May 19, 1970; Hinton, *America on Fire*.

41. Here, I am indebted to Luther Adams—Free Man of Color and Chandan Reddy for their interpretation of the lawlessness inherent to Mississippi's law enforcement. See Adams, "Police Brutality," in Umoja, Stanford, and Young, *Black Power Encyclopedia*; Byrd et al., "Predatory Value."

42. *Mississippi Black Paper*, 19.

43. Walter Johnson has written about the construction of an antebellum "carceral countryside," designed to keep captive Black labor, as well as St. Louis's history of "Black removal—the serial destruction of Black neighborhoods and the transfer of their population according to the reigning model of profit and policing at any given moment." See Johnson, *River of Dark Dreams*, chapter 8; and *Broken Heart of America*, 2. For Black Southern land loss, see Daniel, *Breaking the Land*, chapter 8; Woods, *Development Arrested*, chapter 6; Daniel, *Dispossession*; Kahrl, *The Land Was Ours*; Wexler, *Fire in a Canebreak*; Vann R. Newkirk II, "The Great Land Robbery," *The Atlantic*, September 2019; Kahrl, "From Commons to Capital"; Horowitz, *Katrina*; Dawson, "Hidden in Plain Sight," 144–46; Fraser, "Expropriation and Exploitation in Racialized Capitalism," 166–69; Kahrl, *The Black Tax*.

44. 1890 Census of Agriculture, 43; 1982 Census of Agriculture—State Data, Mississippi, table 1, 1. I calculated total pasturage by combining acres listed as "cropland used only for pasture or grazing," "woodland pasture," and "pastureland and rangeland."

45. Dave Merrill and Lauren Leatherby, "Here's How America Uses Its Land," *Bloomberg*, July 31, 2018; Specht, *Red Meat Republic*.

46. Umoja, *We Will Shoot Back*. For examples outside of Mississippi, see Williams, *Negroes with Guns*; Carmichael and Hamilton, *Black Power*, 46; Jeffries, *Bloody Lowndes*, chapter 3. Carmichael and Hamilton wrote, "Black Power means, for example, that in Lowndes County, Alabama, a black sheriff can end police brutality."

47. Hall et al., *Policing the Crisis*; Camp and Heatherton, *Policing the Planet*.

Chapter 1

1. Winfield Scott Featherston, "But Much Yet Remains to Be Done," handwritten manuscript, ca. 1877, 10, Folder 16, Box 7, Featherston Collection (Archives and Special Collections, J. D. Williams Library, University of Mississippi, Oxford, MS; hereinafter cited as Featherston Collection).

2. Featherston, "But Much Yet Remains," 1–2.

3. Foner, *Reconstruction*, 560–62.

4. Featherston, "But Much Yet Remains," 8, 10, 11.

5. Wells, *Crusade for Justice*, 14.

6. Giddings, *Ida*; Bay, *To Tell the Truth*; Bailey and Tolnay, *Lynched*; Finnegan, *A Deed So Accursed*, 28, table 1.

7. Ida B. Wells, "Southern Horrors," in Royster, ed., *Southern Horrors and Other Writings*, 68.

8. Carole Emberton, "Black Militias," in Finkelman, ed., *Encyclopedia of African American History*, vol. 1, 167–68; Emberton, *Beyond Redemption*; Saville, *The Work of Reconstruction*, 143–51, 177–87.

9. Wells, "Southern Horrors," 70; Ida B. Wells, "A Red Record," in Royster, ed., *Southern Horrors and Other Writings*, 154.

10. Wells-Barnett, *The History of the East St. Louis, Illinois, Riot*, 22.

11. Winfield Scott Featherston, in Historical Data Systems, comp., *American Civil War General Officers* (an Ancestry.com database).

12. Winfield Scott Featherston, biographical sketch, 2, Folder 2, Box 7, Featherston Collection; Ellisor, *The Second Creek War*.

13. 1860 Census, Slave Schedule, Marshall County, Holly Springs, MS, 7.

14. "Appointment of Commissioners," *Semi-Weekly Mississippian*, December 14, 1860, 2; Dew, *Apostles of Disunion*, chapter 2.

15. Dunbar-Ortiz, *An Indigenous Peoples' History*, chapters 4 and 5; Richter, *Facing East from Indian Country*; Grenier, *The First Way of War*; Dimock, *Empire for Liberty*, 8–10, 24.

16. "A law in aid of, and in addition to the regulations of the Governor, for the permanent establishment of the Militia of the Mississippi Territory," subject file: Militia, MDAH.

17. Garrison, *The Legal Ideology of Removal*; Saunt, "Financing Dispossession," 315–37; Dinwoodie, "Evading Indian Removal," 17–41.

18. Johnson, *Soul by Soul*, chapter 1; Harris, "Whiteness as Property," 1707–18; Rothman, *Slave Country*.

19. "An Act, to reduce into one, the several acts concerning Patrols," in *Laws of the State of Mississippi*, 1822, 202; Johnson, *River of Dark Dreams*, chapter 8.

20. Browne, *Dark Matters*; Seigel, *Violence Work*; Rousey, *Policing the Southern City*; Hadden, *Slave Patrols*.

21. *Laws of the State of Mississippi*, 1877, 104, 99; *Laws of the State of Mississippi*, 1880, 635. "Invincibles" was likely a corruption of *Fencibles*, a British name for colonial militias.

22. *Laws of the State of Mississippi*, 1876, 22.

23. *Laws of the State of Mississippi*, 1888, 57; Biennial Report of the Adjutant General of the State of Mississippi, 1890, 1, 6; Biennial Report of the Adjutant General, 1892, 8.

24. Biennial Report of the Adjutant General, 1890, 6.

25. Biennial Report of the Adjutant General, 1892, 4.

26. S. S. Calhoon, quoted in McMillen, *Dark Journey*, 41.

27. Foner, *Reconstruction*, 558–63.

28. Woodward, "Yes, There Was a Compromise," 215–23.

29. Featherston, "Grand Jurors at Oct Term 1881: Marshall County Circuit Court," 1881, Folder 9, Box 9, Featherston Collection.

30. Taylor, *Brokered Justice*, 62–63.

31. Featherston, "Notes for Canvass of 1881," 1881, Folder 17, Box 7, Featherston Collection.

32. Woodward, *The Strange Career of Jim Crow*; Gilmore, *Gender and Jim Crow*; Dailey, *Before Jim Crow*.

33. Taylor, *Brokered Justice*, 62–63; McMillen, *Dark Journey*, 60, 65.

34. *Journal of the Proceedings of the Constitutional Convention of the State of Mississippi* (Jackson, MS: E. L. Martin, 1890), 85.

35. *Proceedings of the Constitutional Convention*, 170.

36. *Proceedings of the Constitutional Convention*, 108.

37. *Proceedings of the Constitutional Convention*, 94. I quote at length because the first independent clause often appears without context. The Prohibition Convention was a separate body that submitted "A Memorial to the Constitutional Convention" through William Thompson Martin, a delegate and railroad president from Adams County.

38. Muhammad, *The Condemnation of Blackness*; McGirr, *The War on Alcohol*.

39. *Proceedings of the Constitutional Convention*, 124, 671.

40. *Proceedings of the Constitutional Convention*, 124.

41. Mancini, *One Dies, Get Another*, chapter 7 and 140–42; Oshinsky, *"Worse Than Slavery,"* 52–53; Haley, *No Mercy Here*; Curtin, *Black Prisoners*.

42. *Proceedings of the Constitutional Convention*, 126.

43. For the twentieth-century recognition of police forces as occupying armies in Black communities, see Balto, *Occupied Territory*, 7–8, 193.

44. Featherston, "Notes on Situation for a Speech," n.d., Folder 5, Box 7, Featherston Collection.

45. Holmes, "The Leflore County Massacre"; Biennial Report of the Adjutant General, 1890, 10.

46. "The Recent Trouble in Leflore County," *Tallahatchie News*, September 5, 1889, 3; Holmes, "The Leflore County Massacre," 267–75; Hahn, *A Nation under Our Feet*, 422–23.

47. Biennial Report of the Adjutant General, 1894, 4.

48. Biennial Report of the Adjutant General, 1894, 10–11. In December 1893, Governor John Marshall Stone pardoned seven white men convicted of whitecapping. See "Valued Christmas Presents," *Weekly C-L*, December 28, 1893, 5; Holmes, "Whitecapping," 165–85.

49. Biennial Report of the Adjutant General, 1894, 8–9.

50. Biennial Report of the Adjutant General, 1892, 7.

51. "The National Guard Bill Passed, etc.," *Vicksburg Evening Post*, March 9, 1892, 1; Biennial Report of the Adjutant General, 1896, 45, 50.

52. Coski, *The Confederate Battle Flag*, 80–82; Cowie, *Freedom's Dominion*, chapter 12; Cox, *No Common Ground*, chapter 1.

53. Johnson, *River of Dark Dreams*, 366–72, 305–8.

54. Unlike the 1894 state flag, the coat of arms survives today. Eric Clark, "The Government of Mississippi: How It Functions," *Mississippi History Now*, http://mshistorynow.mdah.state.ms.us/articles/276/government-of-mississippi-how-it-functions.

55. "Birdsong Guilty," *Natchez Democrat*, December 16, 1908, 4.

56. "A Woman Used a Pistol with Fatal Effect," *Jackson Evening News*, November 25, 1905, 1.

57. "On Witness Stand," *Vicksburg Herald*, December 9, 1906, 1.

58. Smith, *History of the Georgia Militia*, vol. 2, 216, 218; 1850 US Federal Census, District 800, Troup County, GA, James Birdsong, 104a; 1850 US Federal Census, Slave Schedules, District 800, Troup County, GA, Jas Birdsong, 895; War of 1812 Pension Application Files Index, 1812–1815, roll 8, James Birdsong; Compiled Service Records of Confederate Soldiers, Co. F, 46th Ga. Infantry, Lafayette Felix Birdsong.

59. Mississippi, US, Compiled Marriage Index, 1776–1935, Ancestry.com; 1900 Census, Beat 1, Lawrence County, Mississippi; Page 1, Enumeration District 0065, FHL microfilm 1240815. The circumstances around this marriage, one to which Angie Fox could not consent, remain obscure.

60. "Mrs. Birdsong Found Guilty Manslaughter," *Daily C-L*, December 12, 1906, 1; "The Pardon of Mrs. Birdsong," *Vicksburg Evening Post*, July 22, 1907, 7.

61. "An Accessory under Arrest," *JDN*, December 11, 1908, 1.

62. "Gov. Stone, as Commander-in-Chief . . . ," *Daily C-L*, May 16, 1893, 2.

63. "Birdsong, Thomas B., Sr.," Co. E, First Mississippi Infantry, Organization Index to Pension Files of Veterans Who Served between 1861 and 1900, RG 15, Identifier: 2588825, NARA. No one from Mississippi's four volunteer infantry regiments fought in Cuba or the Philippines. Only regular Army soldiers from Mississippi, including Black regulars, fought. See David R. Murray, "Black Regular Troops in the Spanish-Cuban/American War," in Beede, ed., *The War of 1898*, 54.

64. "A Delightful Social Event," *Daily C-L*, May 24, 1892, 4; "The Glorious Fourth," *Daily C-L*, July 12, 1894, 3; "Jeff Davis Volunteers," *Daily C-L*, August 4, 1896, 6.

65. "Dr. Birdsong Gets Life Term," *Hattiesburg Daily News*, December 15, 1908.

66. "Birdsong Begins Term on Rankin County Farm," *Hattiesburg Daily News*, December 18, 1908, 1; "Birdsong Pardoned for Meritorious Service," *Natchez News-Democrat*, August 19, 1915, 2.

67. I grant that knowing one's date of birth is a modern notion in American life that dates to the Progressive Era. However, Birdsong's memory of his date of birth was incredibly inconsistent. He alternated between 1892 and 1894 on official paperwork until the US Army brought this discrepancy to his attention in 1940. He also later remembered leaving home at sixteen—not eighteen, the legal age to join the militia. See Birdsong's Official Military Personnel File, obtained from the National Archives and Records Administration's National Personnel Records Center (hereafter OMPF).

68. Biographical material comes from OMPF.

69. Harris and Sadler, *The Great Call-Up*, 108–9.

70. W. G. Landers to whom it may concern, letter of recommendation, May 3, 1917, OMPF.

71. Johnson, *Revolution in Texas*, 91–92; Martinez, *Injustice Never Leaves You*, 87–88.

72. Jennings, *A Texas Ranger*, 71.

73. Carrigan and Webb, *Forgotten Dead*.

74. Grandin, *The End of the Myth*, 157–58, 283; Webb, *The Texas Rangers*; Swanson, *Cult of Glory*, 2; Paredes, *With His Pistol in His Hand*, 20, 26; Martinez, *Injustice Never Leaves You*, 25.

75. "Colquitt Put Direct Query to President," *Houston Post*, February 28, 1914, 1.

76. "Polk, Texas Highway Patrol, Trooper Hendricks, Captain A. S. Windham, Colonel T. B. Birdsong, Chief Elliott, and Inspector Conner, September 9, 1952," Folder P-248, Box PPO543, Texas Department of Public Safety photographs, Archives and Information Services Division, Texas State Library and Archives Commission.

77. Martinez, *Injustice Never Leaves You*, 130–34.

78. "Infantry Awaits Bandit Attack on Indio Ranch," *Fort Worth Star-Telegram*, December 29, 1917, 2; W. L. Wright to James A. Harley, November 14, 1917, Texas State Library and Archives, RG 401, box 1183, folder 14.

79. Wright to Harley, December 28, 1917.

80. Monica Muñoz Martinez, "Porvenir Massacre," *Handbook of Texas Online*, Texas State Historical Association.

81. Martinez, *Injustice Never Leaves You*, 174, 184–95; "Proceedings of the Joint Committee of the Senate and the House in the Investigation of the Texas State Ranger Force," transcript, 1919, Texas State Library, Online Collections.

82. "Birdsong Portrait Unveiled at MHP," *Daily C-L*, April 30, 1968, 6.

Chapter 2

1. Glen Norse, "Co-Eds Laugh, Men Sing, Drink, as Mississippi Stages Lynch Holiday," *Pittsburgh Courier*, March 24, 1934, 6. "Glen Norse" may be a pseudonym. I have found no other evidence of the writer despite his description as a "Pittsburgh Courier Staff Correspondent."

2. Norse, "Co-Eds Laugh"; "DeSoto Ready for Execution," *Greenwood Commonwealth*, March 14, 1934, 1; "Negroes Pay Penalty for Brutal Crime," *Greenwood Commonwealth*, March 16, 1934; McMillen, *Dark Journey*, 206–8; Oshinsky, *Worse Than Slavery*, 210–13.

3. Norse, "Co-Eds Laugh"; Kenneth Toler, "Guardsmen Ordered to Hanging of Trio," *Commercial Appeal*, March 13, 1934, 3.

4. Norse, "Co-Eds Laugh"; Wood, *Lynching and Spectacle*, chapter 4.

5. See also Kerry James Marshall, "Heirlooms and Accessories," Studio Museum in Harlem, www.studiomuseum.org/artworks/heirlooms-accessories, which redirects the observer to white attendance of a spectacle lynching in Marion, Indiana, in 1930. I search for an unsensational treatment of lynching and capital punishment. See Hartman, *Scenes of Subjection* and Sharpe, *Monstrous Intimacies*, on reproduction of Black subjection.

6. Finnegan, *A Deed So Accursed*, 4–5.

7. Rushdy estimates that white Americans lynched, on average, one Black person every five days for fifty years, from 1880 to 1930. See Rushdy, *American Lynching*, ix. For the latest literature on lynching, anti-lynching activism, and Jim Crow efforts to reform the practice, see Brundage, *Lynching in the New South*; Hill, *Men, Mobs, and Law*, chapter 3; Goldsby, *A Spectacular Secret*; Johnson, *Reforming Jim Crow*, chapter 2; Smith, *Managing White Supremacy*; Kato, *Liberalizing Lynching*.

8. Finnegan, *A Deed So Accursed*, 4–5; Jan Hillegas, Preliminary List of Mississippi Legal Executions (revised), MDAH.

9. "In Brandon Jail," *Daily Commercial Herald*, April 5, 1890, 1; "Lynching Prevented," *Daily Commercial Herald*, April 30, 1890, 1; "Thomas Hung," *C-L*, May 28, 1890, 1; "Anthony Thomas, the Murderer . . . ," *Vicksburg Evening Post*, June 6, 1890, 4. McLaurin was the great-grandfather of twentieth-century comedian Robin Williams.

10. "Statewide Search Misses Murderer," *C-L*, June 4, 1927, 1; "North Greatly Impressed by Mississippi Booster Train," *C-L*, August 30, 1925, 8.

11. "Tall Yellow Negro Drove Auto to Spot Where It Was Found," *C-L*, June 5, 1927, 1, 10; "Negro Sent to Montgomery under Guard," *Sun Herald*, June 6, 1927, 1, 5; "Quick Trial Given Confessed Black Slayer," *C-L*, June 22, 1927, 1, 8; "Company L to Jackson Sunday," *Semi-Weekly Journal*, June 22, 1927, 5; "Burley Pays with His Life," *Sun Herald*, July 22, 1927, 1.

12. "Good Business Is Good Politics," *Semi-Weekly Journal*, June 25, 1927, 3; "Mob Law Condemned by Exchange Club," *C-L*, June 15, 1927, 8; "American Legion Is Strongly Endorsing All Official Action," *C-L*, June 10, 1927, 9; "Final Appropriations Made for Biloxi Encampment," *Sun Herald*, June 24, 1927, 1; Simpson County Murphree Campaign Committee, "An Attempt to Crucify a Faithful Official on a Cross of Duty," *Simpson County News*, August 18, 1927, 5. For more on Bilbo's political career, see Morgan, *Redneck Liberal*, chapters 1 and 2.

13. "Two Accused Hub Slayers in Hinds," *C-L*, December 17, 1931, 8; Cortner, *The Scottsboro Case in Mississippi*, 70.

14. "Two Dozen Prentiss Farmers Jailed in Hunt for Murderers," *C-L*, May 18, 1931, 1; "Slain Officer Buried Today," *Greenwood Commonwealth*, May 18, 1931, 1;

"Eatons Spend Quiet Sunday," *C-L*, June 15, 1931, 1, 7; Theodore G. Bilbo, executive order, June 11, 1931, Box 265, Birdsong Collection, Mississippi Armed Forces Museums.

15. Daniel, *Breaking the Land*, 19–20; Martha H. Swain and Roger D. Tate Jr., "Great Depression," *Mississippi Encyclopedia*, https://mississippiencyclopedia.org/entries/great-depression/.

16. Memo from Birdsong and George C. Ray to Adjutant General, subj. Report on Chemical Warfare Equipment, February 25, 1933, 1, Box 265, Birdsong Collection; "Arrest 5 in Strike Outbreak Here," *Daily Tribune*, November 10, 1933, 1; "Madison Cops Receive 'Timely' Gas Lesson," *Capital Times*, November 8, 1933, 6; "Demonstrate Gas," *Sandusky* (Ohio) *Register*, April 28, 1933, 14.

17. Memo from Birdsong to Thomas J. Grayson, subj. Riot Duty, January 9, 1934, 1, Box 265, Birdsong Collection.

18. "Troops Guard Hernando Courthouse," *Blytheville Courier News*, February 12, 1934, 1; "Trio of Negroes Are Hanged for Assault on Girl," *Decatur Daily*, March 16, 1934. The incident, but not the role of Birdsong, is recorded by McMillen, *Dark Journey*, 206–8; and Oshinsky, *Worse Than Slavery*, 210–13.

19. Carter, *Scottsboro*, 59.

20. Cortner, *The Scottsboro Case in Mississippi*, chapter 1.

21. Virgil Alexis Griffith, dissent, *Brown v. Mississippi*, n.d., 1–3, 6–7, Supreme Court Case File no. 31375, MDAH.

22. Griffith, dissent, *Brown v. Mississippi*, 7. Monica Martinez documents a similar rebuke of lynching as bad diplomatic relations in the 1910 case of Antonio Rodríguez, a Mexican national, murdered in Rocksprings, Texas; see Martinez, *Injustice Never Leaves You*, 42.

23. Testimony of Irena Brown, Mary Shields, and Kate Ellington, trial transcript, March 1934, *Mississippi v. Ed Brown et al.*, 91–102, Supreme Court Case File no. 31375, MDAH; 1930 Census, Beat 1, Kemper County, Mississippi, 5A, Enumeration District 0004, FHL microfilm 2340887.

24. "Escapes Noose: Near Death from Torture," *The Crisis*, April 1935, 119; "Take Torture Case Before US High Court," *Chicago Defender*, November 2, 1935, 2; "Full Text of Mississippi Torture Case Involving Brown, Shields, Ellington," *Chicago Defender*, February 29, 1936, 3; "Mississippi Trio Takes Jail, Fear Trial," *Chicago Defender*, December 19, 1936, 10.

25. For examples of international and internationalist coverage in English, see "Negroes Reprieved," *The Guardian*, February 18, 1936, 5; "Death Sentences Set Aside," *Daily Herald*, February 18, 1936, 11.

26. "Governor Hugh White's Message to Legislature," *Greenwood Commonwealth*, January 21, 1936, 2; "White Program Is Now Ready," *Greenwood Commonwealth*, August 19, 1936, 1; "Industrial Bill Sent to White's Desk," *Enterprise-Journal*, September 18, 1936, 1; "First Application in New Program," *Sun Herald*, December 3, 1936, 1; "Coast Residents Okay Wool Mill," *C-L*, February 14, 1937, 4; Jack Dale, "State Gaining in Industrial Way," *Sun Herald*, October 13, 1937, 1; "Industrial Act Valid Supreme Court Rules," *Greenwood Commonwealth*, February 7, 1938, 1; Cobb, *Selling the South*, chapter 1.

27. Hugh White, *Address of Governor Hugh L. White before the Annual Convention of the Mississippi Press Association* . . . , June 12, 1936, 6, quoted in Cobb, *Selling the South*, 12; Kelley, *Hammer and Hoe*; Ferguson, *Remaking the Rural South*.

28. "Governor to Make Prison Inspection," *Sun Herald*, May 5, 1936, 1.

29. Biennial Report of the Adjutant General of the State of Mississippi, 1936–37, 6.

30. "Quiet Reigns at Parchman after Revolt," *Greenwood Commonwealth*, May 6, 1936, 1.

31. Road Map of Mississippi, September 1936; Road Map of Mississippi, January 1, 1940; in Department of Transportation, State Highway Archive, https://mdot.ms.gov/portal/maps.

32. "Brown Pays Fine in 'J.P.' Court," *C-L*, January 12, 1936, 17; "Confiscated Liquor Fed to the Little Fishes," *C-L*, January 5, 1936, 2.

33. "Rankin Officers Enter New Posts," *C-L*, January 9, 1936, 3; Mrs. Billie O. Stamps-Fuller, Jimmie R. Lindsey, and Davis R. Lindsey, interview by Robert Luckett, November 16, 2009, video, Oral History Division, Margaret Walker Center, Jackson State University; Vogel, *The Scene of Harlem Cabaret*.

34. Stamps-Fuller interview.

35. "Birdsong Heads White's State Vice Squad," *Hattiesburg American*, January 13, 1937.

36. Mississippi Highway Safety Patrol: 2003 Yearbook (Paducah, KY: Turner Publishing, 2003), 16–20; Report of the Adjutant General of the State of Mississippi, 1936–37, 6.

37. Scott Barretta and Jim O'Neal, "Gold Coast—Jackson," Mississippi Blues Trail historical marker, http://msbluestrail.org/blues-trail-markers/gold-coast; Tracy, *Mississippi Moonshine Politics*, chapter 9. For the case of Alabama's most infamous vice district and the active decriminalization of whiteness, see Tammy Ingram, "The South's Sin City: White Crime and the Limits of Law and Order in Phenix City, Alabama," in Wood and Ring, eds., *Crime and Punishment in the Jim Crow South*.

38. Hugh White, address to Joint Session of Mississippi State Legislature, January 1938, quoted in J. L. Warren, House Concurrent Resolution 85, "Commending and Congratulating the Mississippi Highway Patrol as It Celebrates Its 70-Year Anniversary," Regular Session 2008, http://billstatus.ls.state.ms.us/documents/2008/pdf/HC/HC0085SG.pdf.

39. *Laws of the State of Mississippi, Passed at a Regular Session of the Mississippi Legislature Held in the City of Jackson, Commencing Tuesday, January 4, 1938, and Ending Wednesday, April 13, 1938*, chapter 143, Senate Bill 161, The Highway Safety Patrol and Driver's License Act of 1938, 214–29.

40. Mississippi Highway Safety Patrol, Biennial Report, 1938/39, Government Documents Collection, State of Mississippi Documents, J. D. Williams Library, University of Mississippi; "94 Train for 53 Road Patrol Jobs," *Hattiesburg American*, May 16, 1938.

41. "State's Highway Patrol Makes Debut Here Today," *C-L*, June 17, 1938, 1–2. For comparison, see descriptions of the annual Nazi *Reichsparteitag*, commonly referred to as the Nuremberg Rally: Sinclair, "The Nazi Party Rally."

42. "Road Patrol Commissions Given Today," *Daily Herald*, June 17, 1938; "City, County Review of 1938," *Hattiesburg American*, December 31, 1938.

43. "Louisiana Truck Drivers Protest Mississippi Fines," *Daily Herald*, September 6, 1939.

44. Patrolmen activities from this earlier period survive in justice of the peace dockets. See, for example, J.P. Docket, Criminal and Civil, Oktibbeha County, R. L. Whitmire, May 13, 1930, to 1945, Oktibbeha County Justice Court, Starkville, MS; or J.P. Docket, Criminal Cases, District 5, Noxubee County, March 1957 to 1959, Office of the Chancery Clerk, Macon, MS.

45. MHSP, Biennial Reports, 1938/39 through 1943/45.

46. H. Rey Bonney, "Dangerous Policing Powers Asked for Mississippi Highway Patrol," *McComb Daily Journal*, September 30, 1941, 2.

47. Arrest statistics compiled from MHSP, Biennial Report, 1939/41, 1941/43, and 1943/45. Birdsong strenuously avoided the term "state police," emphasizing "safety patrol" into the 1960s, as in the aftermath of the University of Mississippi riot in the fall of 1962. See *Oxford, USA*, MDAH.

48. "Governor Hugh White's Message to Legislature," *Greenwood Commonwealth*, January 21, 1936, 2.

Chapter 3

1. "Preston N.A.A.C.P. Branch Hail Presidents Annual Address," *Jackson Advocate*, January 10, 1948, 1.

2. Sullivan, *Lift Every Voice*; Anderson, *Bourgeois Radicals*; O'Brien, *The Color of the Law*; Dittmer, *Local People*, chapter 1; Evers-Williams and Marable, *The Autobiography of Medgar Evers*, 81–82, 88, 206–7; Daniel, *Breaking the Land*, chapter 8.

3. This contention, that the overlapping hierarchies of race and gender demanded additional advocacy and organizing work from Black women, draws from Sarah Haley's conception of the "racial-gendered order" at the heart of Jim Crow. See *No Mercy Here*, 3; Gilmore, "'You Have Dislodged a Boulder,'" 27.

4. Ruby Hurley to Medgar Evers, March 9, 1955, series 2, Box 2, Folder 18, Medgar Evers Papers, MDAH.

5. "Black Sheriff Feels No Pressure," *Clarksdale Press Register*, May 24, 1979, 10.

6. For the case of Sheriff Willis V. McCall in Lake County, Florida, see King, *Devil in the Grove*, chapter 6, 340.

7. Tammy Ingram, "The South's Sin City: White Crime and the Limits of Law and Order in Phenix City, Alabama," in Wood and Ring, eds., *Crime and Punishment*, chapter 4.

8. 1910 Census: Beat 3, Kemper, Mississippi; Roll: T624_740; Page: 18B; Enumeration District: 0030; FHL microfilm: 1374753; 1940 Census: Moscow, Kemper, Mississippi; Roll: m-t0627–02037; Page: 9A; Enumeration District: 35-11.

9. Leroy E. Carter, "Report of Investigation: Shooting of Matt McWilliams by Sheriff," ca. March 28, 1948, Papers of the NAACP, Part 8: Discrimination in the

Criminal Justice System, 1910–1955, Series B: Legal Department and Central Office Records, 1940–1955, Police brutality general files, M, NAACP/PQ).

10. 1900 Census: Moscow, Kemper, Mississippi; Page: 6; Enumeration District: 0005; FHL microfilm: 1240813; "Harbour-White Announcement," *JDN*, May 1, 1921, 1; "Negro Held on Serious Charge," *C-L*, May 8, 1930, 8.

11. Carter, "Report of Investigation"; "W. E. Belcher, Sr. Dies Following Heart Attack," *Centreville Press*, July 19, 1945, 1.

12. Carter, "Report of Investigation."

13. Rev. Roosevelt Clark, interview by Faye Washington and author, April 26, 2023; 1940 Census, Place: Moscow, Kemper, Mississippi; Roll: m-t0627–02037; Page: 9A; Enumeration District: 35-11.

14. Margaret A. Burnham's Civil Rights and Restorative Justice Project (CRRJ) at Northeastern University's School of Law found McWilliams's death certificate and a single newspaper article ("Clear Sheriff in JP Court," *Kemper County Messenger*, January 9, 1947) that documents Harbour's acquittal at the hands of L. L. Shumate. This evidence has been used by Newton, *Unsolved Civil Rights Murder Cases*. I draw my narrative primarily from the NAACP investigation, which independently recorded the paperwork Nettie McWilliams passed along before her death. Assistant Field Secretary LeRoy E. Carter reported after viewing the family's financial records that Harbour, L. L. Shumate, and his son, John Lloyd Shumate, had bought the tax lien from the Steel City Lumber Company. 1940 Census, De Kalb, Kemper, Mississippi, Roll: T627_2037; Page: 3A, Enumeration District: 35-15; 1930 Census, De Kalb, Kemper, Mississippi; Roll: 1152; Page: 9B; Enumeration District: 0014; Image: 390.0; FHL microfilm: 2340887.

15. Carter, "Report of Investigation"; Leroy Carter to Robert L. Carter, March 26, 1947; Edward Knott Jr. to Leroy Carter, March 11, 1947, Police brutality general files, M, NAACP/PQ.

16. Application for charter, Bluff Springs, MS, June 7, 1947, Box II:C242, Folder 7, NAACP/LOC.

17. 1900 Census, Beat 5, Winston, Mississippi; Page: 5; Enumeration District: 0103; FHL microfilm: 1240834; 1900 Census, Kellis Store, Kemper, Mississippi; Page: 4; Enumeration District: 0007; FHL microfilm: 1240813; 1940 Census, Kellis Store, Kemper, Mississippi; Roll: m-t0627–02037; Page: 2A; Enumeration District: 35-12.

18. Buford Johnson to Gloster Current, January 16, 1928; Johnson to Daisy Lampkin, ca. April 29, 1948, Box II:C96, Folder 18, NAACP/LOC.

19. Johnson to Current, January 15, 1951, Box II:C96, Folder 18, NAACP/LOC.

20. Johnson to Lampkin, ca., April 29, 1948, Box II:C96, Folder 18, NAACP/LOC. Amos 8:4–7 is an exposition on unjust practices by merchants "dealing falsely with balances of deceit" (ASV) or "falsifying the balances by deceit" (KJV). Proverbs 11:1 and 20:23 also deal with the justice of weights and scales. The Johnson and McWilliams families maintain stories about Arnold Harbour in family memory: Elvira Johnson, Lindy Johnson, and Carmel Baldwin, interview by author, July 20, 2021; Faye Washington, interview by author, April 26, 2023.

21. Warranty Deed, Arnold Harbour to L. L. Wilkerson, Deed Record, Book Y, 593, Office of the Kemper County Chancery Clerk, DeKalb, MS; "Merchant Lost on

Hunt Found Safe," *C-L*, December 28, 1962, 12; "Frederick Dale Harbour," obituary, *Meridian Star*, February 22, 2011.

22. "Memorial tributes delivered in Congress to John C. Stennis," in Senate Documents: Nos. 11–12, US Congressional Serial Set, Serial Number 14283, 104th Congress, First Session (Washington, DC: Government Printing Office, 1997), 46, 69, 121–22.

23. This narrative is a composite of legal and epistolary sources that prioritizes the arc of the story relayed by Miller's family. See Papers of the NAACP, Part 08: Discrimination in the Criminal Justice System, 1910–1955, Series B: Legal Department and Central Office Records, 1940–1955, *Miller v. Wiggins* rape case, correspondence, and *Miller v. Wiggins* rape case, legal papers, NAACP/PQ.

24. Gravely, *They Stole Him Out of Jail*.

25. Lonnie J. Broadway, *Leroy Miller v. Marvin Wiggins, Supt., etc.*, Brief and Argument on Behalf of Appellant, Supreme Court of Mississippi, May 31, 1949, Wiggins rape case, legal papers, NAACP/PQ.

26. Though not all propelled by police violence, the civil rights literature abounds with the leadership of everyday women. See Pigee, *The Struggle of Struggles*; Hamlin, *Crossroads at Clarksdale*; Ransby, *Ella Baker*; McGuire, *At the Dark End*; Payne, *I've Got the Light*, chapter 3; Charron, *Freedom's Teacher*.

27. Anonymous to Arthur B. Spingarn, ca. March 17, 1947; E. F. Brown to Lucille Black, March 10, 1947; "Amory Negro Held for Grand Jury Action," clipping from unknown local newspaper, ca. March 12, 1947; R. V. Amison to Franklin H. Williams, April 21, 1947, both in *Miller v. Wiggins* rape case, correspondence, NAACP/PQ.

28. Amison to Eleanor Roosevelt, April 4, 1947, *Miller v. Wiggins* rape case, correspondence, NAACP/PQ.

29. Amison to Williams, April 21, 1947. Notably, Amory's mayor, Fred P. Wright, in whose office Leroy testified to being tortured for five hours, was also a returning white G.I. White Amory voters had elected him the previous fall, November 1946. See Fred P. Wright, obituary, Legacy.com, www.legacy.com/obituaries/name/fred-wright-obituary?pid=144500715&view=guestbook.

30. Unsigned to Spingarn, ca. March 17, 1947, 1, NAACP/LOC, Box II:B125, Folder: Miller v. Wiggins, Correspondence.

31. Papers of the NAACP, Part 08: Discrimination in the Criminal Justice System, 1910–1955, Series B: Legal Department and Central Office Records, 1940–1955, *Patton v. Mississippi* and Leroy Miller case; Broadway to Franklin H. Williams, August 12, 1947, *Miller v. Wiggins* rape case, correspondence, NAACP/PQ. Broadway, *Leroy Miller v. Marvin Wiggins, Supt., etc.*, Petition for Writ of Habeas Corpus, Circuit Court of Monroe County, MS, March 23, 1948, Wiggins rape case, legal papers; Broadway to Williams, March 23, 1948; Judge Raymond T. Jarvis "Opinion and Ruling of the Court," March 23, 1948, Wiggins rape case, correspondence, NAACP/PQ.

32. Williams to Broadway, September 19, 1947; Broadway to Williams, September 27, 1947; memo from Williams, re. *Miller v. Wiggins*, Wiggins rape case, correspondence, NAACP/PQ.

33. Amison to Williams, April 13, 1948, Wiggins rape case, correspondence, NAACP/PQ.

34. *Leroy Miller v. Marvin Wiggins, Supt., etc.*, opinion en banc, Supreme Court of Mississippi, June 13, 1949, *Miller v. Wiggins* rape case, legal papers, NAACP/PQ.

35. Such questions had reigned since Reconstruction and the judiciary's weakening of Fourteenth Amendment protections against violent state actors in decisions like *Cruikshank* (1876); see Hahn, *A Nation under Our Feet*, 292–95.

36. Thurgood Marshall to Clerk, United States Supreme Court, September 9, 1949; Charles Elmore Cropley to Williams, October 17, 1949, Wiggins rape case, correspondence, NAACP/PQ.

37. Amison to Williams, July 26, 1949; Williams to Amison, October 20, 1949, *Patton v. Mississippi* and Leroy Miller case; "Convention Roll Call and Credentials of Voting Delegates," July 5, 1949, Papers of the NAACP, Part 01, Meetings of the Board of Directors, Records of Annual Conferences, Major Speeches, and Special Reports, Annual Convention, 1949, including discrimination in the military, housing, and education, NAACP/PQ.

38. Leroy Miller, Convict no. 18086, Convict Registers microfilm, roll 15218, Book T: 1945–1955, Corrections, Department of Penitentiary, RG 49, MDAH.

39. Malcolm Wright Jr., interview by author, May 31, 2012, U-0939, Southern Oral History Program Collection, University of North Carolina at Chapel Hill.

40. Tony Vartan, "Slain Negro's Widow Is First Witness Today as White Youth Faces Trial Jury," *Tupelo Daily News*, April 1, 1950; "Youth Expected to Take Stand: Pittsboro Jury to Get Case This Afternoon," *Tupelo Daily Journal*, April 2, 1950, emphasis mine; "Chickasaw County Youth Cleared in Killing Case," *Tupelo Daily Journal*, April 5, 1950.

41. Wright interview.

42. "Bolen Trial Due to Begin Today," *Tupelo Daily Journal*, October 28, 1949, 1; "Jury Completed for Case Facing Trial in Okolona," *Tupelo Daily Journal*, October 29, 1949, 1; "Sentence Four for Beating Road Patrolman," *Hattiesburg American*, October 31, 1949, 1. For examples of the family's prior run-ins with the law, see "Okolonans Fined in City Tribunal," *Tupelo Daily Journal*, January 7, 1947, 1.

43. Estimated mileage and pavement statistics for Chickasaw County are calculated from the Mississippi Department of Transportation's State Highway Map Archive, https://mdot.ms.gov/portal/maps; Heber Ladner, ed., *Mississippi Blue Book: Statistical Register of State, 1945–1949*, chapter 423, Laws of the State of Mississippi, 1948, 128–29. 1950 Census of Agriculture, vol. 1, part 22, chapter B, 71, 57. MHSP, Biennial Report, 1949/51, 14–15.

44. *State of Mississippi v. Tommy Booker*, no. 1360, court transcript of Bessie Kate Bell (Court Reporter), Lowndes County Circuit Court Miscellaneous Cases, 1953 to 1955, Billups-Garth Archives, Columbus and Lowndes County Public Library, Columbus, MS.

45. *State v. Booker*, court transcript. There were no paramedics at this point in Lowndes County. The nearest funeral home transported the injured to hospital.

46. *State v. Tommy Booker*, court transcript.

47. Seiler, *Republic of Drivers*; Seo, *Policing the Open Road*; Sorin, *Driving While Black*.

48. Mississippi State Conference of NAACP Branches, press release, November 2, 1952, Box II:C98, Folder 2, NAACP/LOC. Hugh White, who had founded the Highway Patrol in 1938, served as governor again between 1952 and 1956.

49. Beito and Beito, *Black Maverick*.

50. "The Accomplishments and Objectives of the Regional Council of Negro Leadership of Mississippi," ca. 1955, Box II:A422, Folder 6, NAACP/LOC; Dittmer, *Local People*, 33.

51. C. J. McGehee, *Booker v. State*, no. 39071, opinion, April 5, 1954.

52. Tommy Booker, Convict no. 22529, Convict Registers microfilm, roll 15220, Book V: 1952–1964, Corrections, Department of Penitentiary, RG 49, MDAH.

53. The Forced Trajectory Project's work is available at www.forcedtrajectory.com/. They collaborate closely with the After Violence Project, https://afterviolenceproject.org/.

54. Payne, *I've Got the Light*, 77–102; Ransby, *Ella Baker*; Anderson, *Eyes off the Prize*.

Chapter 4

1. 1900 Census, Beat 4, Newton County, MS, roll 822, 15; 1910 Census, Beat 4, Newton County, MS, roll T624_753, 4B; "Tobe Falkner," MS, World War I Service Cards, 1917–1919, Ancestry.com; 1920 Census, Beat 4, Newton County, MS, roll T625_888, 4A; 1930 Census, Beat 4, Newton County, MS, 5A; 1940 Census, Newton Town, Newton County, MS, roll m-t0627–02053, 6A; 1950 Census, Newton County, MS, roll 4680, sheet 29.

2. "Hard Gunfight Upstate Ended with One Dead," *Enterprise Journal*, February 21, 1952, 1; Erle Johnston, "Negro Is Slain in Blazing Gun Battle," *C-L*, February 21, 1952, 1; "Barricaded Man Is Killed; 2 Others Shot," *Delta Democrat-Times*, February 21, 1952, 1.

3. "Stephens Funeral Held at Lawrence," *Newton Record*, August 7, 1958, 1.

4. "Negro Citizens in Three Counties Terrorized . . . ," *Jackson Advocate*, March 1, 1952, 1–2.

5. "Negro Citizens in Three Counties"; "Tenant Farmer, 65, Killed By 35 Cops," *Chicago Defender*, March 1, 1952, 21.

6. See, for example "Jasper County Tenant Farmer 15 Year Old Son Held for Slaying White Cattle Dealer," *Jackson Advocate*, July 23, 1949, 4; "Humphreys County Violence," *Jackson Advocate*, December 10, 1949, 1; Umoja, *We Will Shoot Back*, 23–25; "Violence Toll Reaches Nine," *C-L*, May 11, 1959, 1; "Clarksdale Negro Who Killed Man Is Slain," *Delta Democrat-Times*, May 11, 1959, 1.

7. Mississippi Cattlemen's Association, *News Letter* 1, no. 3 (July 10, 1948), Cattlemen's Association MS, subject file, MDAH; Bureau of Agricultural Economics, United States Department of Agriculture, *The Cotton Situation*, June/July 1951.

8. Polyani, *The Great Transformation*, chapter 3; Wood, *The Origin of Capitalism*, chapter 5; Padmore, *Life and Struggles*, chapter 1.

9. Roane, "Plotting the Black Commons."

10. Vann R. Newkirk II, "The Great Land Robbery," *The Atlantic*, September 2019, section 3; McMillen, *Dark Journey*; Kirby, *Rural Worlds Lost*; Kahrl, *The Land Was Ours*; Daniel, *Dispossession*. In 1950, Mississippi had 94,000 Black tenant farms; in 1974, the federal government didn't bother to disaggregate by race, listing 3,824 total.

11. For the "logic of dominion" born in the nineteenth century, see Dimock, *Empire for Liberty*.

12. This vignette is a composite of James Gale Carr's career scrapbook, including Marie Wathen, "Shelby County Maintains the Model for Modern and Intelligent Penal Management," *Commercial Appeal*, May 26, 1935, 55; Clifford Farmer, "Shelby County Penal Farm Near Memphis Gives Many Interesting Facts for Use Here," n.d., unknown Missouri newspaper, in Box 1, Gale Carr Papers, Special Collections, Mitchell Memorial Library, Mississippi State University, Starkville, MS; 1940 Census, Lee County, Mississippi; Roll: m-t0627–02042; Page: 14A; Enumeration District: 41-20.

13. See Carr Papers for biography and promotional materials. Both Talitha Leflouria and Sarah Haley have shown the opportunity for knowledge creation in rural penal institutions. See Leflouria, *Chained in Silence*; Haley, *No Mercy Here*.

14. Eleanor Roosevelt, "My Day, November 22, 1937," *Eleanor Roosevelt Papers Digital Edition* (2017), www2.gwu.edu/~erpapers/myday/displaydoc.cfm?_y=1937&_f=md054805.

15. Blade, *Tupelo Man*, chapter 4. At the time, the USDA's agricultural extension service, formed under the 1914 Smith-Lever Act, was legally segregated in Southern states. In Mississippi, extension agents who visited farmers to expose them to scientific or progressive technologies and techniques operated out of a public land-grant university. White extension agents worked from Mississippi State College (now Mississippi State University) in Starkville, while African American agents operated from Alcorn Agricultural and Mechanical College (now Alcorn State University), near Natchez.

16. Those states bordering Mississippi include Alabama, Arkansas, Louisiana, and Tennessee. My use of the rate of farm/farm operator per 100,000 residents is necessary due to varied counting methods for agrarians across time. For instance, the Census of Agriculture only regularly tabulated the number of farms/farm operators, not the population of those farms. Only in 1930 did the population census track farm dwellers in its wider count of rural residents.

17. This can be seen by tracking the number of "nonwhite farms owned," "acres owned by nonwhite farmers," and "nonwhite farm operators" in the Mississippi over this period. For instance, in 1954, the number of Black farmers was just above 100,000; by 1959, it had fallen below 60,000. See US Bureau of the Census, Census of Agriculture, http://agcensus.mannlib.cornell.edu/.

18. Blade, *Tupelo Man*, 91–94. William Minga Swoope, interview by Ryan Semmes, June 11, 2012, Lloyd-Ricks-Watson Project, Mississippi State University Libraries, https://msstate.contentdm.oclc.org/digital/collection/lrw/id/996/rec/4.

19. For the roots of America's beef industry, see Specht, *Red Meat Republic*; for the industrial cow-calf turn, see Hamilton, *Trucking Country*, 139–45.

20. Daniel, *Breaking the Land*, 170–71.

21. Biennial Report of the Superintendent, Physician and Chaplain of the Mississippi Penitentiary, to the Legislature of Mississippi, 1947/49, 16.

22. Taylor, *Brokered Justice*, 160.

23. Fiftieth Biennial Report of the Mississippi State Hospital, July 1953 to June 1955, 26–27, 33, 13, 31, 42.

24. US Department of Agriculture, National Agricultural Statistics Service, Total Cattle, Cows, Beef—Inventory, on January 1, https://quickstats.nass.usda.gov/results/37AF44F0-2756-3712-AE6C-43C32447DDEF; Mississippi State Board of Health, *Vital Statistics: Mississippi*, 1963, table 1. The number of beeves peaked in 1975, using this counting method, at 1.5 million.

25. Alan L. Olmstead and Paul W. Rhode, "Beef, Veal, Pork, and Lamb-Slaughtering, Production, and Price: 1899–1999," table Da995-1019 in *Historical Statistics of the United States*, ed. Carter, Carter, et al., http://dx.doi.org/10.1017/ISBN-9780511132971.Da661-1062.

26. Daniel, *Breaking the Land*.

27. 1910 Census, Place: Beat 5, Lowndes, MS, Roll: T624_750, Page: 5A, Enumeration District: 0051, FHL microfilm: 1374763.

28. Swoope interview. Several of Walter Swoope's first cousins once removed were extension agents in the white system.

29. "Cattlemen Organize State Association," *Commercial Appeal*, May 24, 1946, 1; Ross, ed., *History of the Mississippi Beef Cattle Industry*, 427–28.

30. Black farmers fought to desegregate cattle sale barns in the 1960s; see Daniel, *Dispossession*, 45.

31. Mississippi Cattlemen's Association, *News Letter* 1, no. 4 (December 10, 1948), Cattlemen's Association MS, subject file, MDAH.

32. See Folders 3-34 and 3-35, Box 3, subseries 3, series 1, Eastland Collection, University of Mississippi; Ross, *History of the Mississippi Beef Cattle Industry*, 61.

33. Mississippi Legislature, "Hand Book: Biographical Data of Members of Senate and House, Personnel of Standing Committees, 1964 Session" (1964), University of Mississippi, State of Mississippi Government Documents, https://egrove.olemiss.edu/sta_leghb/11.

34. Paul F. Newell, "Mississippi Commercial Cattlemen's List," April 1947, 15, Cattlemen's Association MS, subject file, MDAH.

35. 1940 Census, Jefferson, MS, Roll: m-t0627-02034, Page: 3A, Enumeration District: 32-33; Irma Fitzgerald Bailey, obituary, Find-A-Grave memorial 196644395, www.findagrave.com/memorial/196644395/irma-bailey.

36. Minutes of Race Relations Committee, Delta Council, March 15, 1949, 9, Box 37, Walter Sillers Jr. Papers, Delta State University Library, Cleveland, MS, quoted in Woodruff, "Mississippi Delta Planters," 282–83. I reproduce this version of McLaurin's language but admit that I cannot know its path to transcription. The Delta Council's minutes taker was almost certainly white. They may have transcribed verbatim, heard what they wanted to hear, or warped McLaurin's meaning.

37. Mississippi's non-white farm owners claimed over 2 million acres in 1950; by 1960 that number had fallen to 1.7 million acres, a decrease of 15 percent. Coahoma

County's total was 11,678 acres in 1950 and 9,139 acres in 1960. See 1950 AgCensus, Mississippi, chapter B, County Table 2a, Farms by Color and Tenure, 68-69; 1959 AgCensus, Statistics for Counties, table 3, Farms and Farm Acreage by Color and Tenure, 140-41.

38. Fannie Lou Hamer quoted in Jerry DeMuth, "'Tired of Being Sick and Tired,'" *The Nation*, June 1, 1964, 1.

39. Asch, *The Senator and the Sharecropper*, 48; Kai Lee, *For Freedom's Sake*, 15.

40. Cornelius Toole Sr., interview by Eleanor Green and Emily Weaver, Mound Bayou, MS, May 19, 2006, transcript, 2-4, in Delta Black Farmers Oral History Project 2006-2007, Delta State University Library, Cleveland, MS; Crosby, *A Little Taste of Freedom*, 5.

41. Mississippi Cattlemen's Association, *News Letter* 1, no. 1 (March 1, 1948), Cattlemen's Association MS, subject file, MDAH.

42. 1950 AgCensus, Mississippi, chapter A, State Table 3, "Farms by Color and Tenure of Operator: Censuses of 1920 to 1950," 4.

43. Blevins, *Cattle in the Cotton Fields*, 85.

44. Mississippi Cattlemen's Association, *News Letter* 1, no. 3 (July 10, 1948), MDAH.

45. "Cattlemen Set Annual Meet Here," *JDN*, December 17, 1948; Cookman, "'Plane-Dirt' Farmers," 111.

46. Noxubee County's total was 1,924 sharecroppers in 1950 and 1,027 in 1959; 556 Black farmers owned 45,720 acres in 1950 and 420 owned 31,684 acres in 1959. See 1950 AgCensus, Mississippi, chapter B, County Table 2a, Farms by Color and Tenure, 68-69; 1959 AgCensus, Statistics for Counties, table 3, Farms and Farm Acreage by Color and Tenure, 140-41.

47. "Cattlemen Hit at Socialism," *Greenwood Commonwealth*, January 20, 1950, 1; "A. B. Freeman Is Named State Cattlemen's Head," *C-L*, January 20, 1950.

48. Burgin, *The Great Persuasion*.

49. Daniel, *Dispossession*, chapter 8.

50. Ross, *History of the Mississippi Beef Cattle Industry*, 427-32; Mississippi Highway Safety Patrol, Biennial Report, 1949/51, Government Documents Collection, State of Mississippi Documents, J. D. Williams Library, University of Mississippi, Oxford, MS; *Laws of the State of Mississippi, Passed at a Regular Session of the Mississippi Legislature Held in the City of Jackson, Commencing on Tuesday, January 6, 1950 and Ending Wednesday, April 20, 1950* (Jackson, 1950), House Bill 620, chapter 112, 105-6, and House Bill 496, chapter 394, 465-67.

51. *Laws of the State of Mississippi, Passed at a Regular Session of the Mississippi Legislature Held in the City of Jackson, Commencing Tuesday, January 8, 1946, Ending Wednesday, April 10, 1946* (Jackson, 1946), chapter 278, House Bill 211, 448-49; and chapter 420, House Bill 519, 679-86.

52. Mississippi Highway Safety Patrol, Biennial Report, 1949/51; *Laws of the State of Mississippi, Passed at a Regular Session of the Mississippi Legislature Held in the City of Jackson, Commencing on Tuesday, January 6, 1950 and Ending Wednesday, April 20, 1950* (Jackson, 1950), Senate Bill 577, 104-5.

53. Mississippi Highway Safety Patrol, Biennial Reports, 1949/51, 1951/53, 1961/63, 1967/69.

54. Mississippi Highway Safety Patrol, Biennial Report, 1953/55.

55. For the violent year of 1955, see Tyson, *The Blood of Emmett Till*, 69–72, 118–20. Night riders also attempted to kill Gus Courts, an associate of George Lee, in 1955.

56. Mississippi Highway Safety Patrol, Biennial Report, 1957/59, 56.

57. "Authorities Made Charge of Cattle Theft in Arrest," *Newton Record*, May 12, 1955; Mississippi Highway Safety Patrol, Biennial Report, 1953/55.

58. Charles A. Marx, interview by Orley B. Caudill, October 28, 1976, transcript, 30–33, University of Southern Mississippi, Center for Oral History and Cultural Heritage.

59. "State Cattle Thefts under Investigation," *C-L*, April 19, 1951, 10. The census of 1950 was the first to report a majority white population (55 percent) in Mississippi since 1830.

60. Mississippi Highway Safety Patrol, Biennial Report, 1949/51 to 1959/61; Biennial Report of the Superintendent, Physician and Chaplain of the Mississippi Penitentiary, to the Legislature of Mississippi, 1947/49 to 1959/61.

61. "State Cattle Thefts under Investigation."

62. "Sound Legislation to Reduce Cattle Thefts," *C-L*, March 7, 1952, 10.

63. Arrest, conviction, and return statistics come from Biennial Reports between 1949/51 and 1959/61.

64. Oshinsky, *Worse Than Slavery*, 225.

65. Register of Persons Convicted of Crime, vol. 1, Lowndes County; Ted Ownby, "Prohibition," *Mississippi Encyclopedia*, https://mississippiencyclopedia.org/entries/prohibition/.

66. J.P. Docket, Beat 4, Oktibbeha County; 1940 Census, Oktibbeha, MS; Roll: m-t0627–02055; Page: 2A; Enumeration District: 53-16.

67. Register of Persons Convicted of Crime, vol. 1, Lowndes County; 1920 Census, Columbus, Ward 4, Lowndes, MS, Roll: T625_885, Page: 23B, Enumeration District: 42; 1940 Census, Columbus, Lowndes, MS, Roll: m-t0627–02046, Page: 13B, Enumeration District: 44-10. Hunting and fishing charges are common in justice of the peace dockets.

68. Mississippi Agricultural and Mechanical College, *The Reveille* 20 (1924), 67; L. V. Henson to Stennis, October 29, 1954, series 29, Box 1, Folder 7, in Stennis Papers; Mississippi Association of County Agricultural Agents, "History," published November 2002, 9, www.mscountyagent.com/pdfs/history.pdf.

69. Henson to Stennis.

70. Ross, *History of the Mississippi Beef Cattle Industry*.

71. Ross, *History of the Mississippi Beef Cattle Industry*, 218.

72. Charles M. Hills, "At Parchman Book Bindery For State," *C-L*, October 18, 1964, 7.

Chapter 5

1. Elton Deanes Sr., interview by author, May 22, 2012, U-0928; Elton Dean Jr., interviews by author, May 22, 2012, U-0926, and June 6, 2012, U-0927, all in Southern

Oral History Program Collection, University of North Carolina at Chapel Hill; 1880 Census, Beat 4, Clay County, MS, Roll 644, 263B, Enumeration District 045; 1910 Census, Beat 4, Clay County, MS, Roll T624_736, 5A, Enumeration District 0070, FHL microfilm no. 1374749; 1940 Census, Clay County, MS, Roll m-t0627-02016, 2A, Enumeration District 13-13A; Deed of Sale from Lacy M. Whitfield to Payton Deanes, November 16, 1874, Colfax County, MS; Deed of Sale from W. W. Whitfield to Peyton Deanes, March 28, 1877, Clay County, MS; Deed of Sale from Frank Myers to Peyton Deanes, May 8, 1906, Clay County, MS, in possession of Elton Dean Jr.

2. Elton Deanes Sr., interview.

3. Elton Deanes Sr., interview; Zach Van Landingham to John K. Wilson, April 24, 1959, SCR ID #2-88-0-11-1-1-1; Wilson to Van Landingham, April 27, 1959, SCR ID #2-88-0-18-1-1-1, MSSC.

4. Robert B. Patterson, "Robert Boyd Patterson Autobiographical Sketch: For My Children," January 2001, subject file: "Patterson, Robert Boyd," MDAH; McMillen, *The Citizens' Council*, chapter 2; Evers and Peters, *For Us, the Living*, 232–34.

5. McMillen, *The Citizens' Council*, chapter 8; Rolph, *Resisting Equality*, chapter 2.

6. Association of Citizens' Councils, "The Citizens' Council," pamphlet, Winona, MS, 1954, 2–3, emphasis in original, call no. 325.26 As7, General Collection, MDAH.

7. Falerios, *"Give me Something I Can't Do,"* 34, 41, 169; "Robert Boyd Patterson of Carrollton, Mississippi, 1921–2017," obituary, Williams & Lord Funeral Home, ca. September 21, 2017, www.williamsandlord.com/obituary/robert-patterson-sr.

8. Patterson, "Robert Boyd Patterson Autobiographical Sketch," 10–15; Ross, *History of the Mississippi Beef Cattle Industry*, 319.

9. "Eastland Advises Group to Avoid Violence; Urges Legal Resistance," *Greenwood Commonwealth*, February 11, 1956; McGuire, *At the Dark End of the Street*, chapter 1.

10. Bartley, *The Rise of Massive Resistance*; Lassiter and Lewis, *The Moderates' Dilemma*, introduction; Kruse, *White Flight*; Crespino, *In Search of Another Country*; Daniel, *Dispossession*; McRae, *Mothers of Massive Resistance*. T. R. M. Howard is a well-known instance of an activist being forced to leave. See Beito and Beito, *Black Maverick*, 166–70.

11. For the Warren Court's original rationale toward implementation, see Klarman, *From Jim Crow to Civil Rights*. For an antidote to this orthodox interpretation that emphasizes modernizing white Southern compliance, see Bell, "*Brown v. Board of Education*." 1954 Census of Agriculture, vol. 1, pt. 33, chapter B, tables 2 and 2a, 73, 78, available through United States Department of Agriculture, Census of Agriculture Historical Archive, http://agcensus.mannlib.cornell.edu/AgCensus/; Population Census reports: 1950 Census, table 5, 24–28; 1960 Census, table 6, 26–10.

12. Emmett J. Stringer, "Biographical Sketch," ca. December 1954; Stringer and J. L. Allen, "Financial Statement for the Year Ending December 31, 1953," BoxII:C96, Folder 9, NAACP/LOC.

13. "Kick-Off Mass Meeting" program, October 30, 1955, BoxII:C96, Folder 9, NAACP/LOC.

14. Memo from Stringer to All Members and Friends, December 19, 1953; Stringer to Hurley, February 9, 1953, BoxII:C96, Folder 9, NAACP/LOC. Hurley to Roy Wilkins, January 13, 1953, Papers of the NAACP, Part 25: Branch Department Files, Series A: Regional Files and Special Reports, 1941–1955, Southeast Regional Office correspondence, 1953, NAACP/PQ.

15. Stringer, "The Big-Three of First Class Citizenship," speech delivered at the Annual Meeting of the Cleveland, Ohio, Branch of the NAACP, December 12, 1954, Box II:C96, Folder 9, NAACP/LOC.

16. Memorandum from Stringer, December 13, 1953; Report from the November 1954 State Convention, n.d.; Secretary Report, June 14, 1954; Memorandum from Williams, December 22, 1954, in Bracey, Harley, and Meier, eds., *Papers of the NAACP, Part 26: Selected Branch Files, 1940–1955, Series A: The South*, reel 15. Dittmer, *Local People*, 45–47. For the weaponization of these petitions by Citizens' Councils, see Berrey, *The Jim Crow Routine*, 127–29.

17. Memorandum from Current, December 13, 1954; News Release from Hurley, Birmingham, AL, September 9, 1954; Report from the November 1954 Memorandum from Current, December 26, 1954 in Bracey, Harley, Meier, eds., *Papers of the NAACP*. Dittmer, *Local People*, 46. Gloster Current reported Stringer's confidential motivations for withdrawing as strictly financial, despite public announcements that downplayed the role of white intimidation.

18. See, generally, Memorandum to the Board from Mr. Current, re: Digest of the Report . . . , December 13, 1954; Wilkins to Stringer, February 7, 1955; Wilkins to Alfred Baker Lewis, March 1, 1955, Mississippi Pressures, Box II:A422, Folders 2, 4, 5, and 6, NAACP/LOC. Providing for inflation, the Stringers' loans would equal some $44,000 in 2022. For more on the Tri-State Bank, see Baradaran, *The Color of Money*, 319n94.

19. 1920 Census: Beat 3, Leflore, MS; Roll: T625_883; Page: 15A; Enumeration District: 85; 1930 Census: Beat 5, Sunflower, MS; Roll: 1166; Page: 8B; Enumeration District: 0027; FHL microfilm: 2340901; 1940 Census: Lowndes, MS; Roll: m-t0627-02046; Page: 6B; Enumeration District: 44-23; Memo from Henry Lee Moon to Editors, August 4, 1955, in Papers of the NAACP, Part 18: Special Subjects, 1940–1955, Series C: General Office Files: Justice Department—White Supremacy, Mississippi racial discrimination, economic intimidation, and violence, NAACP publicity; and postcard to Calab Lide [sic], Box II:A422, Folder 2, NAACP/PQ. Tyson, *The Blood of Emmett Till*, 110.

20. Stringer, "The Big-Three of First Class Citizenship."

21. Stringer to Black, October 11, 1955 (emphasis in original), Box III:C73, Folder 9, NAACP/LOC.

22. Membership Reports, Columbus, Mississippi, Youth Chapter, Box II:E80, Folder 11, NAACP/LOC. Dittmer, *Local People*, 46; "Oxford, Miss.," *Pittsburgh Courier*, May 29, 1943, 16. For more on the role of Mississippi women in gender-exclusive organizing, see Hamlin, *Crossroads at Clarksdale*, chapter 2.

23. Wilkins to J. E. Walker, February 7, 1955; Wilkins to Hubert T. Delany; Roy Wilkins to Stringer, February 7, 1955; Wilkins to Stringer, February 17, 1955, Box II:A422, Folder 5, NAACP/LOC.

24. These and following statistics come from a database created from Register of Persons Convicted of Crime, vols. 1–3, Office of the Circuit Clerk, Columbus, Lowndes County, MS. C. M. Marihugh digitized data as a research assistant. I performed statistical inquires using SQL.

25. For another important interrogation of the focus on post-1968 America as a starting place for mass imprisonment, see Bardes, *The Carceral City*, 2–3.

26. Biennial Report of the Superintendent, Physician, and Chaplain of the Mississippi Penitentiary, 1959–1961, 16, call no. 552SP.1:Bi1959/1961, MDAH.

27. Clerks marked some white women with gendered courtesy titles. See, for example, the case of Mattie Raines from November 1955, where authorities charged her, a white woman, with court costs (but apparently not fines) for lacking a beer license, a café license, a beer permit, and a music machine license. 1950 Census, Beat 5, Lowndes County, MS, Enumeration District 44-54, 5.

28. E. J. Stringer, Program for 1955, Columbus Branch, February 20, 1955, 1, in Folder 9, Box II:C96, NAACP/LOC.

29. Stringer to Black, February 20, 1957, Box III:C73, Folder 9, NAACP/LOC.

30. Stuart Covington, "Citizens' Council to Probe NAACP Man's TV Stint," *Birmingham News*, February 7, 1961, 4; "TV Appearance of Dentist Hit," *Commercial Dispatch*, February 7, 1961; "McKellar Heads Citizens Council," *C-L*, November 2, 1956, 24; Stringer to Current, July 16, 1965; "Youth Day, Mt. Olive Baptist Church," program, July 11, 1965, Box III:C73, Folder 9, NAACP/LOC; "Young Dentist Crusades for Freedom in Dixie," *New York Age*, July 9, 1955, 7.

31. Tell, *Remembering Emmett Till*, 1, 255n1; Till-Mobley and Benson, *Death of Innocence*; Whitfield, *Death in the Delta*; Gorn, *Let the People See*; Tyson, *The Blood of Emmett Till*; Ewing, "I Saw Emmett Till This Week at the Grocery Store," in *1919, Poems*. Tyson has earned significant scrutiny for his unsubstantiated reporting of Carolyn Bryant's recantation in an oral history interview. His archival research and general narrative remain historiographically influential.

32. Tyson, *The Blood of Emmett Till*, chapter 12; Anderson, *Emmett Till*, 68, 105, 178.

33. Gorn, *Let the People See*; Tyson, *The Blood of Emmett Till*.

34. Huie, "The Shocking Story of Approved Killing in Mississippi," *Look*, January, 24, 1956.

35. Jesse Jackson, interview by Ed Gordon, December 5, 2005, transcript, www.npr.org/2005/12/05/5039020/jesse-jackson-recalls-bus-boycott; Tell, *Remembering Emmett Till*, 135–44.

36. "Vicksburg Negro Held in Murder," *C-L*, June 21, 1949, 1, 4.

37. "Hinton's Death Sentence Upheld by Supreme Court," *Enterprise-Journal*, April 11, 1950, 1, 6.

38. Levine, *Bella Abzug*, 49–56; Mitford, *A Fine Old Conflict*, 176–92; "Willie McGee Files Suit for Damages," *C-L*, May 6, 1951, 1; "McGee Dies in Chair," *Hattiesburg American*, May 8, 1951, 1, 13; Walker, *The Ghost of Jim Crow*, 18.

39. "Scarbrough New Head of State Safety Patrol," *Biloxi Daily Herald*, March 26, 1956, 1; "Scarbrough Is Named to State Patrol Post," *JDN*, March 26, 1956; "Scarbrough, Ex-Patrol Chief, Dies," *C-L*, March 29, 1968; MHSP Biennial Report, 1955/57.

Tom Scarbrough's beef affiliation shows on his stationery; see Scarbrough to Thomas G. Abernethy, October 17, 1952, in Box 17, Folder 17.3, Thomas G. Abernethy Collection, Archives and Special Collections, J. D. Williams Library, The University of Mississippi, Oxford, MS; "Scarbrough Replaces Birdsong as Chief of Highway Patrol," *C-L*, March 27, 1956, 1.

40. Berrey, *The Jim Crow Routine*, 140; Walker, *The Ghost of Jim Crow*, 27–31; Walker, "The Violent Bear It Away," 479–80. In fact, a Philadelphia, MS, policeman named Lawrence Rainey, who later took part in the 1964 Klan murder of Andrew Goodman, Charles Schwerner, and James Earl Chaney, killed Luther Jackson on October 30, 1959; see Dittmer, *Local People*, 79.

41. MHSP Biennial Report, 1955/57.

42. MHSP Biennial Report, 1955/57; Scarbrough quoted in MHSP Biennial Report, 1957/59, 56.

43. Taylor, *Brokered Justice*, 152–63; Prison Commission, Folder 28, Box 15, series 37, John C. Stennis Papers, Mississippi State University.

44. Taylor, *Brokered Justice*, 147; Sam Johnson, "Capitol Column," *Sun Herald*, 1, 6; LaChance, *Executing Freedom*, introduction. For comparison, California instituted its gas chamber in 1938 and stopped in 1967; see Christianson, *The Last Gasp*, table 1, p. 3.

45. Taken together, the patrol's program matches something like the opposite of Ruth Wilson Gilmore's aspiration for "life-affirming institutions."

46. Anderson, *Slow, Calculated Lynching*.

47. Rowe-Sims, "The Mississippi State Sovereignty Commission," passim, 39.

48. Zack J. Van Landingham to Henry Harris, April 24, 1959, SCR ID #2–88–0–14–1-1-1; Van Landingham to D. A. Vaughn, April 24, 1959, SCR ID #2–88–0-7-1-1-1; Van Landingham to Director, April 23, 1959, SCR ID #2–88–0-17-1-1-1 to 2-1-1 in MSSC; Tommie Valentine and Brenda Valentine, interview by author, June 18, 2012, U-0934, Southern Oral History Program Collection, University of North Carolina at Chapel Hill.

49. Tommie Valentine, Brenda Valentine, and Eddie Valentine, interview by author, January 7, 2013; Deed Record, vol. 94, 493–94, Office of the Chancery Clerk, West Point, Clay County, MS.

Chapter 6

1. "Johnson Would Aid Well-Being of State," *C-L*, July 21, 1959, 8.

2. Historians generally render Johnson as the progressive foil to Barnett. Joseph Crespino argues that Johnson's moderate inclinations were one of his largest political liabilities until his association with the Barnett administration allayed doubts. See Crespino, *In Search of Another Country*, 9–91. Paul B. Johnson Jr., interview by John Jones, June 20, 1980, transcript, MDAH.

3. "The Next Governor of Mississippi," *C-L*, August 28, 1951, 4; Derr, "The Triumph of Progressivism," 43.

4. "Johnson Urges Inspection of Cars, Driver Recheck," *C-L*, November 5, 1959, 1, 14.

5. "Johnson Urges Inspection of Cars, Driver Recheck."

6. Paul Johnson's lone biographer remains Reid Derr, who argues that his administration amounted to the state's actualization of the Progressive Era some fifty years late. See Derr, "The Triumph of Progressivism."

7. Robert Parris Moses, "Reflections from Bob Moses on the Mississippi Theater of the Civil Rights Movement on the Occasion of the Passing of John Doar," undated, ca. November 11, 2014, 1, 4, Civil Rights Movement Archive, crmvet.org, www.crmvet.org/comm/1411_doar-moses.pdf. Moses's analysis resonates with Dan Berger's theory of the Black freedom struggle as "an American foco," or *foquismo*, the revolutionary theory formulated by, among others, Che Guevara during the Cuban Revolution of 1959. See Berger, *Captive Nation*, 43, as well as other grassroot studies such as Hamlin, *Crossroads at Clarksdale*, chapter 1; and Crosby, *A Little Taste of Freedom*, chapters 5 and 6.

8. Moses, "Reflections," 1.

9. The ICC's order came through *Sarah Keys v. Carolina Coach Company* (1955), in which the commission applied the Supreme Court's refutation of *Plessy v. Ferguson* in *Brown* to interstate transportation and accommodation. This built on the Supreme Court's original busing case, *Irene Morgan v. Virginia* (1946), and the later confirmation in *Bruce Boynton v. Virginia* (1960).

10. The Freedom Rides enjoy a robust historical record and literature. See Berrey, *The Jim Crow Routine*, chapter 4; Branch, *Parting the Waters*, chapter 12; Farmer, *Lay Bare the Heart*, chapters 1, 2, 3, 17, 18, 19; Arsenault, *Freedom Riders*. An excellent photographic history documents the Highway Patrol's presence; see Etheridge and Wilkins, *Breach of Peace*.

11. Farmer, *Lay Bare the Heart*, 207; and quoted in Arsenault, *Freedom Riders*, 188.

12. "Citizens' Council Urges 'Let Authorities Handle,'" *C-L*, May 24, 1961, 1.

13. "Bomb Threat Welcomes Riders to Mississippi," *Delta Democrat-Times*, May 24, 1961, 1; Edmund Noel, "Trip from Meridian Quiet under Escort," *C-L*, May 25, 1961, 1.

14. Arsenault, *Freedom Riders*, 218, 225, 233–37.

15. Ruth Wilson Gilmore and Craig Gilmore, "Beyond Bratton," in Camp and Heatherton, eds., *Policing the Planet*, 197.

16. Silver, *Freedom Rider Diary*, 40–42, 53–54.

17. Joan Trumpauer Mulholland, interview in *American Experience: Freedom Riders*, PBS, www.pbs.org/wgbh/americanexperience/films/freedomriders/.

18. Silver, *Freedom Rider Diary*, 81, 83; Farmer, *Lay Bare the Heart*, 28–29.

19. *American Experience: Freedom Riders*; Farmer, *Lay Bare the Heart*, 210.

20. Meredith expounded on his white, Black, and Choctaw identity in several self-published books from the 1990s. See Meredith, *The Choctaw Nation*; Meredith, *The Father of White Supremacy*.

21. Eagles, *The Price of Defiance*, 301–5.

22. Oxford's desegregation crisis also enjoys a robust literature, with interpretations and emphases varying from the rise of the Kennedys to the militaristic nature of the counterinsurgency, and most recently the future of de facto segregated education: Branch, *Parting the Waters*, chapter 17; Doyle, *An American Insurrection*;

Eagles, *The Price of Defiance*. For descriptions of the two homicide victims, see Eagles, *The Price of Defiance*, chapter 18, esp. 306, 364-65.

23. Eagles, *The Price of Defiance*, 275-76.

24. Eagles, *The Price of Defiance*, 301, 322-23; Doyle, *An American Insurrection*, 86-90; Crespino, *In Search of Another Country*, 115-19.

25. See Biographical/Historical note to W. G. Bud Gray Papers, Special Collections, University of Southern Mississippi.

26. Eagles, *The Price of Defiance*, 354.

27. Eagles, *The Price of Defiance*, 358.

28. Eagles, *The Price of Defiance*, chapter 18, esp. 354-56; Doyle, *An American Insurrection*, chapter 13; George M. Yarbrough, interview by Orley B. Caudill, February 21, 1980, Mississippi Oral History Program, University of Mississippi. Doyle argues that as highway patrolmen received increasingly flawed information and received tear gas they planned to mutiny and mount an internal insurrection against the US marshals. In this narrative, Johnson and Birdsong halted the efforts of rogue patrolmen. See Doyle, *An American Insurrection*, 220-23.

29. "Federal Troops Take Over at University," *The Conservative*, October 4, 1962, 1.

30. "Our People Have Right to Know All the Facts," *Enterprise-Journal*, October 9, 1962, 2.

31. "Oxford Mayor Tells Why He Asked Aid of Army," *C-L*, October 6, 1962, 5.

32. Gavin Scott, "Oxford Mayor Tells Why He Asked Army for help," *Hattiesburg American*, October 6, 1962, 9.

33. Charles M. Hills, "Yarbrough Riot Story," *C-L*, October 21, 1962, section D, 3.

34. Charles M. Hills, "Legislature Standing By; Senate Lauds Patrolmen," *C-L*, October 4, 1962, 1, 14.

35. Raiford, *Imprisoned in a Luminous Glare*, 94; Lyon, *Memories of the Southern Civil Rights Movement*, 60.

36. Asch, *The Senator and the Sharecropper*, 48; Kai Lee, *For Freedom's Sake*, 15.

37. Kai Lee, *For Freedom's Sake*, 18.

38. Kai Lee, *For Freedom's Sake*, 21-22; Roberts, *Killing the Black Body*, 90. "Genocide in Mississippi," SAVF-SNCC, Social Action vertical file, ca. 1930-2002, Archives Main Stacks, Mss 577, Box 47, Folder 16, WHS.

39. Fannie Lou Hamer, "Testimony before the Credentials Committee at the Democratic National Convention," August 22, 1964, quoted in Brooks and Houck, eds., *The Speeches of Fannie Lou Hamer*, chapter 4; Payne, *I've Got the Light*, 154-55.

40. The Winona affair generated volumes of published primary evidence and secondary analysis, owing to its sadistic content, the roles of multiple governments, and the testimony of Hamer throughout the civil rights struggle. See Branch, *Parting the Waters*, chapter 19; Payne, *I've Got the Light*, 225-35, 285, 309; Dittmer, *Local People*, 170-73; Brooks and Houck, eds., *The Speeches of Fannie Lou Hamer*.

41. The most recent narrative of the Montgomery County jail saga comes in Houck, "Fannie Lou Hamer on Winona." Houck accessed the manuscript collection surrounding *US v. Patridge, et al*. I build from Houck's statement of the facts and

his partial reproduction of the court transcript in Brooks and Houck, *The Speeches of Fannie Lou Hamer*, 7–35.

42. Basinger's assignment found in MHSP Biennial Report, 1957/59. For testimony of the arrest sequence, see Brooks and Houck, *The Speeches of Fannie Lou Hamer*, 8–11. Ponder's verbal interchange can be found in most of Hamer's recollections of the affair; see Annell Ponder, affidavit, quoted in *Mississippi Black Paper*.

43. Fannie Lou Hamer, "America Is a Sick Place, and Man Is on the Critical List," speech, May 27, 1970, quoted in Brooks and Houck, *The Speeches of Fannie Lou Hamer*, 113; Hamer, federal court testimony, quoted in Brooks and Houck, *The Speeches of Fannie Lou Hamer*, 13–15.

44. The officers' torture of Guyot transgressed assumptions of heteronormativity. Regina Kunzel has theorized carceral institutions as sites of sexuality formation and expression; this might be extrapolated to the fluidity of performance by punishers as well. See Kunzel, *Criminal Intimacy*.

45. Kai Lee, *For Freedom's Sake*, 29–30; Hamer, federal court testimony, 16–17.

46. Hamer, federal court testimony, 15–16.

47. Historians of the long civil rights movement have focused on the ubiquitous sexual threat that white civilians and lawmen posed to Black women and the activism geared to resist it. McGuire's focus on Bessie Turner and case study of Joan Little's self-defense in the Beaufort County, North Carolina, jail are important examples to establish the systemic nature of this violence; see McGuire, "'It Was Like All of Us'"; Feimster, *Southern Horrors*; McGuire, *At the Dark End of the Street*, 196–97 and chapter 8; Greene, *Free Joan Little*.

48. For more on the trial in US district court, an often omitted denouement, see Brooks and Houck, *The Speeches of Fannie Lou Hamer*, 7–8; Houck, "Fannie Lou Hamer on Winona," 20–21.

49. Hamer, "America Is a Sick Place"; Kai Lee, *For Freedom's Sake*, 56–57.

50. John F. Kennedy, "Radio and Television Report to the American People on Civil Rights," June 11, 1963, available online at Gerhard Peters and John T. Woolley, *The American Presidency Project*, www.presidency.ucsb.edu/ws/?pid=9271.

51. Hamer, interview by unknown SNCC publicist, ca. March 17, 1964, transcript, www.crmvet.org/nars/63_flh_winona.pdf.

52. Crespino, *In Search of Another Country*, 67, 116. "Stand Tall with Paul" campaign brochure, ca. 1963, Box 2, Folder 6, Miller (Michael J.) Civil Rights Collection, University of Southern Mississippi, McCain Library and Archives, Special Collections.

53. Claude Sitton, "New Mississippi Governor Gives Anti-Hatred Vow at Inaugural," *New York Times*, January 22, 1964, 1.

54. Governor Paul B. Johnson Jr., Address to Joint Session of the Mississippi Legislature, March 3, 1964, Box 91, Folder 26, PBJ (emphasis in original).

55. My argumentation is deeply indebted to historians of white supremacist ideology and epochs, especially in the South, such as Woodward, *The Strange Career*; Ward, *Defending White Democracy*; Berrey, *The Jim Crow Routine*. It also builds from the emphasis on Cold War public relations charted by Dudziak, *Cold War Civil Rights*.

56. Johnson, address, March 3, 1964.

57. House Bill 564's full title was the Mississippi Law Enforcement Officers' Training Academy Act of 1964. Its text can be found in numerous sources: General Laws of Mississippi, 1964, chapter 143, House Bill 564, or the Mississippi Law Enforcement Officers' Training Academy Act of 1964. United States Commission on Civil Rights, *Law Enforcement: A Report on Equal Protection in the South* (Washington, DC: Government Printing Office, 1965), 90; "The Mississippi Legislature—1964," June 2, 1964, Congress of Racial Equality Papers, Southern Regional Office Records, 1954–1966, Wisconsin Historical Society, Madison, WI, Freedom Summer Collection, Mss 85 (hereafter cited as CORE), Box 8, Folder 10; Kenneth W. Fairly, interview by Reid Derr, July 7, 1993, transcript, University of Southern Mississippi Digital Collections.

58. "PBJ Welcomes New Patrolmen," *Delta Democrat-Times*, September 1, 1964, 1; Governor Paul B. Johnson, Jr., address to the graduating class of the Mississippi Highway Patrol, August 31, 1964, transcript, MDAH, AU 095, 6.

59. Johnson, address to the graduating class, 1.
60. Bederman, *Manliness and Civilization*, conclusion.
61. Johnson, address to the graduating class, 1.
62. Johnson, address to the graduating class, 5.
63. Johnson, address to the graduating class, 4.
64. Johnson, address to the graduating class, 1–2.
65. Johnson, address to the graduating class, 3.
66. Fairly interview.

Chapter 7

1. "Clay County Freedom Democratic Party Struggle," SCR ID #2-88-0-51-1-1-1; Tom Scarbrough, "Report on Clay County," July 21, 1965, SCR ID #2-88-0-55-2-1-1 to 3-1-1 in MSSC; David M. Tobis, interview by anonymous Stanford University student, MFDP Chapter 76, KZSU Project South Interviews, Collection Number SC0066, Department of Special Collections and University Archives, Cecil H. Green Library, Stanford University, Stanford, CA (hereafter cited as Project South); David Tobis, "You've Just Got to Keep On Keeping On," *Berkshire Eagle*, August 21, 1965.

2. Tobis interview.
3. Scarbrough, "Report on Clay County."
4. Tobis interview.
5. MHSP Biennial Report, 1963/65. As per the 1938 law establishing the Highway Patrol, all fines fell due to the justice of the peace in the jurisdiction where patrolmen wrote citations.

6. T. B. Birdsong to Kenneth Phillips, March 25, 1964; Phillips to Birdsong, March 27, 1964; Memo from Birdsong to all law enforcement officers, August 1964, Box 144, Folders 2 and 9, PBJ.

7. Memo from Birdsong to all law enforcement officers, August 1964, Box 2, Folder 9, PBJ.

8. Elton Deanes Sr., interview by author, May 22, 2012, U-0928, Southern Oral History Program Collection, University of North Carolina at Chapel Hill.

9. Deanes interview.

10. Deanes interview. For finer points of ASCS committee work, see Daniel, "African American Farmers," 20–22, 16–18; Jeffries, *Bloody Lowndes*, chapter 4.

11. Deanes interview; Daniel, "African American Farmers," 5, 15.

12. Daniel, *Dispossession*.

13. Eddie Valentine, Tommie Valentine, and Brenda Valentine, interview by author, January 7, 2013. Like the Jim Crow operation of the local ASCS, white elites also dominated the county's FmHA office. Tommie Valentine's wife, Brenda Grove, learned the difference a friendly face at the FmHA could make before meeting Tommie or moving to Pheba. Her family sharecropped near Carthage, in Leake County, until they purchased their first eighty-eight acres with an FmHA loan in 1967. They had tried to make the leap to landownership before, only to be turned down by all-white FmHA agents. But in 1967, a Black schoolteacher from the Grove family's community integrated the Leake County FmHA and secured their loan for a property twenty-five miles from their previous farm. The promissory note called for yearly payments of $300, an amount often hard to net by growing cotton and corn, but the Groves paid it. For Brenda Valentine's family, an integrated FmHA made the climb to landownership possible. Tommie Valentine and Brenda Valentine, interview by author, June 18, 2012, Southern Oral History Program Collection, Interview U-0934.

14. Daniel, "African American Farmers," 5, 16, 19–20; "ASCS ELECTION" handbill, ca. November 2, 1965, in Box 2, Dora Adams Papers, Mss 667, 1955–1991, Special Collections, Mitchell Memorial Library, Mississippi State University (hereinafter Dora Adams Papers); "Freedom School Newspaper," no author, July 15, 1965, published by the Church of God in West Point, in Folder 1, Civil Rights Collection, 1963–1965, Mss 175, Special Collections, Mitchell Memorial Library, Mississippi State University (hereinafter Civil Rights Collection); Sam Carr, interview by unknown Stanford University student, Aberdeen, MS, summer 1965, MFDP Chapter 3, in Project South.

15. Carr interview; "ASCS ELECTION" handbill.

16. Carr interview.

17. For studies of COFO organizing in other local movements, see Dittmer, *Local People*; Payne, *I've Got the Light*; Umoja, *We Will Shoot Back*; Daniel, "African American Farmers"; Sturkey, "I Want to Become a Part of History."

18. B. Cowart, Mississippi Livestock Theft Bureau Case Report, "Starkville, Aberdeen and West Point COFO Workers," August 3, Box 144, Folder 9, PBJ. Cowart's handwritten notes from this meeting do not survive in the archive.

19. Instances of each type of surveillance and harassment occur later in this chapter, and are substantiated by investigative reports in Series II, Sub-Series 10: Highway Patrol, PBJ. Such documents are generally classified and in custody of the Mississippi Department of Public Safety. Librarians incidentally archived these reports with the rest of Johnson's papers. For one example of activist knowledge of such activities and attempts to counter such surveillance, see Hamlin, "Undercover for the Movement."

20. 1910 US Federal Census, Beat 4, Harrison County, Mississippi, Roll 276, Page 1A, Enumeration District 0237; 1940 Census, Saucier, Harrison County, Missis-

sippi, Roll T627_2025, Page 2A, Enumeration District 24-40; B. Cowart, US World War II Army Enlistment Records, 1938–1946, RG 64, NARA at College Park. "Selection of a Jury," *Delta Democrat-Times*, March 3, 1949; "Hearing Postponed in Manslaughter Case Jackson," *Delta Democrat-Times*, March 9, 1949.

21. B. Cowart, Mississippi Livestock Theft Bureau Case Report, "Starkville, Aberdeen and West Point COFO workers," August 3, 1964; Cowart, Mississippi Livestock Theft Bureau Case Report, August 13, 1964, Box 144, Folder 9, PBJ.

22. Cowart, Inter-Office Memorandum, August 6, 1964; Cowart, Mississippi Livestock Theft Bureau Case Report, "Wayne David Anderson, w/m," August 19, 1964, in Box 144, Folder 9; Cowart, Mississippi Livestock Theft Bureau Case Report, September 7, 1964; Lloyd Bean and John Gray, Mississippi Bureau of Identification Case Report, "COFO Workers Arrested at West Point, Mississippi," November 2, 1964, Box 145, Folder 3, PBJ. Cole, *Suspect Identities*.

23. Cowart, Mississippi Livestock Theft Bureau Case Report, August 13, 1964, Box 144, Folder 9, PBJ.

24. Lloyd Bean, Mississippi Bureau of Identification Case Report, "COFO Meeting, Mt. Olive Baptist Church, West Point, Mississippi," November 2, 1964, Box 145, Folder 3; Memo from Charles E. Snodgrass to Chief A. D. Morgan, July 21, 1964, Box 144, Folder 8, PBJ.

25. Fred McKay, "Report No. 9: Report Reference COFO Citizens Band Operations in Mississippi," August 19, 1964, Box 144, Folder 9; McKay, "Mississippi Highway Patrol Report Reference Citizens Band Activities in Mississippi," November 25, 1964, Box 145, Folder 3, PBJ. Unnamed source to Stennis, August 21, 1965, Folder 3, Box 5, Series 1, Stennis Papers.

26. Cowart, Mississippi Livestock Theft Bureau Case Report, August 20, 1964, Box 144, Folder 9, PBJ.

27. Lloyd Bean and John Gray, Mississippi Bureau of Identification Case Report, "Information Concerning Ku Klux Klan, Chickasaw County, MS," November 2, 1964, Box 145, Folder 3, PBJ; Resident Agent Lawrence W. Gorman, Informant Report from Member of White Knights of the Ku Klux Klan of Mississippi, West Point, MS, August 26, 1965, part of FBI file 157-JN-3738, RG 65, NARA. For FBI informants in the KKK, see Gage, *G-Man*, chapter 51.

28. Lloyd Bean and John Gray, Mississippi Bureau of Identification Case Report, "Information Concerning Ku Klux Klan, Chickasaw County"; Lloyd Bean and John Gray, Mississippi Bureau of Identification Case Report, "Information Concerning Ku Klux Klan, Clay County, Mississippi," November 2, 1964, Box 145, Folder 3, PBJ.

29. Cowart, Mississippi Livestock Theft Bureau Case Report, "St. Peters Baptist Church Fire, Friday 8-28-64, West Point, Miss.," August 28, 1964; Cowart, Mississippi Bureau of Identification Case Report, "Attempt to Burn New St. Peters Missionary Baptist Church Located One Mile South of West Point City Limits on Tibbe Road on the Night of 27 August 1964," August 28, 1964, Box 144, Folder 9; Mississippi Bureau of Identification Case Report, "Bombing of Negro Church Located Approximately Four Miles North of Aberdeen, Mississippi 9 September 1964, Monroe County," September 11, 1964; Cowart, Mississippi Livestock Theft Bureau Case

Report, "Shady Grove Baptist Church for Negroes, Burned at 10:15 p.m., Friday Night, September 18, 1964," September 20, 1964, Box 145, Folder 1, PBJ.

30. Snodgrass to Birdsong and Morgan, "Klan Meeting," November 16, 1965, Box 146, Folder 4; Mississippi Bureau of Identification Case Report, "Burning of KKK Cross, Beatles Records & Wigs . . . Tupelo, MS," August 16, 1966, Box 147, Folder 6; Lloyd Bean, Mississippi Bureau of Identification Case Report, "Ku Klux Klan, Chickasaw County," November 9, 1964; Lloyd Bean and John Gray, Mississippi Bureau of Identification Case Report, "Information Concerning Ku Klux Klan, Chickasaw County, Mississippi," November 2, 1964; Lloyd Bean and John Gray, Mississippi Bureau of Identification Case Report, "Information Concerning Ku Klux Klan, Clay County, Mississippi," November 2, 1964, Box 145, Folder 3; Snodgrass to Birdsong and Morgan, "Attempted Arson," January 20, 1966, Box 146, Folder 6, PBJ.

31. MHSP Biennial Report, 1963/65, 31–32.

32. MHSP Biennial Report, 1963/65, 31–32; Derr, "The Triumph of Progressivism," 194–98.

33. "Pheba, Mississippi" activity report, August 16, 1965, in Box 2, Dora Adams Papers; Michael Royce, "Mississippi Freedom Summer in Eight Vignettes," *Fringe Magazine*, June 6, 2011, www.sundresspublications.com/bestof/2011/roycem.htm; Michael Royce, Zoom interview by author, October 16, 2023. Since 1965, Reuss has legally changed his family name to the phonetic spelling.

34. Royce, "Mississippi Freedom Summer"; MHSP organizational memo, "Information Received from Dan Davis—West Point," August 6, 1965, Box 146, Folder 1, PBJ.

35. Royce, "Mississippi Freedom Summer."

36. Royce interview.

37. Debate of Henry Reuss and Thomas Abernethy, *Congressional Record: House*, August 10, 1965, 19912–18; "By Valor and Arms," *Washington Post*, August 10, 1965, A10.

38. "President Lyndon B. Johnson Signs the Voting Rights Act in 1965," *New York Daily News*, August 7, 1965.

39. Tommie Valentine and Brenda Valentine interview, June 18, 2012; Dan Davis, Mississippi Bureau of Investigation Case Report, "Shooting into COFO House," August 8, 1965, Box 146, Folder 1, PBJ.

40. Dan Davis, Mississippi Bureau of Identification Case Report, August 8, 1965, "Shooting into COFO House, Pheba, MS . . . Shooting into Vernon Valentine's, Negro Male, House, Pheba, MS," Box 146, Folder 1, PBJ; Lynn P. Smith, interview by E. Avery Rollins, July 21, 2008, transcript, National Law Enforcement Museum, Washington, DC, Society of Former Special Agents of the FBI Oral History Collection, Digital Collection, www.nleomf.org/museum/the-collection/oral-histories/.

41. Smith interview; Donald J. Cesare, interview by Brian R. Hollstein, October 16, 2006, transcript, Society of Former Special Agents of the FBI Oral History Collection; "Lynn Smith: Obituary," *C-L*, March 22, 2010.

42. Smith interview; "FDP County Reports: December 6–December 14, 1965," SCR ID #2-165-5-51-1-1-1, MSSC; Tommie Valentine and Brenda Valentine interview, June 18, 2012; Daniel, *Dispossession*, 113; Tommie Valentine and Brenda Valentine, interview by author, May 4, 2023.

43. In the case of Stokely Carmichael and the Lowndes County, Alabama, movement, one community ballot had over sixty Black candidates. See Daniel, "African American Farmers," 20–22; "FDP County Reports: December 6–December 14, 1965," SCR ID #2-165-5-51-1-1-1, MSSC. Later in life, Vernon Valentine was elected to his county USDA committee; his son Tommie Valentine served on the committee as of 2023.

44. "FDP County Reports: December 6–December 14, 1965," SCR ID #2-165-5-51-1-1-1, MSSC; Valentine, Valentine, and Valentine interview. The arson in Pheba was part of a countywide spree. Night riders had attempted to burn a Black grocery store in West Point on September 21, 1965. According to Sheriff Strickland, the Molotov cocktail failed to ignite because the wick was improperly soaked in the bomb's flammable component. Scarbrough, "Report on Clay County," September 30, 1965, SCR ID #2-88-0-58-1-1-1, MSSC.

Chapter 8

1. Earl Robert Poe, statement to Joseph A. Sullivan, Meridian, MS, November 11, 1964, MIBURN Casefile, pt. 3, 77–78, FBI Vault, vault.fbi.gov/Mississippi%20Burning%20%28MIBURN%29%20Case.

2. McAdam, *Freedom Summer*, chapter 3; and Dittmer, *Local People*, chapter 11.

3. Dittmer, *Local People*, 280–85; Ellen Barry, "Arrest Made in 1964 Civil Rights Killings," *Los Angeles Times*, January 7, 2005; testimony of James Jorden, Trial Transcripts in the Case *United States v. Price, et al.*, vol. 2, pt. 5, October 1967, 951–52, www.justice.gov/crt/foia/file/670996/download; report of excavation of dam site, August 12, 1964, 6, MIBURN Casefile, pt. 5, FBI Vault, 285; Cagin and Dray, *We Are Not Afraid*, 55, 359.

4. John Lewis, draft speech for the March on Washington, ca. August 28, 1963, Hank Werner Papers, box 2, folder 5, Wisconsin Historical Society.

5. Zinn, *SNCC*, 190–91; Forman, *The Making of Black Revolutionaries*, 379–82; Garrow, *Bearing the Cross*, 282.

6. Du Bois, *Black Reconstruction*, 182, 187.

7. Zinn, *SNCC*. Zinn also gave trainings to SNCC volunteers on American history; see Ransby, *Ella Baker*, 314–19.

8. For revolutionary prison- and police-based critique of "reformism," see Jackson, *Blood in My Eye*, 135, 172.

9. Berger, Kaba, and Stein, "What Abolitionists Do." For more on abolitionist and non-reformist reforms, see Davis, *Abolition Democracy*; Akbar, "An Abolitionist Horizon"; McLeod, "Envisioning Abolition Democracy."

10. Umoja, "1964"; Akinyele Omowale Umoja, "'It's Time for Black Men . . .': The Deacons for Defense and the Mississippi Movement," in Ownby, ed., *The Civil Rights Movement*; Umoja, *We Will Shoot Back*, 154–59; Cobb, *This Nonviolent Stuff'll Get You Killed*; Williams, *Negroes with Guns*; Strain, "We Walked like Men"; Jeffries, *Bloody Lowndes*.

11. Robin D. G. Kelley, "Change from the Roots: What Abolition Looks Like, from the Panthers to the People" in Kaepernick, ed., *Abolition for the People*, 93.

12. Annell Ponder, COFO Executive Committee meeting minutes, July 10, 1964, 1, COFO records, Z: Accessions, M79-423, WHS.

13. Ponder, COFO Executive Committee meeting minutes.

14. See *Council of Federated Organizations, et al., v. Lawrence A. Rainey, et al.*, US District Court for the Southern District of Mississippi, Jackson Division: Civil Action No. 3599, July 10, 1964, Arthur Kinoy papers, Z: Accessions, M2007-010, Box 8, Folder 20, WHS.

15. Kinoy, *Rights on Trial*, 115-17, 151-57; Paul Lewis, "Arthur Kinoy Is Dead at 82," *New York Times*, September 20, 2003; Christopher Reed, "Obituary: Arthur Kinoy," *The Guardian*, September 27, 2003.

16. "Minutes of Meeting of Legal Advisory Committee," October 3, 1964, Box 1, Folder 14, Benjamin E. Smith Papers, WHS.

17. *COFO v. Rainey*, 2-3.

18. *COFO v. Rainey*, 6, 8, 10 (emphasis added).

19. *COFO v. Rainey*, 3-5.

20. *COFO v. Rainey*, 10.

21. Kinoy, *Rights on Trial*, 250-51. Though activists do not mention the United Nations, their description of a neutral peacekeeping force was reminiscent of the UN's internationalist peacekeeping campaigns of the 1950s and '60s. See Anderson, *Eyes off the Prize*; Tudor, *Blue Helmet Bureaucrats*.

22. For the NAACP approach, see Krinitsky, "The Politics of Crime Control," chapter 6; King, *Devil in the Grove*.

23. Carmichael and Hamilton, *Black Power*, 46.

24. Kinoy, *Rights on Trial*, 252.

25. Kinoy, interview by Kay Mills, Newark, NJ, February 19, 1990, quoted in Mills, *This Little Light*, 147-48.

26. William L. Chaze, "Mississippi Leading Nation as Most Law-Abiding State," *C-L*, July 21, 1964, 1, 10; Flamm, *In the Heat*.

27. *COFO v. Sidney Mize*, December 22, 1964, 339 F.2d 898 (5th Cir. 1964), https://law.justia.com/cases/federal/appellate-courts/F2/339/898/5302/.

28. "Minutes of Meeting of Legal Advisory Committee," October 3, 1964.

29. "Brief for Petitioners-Appellants," *COFO v. Rainey*, 11-12, ca. October 1964, Box 9, Folder 19, Kinoy Papers, WHS.

30. "Affidavits," 9, Social Action Vertical File—SNCC, Mss 577, Box 47, Folder 16, WHS.

31. Edward Hollander, audio recording of James Earl Chaney memorial service, August 16, 1964, Audio 369A, WIHVH2870-A, WHS.

32. Hollander, audio.

33. "Hear! Hear! How Our Brothers Died for Freedom," CORE poster, ca. August 1964, Danny Lyon Collection, Magnum Photos; Martin B. Stiles, "Rights Rally Raises $7,000," *The Record*, July 20, 1964, 1, 12.

34. Fannie Lee Chaney, "An Address by Mrs. Fannie Lee Chaney of Meridian, Mississippi at the Metropolitan A.M.E. Church in Harlem," *Freedomways* 5, no. 2: 290-91.

35. Douglas Martin, "Fannie Lee Chaney, 84, Mother of Slain Civil Rights Worker, Is Dead," *New York Times*, March 24, 2007; Wilford S. Shamlin, "Chaneys Have Yet to Heal," *Courier-Post*, January 16, 2005, 6; Fannie Lee Chaney, video of testimony, *Mississippi v. Edgar Ray Killen*, June 18, 2005, www.c-span.org/video/?187272-1/mississippi-v-edgar-ray-killen-day-4.

36. Singh, ed., *Climbin' Jacob's Ladder*, introduction; Greene, "Ruby Dee, Ossie Davis"; Ruby Dee, "Ben Is Going to Take His Big Brother's Place," *What If I Am a Woman?* vol. 2 (Folkways Records, 1977), track 2.

37. Chaney, "An Address," 290–91.

38. Chaney, "An Address." I take "outdoors" to mean "out-of-doors" or homeless.

39. Chaney, "An Address."

40. See "Gave Equal Protection, Pike Sheriff Declares," *C-L*, November 19, 1964, sec. A, 5; *City of Greenwood v. Peacock*, 384 US 808 (1966); Kinoy, "The Constitutional Right of Negro Freedom," 434–41.

41. "Brief for Petitioners-Appellants," *COFO v. Rainey*, 57.

42. Hinton, *From the War on Poverty*, chapter 2.

43. "Brief for Petitioners-Appellants," *COFO v. Rainey* (emphasis in original).

44. James Saggus, teletype numbered A41NU, AP 16, Box 46, Folder 677, Bureau Records, 1938–2009, Washington, DC, Bureau Collection, Associated Press Corporate Archives.

45. "FBI Director J. Edgar Hoover Says FBI Won't Protect Civil Rights Workers," video, AP Archive, https://youtu.be/5nfgzrkx5vA.

46. This fact has been more deduced than proven. See Jerry Mitchell, "Who's the 'Hero' with No Name?" *C-L*, January 7, 2001, 1, 9A; Jerry Mitchell, "Mr. X 'Unsung Hero' in Slaying of 3 Men," *C-L*, June 12, 2005, 1, 12A; Mitchell, *Race against Time*, 303–4, 400.

47. See Cagin and Dray, *We Are Not Afraid*, 43, 410, 477, 483; J. Edgar Hoover to Johnson, August 10, 1964, Folder 14, Box 114, PBJ.

48. Jerry Mitchell, "The Mystery of Mr. X," *C-L*, January 7, 2001, 9A.

49. Mitchell, *Race against Time*, 304.

50. Mitchell, *Race against Time*, 304. Sullivan went to his grave denying that Maynard King was Mr. X.

51. Robert H. Gordon, "Emergency Powers Have Gone Unused," *C-L*, August 16, 1964, sec. E, 3.

52. "In Ruleville: Cross Burned at Mayor's Home," *Delta Democrat-Times*, August 21, 1964, 1. The mayor, Charles Dorrough, was president of the Mississippi Manufacturers' Association.

53. "Two Train for Highway Patrol," *Yazoo Herald*, September 3, 1964, sec. 2, 1; "Two Patrolmen Are Assigned," *Enterprise-Journal*, September 9, 1964, 8.

54. "APWR Rejects Lawlessness," *Enterprise-Journal*, August 4, 1964, 3.

55. Ward, ed., *Mississippi Black Paper* (2017), introduction.

56. *Mississippi Black Paper* (1965), 6–7, 14, 4–6, 17–24, 59–63. For a history of Vera Mae Pigee and the long Clarksdale movement, see Hamlin, *Crossroads at Clarksdale*; Pigee, *The Struggle of Struggles*.

57. *Mississippi Black Paper* (1965), 88–89. Ward, *Mississippi Black Paper* (2017), xix.

58. *Mississippi Black Paper* (1965), 88–89.

59. Tom Etheridge, "Liberal Cleric Blasts State in New Book Based on COFO 'Affidavits,'" *C-L*, July 30, 1965, 10.

60. Hodding Carter III, "Introduction," in *Mississippi Black Paper* (1965).

61. Carter, "Introduction."

62. Memo from Joseph M. Fox to Robert L. Bernstein, re: *Mississippi Black Paper*, February 9, 1965, folder: *Mississippi Black Paper*, Box 700, Random House Records, Rare Book and Manuscript Library, Columbia University in the City of New York.

63. Walker Percy, "The Fire This Time," *New York Review of Books*, July 1, 1965; Hamlin, *Crossroads at Clarksdale*, chapter 4.

64. Berger, *Captive Nation*, 30; Berger and Hobson, eds., *Remaking Radicalism*, sec. B. For a keen analysis of the 2005 murder trial of James Chaney's killers and other twenty-first-century civil rights cold case investigations, see Berger, "Rescuing Civil Rights."

65. Gilmore, "Prisons and Class Warfare," in *Abolition Geography*, 267.

66. "Meridian Project Report: Sept. 26–Oct. 9, 1964," October 1964, 2, MFDP, Lauderdale County (MS) records, 1964–1966, Microform 55, Reel 2, Segment 53; "Progress and Problems of the COFO Community Centers," 1, 1964, CORE, Mississippi 4th Congressional District records, 1961–1966, Microform 793, Reel 1, Segment 8; Rita Schwerner, "Meridian Community Center," October 19, 1964; Eric and Elaine Weinberger, "Weekly Report from the Meridian Community Center, ending October 9," October 1964, 1–2; and Eric Weinberger to Marvin Rich, October 21, 1964, Scholarship, Education and Defense Fund for Racial Equality records, 1944–1976, Archives Main Stacks, Mss 546, Box 1, Folder 14; Agnes Smith to Eric Weinberger, October 24, 1966, MFDP, Lauderdale County records, 1964–1966, Microform 55, Reel 1, Segment 11, WHS. Payne, *I've Got the Light of Freedom*, 251–52; Sojourner with Reitan, *Thunder of Freedom*, chapter 4.

67. Julia Chaney-Moss, phone interview by author, June 5, 2024.

68. Sanders, *A Chance for Change*, 32–33, 48; Hamlin, *Crossroads at Clarksdale*, 212–39; Walker, "'Some Time We Have Trouble in Getting Mail.'"

69. "Softly Singing Marchers Walk Past Philadelphia," *Hattiesburg American*, June 21, 1965, 1.

Chapter 9

1. "Mrs. Lucinda Ranchers Version of the Demonstrations in Jackson," MFDP *Newsletter*, vol. 5, July 7, 1965, 5. Lucinda Rancher was likely a Black woman documented as being born in 1935, living in Meridian and working as a maid in 1959. See Meridian, Lauderdale County, Mississippi, Roll 1190, 6, Enumeration District 38-30, 1950 Census; and *Meridian City Directory* (Richmond, VA: R. L. Polk, 1959), 244.

2. Dittmer, *Local People*, 344–46; Paul L. Montgomery, "472 Are Arrested in Jackson March," *New York Times*, June 15, 1965, 1.

3. "Mrs. Lucinda Ranchers Version," 5.

4. Robert W. Park, "Letter from the Jackson Fair Grounds Compound," June 1965, Robert W. Park Papers, Archives Main Stacks SC658, WHS. The blank appears in the original; I take Park to mean testicles. The account of Gwendolyn "Gwen" Robinson (later Zoharah Simmons) confirms this interpretation in a memory of what is almost certainly the same scene. See Berger, *Stayed on Freedom*, chapter 6.

5. Akinyele Umoja has documented the armed self-defense that often made Mississippi's Black freedom struggle possible. Much of his evidence emerged from northeast Mississippi, where Umoja himself organized. See Umoja, *We Will Shoot Back*, chapters 6, 7, and 8; Strain, "'We Walked Like Men'"; Hill, *Deacons for Defense*, chapter 11. For the electoral realignment of Mississippi politics after 1965, see Dittmer, *Local People*, chapter 18; Danielson, *After Freedom Summer*. For the War on Poverty, see Sanders, *A Chance for Change*; de Jong, *You Can't Eat Freedom*.

6. Stuart Schrader traces the hegemony of "police-led counterinsurgency" as a security practice in the Cold War era. He also captures how militarized police strategists came to understand Mississippi in ways similar to other hot spots in the Cold War. One military college instructor extolled the maintenance of "law and order whether in California, Pennsylvania, Mississippi, or the rice paddies and jungles of Vietnam," in a 1966 article titled "Police-Military Relations in a Revolutionary Environment." See Schrader, *Badges without Borders*, 13, 240.

7. See SNCC *Newsletter*, special issue, "The Freedom Walk, 1963," May 3, 1963, 1, Social Action Vertical File—COFO, Archives Main Stacks, Mss 577, Box 46, Folder 47, WHS; McWhorter, *Carry Me Home*, 489; Fager, *Selma, 1965*, 37, 54, 65; Flamm, *In the Heat*, 90. Survivors of the Chicago Police Department's torture ring led by John Burge reported the use of cattle prods. See Brundage, *Civilizing Torture*, 320–34.

8. Carmichael with Thelwell, *Ready for Revolution*, 202–3; Dittmer, *Local People*, 96.

9. "FBI Agents in Mississippi Chums of Racist Cops," *The Militant* 28, no. 28 (July 27, 1964): 3; Bill to family, July 17, 1964, in Martinez, ed., *Letters from Mississippi*, 175.

10. "Mississippi Exposition Promises to Be the Best," *Hattiesburg Daily News*, September 22, 1907, 3.

11. "Huge State Fair Program Viewed," *C-L*, September 2, 1937, 16; "Major Improvements Are Made in Plant for Mississippi Fair," *Enterprise-Journal*, September 19, 1955, 7.

12. "New Building Ready for State Fair Next Month," *Sun Herald*, September 25, 1957, 3; John Hall, "Jackson 'Motel' Ready for Riots," *Orlando Evening Sun*, July 8, 1965, 32; Dittmer, *Local People*, 345.

13. Benton-Cohen, *Borderline Americans*, chapter 7; Hinnershitz, *Japanese American Incarceration*, 28, 106; Nakai Havey, *Gasa Gasa Girl*, 1; Nakano with Nakano, *Within the Barbed Wire Fence*, 12–13. A. Naomi Paik theorizes "the camp" as a place "to remove [the detained] from any community that might receive [their] act of bearing witness," a place where "rightlessness" reigns. See Paik, *Rightlessness*, 1–2.

14. McWhorter, *Carry Me Home*, 403.

15. Ed King, quoted in Seeger and Reiser, *Everybody Says Freedom*, 144–46. This story is uncorroborated for 1963, but activists complained of incessant mosquito fogging again in the summer of 1965; see Hall, "Jackson 'Motel'"; Ian McCrae, W. Raymond Berry, and John M. Pratt, Statement Presented to Congressional Briefing, June 22, 1965, 1, SCR ID #99-121-0-8-1-1-1, MSSC. John Lewis endured the insecticide of a restaurant owner in Nashville, Tennessee, on November 10, 1960; see Meachem, *His Truth Is Marching On*, 76–78.

16. Evers, *For Us, the Living*, 281; Gwin, *Remembering Medgar Evers*, 7.

17. Jack Langguth, "Wilkins Is Seized in Jackson, Miss.," *New York Times*, June 2, 1963, 70. See photos taken by Matt Herron, including "Mass Arrests," June 24, 1965, TKS2020136, https://www.topfoto.co.uk/asset/4130577.

18. Ira Grupper, interview by Sheila Michaels, October 4, 2000, 2, 11–13, Oral History Archives, Columbia University Libraries.

19. Park, "Letter from the Jackson Fair," 3; McCrae, Berry, and Pratt, Statement, 1.

20. McCrae, Berry, and Pratt, Statement, 1.

21. Annie Mae King, statement taken by ML, Atlanta, GA, June 1965, in Emergency Bulletin #2 from the New York Office of SNCC, 1, Dunlap—Mississippi Freedom Project, Papers, Z: Accessions, M2000-007, Box 2, Folder 6, WHS; 1940 Census, Sunflower, Mississippi, Roll m-t0627-02067, 9A, Enumeration District 67-30; Boston Friends of SNCC, report beginning "and nurses from the Medical Committee for Human Rights," June 21, 1965, marked p. 2, SAVF-SNCC, Archives Main Stacks, Mss 577, Box 47, Folder 13, WHS. The report of miscarriages is credited to Phyllis Cunningham; see Dittmer, *The Good Doctors*, 67–68 and passim. I am grateful to Micah Jones for introducing me to the stories of Annie Mae King and Maggie Lee Gordon from her own research on the Mississippi State Fair. See Jones, "The Price of Freedom."

22. Maggie Gordon, statement taken by ML, Atlanta, GA, June 1965, in Emergency Bulletin #2 from the New York Office of SNCC, 4, Dunlap—Mississippi Freedom Project, Papers, Z: Accessions, M2000-007, Box 2, Folder 6, WHS, 4; 1950 Census, Holmes, Mississippi; Roll 3256, 25, Enumeration District 26-56.

23. "Negro Woman Attacks Jackson Police Officers," *C-L*, June 17, 1965, 3.

24. "John Bell Williams Says Brutality Reports Untrue," *Greenwood Commonwealth*, June 30, 1965, 1. See Haley, *No Mercy Here*, 252, for Jim Crow modernity's denial of womanhood to Black women.

25. Gordon, statement; "Maggie Gordon's House Burned," MFDP *Newsletter*, vol. 5, July 7, 1965, 11. Maggie Gordon died in 1978, at age forty-five; see Maggie Lee Gordon, Find-a-Grave Memorial ID 242916273.

26. "Educators Find 'Kind of Terror' in Jackson, Miss.," *York Daily Record*, June 26, 1965, 2.

27. McCrae, Berry, and Pratt, statement, 1; "Jackson Brutality Charged by Clerics," *New York Times*, June 23, 1965, 19; Leslie H. Whitten, "A Torture Camp in Mississippi," *San Francisco Examiner*, June 23, 1965, 1, 9.

28. "The Injunction," MFDP *Newsletter*, vol. 5, July 7, 1965, 4; Hall, "Jackson 'Motel.'"

29. "Controversial Appointee," *New York Times*, June 19, 1965, 14; Luckett, *Joe T. Patterson*, 164–66.

30. Larson, *Walk with Me*, chapters 10–11.

31. Statement of Mrs. Victoria J. Gray, in *Nomination of James P. Coleman: Hearings before a Special Subcommittee of the Committee of the Judiciary, United States Senate* (Washington: US Government Printing Office, 1965), 89–91.

32. Testimony of John Lewis . . . before the Senate Judiciary Subcommittee, July 1965, 1–2, SAVF-SNCC, Box 47, Folder 13.

33. Statement of Hon. Nicholas de B. Katzenbach, in *Nomination of James P. Coleman*, 3–7.

34. Lyndon Johnson, "The President's Address to the Nation on Civil Disorders," July 27, 1967, American Presidency Project, www.presidency.ucsb.edu/documents/the-presidents-address-the-nation-civil-disorders.

35. Nixon, "What Has Happened to America?" *Reader's Digest* 46 (October 1967): 49–54.

36. Excerpt from Gov. Johnson's message to the Legislature, January 5, 1966; Excerpts from Governor Johnson speaking at graduation of Highway Patrol, October 14, 1966; Item No. 3—"Statements on Law Enforcement by Gov. Paul B. Johnson, Jr.," Series 2808, Box 12453, MDAH.

37. Johnson quoted in "Suit Filed in Natchez," *Enterprise-Journal*, September 8, 1965, 7; Derr, "The Triumph of Progressivism," 407–10, 414; Hill, *The Deacons for Defense*, chapter 11.

38. Johnson, Organizational Meeting—State Crime Commission, September 7, 1967, Box 100, Folder 18, PBJ.

39. Frank Loesser, "Praise the Lord and Pass the Ammunition," in Ravitch, ed., *The American Reader*, 287.

40. Borne, *Troutmouth*, chapters 1 and 2; Gage, *G-Man*, chapter 5, 118–19, 121, 496–97.

41. For Clegg's official FBI biography, see www.fbi.gov/news/stories/2010/july/national-academy/image/hugh-clegg/view; J. Edgar Hoover to John C. Stennis, June 23, 1950, Declassified Subject File of John C. Stennis, RG 65, NARA.

42. "Crime Group Meets Tuesday at Capital," *C-L*, December 13, 1967, 15; Sturkey, *Hattiesburg*, 217, 220, 260; "Walter Washington," *C-L*, December 4, 1999, 19; Bristow, *Steeped in the Blood*, chapter 2; Investigation of L. S. Alexander, October 25, 1962, 2, SCR ID #2-55-10-6-2-1-1, MSSC. Commission records are inadequate to explain the substance of the men's individual roles in crafting the commission's findings and recommendations. One possibility, as the legal scholar James Forman Jr. has shown of Black leaders elsewhere, is that they participated willingly in hopes of protecting Black Mississippians from violence and property crime perpetrated by what the Black middle class believed to be a desperate criminal underclass. See Forman, *Locking Up Our Own*.

43. "Mississippi Seats First Negro Legislator in 74 Years," *New York Times*, January 3, 1968, 1.

44. Brady, *Black Monday*, 11–14, 45–46.

45. Mississippi Crime Commission, roster, SCR ID #99-107-0-5-1-1-1, MSSC.

46. MHSP Press Release, February 20, 1964, Box 144, Folder 3, PBJ; "Report Number One: Mississippi Crime Commission," February 1968, Series 2808, Box 12453, MDAH; Address of Johnson at MHSP School Graduation, Mississippi Law Enforcement Officers' Training Academy, October 14, 1966, Box 97, Folder 27, PBJ; "Report Number One," 6.

47. Pettengill, dir., *Riotsville, U.S.A.*

48. Harpole to Johnson, December 12, 1964, Box 144, Folder 9, PBJ.

49. "Report Number One"; Kenneth W. Fairly, interview by Reid Derr, July 7, 1993, transcript, University of Southern Mississippi Digital Collections.

50. "Report Number One," 22.

51. "Report Number One," 29–32.

52. "Report Number One," 24; Speech by Marshall G. Bennett before Youth Court Judges and Welfare Department, Series 2808, Box 12453, MDAH; "Law Enforcement Meeting Opens at Northwest Today," *C-L*, October 3, 1967, 8.

53. "Report Number One," 25.

54. Hugh Clegg, interview by Mike Garvey, October 1, 1975, Center for Oral History and Cultural Heritage, University of Southern Mississippi; "Report Number One"; Item No. 7—"Purpose of the Commission," Items for Consideration by the Miss. Crime Commission, Series 2808, Box 12453, MDAH.

55. Commission on Law Enforcement and Administration of Justice, *The Challenge of Crime*, 55–60, 83, 133; Memo from Ramsey Clark to Mississippi Crime Commission, February 7, 1968, Series 2808, Box 12453, MDAH; National Advisory Commission on Civil Disorders, *Report*, 180–81.

56. Item No. 4—"Historical," Items for Consideration by the Miss. Crime Commission, Series 2808, Box 12453, MDAH. Vesla Weaver has called the LEAA the "creation of a major federal crime bureaucracy," marking the birth of "the modern criminal justice system." See Vesla M. Weaver, "The Significance of Policy Failures in Political Development: The Law Enforcement Assistance Administration and the Growth of the Carceral State" in Jenkins and Patashnik, eds., *Living Legislation*, 221–23. Memo from Johnson to Joe Patterson, December 12, 1967, 99-107-0-7-1-1-1; and Johnson, draft of Mississippi Crime Commission final report, 99-46-0-1-1-1-1 through -1-41-1-1, MSSC.

57. MHSP Press Release, February 20, 1964, Box 144, Folder 3, PBJ; "Report Number One"; Address of Johnson at MHSP School Graduation; "Grant Awarded," *Delta Democrat-Times*, November 12, 1966, 2.

58. "5 State Educational Institutions to Get Federal Grants," *Hattiesburg American*, December 31, 1968, 3.

59. Hinton, *America on Fire*, 10, 304, 315–16.

60. "Ex-Local Patrolman Appointed by JBW," *Delta Democrat-Times*, January 17, 1968, 1; "Birdsong Portrait Unveiled at MHP," *C-L*, April 30, 1968, 6.

61. Bristow, *Steeped in the Blood*, chapter 1; Moody, *Coming of Age*, chapter 22.

62. Charles M. Hills Jr., "Governor Unveils Agency, Touches on Other Topics," *C-L*, March 18, 1969, 10.

63. Mississippi Division of Law Enforcement Assistance, 1972 Annual Report, December 1972, in folder: Lowndes County Project—Law Enforcement Assistance, Box 3, Tombigbee Council on Human Relations records, Special Collections Department, Mississippi State University Libraries, Starkville; Sophie R. Dales, "Federal Grants to State and Local Governments, 1968–69," *Social Security Administration Bulletin* 33, no. 10 (October 1970): 31–35; Hinton, *From the War on Poverty*, 2.

64. Laws of the State of Mississippi, 1958, 108; Laws of the State of Mississippi, 1968, 156; MDLEA, 1972 Annual Report.

65. Ronni Patriquin, "If Prison Plan Not Implemented State May Lose LEAA Funding," *C-L*, February 28, 1976, 9.

66. MDLEA, 1972 Annual Report.

67. John Carr, "Former Ministry Worker Killed in Rioting," *Delta Democrat-Times*, May 12, 1967, 1; Dittmer, *Local People*, 413.

68. Memo from Civil Rights Division to Chief re: Trooper Lloyd Silas Jones, US Department of Justice, file no. 144-41-3570, www.justice.gov/crt/case-document/file/951851/download (accessed November 29, 2023); "Lloyd Jones Gets Broken Foot," *Simpson County News*, July 29, 1948, 4; "Highway Patrol Will Train 41 Recruits," *C-L*, July 29, 1956, 4.

Chapter 10

1. Jerome Mangum, interview by author, August 3, 2022.

2. Mangum interview.

3. *Fiftieth Biennial Report of the Mississippi State Hospital*, July 1953 to June 1955, 26–27; photo of J. W. Patrick family farm, May 17, 1957, Langfitt (Howard) Farm Family of the Week Collection, Mississippi State University Libraries, https://scholarsjunction.msstate.edu/mss-langfitt-photos/4837/.

4. Spofford, *Lynch Street*, 105–13.

5. The facts of the Jackson State shooting appear in Carter Dalton Lyon, "Jackson State College Killings," *Mississippi Encyclopedia*, http://mississippiencyclopedia.org/entries/jackson-state-college-killings-may-14-1970/; President's Commission on Campus Unrest (the Scranton Commission), *The Report of the President's Commission on Campus Unrest* (Washington: US Government Printing Office, 1970), 411–66, https://files.eric.ed.gov/fulltext/ED083899.pdf; Bristow, *Steeped in the Blood*, chapter 3; Constance Iona Slaughter to John P. Adams, April 8, 1974, in Slaughter-Harvey's personal archive, Forest, MS (hereinafter CISH).

6. President's Commission on Campus Unrest, *Report*, 434.

7. Constance Iona Slaughter-Harvey, interviews by author, Forest, MS, January 2, 2019, and July 10, 2022. See *Myrtle Green Burton et al. v. John Bell Williams, et al.*, CISH. Bristow, *Steeped in the Blood*. For more on the Black sniper canard, see Fannie Lou Hamer, "America Is a Sick Place," May 27, 1970, in Brooks and Houck, eds., *The Speeches of Fannie Lou Hamer*, 124; Hinton, *America on Fire*, chapter 4.

8. Slaughter-Harvey, interview by Verna Myers, June 4, 2010, 8, American Bar Association, Women Trailblazers Project.

9. Mangum interview.

10. "Plaintiffs' Post-Trial Memorandum of Law," *Morrow v. Crisler*, August 6, 1971, 5–6, CISH. *Morrow v. Crisler* lasted over nine years. Its title changed as the lead defendant, the commissioner of public safety, changed from Giles Crisler to W. O. Dillard to James Finch.

11. "Plaintiffs' Memorandum of Law in Opposition to Defendants' Motion to Dismiss," ca. July 1970, 5 (emphasis in original), CISH.

12. "Plaintiffs' Post-Trial Memorandum of Law," *Morrow v. Crisler*, 7, 4–5, 15.

13. "Plaintiffs' Post-Trial Memorandum of Law," 5.

14. "Plaintiffs' Post-Trial Memorandum of Law," 17–18.

15. "Petition for Rehearing and Petition for Rehearing En Banc," *Morrow v. Crisler*, 6, CISH.

16. "Petition for Rehearing and Petition for Rehearing En Banc," 6–7.

17. *Morrow v. Crisler*, March 27, 1974, 491 F.2d 1053 (5th Cir. 1974), https://law.justia.com/cases/federal/appellate-courts/F2/491/1053/453025/; "Plaintiffs' Memorandum of Law in Support of Motion for Temporary Restraining Order and/or Preliminary Injunction," *Morrow v. Dillard*, May 15, 1974, CISH; Slaughter-Harvey, interview by author, January 2, 2019.

18. Senate Bill 1957, "Uniform Controlled Substances Act," April 16, 1971, in General Laws of Mississippi (1971), 802–32. For the carceral pitfalls of medicalized drug enforcement in the case of Texas, see Treviño, "Mexican Americans and the War on Narcotics."

19. Senate Bill 1609, May 19, 1972, in General Laws of Mississippi (1972), 798–823; Report of Kenneth W. Fairly, Mississippi Bureau of Narcotics, 1973 and 1974, RG 53, 711.7:MP, MDAH.

20. James Harvey et al., survey tabulation, folder: Mississippi Council on Human Relations—Newsletters, Box 4, Tombigbee Council on Human Relations Records, Manuscripts Unit, Division of Archives and Special Collections, Mississippi State University Libraries, hereafter TCHR.

21. Donna Myhre, "Notes for West Point Project: Ruby Smith . . . ," ca. February 1971, Folder: West Point—Report Resource Material, Box 8, TCHR.

22. "Biographical Note," no date; obituary in funeral program, after February 7, 1990; policy from Aetna Life Insurance Company, December 11, 1961, Box 1, in Dora Adams Papers, Special Collections, Mitchell Memorial Library, Mississippi State University; Jan Hillegas to friend, September 30, 1964SCR ID #2-88-0-45-1-1-1; and Hillegas to file, September 14, 1997, SCR ID #50-8-0-1-5-1-1, MSSC.

23. "Negroes Submit New Grievance List," *Hattiesburg American*, June 28, 1967, 1.

24. "Alleged Brutality," *Hattiesburg American*, April 24, 1978, 9; Umoja, *We Will Shoot Back*, chapter 8.

25. "Welfare Group Calls for Rally This Saturday," *Simpson County News*, April 12, 1979, 3; "NAACP Calls for Dismissal of Hilliard," *C-L*, February 13, 1979, 19.

26. "Alleged Brutality," *Hattiesburg American*, April 24, 1978, 9; "Sheriff Suit Is Dismissed," *Picayune Item*, April 30, 1978, 2.

27. "Tupelo Blacks to Stage Rally," *Hattiesburg American*, February 28, 1978, 15.

28. "Suggested Items of Clothing and Equipment Needed by Sheriff and One Deputy Beginning 1 January 1972," September 1970, 153; and "Budget of Estimated Receipts and Disbursements for Fiscal Year Ending September 30, 1971," September 1970, 162, in Supervisors Minute Book, vol. 32, Office of the Winston County Chancery Clerk, Louisville, MS.

29. Memo from B. A. Hammond to President of Board of Supervisors, Chancery Clerk, and Sheriff, re: "$9,000.00 Law Enforcement Assistance allotment to your county," June 3, 1971, 574–75, in Supervisors Minute Book, vol. 32, Winston County. Payne, *I've Got the Light*, 171; Michael Sayer, affidavit, in *Mississippi Black Paper* (1965), 83–84.

30. "Order," June 8, 1971, 573, 575–82, in Supervisors Minute Book, vol. 32, Winston County. For a description of "Riot Hand Grenades," see *Department of the Army Field Manual, 19-15, Civil Disturbances and Disasters* (Washington: US Government Printing Office, 1968), sec. 7, 25. Notably, only Roper Supply Company seemed to know that by "baseball grenades," county governments meant those filled with tear gas. The distinction appears nowhere on sheriff department wish lists, and we might reasonably infer that officials expected military-grade fragmentation grenades.

31. Umoja, *We Will Shoot Back*, chapter 8.

32. "Order Approving Law Enforcement Grant and Authorizing Filing of Application for Action Project Grant," June 22, 1971, 65–66, in Minute Book, Board of Supervisors, vol. 45, Office of the Alcorn County Chancery Clerk, Corinth, MS; "In the Matter of Matching Funds for Law Enforcement Assistance Regional Council No. 1," April 3, 1972, 467, in Supervisors Minutes, vol. 58, Office of the Lee County Chancery Clerk, Tupelo, MS; "Order Declaring an Emergency Situation with Reference to the Alcorn County, Mississippi Jail," July 3, 1973, Alcorn County Minute Book, Board of Supervisors, vol. 48, 15; "Budget of Estimated Receipts and Disbursements for Fiscal Year Ending September 30, 1973," August 10, 1972, 579, in Supervisors Minutes, vol. 25, Office of the Union County Chancery Clerk, New Albany, MS.

33. Mississippi Division of Law Enforcement Assistance, *1972 Annual Report*, December 1972, 6–7 and passim., in folder: Lowndes County Project—Law Enforcement Assistance, Box 3, TCHR. For an incidence of intern employment, see "Order Authorizing Participation by Alcorn County, Mississippi in LEAA Internship Program," 586, in Minute Book, Board of Supervisors, vol. 48, Alcorn County Chancery Clerk. Ronni Patriquin, "If Prison Plan Not Implemented State May Lose LEAA Funding," *C-L*, February 28, 1976, 9.

34. Hinton, *From the War on Poverty*, 136.

35. "Budget of Estimated Receipts and Disbursements for Fiscal Year Ending September 30, 1971," 171–73; "Budget of Estimated Receipts and Disbursements for Fiscal Year Ending September 30, 1972," 381–84, in Minutes, Board of Supervisors, vol. 5; "Budget of Estimated Receipts and Disbursements for Fiscal Year Ending September 30, 1975," 149–53; "Budget of Estimated Receipts and Disbursements for Fiscal Year Ending September 30, 1976," 465–69, in Minutes, Board of Supervisors, vol. 10, Office of the Kemper County Chancery Court, DeKalb, MS. Standardized

line items for public safety include the sheriff's office, fire department, correctional institutions, justice of the peace courts, and constables; welfare services include county health departments, vital statistics, paupers, tuberculosis patients, food stamps, and child welfare services.

36. For a history of red squads and their history in the 1970s, see Davis, *Police against the Movement*.

37. Rowe-Sims, "The Mississippi State Sovereignty Commission," 29–31; Crespino, *In Search of Another Country*, 131–43.

38. Muhammad Ahmad, "We Are All Prisoners of War," in handbill produced by African Prisoners of War Solidarity Day Committee, SCR ID #99-24-0-1-3-1-1, MSSC. For Ben Chaney's life in revolutionary Black politics, see Hank Klibanoff, "The Lasting Impact of a Civil Rights Icon's Murder," *Smithsonian Magazine*, December 2008, 12–14. For a history that further explains the currents in Black liberation struggles that could bring Ben Chaney into the Black Panther Party and Black Liberation Army, see Burton, *Tip of the Spear*.

39. Onaci, *Free the Land*, 40.

40. Institutional histories of the Sovereignty Commission include Calvin Trillin, "State Secrets," *New Yorker*, May 29, 1995, 54–64; Rowe-Sims, "The Mississippi State Sovereignty Commission"; Katagiri, *The Mississippi State Sovereignty Commission*; Irons, *Reconstituting Whiteness*. Seminal histories that utilize Sovereignty Commission files include Dittmer, *Local People*; Crespino, *In Search of Another Country*; Arsenault, *Freedom Riders*; Berrey, *The Jim Crow Routine*; Rolph, *Resisting Equality*. One could scarcely imagine a *new* book without reference to the digitized archive.

41. Rowe-Sims argues that for Johnson, "above all, Mississippi had to appear to be law-abiding." See "The Mississippi State Sovereignty Commission," 45–46.

42. Rowe-Sims, "The Mississippi State Sovereignty Commission," 49–50. See also correspondence between Paul Johnson, T. B. Birdsong (commissioner of public safety), and other administrators in subseries 10, series II, PBJ.

43. See for instance the front page of the *C-L* in June and July 1971. This coverage wholly overtook the contemporaneous lawsuit to desegregate the Highway Patrol, *Morrow v. Crisler*.

44. The *C-L* covered the Watergate saga with momentary coverage of jail reform lawsuits from across the state; see February through June 1973. For instance, courts ruled for major reforms in the Hinds County jail on June 19, 1973, and while the trial did not make local news, this precedent radiated to movements across the state; see folder: Court Decision Concerning Hinds County, Box 3, TCHR.

45. *Journal of the House of Mississippi*, regular session, 1278, quoted in Katagiri, *The Mississippi State Sovereignty Commission*, 225.

46. W. F. Minor, "Sovereignty Unit's Role in Race Relations Bared," *Times-Picayune*, May 5, 1968, 1; W. F. Minor, "'Espionage' Over; What About Files?" *Times-Picayune*, April 22, 1973, 1.

47. Rowe-Sims, "The Mississippi State Sovereignty Commission," 51–52.

48. W. F. Minor, "What Lurks in Commission Files?" *Delta Democrat-Times*, January 31, 1977, 4.

49. Buckley and Banks quoted in Katagiri, *The Mississippi State Sovereignty Commission*, 227–28.

50. W. F. Minor, "'Redneck Gestapo' Files Dog Legislators' Conscience," *Capital Reporter*, February 3, 1977, 1.

51. Steve Cannizaro, "ACLU Suit Charges Illegal Surveillance," *C-L*, February 19, 1977, 1; Rowe-Sims, "The Mississippi State Sovereignty Committee," 54; Katagiri, *The Mississippi State Sovereignty Commission*, 230; Newman, *Divine Agitators*; and Berger, *Stayed on Freedom*.

52. James Young, "Senate OK's Seal on Secret Files," *Commercial Appeal*, March 3, 1977, 11; Rowe-Sims, "The Mississippi State Sovereignty Commission," 51–52.

53. Filing, *American Civil Liberties Union of Mississippi, Inc., et al. v. Cliff Finch, Governor of the State of Mississippi et al.*, February 18, 1977, Box 1, Folder 3, series I, Faulkner (Leesha) Civil Rights Collection, McCain Library, University of Southern Mississippi, Hattiesburg, MS. James Finch was of no known relation to Cliff Finch.

54. "Anti-Surveillance Suit Survives Court Test," *C-L*, May 21, 1977, 3; *The Police Threat*, chapter 8; Ashaki M. Binta and Ken Lawrence, "Mississippi Spies," *Southern Exposure* 9, no. 3 (October 1981): 82–86; Berger, *Stayed on Freedom*, chapter 13.

55. Patrick O'Rourke, quoted in Steve Cannizaro, "ACLU Begins Probes," *C-L*, June 22, 1977, 1B.

56. W. F. Minor, "Shades of Richard Nixon? Summer Seeks Executive Privilege," *Capital Reporter*, July 7, 1977, 1.

57. A. F. Summer, court filing, quoted in Minor, "Shades of Richard Nixon?" Mississippi passed its first open records law in 1983.

58. Rowe-Sims, "The Mississippi State Sovereignty Commission," 54–58; Katagiri, *The Mississippi State Sovereignty Commission*, 230–42.

59. *The Police Threat*, 59.

60. Bristow, *Steeped in the Blood*, chapter 3.

61. For one kickback and fraud case against the Highway Patrol and local police use of roadblocks, see "Jury Blasts Patrolmen, Clinton PD," *C-L*, April 10, 1968, 1, 14.

62. Fernández, *The Young Lords*, 12; Joseph Goldstein, "Old New York Police Surveillance Is Found, Forcing Big Brother out of Hiding," *New York Times*, June 16, 2016.

Conclusion

1. Elijah Pierce, interview in the documentary *Elijah Pierce: Wood Carver*, 1974, available through Folkstreams.net.

2. Pierce, interview in *Elijah Pierce: Sermons in Wood*, 1980, available through Folkstreams.net.

3. Pierce, interview in *Elijah Pierce: Wood Carver*; "Folk Artist Dies," *Daily News*, May 9, 1984, 17; Gaylen Moore, "The Vision of Elijah," *New York Times Magazine*, August 26, 1979, 28–30, 34.

4. Pierce, interview in *Elijah Pierce: Sermons in Wood*; Dan Kane, "The Son of a Slave and a Columbus Barber, Artist Elijah Pierce Endures," *Repository*, February 1, 2018.

5. Nadja Sayej, "Elijah Pierce: The Woodcarver Who Grappled with Civil Rights and Racism," *The Guardian*, September 28, 2020; Roberts, ed., *Elijah Pierce*, 162, 101.

6. Pierce, quoted by Zoé Whitley and Nancy Ireson, "Curator Conversation: Elijah Pierce's America," Barnes Foundation, streamed live on September 23, 2020, *YouTube*, www.youtube.com/watch?v=tuPAdd56Y5c.

7. Jane L. Levere, "Woodcarver in a Timely Spotlight," *New York Times*, October 25, 2020, sec. F, 4.

8. Laws of the State of Mississippi, 1954, 105–6; Laws of the State of Mississippi, 1980, 349, 310–12, 508–12, 63–64, 292–94.

9. Vera Institute of Justice, "Incarceration Trends," https://trends.vera.org/state/MS.

10. Christine Hauser, "Two Black Men, One Shot in the Mouth," *New York Times*, March 29, 2023; Jesus Jiménez, "Mississippi Deputies Are 'Terminated,'" *New York Times*, June 28, 2023.

11. Brian Howey and Nate Rosenfeld, "How a 'Goon Squad' of Deputies Got Away with Years of Brutality," *Mississippi Today*, November 30, 2023; Nate Rosenfield, Brian Howey, and Jerry Mitchell, "'Did You Tase Him in the Face!?' Inside 'Goon Squad' Deputies' Group Chat," *Mississippi Today*, May 29, 2024.

12. Howey and Rosenfeld, "How a 'Goon Squad.'"

13. Nate Rosenfeld and Brian Howey, "Stories of Alleged Brutality by a Mississippi Sheriff's Department," *Mississippi Today*, December 23, 2023; "Stun Gun Reactions Vary Across Country," *C-L*, May 1, 1985, 3.

14. Steph Quinn, Mukta Joshi, and Jerry Mitchell, "'You're His Property,'" *New York Times*, March 31, 2025, A14; Jerry Mitchell, "Justice Department Says Mississippi Town Violates Residents' Rights," *Mississippi Today*, September 26, 2024.

15. Consent Decree, *US v. Police Department of Baltimore City*, January 12, 2017, 2–3; April J. Anderson, "Reforming Patterns of Unconstitutional Policing," Congressional Research Service, June 15, 2020, https://crsreports.congress.gov/product/pdf/LSB/LSB10494; Merrick B. Garland, remarks at the Civil Rights Division's 65th anniversary, December 6, 2022.

16. Biden, State of the Union Address, March 1, 2022, www.whitehouse.gov/state-of-the-union-2022/.

17. Micah Herskind, "This Is the Atlanta Way: A Primer on Cop City," *Scalawag*, May 2023, https://scalawagmagazine.org/2023/05/cop-city-atlanta-history-timeline.

18. "Bryan Bailey Earns Metro Top Cop Award," *Times-Journal*, December 12, 1999, 21.

19. Rankin County Board of Supervisors, meeting transcript, March 16, 2020, https://docplayer.net/amp/187408182-Agenda-rankin-county-board-of-supervisors-jay-bishop-presiding-monday-march-16-00-am.html; Randy Gray to Rankin County Board of Supervisors, June 15, 2022, with attached Non-Compensated Special Contract Investigator Contract between Christian Dedmon and Mississippi Bureau of Narcotics. This public record is available on Scribd, www.scribd.com/document/663379641/Christian-Dedmon-special-agent-contract-with-MBN.

20. Capitol Complex Improvement District, Master Plan, October 2023, www.dfa.ms.gov/sites/default/files/CCID%20Home/Master%20Plan%20Documents/CCID%20Master%20Plan%20Update_FINAL%20Oct%202023_0.pdf; Geoff Pender, "'Out to Get Jackson': Bill to Create Separate Courts, Police for Part of Capital City Advances over Protest," *Mississippi Today*, March 30, 2023.

21. Tate Reeves and Sean Tindell, press conference, streamed live on July 14, 2021, *Facebook*, www.facebook.com/tatereeves/videos/1155778911614185/.

22. Geoff Pender, "Mississippi DPS Expands Police Power with Takeover of MDOT, Capitol Police, City Interstates," *Mississippi Today*, April 12, 2021; Rick Rojas, "A Mother's Search for Her Son Leads to a Pauper's Grave and More Questions," *New York Times*, November 19, 2023.

23. Reeves and Tindell, press conference.

24. Reports on Department of Public Safety budgets and spending are available through MAGIC, a user interface available at transparency.ms.gov.

25. For one important watershed in local immigration enforcement, Bill Clinton's Illegal Immigration Reform and Immigrant Responsibility Act (IIRIRA), see Macías-Rojas, *From Deportation to Prison*, introduction; Coleman, *The Walls Within*, chapter 6.

26. Sam Bloch, "ICE Raids Seven Mississippi Chicken Plants," *The Counter*, August 8, 2019, https://thecounter.org/ice-raid-mississippi-poultry-plants-undocumented-immigrants-koch/; "The Ongoing Harms of Trump-era Mississippi Raids and Immigration Prosecutions," National Immigrant Justice Center, January 25, 2024, https://immigrantjustice.org/research-items/explainer-ongoing-harms-trump-era-mississippi-raids-and-immigration-prosecutions; Isabelle Taft, "ICE Raids Upended Life for Families, but They're Still Working," *New York Times*, November 7, 2024, 20A.

27. Phil Bryant, "Crime and Illegal Immigration in Mississippi: A Report from the 2007 Summit," Mississippi Office of the State Auditor, 2, https://www.osa.ms.gov/sites/default/files/osa/files/reports/07Crime%20and%20Illegal%20Immigration%20in%20Mississippi%3A%20A%20Report%20From%20The%202007%20Summit.pdf; Maggie Quinlan, "Asylum Seeker in Texas Faces Deportation After Complying as Witness," *Austin Chronicle*, www.austinchronicle.com/daily/news/2025-02-27/asylum-seeker-in-texas-faces-deportation-after-complying-as-witness/.

28. Mina Corpuz, "Mississippi AG Joins ICE Roundup of Undocumented Migrants," *Mississippi Today*, March 27, 2025, https://mississippitoday.org/2025/03/27/mississippi-ag-joins-ice-roundup-of-undocumented-migrants/; "Mississippi Attorney General Announced Partnership with ICE," *WLOX*, March 28, 2025, www.wlox.com/2025/03/28/mississippi-attorney-general-announces-partnership-with-ice/.

29. Illan Ireland, "Immigrant Bounty Hunting Bill Dead," *Mississippi Free Press*, February 11, 2025, www.mississippifreepress.org/immigrant-bounty-hunting-bill-dead-but-fears-live-on-for-vulnerable-mississippi-communities/; Jacob Wilt, "Mississippi Bill Would Create Immigration Enforcement Division," *Commercial Appeal*, February 24, 2025, www.commercialappeal.com/story/news/local/mississippi/2025/02/24/mississippi-ice-bill-immigration-desoto-county-da/80031486007/.

30. See Mississippi-founded Study and Struggle's latest campaign: Free the Mississippi Five, www.studyandstruggle.com/ms5. See campaigns to close Mississippi's private ICE prisons: Ashton Pittman, "Close Adams County ICE Facility," *Mississippi Free Press*, April 28, 2021, www.mississippifreepress.org/close-adams-county-ice-facility-mississippi-aclu-tells-biden-alleging-torment/. For national projects, see Amna Akbar, "The Fight against Cop City," *Dissent*, Spring 2023, www.dissentmagazine.org/article/the-fight-against-cop-city/; McClellan and Morgan, "Toward Abolitionist Remedies"; Savannah Kumar, "ACLU of Texas and Austin Justice Coalition File Public Information Requests into Partnership between Texas DPS and Austin Police Department," press release, ACLU of Texas, April 4, 2023; Idris Robinson, "How It Might Should Be Done," *Ill Will*, August 16, 2020, https://illwill.com/how-it-might-should-be-done.

Bibliography

Primary Sources

Archives
Austin, TX
    Texas State Library and Archives Commission
        RG 401, Texas Adjutant General's Department Ranger Records
        Texas Department of Public Safety Photographs
Cleveland, MS
    Delta State University Library
        Delta Black Farmers Oral History Project, 2006–2007
Columbus, MS
    Billups-Garth Archives, Columbus and Lowndes County Public Library
    Lowndes County Circuit Court
Corinth, MS
    Office of the Alcorn County Chancery Clerk
DeKalb, MS
    Office of the Kemper County Chancery Clerk
Forrest, MS
    Personal Papers of Constance Iona Slaughter-Harvey
Hattiesburg, MS
    Mississippi Armed Forces Museum
        Thomas B. Birdsong Collection
    University of Southern Mississippi
        Center for Oral History and Cultural Heritage
        McCain Library and Archives
            Special Collections
                Charles A. Marx Papers
                Faulkner (Leesha) Civil Rights Collection
                Johnson (Paul B.) Family Papers
                Miller (Michael J.) Civil Rights Collection
                W. G. Bud Gray Papers
Houston, MS
    Office of the Chickasaw County Circuit Clerk
Ithaca, NY
    Cornell University
        Albert R. Mann Library
            US Department of Agriculture Census of Agriculture Historical Archive

Jackson, MS
    Mississippi Department of Archives and History
        Digital Archives
        General Collection
        Photograph Collections
        Medgar Evers Papers
        Mississippi State Sovereignty Commission Files
        RG 49, Corrections
        State Government Records
        State Publications
        Subject Files
        Supreme Court Case Files
Louisville, MS
    Office of the Winston County Chancery Clerk
Macon, MS
    Office of the Noxubee County Chancery Clerk
Madison, WI
    Wisconsin Historical Society
        Arthur Kinoy Papers
        Benjamin E. Smith Papers
        Bryan R. Dunlap Papers, 1964–1972, 1994
        Congress of Racial Equality Papers, Southern Regional Office Records, 1954–66
        Council of Federated Organizations Records
        Edward Hollander Recordings
        Michael Lipsky and David J. Olson Papers, 1935–1981
        Robert W. Park Papers
        Scholarship, Education and Defense Fund for Racial Equality Records
        Social Action Vertical File—COFO
        Social Action Vertical File—SNCC
New Albany, MS
    Office of the Union County Chancery Clerk
New York, NY
    Columbia University Libraries
        Oral History Archives
        Rare Book & Manuscript Library
            Random House Records
Oxford, MS
    University of Mississippi
        J. D. Williams Library
            Archives and Special Collections
                Featherston Collection
                James O. Eastland Collection
                Thomas G. Abernethy Collection
            Government Documents Collections

Stanford, CA
   Stanford University
      Cecil H. Green Library
         Department of Special Collections and University Archives
            KZSU Project South Interviews, Collection Number SC0066
Starkville, MS
   Mississippi State University
      Mitchell Memorial Library
         Congressional and Political Research Center
            John C. Stennis Collection
         Special Collections
            Clay County Civil Rights Movement Collection
            Dora Adams Papers
            Gale Carr Papers
            Tombigbee Council on Human Relations Records
   Oktibbeha County Justice Court
Tupelo, MS
   Office of the Lee County Chancery Clerk
Washington, DC
   Associated Press Corporate Archives
      Bureau Collection
         Washington, DC, Bureau Records
   George Washington University
      Columbian College of Arts and Sciences
         The Eleanor Roosevelt Papers Project
   Howard University
      Moorland-Spingarn Research Center
         Ralph J. Bunche Oral History Collection
   Library of Congress, Manuscript Division
      Records of the NAACP
   National Archives and Records Administration
      RG 29, Records of the Bureau of the Census
      RG 65, Federal Bureau of Investigation Records
   National Law Enforcement Museum
      Society of Former Special Agents of the FBI Oral History Collection
   US Department of Agriculture
      National Agricultural Statistics Service
West Point, MS
   Bryan Public Library

Periodicals

Berkshire Eagle (Pittsfield, MA)
Biloxi Daily Herald (MS)
Birmingham News (AL)
Blytheville Courier News (AR)
Capital Reporter (Jackson, MS)
Capital Times (Madison, WI)
Centreville Press (Centreville, AL)
Chicago Defender

Commercial Appeal (Memphis, TN)
Commercial Dispatch (Columbus, MS)
Courier-Post (Camden, NJ)
Conservative (Carrollton, MS)
Daily Herald (London)
Daily News (Troy, OH)
Daily Tribune (Wisconsin Rapids, WI)
Decatur Daily (AL)
Delta Democrat-Times (Greenville, MS)
Enterprise-Journal (McComb, MS)
Greenwood Commonwealth (MS)
The Guardian (London)
Hattiesburg American (MS)
Hattiesburg Daily News (MS)
Jackson Advocate (MS)
Jackson Clarion-Ledger (MS)
Jackson Daily News (MS)
Kemper County Messenger (DeKalb, MS)
Los Angeles Times
McComb Daily Journal (MS)
Meridian Star (MS)
Newton Record (MS)
New York Daily News
New Yorker
New York Times
New York Times Magazine
Pittsburgh Courier
The Record (Hackensack, NJ)
Repository (Canton, OH)
San Francisco Examiner
Semi-Weekly Journal (McComb, MS)
Semi-Weekly Mississippian (Jackson, MS)
Simpson County News (Mendenhall, MS)
Sun Herald (Biloxi, MS)
Tallahatchie News (Charleston, MS)
Times-Journal (Selma, AL)
Times-Picayune (New Orleans, LA)
Tupelo Daily Journal (MS)
Tupelo Daily News (MS)
Washington Bee
Washington Post
Yazoo Herald (Yazoo City, MS)
York Daily Record (PA)

Interviews

Carr, Sam. Interview by anonymous Stanford University Student, summer 1965.
Cesare, Donald J. Interview by Brian R. Hollstein, October 16, 2006.
Chaney-Moss, Julia. Telephone interview by author, June 5, 2024.
Clark, Rev. Roosevelt. Interview by Faye Washington and author, April 26, 2023.
Clegg, Hugh H. Interview by Mike Garvey, October 1, 1975.
Dean, Elton, Jr. Interview by author, May 22, 2012, and June 6, 2012.
Deanes, Elton, Sr. Interview by author, May 22, 2012.
Fairly, Kenneth W. Interview by Reid Derr, July 7, 1993.
Grupper, Ira. Interview by Sheila Michaels, October 4, 2000.
Hamer, Fannie Lou. Interview by unknown SNCC publicist, ca. March 17, 1964.
Jackson, Jesse. Interview by Ed Gordon, December 5, 2005.
Johnson, Elvira, Lindy Johnson, and Carmel Baldwin. Interview by author, July 20, 2021.
Johnson, Paul B., Jr. Interview by John Jones, June 20, 1980.
Kinoy, Arthur. Interview by Kay Mills, February 19, 1990.
Mangum, Jerome. Interview by author, August 3, 2022.
Marx, Charles A. Interview by Orley B. Caudill, October 28, 1976.
Royce, Michael. Interview by author via Zoom, October 16, 2023.
Slaughter-Harvey, Constance Iona. Interview by author, January 2, 2019, and July 10, 2022.
Slaughter-Harvey, Constance Iona. Interview by Verna Myers, June 4, 2010.

Smith, Lynn P. Interview by E. Avery Rollins, July 21, 2008.
Stamps-Fuller, Mrs. Billie O., Jimmie R. Lindsey, and Davis R. Lindsey. Interview by Robert Luckett, November 16, 2009.
Swoope, William Minga. Interview by Ryan Semmes, June 11, 2012.
Tobis, David M. Interview by anonymous Stanford University student, summer 1965.
Toole, Cornelius, Sr. Interview by Eleanor Green and Emily Weaver, May 19, 2006.
Valentine, Tommy, and Brenda Valentine. Interview by author, June 18, 2012, January 7, 2013, and May 4, 2023.
Valentine, Tommy, Brenda Valentine, and Eddie Valentine. Interview by author, January 7, 2013.
Washington, Faye. Interview by author, April 26, 2023.
Wright, Malcolm, Jr. Interview by author, May 31, 2012.
Yarbrough, George M. Interview by Orley B. Caudill, February 21, 1980.

Published Primary Sources

Biennial Reports of the Adjutant General of the State of Mississippi, 1890–96, 1936.
Biennial Reports of the Superintendent, Physician and Chaplain of the Mississippi Penitentiary, 1947–61.
Bracey, John H., Jr., Sharon Harley, and August Meier, eds. *Papers of the NAACP*. Microfilm. University Publications of America, 1986.
Chaney, Fannie Lee. "An Address by Mrs. Fannie Lee Chaney of Meridian, Mississippi at the Metropolitan A.M.E. Church in Harlem." *Freedomways* 5, no. 2 (1965): 290–91.
Civil Rights Congress. *We Charge Genocide: The Crime of Government against the Negro People*. Civil Rights Congress, 1951.
Commission on Law Enforcement and Administration of Justice. *The Challenge of Crime in a Free Society*. Government Printing Office, 1967.
Department of the Army. *Field Manual 19-15, Civil Disturbances and Disasters*. Government Printing Office, March 1968.
Department of Public Safety, Mississippi Highway Safety Patrol. Biennial and Annual Reports, 1938/1939 to 1980/1981.
Fiftieth Biennial Report of the Mississippi State Hospital. July 1953 to June 1955.
Journal of the Proceedings of the Constitutional Convention of the State of Mississippi. E. L. Martin, 1890.
Ladner, Heber, ed. *Mississippi Blue Book: Statistical Register of State, 1945–1949*.
Laws of the State of Mississippi, 1822, 1876, 1877, 1880, 1888, 1938, 1946, 1948, 1950, 1954, 1958, 1964, 1968, 1971, 1972, 1980.
National Advisory Commission on Civil Disorders. *Report*. Washington, DC: Government Printing Office, 1968.
President's Commission on Campus Unrest. *The Report of the President's Commission on Campus Unrest*. Government Printing Office, 1970.
United States Commission on Civil Rights. *Law Enforcement: A Report on Equal Protection in the South*. Government Printing Office, 1965.

Secondary Sources

Abbott, Richard H. "Black Regular Troops in the Philippine War." In *The War of 1898 and U.S. Interventions, 1898-1934*, edited by Benjamin R. Beede, 54. Routledge, 1994.

Adler, Jeffrey S. *Murder in New Orleans: The Creation of Jim Crow Policing*. University of Chicago Press, 2019.

Akbar, Amna A. "An Abolitionist Horizon for (Police) Reform." *California Law Review* 108, no. 6 (December 2020): 1781-846.

Alexander, Michelle. *The New Jim Crow: Mass Incarceration in the Age of Colorblindness*. New Press, 2010.

Anderson, Carol. *Bourgeois Radicals: The NAACP and the Struggle for Colonial Liberation, 1941-1960*. Cambridge University Press, 2015.

———. *Eyes off the Prize: The United Nations and the African American Struggle for Human Rights, 1944-1955*. Cambridge University Press, 2003.

Anderson, Devery S. *Emmett Till: The Murder That Shocked the World and Propelled the Civil Rights Movement*. University Press of Mississippi, 2015.

———. *Slow, Calculated Lynching: The Story of Clyde Kennard*. University Press of Mississippi, 2023.

Arsenault, Raymond. *Freedom Riders: 1961 and the Struggle for Racial Justice*. Oxford University Press, 2006.

Arsiniega, Brittany, and Matthew Guariglia. "Police as Supercitizens." *Social Justice* 48, no. 4 (December 2022): 33-58.

Asch, Chris Myers. *The Senator and the Sharecropper: The Freedom Struggles of James O. Eastland and Fannie Lou Hamer*. University of North Carolina Press, 2011.

Bailey, Amy Kate, and Stewart E. Tolnay. *Lynched: The Victims of Southern Mob Violence*. University of North Carolina Press, 2015.

Baker, Andrew. *To Poison a Nation: The Murder of Robert Charles and the Rise of Jim Crow Policing in America*. New Press, 2021.

Balto, Simon. *Occupied Territory: Policing Black Chicago from Red Summer to Black Power*. University of North Carolina Press, 2019.

Baradaran, Mehrsa. *The Color of Money: Black Banks and the Racial Wealth Gap*. Belknap Press of Harvard University Press, 2017.

Bardes, John K. *The Carceral City: Slavery and the Making of Mass Incarceration in New Orleans, 1803-1930*. University of North Carolina Press, 2024.

Bartley, Numan V. *The Rise of Massive Resistance: Race and Politics in the South during the 1950s*. Louisiana State University Press, 1999 [1969].

Bay, Mia. *To Tell the Truth Freely: The Life of Ida B. Wells*. Hill and Wang, 2009.

Bechtel, H. Kenneth. *State Police in the United States: A Socio-Historical Analysis*. Greenwood Press, 1995.

Bederman, Gail. *Manliness and Civilization: A Cultural History of Gender and Race in the United States, 1880-1917*. University of Chicago Press, 1995.

Beede, Benjamin R., ed. *The War of 1898 and U.S. Interventions, 1898-1934: An Encyclopedia*. Garland, 1994.

Beito, David T., and Linda Royster Beito. *Black Maverick: T. R. M. Howard's Fight for Civil Rights and Economic Power.* University of Illinois Press, 2009.

Bell, Derrick A., Jr. "*Brown v. Board of Education* and the Interest-Convergence Dilemma." *Harvard Law Review* 93, no. 3 (January 1980): 518–33.

Benton-Cohen, Katherine. *Borderline Americans: Racial Division and Labor War in the Arizona Borderlands.* Harvard University Press, 2009.

Berger, Dan. *Captive Nation: Black Prison Organizing in the Civil Rights Era.* University of North Carolina Press, 2014.

———. "Rescuing Civil Rights from Black Power: Collective Memory and Saving the State in Twenty-First-Century Prosecutions of 1960s-Era Cases." *Journal for the Study of Radicalism* 3, no. 1 (April 1, 2009): 1–27.

———. *Stayed on Freedom: The Long History of Black Power through One Family's Journey.* Basic Books, 2023.

Berger, Dan, and Emily Hobson, eds. *Remaking Radicalism: A Grassroots Documentary Reader of the United States, 1973–2001.* University of Georgia Press, 2020.

Berger, Dan, Mariame Kaba, and David Stein. "What Abolitionists Do." *Jacobin*, January 26, 2021.

Berrey, Stephen A. *The Jim Crow Routine: Everyday Performances of Race, Civil Rights, and Segregation.* University of North Carolina Press, 2015.

Blade, Robert. *Tupelo Man: The Life and Times of George McLean, a Most Peculiar Newspaper Publisher.* University Press of Mississippi, 2012.

Blevins, Brooks. *Cattle in the Cotton Fields: A History of Cattle Raising in Alabama.* University of Alabama Press, 2014.

Borne, Ronald F. *Troutmouth: The Two Careers of Hugh Clegg.* University Press of Mississippi, 2015.

Brady, Thomas P. *Black Monday.* Association of Citizens' Councils, 1955.

Branch, Taylor. *Parting the Waters: America in the King Years, 1954–1963.* Simon & Schuster, 1988.

Bristow, Nancy K. *Steeped in the Blood of Racism: Black Power, Law and Order, and the 1970 Shootings at Jackson State College.* Oxford University Press, 2020.

Brooks, Emily M. *Gotham's War within a War: Policing and the Birth of Law-and-Order Liberalism in World War II–Era New York City.* University of North Carolina Press, 2023.

Brooks, Maegan Parker. *Fannie Lou Hamer: America's Freedom Fighting Woman.* Rowman & Littlefield, 2020.

Brooks, Maegan Parker, and Davis W. Houck, eds. *The Speeches of Fannie Lou Hamer: To Tell It Like It Is.* University Press of Mississippi, 2010.

Brown, Simone. *Dark Matters: On the Surveillance of Blackness.* Duke University Press, 2015.

Brundage, W. Fitzhugh. *Civilizing Torture: An American Tradition.* Belknap Press of Harvard University Press, 2018.

———. *Lynching in the New South.* University of Illinois Press, 1993.

Burden-Stelly, Charisse. "Modern U.S. Racial Capitalism: Some Theoretical Insights." *Monthly Review* 72, no. 3 (July–August 2020).

Burgin, Angus. *The Great Persuasion: Reinventing Free Markets since the Depression.* Harvard University Press, 2012.

Burnham, Margaret A. *By Hands Now Known: Jim Crow's Legal Executioners.* W. W. Norton, 2022.

Burton, Orisanmi. *Tip of the Spear: Black Radicalism, Prison Repression, and the Long Attica Revolt.* University of California Press, 2023.

Byrd, Jodi A., Alyosha Goldstein, Jodi Melamed, Nikhil Pal Singh, and Chandan Reddy. "Predatory Value: Economies of Dispossession and Racial Capitalism." *Social Text* 36, no. 2 (2018): 1–18.

Cagin, Seth, and Philip Dray. *We Are Not Afraid: The Story of Goodman, Schwerner, and Chaney, and the Civil Rights Campaign for Mississippi.* Nation Books, 2006.

Camp, Jordan, and Christina Heatherton, eds. *Policing the Planet: Why the Policing Crisis Led to Black Lives Matter.* Verso, 2016.

Carmichael, Stokely, and Charles V. Hamilton. *Black Power: The Politics of Liberation.* Vintage, 1967.

Carmichael, Stokely, with Ekwueme Michael Thelwell. *Ready for Revolution: The Life and Struggles of Stokely Carmichael (Kwame Ture).* Scribner, 2003.

Carrigan, William D., and Clive Webb. *Forgotten Dead: Mob Violence against Mexicans in the United States, 1848–1928.* Oxford University Press, 2013.

Carson, Clayborne. *In Struggle: SNCC and the Black Awakening of the 1960s.* Harvard University Press, 1981.

Carter, Dan T. *The Politics of Rage: George Wallace, the Origins of the New Conservatism, and the Transformation of American Politics.* Louisiana State University Press, 1995.

———. *Scottsboro: A Tragedy of the American South.* Louisiana State University Press, 2007.

Carter, Susan B., Scott Sigmund Gartner, Michael R. Haines, et al., eds. *Historical Statistics of the United States, Earliest Times to the Present: Millennial Edition.* Cambridge University Press, 2006.

Catte, Elizabeth. *What You Are Getting Wrong about Appalachia.* Belt Publishing, 2018.

Charron, Katherine Mellen. *Freedom's Teacher: The Life of Septima Clark.* University of North Carolina Press, 2009.

Chase, Robert T. *We Are Not Slaves: State Violence, Coerced Labor, and Prisoners' Rights in Postwar America.* University of North Carolina Press, 2020.

Christianson, Scott. *The Last Gasp: The Rise and Fall of the American Gas Chamber.* University of California Press, 2010.

Cobb, Charles E., Jr. *This Nonviolent Stuff'll Get You Killed: How Guns Made the Civil War Rights Movement Possible.* Basic Books, 2014.

Cobb, James C. *The Selling of the South: The Southern Crusade for Industrial Development, 1936–1980.* University of Illinois Press, 1993.

Cole, Simon A. *Suspect Identities: A History of Fingerprinting and Criminal Identification.* Harvard University Press, 2001.

Coleman, Sarah R. *The Walls Within: The Politics of Immigration in Modern America.* Princeton University Press, 2021.

Connolly, N. D. B. "The Strange Career of American Liberalism." In *Shaped by the State: Toward a New Political History of the Twentieth Century*, edited by Brent Cebul, Lily Geismer, and Mason B. Williams, 62–95. University of Chicago Press, 2019.

Cookman, Aubrey O. "'Plane-Dirt' Farmers." *Popular Mechanics* 88 (November 1947): 108–11.

Cortner, Richard. *A "Scottsboro" Case in Mississippi: The Supreme Court and Brown v. Mississippi*. University Press of Mississippi, 1986.

Coski, John M. *The Confederate Battle Flag: America's Most Embattled Emblem*. Harvard University Press, 2005.

Cowie, Jefferson. "Defend Liberalism? Let's Fight for Democracy First." *New Republic*, June 21, 2024.

———. *Freedom's Dominion: A Saga of White Resistance to Federal Power*. Basic Books, 2022.

Cox, Karen L. *No Common Ground: Confederate Monuments and the Ongoing Fight for Racial Justice*. University of North Carolina Press, 2021.

Crespino, Joseph. "Mississippi as Metaphor." In *The Myth of Southern Exceptionalism*, edited by Matthew D. Lassiter and Joseph Crespino. Oxford University Press, 2010.

———. *In Search of Another Country: Mississippi and the Conservative Counterrevolution*. Princeton University Press, 2007.

Crosby, Emilye. *A Little Taste of Freedom: The Black Freedom Struggle in Claiborne County, Mississippi*. University of North Carolina Press, 2005.

Curtin, Mary Ellen. *Black Prisoners and Their World: Alabama, 1865–1900*. University Press of Virginia, 2000.

Dabney, Virginius. *Liberalism in the South*. University of North Carolina Press, 1932.

Dailey, Jane. *Before Jim Crow: The Politics of Race in Postemancipation Virginia*. University of North Carolina Press, 2000.

———. *White Fright: The Sexual Panic at the Heart of America's Racist History*. Basic Books, 2020.

Dalrymple, William. *The Anarchy: The East India Company, Corporate Violence, and the Pillage of an Empire*. Bloomsbury, 2019.

Daniel, Pete. "African American Farmers and Civil Rights." *Journal of Southern History* 73, no. 1 (February 2007): 3–38.

———. *Breaking the Land: The Transformation of Cotton, Tobacco, and Rice Cultures since 1880*. University of Illinois Press, 1985.

———. *Dispossession: Discrimination against African American Farmers in the Age of Civil Rights*. University of North Carolina Press, 2013.

Danielson, Chris. *After Freedom Summer: How Race Realigned Mississippi Politics, 1965–1986*. University Press of Florida, 2011.

Davis, Angela Y. *Abolition Democracy: Beyond Empire, Prisons, and Torture*. Seven Stories Press, 2005.

———. "Political Prisoners, Prisons and Black Liberation." In *If They Come in the Morning: Voices of Resistance*. Third Press, 1971.

Davis, Joshua Clark. *Police against the Movement: The Forgotten Sabotage of the Civil Rights Struggle*. Princeton University Press, 2025.

Dawson, Michael C. "Hidden in Plain Sight: A Note on Legitimation Crises and the Racial Order." *Critical Historical Studies* 3, no. 1 (Spring 2016): 143–61.
de Jong, Greta. *A Different Day: African American Struggles for Justice in Rural Louisiana, 1900–1970*. University of North Carolina Press, 2002.
———. *You Can't Eat Freedom: Southerners and Social Justice after the Civil Rights Movement*. University of North Carolina Press, 2016.
De Leon, Adrian. *Bundok: A Hinterland History of Filipino America*. University of North Carolina Press, 2023.
Derr, Reid. "The Triumph of Progressivism: Governor Paul B. Johnson Jr., and Mississippi in the 1960s." PhD dissertation, University of Southern Mississippi, Hattiesburg, 1994.
Derrida, Jacques. *Archive Fever: A Freudian Impression*. University of Chicago Press, 1996.
Dew, Charles B. *Apostles of Disunion: Southern Secession Commissioners and the Causes of the Civil War*. University of Virginia Press, 2001.
Dimock, Wai Chee. *Empire for Liberty: Melville and the Poetics of Individualism*. Princeton University Press, 1994.
Dinwoodie, Jane. "Evading Indian Removal in the American South." *Journal of American History* 108, no. 1 (June 2021): 17–41.
Dittmer, John. *The Good Doctors: The Medical Committee for Human Rights and the Struggle for Social Justice in Health Care*. Bloomsbury Press, 2009.
———. *Local People: The Struggle for Civil Rights in Mississippi*. University of Illinois Press, 1994.
Doyle, William. *An American Insurrection: The Battle of Oxford, Mississippi, 1962*. Anchor Books, 2003.
Dubber, Markus D. *The Police Power: Patriarchy and the Foundations of American Government*. Columbia University Press, 2005.
Du Bois, W. E. B. *Black Reconstruction in America, 1860–1880*. Free Press, 1998 [1935].
———. *Darkwater*. Harcourt Brace, 1920.
Dudziak, Mary L. *Cold War Civil Rights: Race and the Image of American Democracy*. Princeton University Press, 2000.
Dunbar-Ortiz, Roxanne. *An Indigenous Peoples' History of the United States*. Beacon Press, 2014.
Eagles, Charles W. *The Price of Defiance: James Meredith and the Integration of Ole Miss*. University of North Carolina Press, 2009.
Eason, John. *Big House on the Prairie: Rise of the Rural Ghetto and Prison Proliferation*. University of Chicago Press, 2017.
Edgerton, Ronald. *American Datu: John J. Pershing and Counterinsurgency Warfare in the Muslim Philippines, 1899–1913*. University Press of Kentucky, 2020.
Egerton, John. *The Americanization of Dixie: The Southernization of America*. Harper & Row, 1974.
Ellisor, John T. *The Second Creek War: Interethnic Conflict and Collusion on a Collapsing Frontier*. University of Nebraska Press, 2010.

Emberton, Carole. *Beyond Redemption: Race, Violence, and the American South after the Civil War.* University of Chicago Press, 2013.

Etheridge, Eric, and Roger Wilkins. *Breach of Peace: Portraits of the 1961 Mississippi Freedom Riders.* Atlas, 2008.

Evers, Myrlie, with William Peters. *For Us, the Living.* University Press of Mississippi, 1996 [1967].

Evers-Williams, Myrlie, and Manning Marable, eds. *The Autobiography of Medgar Evers: A Hero's Life and Legacy Revealed through His Writings, Letters, and Speeches.* Basic Civitas Books, 2005.

Ewing, Eve L. *1919: Poems.* Haymarket Books, 2019.

Fager, Charles E. *Selma, 1965: The March That Changed the South.* Scribner, 1974.

Falerios, Kenton J. *"Give Me Something I Can't Do": The History of the 82nd Military Police Company from WWI to the Iraq War.* AuthorHouse, 2007.

Farmer, James. *Lay Bare the Heart: An Autobiography of the Civil Rights Movement.* Texas Christian University Press, 1985.

Feimster, Crystal N. *Southern Horrors: Women and the Politics of Rape and Lynching.* Harvard University Press, 2009.

Felber, Garrett. *Those Who Know Don't Say: The Nation of Islam, the Black Freedom Movement, and the Carceral State.* University of North Carolina Press, 2020.

Felker-Kantor, Max. *Policing Los Angeles: Race, Resistance, and the Rise of the LAPD.* University of North Carolina Press, 2018.

Ferguson, Robert Hunt. *Remaking the Rural South: Interracialism, Christian Socialism, and Cooperative Farming in Jim Crow Mississippi.* University of Georgia Press, 2018.

Fernández, Johanna. *The Young Lords: A Radical History.* University of North Carolina Press, 2020.

Fields, Barbara J. "'Origins of the New South' and the Negro Question." *Journal of Southern History* 67, no. 4 (November 2001): 811–26.

Finkelman, Paul, ed. *Encyclopedia of African American History.* Oxford University Press, 2006.

Finnegan, Terence R. *A Deed So Accursed: Lynching in Mississippi and South Carolina, 1881–1940.* University of Virginia Press, 2013.

Flamm, Michael W. *In the Heat of the Summer: The New York Riots of 1964 and the War on Crime.* University of Pennsylvania Press, 2017.

———. *Law and Order: Street Crime, Civil Unrest, and the Crisis of Liberalism in the 1960s.* Columbia University Press, 2005.

Foner, Eric. *Reconstruction: America's Unfinished Revolution, 1863–1877.* Harper & Row, 1988.

Forman, James, Jr. *Locking Up Our Own: Crime and Punishment in Black America.* Farrar, Straus and Giroux, 2017.

Foucault, Michel. *Discipline and Punish: The Birth of the Prison.* Translated by Alan Sheridan. Vintage Books, 1977.

Fraser, Nancy. "Expropriation and Exploitation in Racialized Capitalism: A Reply to Michael Dawson." *Critical Historical Studies* 3, no. 1 (Spring 2016): 166–69.

Gage, Beverly. *G-Man: J. Edgar Hoover and the Making of the American Century.* Penguin, 2022.

Garrison, Tim Alan. *The Legal Ideology of Removal: The Southern Judiciary and the Sovereignty of Native American Nations.* University of Georgia Press, 2002.

Giddings, Paula J. *Ida: A Sword among Lions.* Amistad, 2008.

Gilmore, Glenda Elizabeth. *Gender and Jim Crow: Women and the Politics of White Supremacy in North Carolina, 1896–1920.* University of North Carolina Press, 1996.

Gilmore, Ruth Wilson. *Abolition Geography: Essays toward Liberation.* Edited by Brenna Bhandar and Alberto Toscano. London: Verso, 2022.

———. "Forgotten Places and the Seeds of Grassroots Planning." In *Abolition Geography: Essays toward Liberation*, edited by Ruth Wilson Gilmore. Verso, 2022.

———. *Golden Gulag: Prisons, Surplus, Crisis, and Opposition in Globalizing California.* University of California Press, 2007.

———. "In the Shadow of the Shadow State." In *The Revolution Will Not Be Funded: Beyond the Non-Profit Industrial Complex*, edited by INCITE! Women of Color against Violence. South End Press, 2007.

———. "Race, Prisons, and War: Scenes from the History of US Violence." *Socialist Register* 45 (2009): 73–87.

———. "'You Have Dislodged a Boulder': Mothers and Prisoners in the Post Keynesian California Landscape." *Transforming Anthropology* 8, no. 1–2 (January 1999): 12–38.

Gilmore, Ruth Wilson, and Craig Gilmore. "Restating the Obvious." In *Indefensible Space: The Architecture of the National Insecurity State*, edited by Michael Sorkin. Routledge, 2007.

———. "Beyond Bratton." In *Policing the Planet*, edited by Jordan T. Camp and Christina Heatherton. Verso, 2016.

Go, Julian. "Imperial Origins of American Policing: Militarization and Imperial Feedback in the Early 20th Century." *American Journal of Sociology* 125, no. 5 (2020): 1193–254.

———. *Policing Empires: Militarization, Race, and the Imperial Boomerang in Britain and the US.* Oxford University Press, 2022.

———. "Reverberations of Empire: How the Colonial Past Shapes the Present." *Social Science History* 48, no. 1 (Spring 2024): 1–18.

Goldsby, Jacqueline. *A Spectacular Secret: Lynching in American Life and Literature.* University of Chicago Press, 2006.

Gorn, Elliott J. *Let the People See: The Story of Emmett Till.* Oxford University Press, 2018.

Grandin, Greg. *The End of the Myth: From the Frontier to the Border Wall in the Mind of America.* Metropolitan Books, 2019.

Gravely, William B. *They Stole Him Out of Jail: Willie Earle, South Carolina's Last Lynching Victim.* University of South Carolina Press, 2019.

Gray Fischer, Anne. *The Streets Belong to Us: Sex, Race, and Police Power from Segregation to Gentrification.* University of North Carolina Press, 2021.

Greene, Christina. *Free Joan Little: The Politics of Gender, Race, and Imprisonment*. University of North Carolina Press, 2020.
Greene, Robert, II. "Ruby Dee, Ossie Davis, and the Black Public Sphere." *U.S. Intellectual History Blog*, June 15, 2014. https://s-usih.org/2014/06/ruby-dee-ossie-davis-and-the-black-public-sphere/.
Grenier, John. *The First Way of War: American War Making on the Frontier, 1607–1814*. Cambridge University Press, 2005.
Guariglia, Matthew. "On August Vollmer's 1935 *Crime and State Police*." *The Metropole Blog*, May 31, 2022. https://themetropole.blog/2022/05/31/on-august-vollmers-1935-crime-and-state-police/.
——. *Police and the Empire City: Race and the Origins of Modern Policing in New York*. Duke University Press, 2023.
Gwin, Minrose. *Remembering Medgar Evers: Writing the Long Civil Rights Movement*. University of Georgia Press, 2013.
Hadden, Sally E. *Slave Patrols: Law and Violence in Virginia and the Carolinas*. Harvard University Press, 2001.
Hahamovitch, Cindy. "The 'Profane Margins' of the State: Florida Sheriff Walter R. Clark and the Local History of Crime, Policing, and Incarceration." *Journal of American History* 110, no. 4 (March 2024): 643–66.
Hahn, Steven. *Illiberal America: A History*. W. W. Norton, 2024.
——. *A Nation under Our Feet: Black Political Struggles in the Rural South from Slavery to the Great Migration*. Harvard University Press, 2003.
Hale, Grace Elizabeth. *In the Pines: A Lynching, a Lie, a Reckoning*. Little, Brown, 2023.
Haley, Sarah. *No Mercy Here: Gender, Punishment, and the Making of Jim Crow Modernity*. University of North Carolina Press, 2016.
Hall, Stuart, Charles Critcher, Tony Jefferson, et al. *Policing the Crisis: Mugging, the State, and Law and Order*. Macmillan, 1978.
Hamilton, Shane. *Trucking Country: The Road to America's Wal-Mart Economy*. Princeton University Press, 2008.
Hamlin, Françoise N. *Crossroads at Clarksdale: The Black Freedom Struggle in the Mississippi Delta after World War II*. University of North Carolina Press, 2012.
——. "Undercover for the Movement: The Story of Stanley Boyd." *Journal of Civil and Human Rights* 6, no. 1 (April 1, 2020): 1–30.
Harris, Charles H., and Louis R. Sadler. *The Great Call-Up: The Guard, the Border, and the Mexican Revolution*. University of Oklahoma Press, 2015.
Harris, Cheryl I. "Whiteness as Property." *Harvard Law Review* 106, no. 8 (1993): 1707–18.
Hartman, Saidiya. *Scenes of Subjection: Terror, Slavery, and Self-Making in Nineteenth-Century America*. Oxford University Press, 1997.
Hartz, Louis. *The Liberal Tradition in America: An Interpretation of American Political Thought since the Revolution*. Harcourt, Brace, 1955.
Harvey, David. *The New Imperialism*. Oxford University Press, 2005.
Haslett, Tobi. "Magic Actions: Looking Back on the George Floyd Rebellion." *N+1* 40 (2021).

Hernández, Kelly Lytle. *City of Inmates: Conquest, Rebellion, and the Rise of Human Caging in Los Angeles, 1771–1965*. University of North Carolina Press, 2017.

——. *Migra! A History of the U.S. Border Patrol*. University of California Press, 2010.

Hersey, Mark D. *My Work Is That of Conservation: An Environmental Biography of George Washington Carver*. University of Georgia Press, 2011.

Hill, Lance. *The Deacons for Defense: Armed Resistance and the Civil Rights Movement*. University of North Carolina Press, 2004.

Hill, Laura Warren. *Strike the Hammer: The Black Freedom Struggle in Rochester, New York, 1940–1970*. Cornell University Press, 2021.

Hill, Rebecca. *Men, Mobs, and Law: Anti-Lynching and Labor Defense in U.S. Radical History*. Duke University Press, 2008.

Hinnershitz, Stephanie. *Japanese American Incarceration: The Camps and Coerced Labor during World War II*. University of Pennsylvania Press, 2021.

Hinton, Elizabeth. *America on Fire: The Untold History of Police Violence and Black Rebellion since the 1960s*. Liveright, 2021.

——. *From the War on Poverty to the War on Crime: The Making of Mass Incarceration in America*. Harvard University Press, 2017.

Holmes, William F. "The Leflore County Massacre and the Demise of the Colored Farmers' Alliance." *Phylon* 34, no. 3 (1973): 267–74.

——. "Whitecapping: Anti-Semitism in the Populist Era." *American Jewish Historical Quarterly* 63, no. 3 (March 1974): 244–61.

Horowitz, Andy. *Katrina: A History, 1915–2015*. Harvard University Press, 2020.

Hosbey, Justin, and J. T. Roane. "A Totally Different Form of Living: On the Legacies of Displacement and Marronage as Black Ecologies." *Southern Cultures* 27, no. 1 (2021): 68–73.

Houck, Davis W. "Fannie Lou Hamer on Winona: Trauma, Recovery, Memory." In *Social Controversy and Public Address in the 1960s and Early 1970s: A Rhetorical History of the United States*, vol. 9, edited by Richard J. Jensen, 1–38. Michigan State University Press, 2017.

Hudson, Peter James. "Racial Capitalism and the Dark Proletariat." *Boston Review*, February 20, 2018.

Hulsether, Lucia. *Capitalist Humanitarianism*. Duke University Press, 2023.

Hurston, Zora Neale. *Of Mules and Men*. Harper & Row, 1935.

Immerwahr, Daniel. *How to Hide an Empire: A History of the Greater United States*. Farrar, Straus and Giroux, 2019.

Irons, Jenny. *Reconstituting Whiteness: The Mississippi State Sovereignty Commission*. Vanderbilt University Press, 2010.

Jackson, George. *Blood in My Eye*. Random House, 1972.

Jeffries, Hasan Kwame. *Bloody Lowndes: Civil Rights and Black Power in Alabama's Black Belt*. New York University Press, 2009.

Jenkins, Destin. "Ghosts of the Past: Debt, the New South, and the Propaganda of History." In *Histories of Racial Capitalism*, edited by Destin Jenkins and Justin Leroy, 185–213. Columbia University Press, 2021.

Jenkins, Jeffery A., and Eric M. Patashnik, eds. *Living Legislation: Durability, Change, and the Politics of American Lawmaking.* University of Chicago Press, 2012.

Jennings, N. A. *A Texas Ranger.* University of Oklahoma Press, 1997 [1899].

Jett, Brandon T. *Race, Crime, and Policing in the Jim Crow South: African Americans and Law Enforcement in Birmingham, Memphis, and New Orleans, 1920–1945.* Louisiana State University Press, 2021.

Johnson, Benjamin H. *Revolution in Texas: How a Forgotten Rebellion and Its Bloody Suppression Turned Mexicans into Americans.* Yale University Press, 2003.

Johnson, Kimberly S. *Reforming Jim Crow: Southern Politics and State in the Age before Brown.* Oxford University Press, 2010.

Johnson, Walter. *The Broken Heart of America: St. Louis and the Violent History of the United States.* Basic Books, 2020.

———. *River of Dark Dreams: Slavery and Empire in the Cotton Kingdom.* Harvard University Press, 2013.

———. *Soul by Soul: Life inside the Antebellum Slave Market.* Harvard University Press, 1999.

Jones, Micah Camille. "The Price of Freedom: Race, Consumption, and the Long Black Freedom Struggle, 1915–1964." PhD dissertation, Yale University, 2023.

Jones, William P. *The March on Washington: Jobs, Freedom, and the Forgotten History of Civil Rights.* W. W. Norton, 2013.

Kaepernick, Colin, ed. *Abolition for the People: The Movement for a Future without Policing and Prisons.* Kaepernick Publishing, 2021.

Kahrl, Andrew W. *The Black Tax: 150 Years of Theft, Exploitation, and Dispossession in America.* University of Chicago Press, 2024.

———. "From Commons to Capital: The Creative Destruction of Coastal Real Estate, Environments, and Communities in the US South." *Transatlantica* 2 (2020).

———. *The Land Was Ours: How Black Beaches Became White Wealth in the Coastal South.* Harvard University Press, 2012.

Kai Lee, Chana. *For Freedom's Sake: The Life of Fannie Lou Hamer.* University of Illinois Press, 2000.

Kang-Brown, Jacob, and Ram Subramanian. "Out of Sight: The Growth of Jails in Rural America." Vera Institute of Justice, 2017.

Kaplan, Amy. *The Anarchy of Empire in the Making of U.S. Culture.* Harvard University Press, 2002.

Katagiri, Yasuhiro. *The Mississippi State Sovereignty Commission: Civil Rights and States' Rights.* University Press of Mississippi, 2001.

Kato, Daniel. *Liberalizing Lynching: Building a New Racialized State.* Oxford University Press, 2016.

Kelley, Robin D. G. *Hammer and Hoe: Alabama Communists during the Great Depression.* University of North Carolina Press, 1990.

———. "Insecure: Policing under Racial Capitalism." *Spectre Journal*, August 17, 2020.

Key, V. O., Jr. *Southern Politics in State and Nation.* Alfred A. Knopf, 1949.

Khalili, Laleh. *Time in the Shadows: Confinement in Counterinsurgencies*. Stanford University Press, 2013.

King, Gilbert. *Devil in the Grove: Thurgood Marshall, the Groveland Boys, and the Dawn of a New America*. HarperCollins, 2012.

King, P. Nicole. "Reckoning with Regionalism: Race, Place, and Power in Urban History." *Journal of Urban History* 47, no. 1 (January 1, 2021): 209–14.

King, Shannon. *The Politics of Safety: The Black Struggle for Police Accountability in La Guardia's New York*. University of North Carolina Press, 2024.

Kinoy, Arthur. "The Constitutional Right of Negro Freedom." *Rutgers Law Review* 21, no. 3 (1967): 434–41.

———. *Rights on Trial: The Odyssey of a People's Lawyer*. Harvard University Press, 1983.

Kirby, Jack Temple. *Rural Worlds Lost: The American South, 1920–1960*. Louisiana State University Press, 1987.

Klarman, Michael J. *From Jim Crow to Civil Rights: The Supreme Court and the Struggle for Racial Equality*. Oxford University Press, 2004.

Kolsky, Elizabeth. "The Colonial Rule of Law and the Legal Regime of Exception: Frontier 'Fanaticism' and State Violence in British India." *American Historical Review* 120, no. 4 (2015): 1218–46.

Krinitsky, Nora. "The Politics of Crime Control: Race, Policing, and Reform in Twentieth-Century Chicago." PhD dissertation, University of Michigan, 2017.

Kruse, Kevin M. *White Flight: Atlanta and the Making of Modern Conservatism*. Princeton University Press, 2005.

Kunzel, Regina. *Criminal Intimacy: Prison and the Uneven History of Modern American Sexuality*. University of Chicago Press, 2008.

Kuzmarov, Jeremy. *Modernizing Repression: Police Training and Nation-Building in the American Century*. University of Massachusetts Press, 2012.

LaChance, Daniel. *Executing Freedom: The Cultural Life of Capital Punishment in the United States*. University of Chicago Press, 2016.

Larson, Kate Clifford. *Walk with Me: A Biography of Fannie Lou Hamer*. Oxford University Press, 2021.

Lassiter, Matthew D., and Andrew B. Lewis, eds. *The Moderates' Dilemma: Massive Resistance to School Desegregation in Virginia*. University Press of Virginia, 1998.

Lassiter, Matthew D., and Joseph Crespino, eds. *The Myth of Southern Exceptionalism*. Oxford University Press, 2010.

Leflouria, Talitha L. *Chained in Silence: Black Women and Convict Labor in the New South*. University of North Carolina Press, 2015.

Levine, Susan. *Bella Abzug: An Oral History*. Farrar, Straus and Giroux, 2008.

Link, William A. *The Paradox of Southern Progressivism, 1880–1930*. University of North Carolina Press, 1992.

Luckett, Robert. *Joe T. Patterson and the White South's Dilemma: Evolving Resistance to Black Advancement*. University Press of Mississippi, 2015.

Macías-Rojas, Patrisia. *From Deportation to Prison: The Politics of Immigration Enforcement in Post-Civil Rights America*. NYU Press, 2016.

Maclean, Nancy. *Behind the Mask of Chivalry: The Making of the Second Ku Klux Klan*. Oxford University Press, 1995.

Mancini, Matthew J. *One Dies, Get Another: Convict Leasing in the American South, 1866–1928*. University of South Carolina Press, 1996.

Mann, Michael. *The Dark Side of Democracy: Explaining Ethnic Cleansing*. Cambridge University Press, 2005.

Martinez, Elizabeth Sutherland, ed. *Letters from Mississippi*. McGraw-Hill, 1965.

Martinez, Monica Muñoz. *The Injustice Never Leaves You: Anti-Mexican Violence in Texas*. Harvard University Press, 2018.

Marx, Karl. *Capital: A Critique of Political Economy*. Translated by Ben Fowkes. Penguin Classics, 1990.

———. "The Eighteenth Brumaire of Louis Bonaparte." In *Karl Marx: Selected Writings*, edited by Lawrence H. Simon. Hackett, 1994.

Mayo, Katherine. *Justice to All: The Story of the Pennsylvania State Police*. G. P. Putnam's Sons, 1917.

McAdam, Doug. *Freedom Summer*. Oxford University Press, 1988.

McClellan, Cara, and Jamelia N. Morgan. "Toward Abolitionist Remedies: Police (Non)Reform Litigation after the 2020 Uprisings." *Fordham Urban Law Journal* 51 (2024): 635.

McCoy, Alfred W. *Policing America's Empire: The United States, the Philippines, and the Rise of the Surveillance State*. University of Wisconsin Press, 2009.

McGirr, Lisa. *The War on Alcohol: Prohibition and the Rise of the American State*. W. W. Norton, 2015.

McGuire, Danielle L. *At the Dark End of the Street: Black Women, Rape, and Resistance—A New History of the Civil Rights Movement from Rosa Parks to the Rise of Black Power*. Vintage, 2010.

———. "'It Was Like All of Us Had Been Raped': Sexual Violence, Community Mobilization, and the African American Freedom Struggle." *Journal of American History* 91, no. 3 (2004): 906–31.

McLeod, Allegra. "Envisioning Abolition Democracy." *Harvard Law Review* 132, no. 6 (April 2019): 1613–49.

McMillen, Neil R. *The Citizens' Council: Organized Resistance to the Second Reconstruction, 1954–64*. University of Illinois Press, 1994 [1971].

———. *Dark Journey: Black Mississippians in the Age of Jim Crow*. University of Illinois Press, 1989.

McRae, Elizabeth Gillespie. *Mothers of Massive Resistance: White Women and the Politics of White Supremacy*. Oxford University Press, 2018.

McWhorter, Diane. *Carry Me Home: Birmingham, Alabama, the Climactic Battle of the Civil Rights Revolution*. Simon & Schuster, 2001.

Meacham, Jon. *His Truth Is Marching On: John Lewis and the Power of Hope*. Random House, 2020.

Melamed, Jodi. "Racial Capitalism." *Critical Ethnic Studies* 1, no. 1 (2015): 76–85.

Meredith, James. *The Choctaw Nation: 1540–1830*. James Meredith Books, 1995.

———. *The Father of White Supremacy*. James Meredith Books, 1995.

Miles, Tiya. *Ties That Bind: The Story of an Afro-Cherokee Family in Slavery and Freedom*. University of California Press, 2005.
Mills, Charles W. *The Racial Contract*. Cornell University Press, 1997.
Mills, Kay. *This Little Light of Mine: The Life of Fannie Lou Hamer*. University Press of Kentucky, 2007.
Mississippi Black Paper: Fifty-Seven Negro and White Citizens' Testimony of Police Brutality, the Breakdown of Law and Order and the Corruption of Justice in Mississippi. Random House, 1965.
Mississippi Highway Safety Patrol. *2003 Yearbook*. Turner Publishing, 2003.
Mitchell, Jerry. *Race against Time: A Reporter Reopens the Unsolved Murder Cases of the Civil Rights Era*. Simon & Schuster, 2020.
Mitford, Jessica. *A Fine Old Conflict*. Alfred A. Knopf, 1977.
Moody, Anne. *Coming of Age in Mississippi*. Dell, 1968.
Morgan, Chester M. *Redneck Liberal: Theodore G. Bilbo and the New Deal*. Louisiana State University Press, 1999.
Muhammad, Khalil Gibran. *The Condemnation of Blackness: Race, Crime, and the Making of Modern Urban America*. Harvard University Press, 2010.
Murakawa, Naomi. *The First Civil Right: How Liberals Built Prison America*. Oxford University Press, 2014.
Murphy, Mary-Elizabeth B. *Jim Crow Capital: Women and Black Freedom Struggles in Washington, D.C., 1920–1945*. University of North Carolina Press, 2018.
Musgrave, Paul. "Bringing the State Police In: The Diffusion of U.S. Statewide Policing Agencies, 1905–1941." *Studies in American Political Development* 34, no. 1 (April 2020): 3–23.
Nakai Havey, Marie. *Gasa Gasa Girl Goes to Camp: A Nisei Youth behind a World War II Fence*. University of Utah Press, 2014.
Nakano, Takeo, with Leatrice Nakano. *Within the Barbed Wire Fence: A Japanese Man's Account of His Internment in Canada*. University of Toronto Press, 1980.
Neocleus, Mark. *The Fabrication of Social Order: A Critical Theory of Police Power*. Pluto Press, 2000.
Newman, Mark. *Divine Agitators: The Delta Ministry and Civil Rights in Mississippi*. University of Georgia Press, 2004.
Newport, Melanie D. *This Is My Jail: Local Politics and the Rise of Mass Incarceration*. University of Pennsylvania Press, 2022.
Newton, Michael. *Unsolved Civil Rights Murder Cases, 1934–1970*. McFarland & Company, 2006.
Nixon, Rob. *Slow Violence and the Environmentalism of the Poor*. Harvard University Press, 2011.
O'Brien, Gail Williams. *The Color of the Law: Race, Violence, and Justice in the Post–World War II South*. University of North Carolina Press, 1999.
O'Brien, Michael. "C. Vann Woodward and the Burden of Southern Liberalism." *American Historical Review* 78, no. 3 (June 1973): 589–604.
———. *The Idea of the American South, 1920–1941*. Johns Hopkins University Press, 1979.

Olmstead, Alan L., and Paul W. Rhode. "Beef, Veal, Pork, and Lamb—Slaughtering, Production, and Price: 1899–1999." Table Da995-1019 in *Historical Statistics of the United States, Earliest Times to the Present*, edited by Susan B. Carter, Scott Sigmund Carter, et al. Cambridge University Press, 2006.

Onaci, Edward. *Free the Land: The Republic of New Afrika and the Pursuit of a Black Nation-State*. University of North Carolina Press, 2020.

Oshinsky, David M. *Worse Than Slavery: Parchman Farm and the Ordeal of Jim Crow Justice*. Free Press, 1996.

Ownby, Ted, ed. *The Civil Rights Movement in Mississippi*. University Press of Mississippi, 2013.

Padmore, George. *Life and Struggles of Negro Toilers*. Red International Labour Unions Magazine, 1931.

Paik, A. Naomi. *Rightlessness: Testimony and Redress in U.S. Prison Camps since World War II*. University of North Carolina Press, 2016.

Paredes, Américo. *With His Pistol in His Hand: A Border Ballad and Its Hero*. University of Texas Press, 1958.

Payne, Charles M. *I've Got the Light of Freedom: The Organizing Tradition and the Mississippi Freedom Struggle*. University of California Press, 2007 [1995].

Pelot-Hobbs, Lydia. *Prison Capital: Mass Incarceration and Struggles for Abolition Democracy in Louisiana*. University of North Carolina Press, 2023.

Perkinson, Robert. *Texas Tough: The Rise of America's Prison Empire*. Metropolitan Books, 2010.

Pettengill, Sierra, dir. *Riotsville, U.S.A.* Magnolia Pictures, 2022.

Petty, Adrienne Monteith. *Standing Their Ground: Small Farmers in North Carolina since the Civil War*. Oxford University Press, 2013.

Petty, Adrienne Monteith, and Mark R. Schultz. *Breaking New Ground: African American Landownership since the Civil War*. Oxford University Press, forthcoming.

Pigee, Vera. *The Struggle of Struggles*. University Press of Mississippi, 2023 [1975].

Pishko, Jessica. *The Highest Law in the Land: How the Unchecked Power of Sheriffs Threatens Democracy*. Dutton, 2024.

Pliley, Jessica R. *Policing Sexuality: The Mann Act and the Making of the FBI*. Harvard University Press, 2014.

The Police Threat to Political Liberty: Discoveries and Actions of the American Friends Service Committee Program on Government Surveillance and Citizens' Rights. American Friends Service Committee, 1979.

Polyani, Karl. *The Great Transformation: The Political and Economic Origins of Our Time*. Beacon Press, 2001 [1944].

Prifogle, Emily Alise. "Cows, Cars, and Criminals: The Legal Landscape of the Rural Midwest, 1920–1975." PhD dissertation, Princeton University, 2019.

Prince, K. Stephen. *The Ballad of Robert Charles: Race, Violence, and Memory in the Jim Crow South*. University of North Carolina Press, 2016.

Purnell, Brian. *Fighting Jim Crow in the County of Kings: The Congress of Racial Equality in Brooklyn*. University Press of Kentucky, 2013.

Purnell, Brian, and Jeanne Theoharis, eds. *The Strange Careers of the Jim Crow North: Segregation and Struggle outside the South*. New York University Press, 2019.

Randolph, Justin. "The Jim Crow Militia: Paramilitary Police Reform and Law-and-Order Liberalism in Mississippi." *Journal of Southern History* 90, no. 2 (May 2024): 285–324.

Ransby, Barbara. *Ella Baker and the Black Freedom Movement: A Radical Democratic Vision*. University of North Carolina Press, 2003.

Ravitch, Diane, ed. *The American Reader: Words That Moved a Nation*. HarperCollins, 1990.

Ray, Gerda W. "From Cossack to Trooper: Manliness, Police Reform, and the State." *Journal of Social History* 28, no. 3 (April 1, 1995): 565–86.

Reid, Debra A., and Evan P. Bennett, eds. *Beyond Forty Acres and a Mule: African American Landowning Families since Reconstruction*. University Press of Florida, 2012.

Richter, Daniel K. *Facing East from Indian Country: A Native History of Early America*. Harvard University Press, 2001.

Roane, J. T. "Plotting the Black Commons." *Souls* 20, no. 3 (2018): 239–66.

Roberts, Dorothy. *Killing the Black Body: Race, Reproduction, and the Meaning of Liberty*. Vintage, 1997.

Roberts, Norma J., ed. *Elijah Pierce: Woodcarver*. Columbus Museum of Art, 1992.

Robinson, Cedric J. *Black Marxism: The Making of the Black Radical Tradition*. University of North Carolina Press, 2000.

Rolph, Stephanie. *Resisting Equality: The Citizens' Council, 1954–1989*. Louisiana State University Press, 2018.

Ross, Jim Buck, ed. *History of the Mississippi Beef Cattle Industry*. Mississippi Department of Corrections, 1985.

Rothman, Adam. *Slave Country: American Expansion and the Origins of the Deep South*. Harvard University Press, 2005.

Rousey, Dennis C. *Policing the Southern City: New Orleans, 1805–1889*. Louisiana State University Press, 1996.

Rowe-Sims, Sarah. "The Mississippi State Sovereignty Commission: An Agency History." *Journal of Mississippi History* 61, no. 1 (1999): 29–58.

Royster, Jacqueline Jones, ed. *Southern Horrors and Other Writings*. Bedford Books, 1997.

Rushdy, Ashraf H. A. *American Lynching*. Yale University Press, 2012.

Sanders, Crystal R. *A Chance for Change: Head Start and Mississippi's Black Freedom Struggle*. University of North Carolina Press, 2016.

Saunt, Claudio. *Black, White, and Indian: Race and the Unmaking of an American Family*. Oxford University Press, 2006.

———. "Financing Dispossession: Stocks, Bonds, and the Deportation of Native Peoples in the Antebellum United States." *Journal of American History* 106, no. 2 (September 2019): 315–37.

Saville, Julie. *The Work of Reconstruction: From Slave to Wage Laborer in South Carolina, 1860–1870*. Cambridge University Press, 1994.

Schoenfeld, Heather. *Building the Prison State: Race and the Politics of Mass Incarceration.* University of Chicago Press, 2018.

Schrader, Stuart. *Badges without Borders: How Global Counterinsurgency Transformed American Policing.* University of California Press, 2019.

Schultz, Mark Roman. *The Rural Face of White Supremacy: Beyond Jim Crow.* University of Illinois Press, 2005.

Schwartz, Joanna. *Shielded: How the Police Became Untouchable.* Viking, 2023.

Seeger, Pete, and Bob Reiser. *Everybody Says Freedom: A History of the Civil Rights Movement in Songs and Pictures.* W. W. Norton, 1989.

Seigel, Micol. "Always Already Military: Police, Public Safety, and State Violence." *American Quarterly* 71, no. 2 (June 2019): 519–39.

———. "On the Critique of Paramilitarism." *Global South* 12, no. 2 (October 1, 2018): 166–83.

———. "The Dilemma of 'Racial Profiling': An Abolitionist Police History." *Contemporary Justice Review* 20, no. 4 (October 2017): 474–90.

———. *Violence Work: State Power and the Limits of Police.* Duke University Press, 2018.

Seiler, Cotten. *Republic of Drivers: A Cultural History of Automobility in America.* University of Chicago Press, 2008.

Self, Robert O. *American Babylon: Race and the Struggle for Postwar Oakland.* Princeton University Press, 2003.

Seo, Sarah A. *Policing the Open Road: How Cars Transformed American Freedom.* Harvard University Press, 2019.

Sharpe, Christina. *Monstrous Intimacies: Making Post-Slavery Subjects.* Duke University Press, 2010.

Silver, Carol Ruth. *Freedom Rider Diary: Smuggled Notes from Parchman Prison.* University Press of Mississippi, 2014.

Sinclair, Thornton C. "The Nazi Party Rally at Nuremberg." *Public Opinion Quarterly* 2, no. 4 (October 1938): 570–83.

Singh, Nikhil Pal, ed. *Climbin' Jacob's Ladder: The Black Freedom Movement Writings of Jack O'Dell.* University of California Press, 2010.

———. *Race and America's Long War.* University of California Press, 2017.

———. "The Whiteness of Police." *American Quarterly* 66, no. 4 (December 1, 2014): 1091–99.

Smith, Gordon Burns. *History of the Georgia Militia, 1783–1861.* Boyd Publishing, 2000.

Smith, J. Douglas. *Managing White Supremacy: Race, Politics, and Citizenship in Jim Crow Virginia.* University of North Carolina Press, 2002.

Sojourner, Sue [Lorenzi], with Cheryl Reitan. *Thunder of Freedom: Black Leadership and the Transformation of 1960s Mississippi.* University Press of Kentucky, 2013.

Sorin, Gretchen. *Driving While Black: African American Travel and the Road to Civil Rights.* Liveright, 2020.

Spade, Dean. *Normal Life: Administrative Violence, Critical Trans Politics, and the Limits of Law.* Duke University Press, 2015.

Specht, Joshua. *Red Meat Republic: A Hoof-to-Table History of How Beef Changed America*. Princeton University Press, 2019.

Spofford, Tim. *Lynch Street: The May 1970 Slayings at Jackson State College*. Kent State University Press, 1988.

Stein, David. "Why Coretta Scott King Fought for a Job Guarantee." *Boston Review*, January 12, 2018.

Stewart-Winter, Timothy. "Queer Law and Order: Sex, Criminality, and Policing in the Late Twentieth-Century United States." *Journal of American History* 102, no. 1 (2015): 61–72.

Stoler, Ann Laura. *Duress: Imperial Durabilities in Our Times*. Duke University Press, 2016.

Stoll, Steven. *Ramp Hollow: The Ordeal of Appalachia*. Hill and Wang, 2017.

Strain, Christopher B. "'We Walked Like Men': The Deacons for Defense and Justice." *Louisiana History* 38, no. 1 (1997): 43–62.

Sturkey, William. *Hattiesburg: An American City in Black and White*. Harvard University Press, 2019.

———. "I Want to Become a Part of History: Freedom Summer, Freedom Schools, and the Freedom News in Mississippi." *Journal of African American History* 95, nos. 3-4 (June 2010): 348–68.

Sullivan, Patricia. *Lift Every Voice: The NAACP and the Making of the Civil Rights Movement*. New Press, 2009.

Swanson, Doug J. *Cult of Glory: The Bold and Brutal History of the Texas Rangers*. Viking, 2020.

Taylor, William Banks. *Brokered Justice: Race, Politics, and Mississippi Prisons, 1798–1992*. Ohio State University Press, 1993.

Tell, Dave. *Remembering Emmett Till*. University of Chicago Press, 2019.

Thompson, Heather Ann. "Why Mass Incarceration Matters: Rethinking Crisis, Decline, and Transformation in Postwar American History." *Journal of American History* 97, no. 3 (2010): 703–34.

Till-Mobley, Mamie, and Christopher Benson. *Death of Innocence: The Story of the Hate Crime That Changed America*. Random House, 2003.

Toscano, Alberto. *Late Fascism*. Verso, 2023.

———. "The Long Shadow of Racial Fascism." *Boston Review*, February 20, 2018.

Tracy, Janice Branch. *Mississippi Moonshine Politics: How Bootleggers and the Law Kept a Dry State Soaked*. Arcadia Publishing, 2017.

Treviño, ToniAnn. "Mexican Americans and the War on Narcotics: Racialized Policing Practices and Community Responses in the Postwar Texas Borderlands." PhD dissertation, University of Michigan, 2022.

Trouillot, Michel-Rolph. *Silencing the Past: Power and the Production of History*. Beacon Press, 1995.

Tudor, Margot. *Blue Helmet Bureaucrats: United Nations Peacekeeping and the Reinvention of Colonialism, 1945–1971*. Cambridge University Press, 2023.

Ture, Kwame, and Charles V. Hamilton. *Black Power: The Politics of Liberation*. Random House, 1967.

Tyson, Timothy B. *The Blood of Emmett Till*. Simon & Schuster, 2017.

Umoja, Akinyele Omowale. "1964: The Beginning of the End of Nonviolence in the Mississippi Freedom Movement." *Radical History Review* 85 (2003): 201–26.

———. *We Will Shoot Back: Armed Resistance in the Mississippi Freedom Movement*. New York University Press, 2013.

Umoja, Akinyele, Karin L. Stanford, and Jasmin A. Young, eds. *Black Power Encyclopedia*. Greenwood Press, 2018.

Vogel, Shane. *The Scene of Harlem Cabaret: Race, Sexuality, Performance*. University of Chicago Press, 2009.

Vollmer, August, and Alfred E. Parker. *Crime and the State Police*. University of California Press, 1935.

Walker, Anders. *The Ghost of Jim Crow: How Southern Moderates Used* Brown v. Board of Education *to Stall Civil Rights*. Oxford University Press, 2009.

———. "The Violent Bear It Away: Emmett Till and the Modernization of Law Enforcement in Mississippi." *San Diego Law Review* 46, no. 2 (May 1, 2009): 459–504.

Walker, Pamela N. "'Some Time We Have Trouble in Getting Mail. And Everything Else Here': Black Women, Freedom Food and the US Postal System." *Gender & History* 34, no. 3 (January 1, 2022): 673–89.

Ward, Jason Morgan. *Defending White Democracy: The Making of a Segregationist Movement and the Remaking of Racial Politics, 1936–1965*. University of North Carolina Press, 2011.

———, ed. *Mississippi Black Paper*. University of Mississippi Press, 2017.

Weaver, Vesla M. "Frontlash: Race and the Development of Punitive Crime Policy." *Studies in American Political Development* 21, no. 2 (2007): 230–65.

Webb, Walter Prescott. *The Texas Rangers: A Century of Frontier Defense*. University of Texas Press, 1935.

Weber, Max. "Politics as a Vocation." In *From Max Weber: Essays in Sociology*, translated and edited by H. H. Gerth and Wright Mills. Routledge, 2009 [1921].

Wells-Barnett, Ida B. *Crusade for Justice: The Autobiography of Ida B. Wells*. University of Chicago Press, 1970.

———. *The East St. Louis Massacre: The Greatest Outrage of the Century*. The Negro Fellowship Herald Press, 1917.

———. *The Red Record: Tabulated Statistics and Alleged Causes of Lynching in the United States*. Author, 1895.

Wexler, Laura. *Fire in a Canebreak: The Last Mass Lynching in America*. Scribner, 2003.

Whitfield, Stephen J. *A Death in the Delta: The Story of Emmett Till*. Johns Hopkins University Press, 1991 [1988].

Whitlock, Kay, and Nancy A. Heitzeg. *Carceral Con: The Deceptive Terrain of Criminal Justice Reform*. University of California Press, 2021.

Williams, Robert F. *Negroes with Guns*. Wayne State University Press, 1998 [1962].

Williams, Teona. "For 'Peace, Quiet, and Respect': Race, Policing, and Land Grabbing on Chicago's South Side." *Antipode* 53, no. 2 (March 1, 2021): 497–523.

Winston, Ali, and Darwin BondGraham. *The Riders Come Out at Night: Brutality, Corruption, and Cover-Up in Oakland*. Atria Books, 2023.

Wood, Amy Louise. *Lynching and Spectacle: Witnessing Racial Violence in America, 1890–1940*. University of North Carolina Press, 2011.

Wood, Amy Louise, and Natalie J. Ring, eds. *Crime and Punishment in the Jim Crow South*. University of Illinois Press, 2019.

Wood, Ellen Meiksins. *The Origin of Capitalism: A Longer View*. Verso, 2002.

Woodruff, Nan Elizabeth. *American Congo: The African American Freedom Struggle in the Delta*. Harvard University Press, 2003.

———. "Mississippi Delta Planters and Debates over Mechanization, Labor, and Civil Rights in the 1940s." *Journal of Southern History* 60, no. 2 (May 1994): 263–84.

Woods, Clyde. *Development Arrested: The Blues and Plantation Power in the Mississippi Delta*. Verso, 1998.

Woodson, Carter G. *The Rural Negro*. Association for the Study of Negro Life and History, 1930.

Woodward, C. Vann. *Origins of the New South, 1877–1913*. Louisiana State University Press, 1951.

———. *The Strange Career of Jim Crow*. Oxford University Press, 2006 [1954].

———. "Yes, There Was a Compromise of 1877." *Journal of American History* 60 (June 1973): 215–23.

Yarbrough, Fay A. *Choctaw Confederates: The American Civil War in Indian Country*. University of North Carolina Press, 2021.

Zinn, Howard. *SNCC: The New Abolitionists*. Beacon Press, 1964.

Index

Note: Italic page numbers refer to illustrations.

abolitionist police reform, 151–52, 169, 216, 218
ACLU v. Finch, 207, 209
activism: and caring, 169–70; civil rights movement, 3–4, 58; police reform, 14; of NAACP in Kemper County, 62–64; against rural and farm-based violence, 57–58
Adams, Dora, 201
Agricultural Adjustment Act, 42, 137
Agricultural Stabilization and Conservation Service (ASCS), 138–39
agriculture: agricultural justice, 138; "Balance Agriculture with Industry," 46, 54, 70, 176; cotton industry, shift away from, 137; crop allotments, 138; evictions of Black tenant farmers, 42; farm loans, 139; gardening and food supplies, 85; landownership and segregation, 28, 91–92; tenant farming, 76–77, 79, 85. *See also* rurality; sharecropping
alcohol: illegal production of, 90; legality of, 47–48. *See also* prohibition, alcohol
Alcorn Agricultural and Mechanical College, 84
Allen, George, 27
American Civil Liberties Union (ACLU), 207
American Friends Service Committee (AFSC), 207, 209
Americans for the Preservation of the White Race, 155, 165
Amison, Roosevelt V., 66, 67–69

authoritarianism: carceral space, 125, 176; Highway Patrol, role in, 53; and liberalism, 9; pageantry and spectacle of, 50–51; and protection of prisoners, 41–42; racial, 9, 41, 151, 213
autocracy: and Black agrarian displacement, 111; and incarceration, 125, 174; law enforcement on rural roads, 73; and policing, 10–13; and surveillance, 135; and Texas Rangers, 35
automobility, 7, 37; challenges to in rural settings, 69; driver licensure, 7, 72; road systems, 47, 70

Baker, Ella, 154, 169
"Balance Agriculture with Industry" (Hugh White administration), 54, 70, 176
Banks, Fred L., Jr., 206
Barnett, Ross, 115, 118–20
Basinger, John Lutellas, 125, 126–27, 128, 162, 164
beef industry. *See* cattle industry
Bilbo, Theodore G., 41, 42
Birdsong, Angeline Fox, 31
Birdsong, Thomas Butler, Jr.: chemical weapons, National Guard use of, 42; *COFO v. Rainey*, 155; as commissioner of public safety, 50; and FBI, *163*, 163–64; and Freedom Riders, 119; Gold Coast assignment, 49; Highway Patrol, militarization of, 136; Highway Patrol parades, 50–51, *51*; Highway Patrol preparedness, 133; legacy and impact, 10, 15, *34*, *107*, 214,

Birdsong, Thomas Butler, Jr. (cont.) 215–16; and Livestock Theft Bureau, 87; Mississippi Commission on Law Enforcement, role in, 190; as National Guard commander, 38–39, 41; and Parchman Penitentiary riot, 47; Penitentiary Probation and Parole Board, 107–8; retirement of, 189, 190; and state fairgrounds as stockade, 176; surveillance and counterintelligence activities of, 42–43, 136–37; Texas Rangers, 30–37; Tobe Faulkner incident, 75–76; University of Mississippi desegregation efforts of, 120; white criticism of, 52

Black, Hugo, 68

black-market economies, 47–48

Black Panther Party for Self-Defense, 153

Black populations: Black freedom struggle, 9, 13–14, 66, 182; Black militiamen, 20–21, 27–28; Black mothers, organizing by, 14; in 1890 constitution, 24–26; land ownership of, 12, 79, 84–85; land ownership, loss of, 77, 110–11; racial uplift, 72, 74; refugee camps of evicted farmers, 42; as tenant farmers, 75–76

Black United Front, 174

Booker, Tommy, 71–73, 215

bootlegging, 41–42. *See also* prohibition, alcohol

Brady, Tom P., 185–86

Brown, Benjamin, 11, 191, 195, 209

Brown v. Board of Education (1954), 15, 91, 95, 96, 98, 181

Brown v. Mississippi (1935), 38, 44, 46, 60, 64

Bryant, Carolyn, 105

Buckley, Horace L., 206

Burger, N. R., 185, 188

Burton, Myrtle Green, 195, 199

capitalism: and agriculture, 13; inequality and anti-capitalism, 27; and order, 9, 232n30; racial capitalism, 2, 53–54, 59, 230n7; rural, 105

capital punishment, 38–39, 106; electric chair to gas chamber transition, 109; as "legal lynching," 43; statistics, early twentieth century, 39–40

Carmichael, Stokely, 135, 136, 153, 156, 175

Carr, James Gale, 78–80, 246n12

Carter, William Hodding, III, 165, 166–67, 168

cattle equipment, used on detainees, 134, 175–82

cattle industry, 13, 15, 215; artificial insemination in, 78–79; and beef production, 80–81; cross-border raids of, 36; and enclosure, 58, 86; and law enforcement, 107–8; Mississippi Cattlemen's Association, 83–86; Mississippi Livestock Theft Bureau, 86–93; origin myth of, 88; and prison, 77–83; and rural violence, 75–77; technological innovation in, 79–80; Texas Cattle Raisers Association, 35, 36. *See also* Livestock Theft Bureau

Chaney, Ben, Jr., 158, 160–61, 204

Chaney, Fannie Lee: activism of, 149, 151, 169–70, 223; *COFO v. Rainey*, 154, 158–62; legacy of and family's activism, 216; son's memorial service, 159; surveillance of, 204

Chaney, James Earl, 149–50, 151, 154; memorial service of, 158–59, 159. See also *COFO v. Rainey*

Chaney-Moss, Julia, 169

chemical weapons, 42

Chiang Kai-shek, 10

Chicago Defender, 45–46, 76, 105

Chomsky, Noam, 178

Citizens' Councils, 94–95, 96, 100, 202; archival material, 109–10; *COFO v. Rainey*, 155; in Columbus, MS, 104; intimidation campaigns, 101–2;

Oxford, USA (film), 128; response to Freedom Riders, 118; and surveillance and counterintelligence, 136; and violence in Columbus, MS, 101
Civil Rights Act (1866), 156, 216
Civil Rights Act (1964), 150, 153, 154, 189; Title VII, 196
Civil Rights Congress, 77, 106; *We Charge Genocide*, 75
Clark, Ramsey, 188
Clark, Robert G., Jr., 185
Clegg, Hugh H., 184–85, 186, 188
coat of arms, Mississippi, 29–30, *30*
COFO v. Rainey, 16, 153–58, 216; activism for national audience, 165–66; Fannie Lee Chaney's organizing, 158–62; and grassroots organizing, 156–58
Coleman, James Plemon: archival material, Citizens' Council, 109–10; cattlemen in criminal legal system, 176, 186, 191; as circuit judge, 217; governorship of, 106–8, *107*, 116; loss to Johnson (1963), 128; Mississippi State Sovereignty Commission, 109–10, 133, 204; police expansion under, 116, 215; and white supremacy and segregation, 95, 99, 156, 179–82
colonialism, 7, 11
Colored Farmers' Alliance, 27–28
Communist Party of the United States (CPUSA), 46–47
concentration camps, 176, 177, 178
confessions, coerced, 1, 44, 64, 66
Congress of Racial Equality (CORE), 15, 117–18; Freedom Summer murders, 149–50
convict lease system, 13, 26
Cop City, 220–21
cotton economy: and enslavement, 22–23; failure of, 91; production, 42; shift away from, 76, 137
Council of Federated Organizations (COFO), 124, 142–43, 150; communications intercepted by, 143; Community Centers, 169; Freedom Schools (Mississippi Summer Project), 129–30, 140; Freedom Vote campaign (1963), 128; and Highway Patrol, 140–41; local organization work, 137; Mississippi Freedom Democratic Party (MFDP), 133–34; non-reformist police reform, 152–53. See also *COFO v. Rainey*
counterinsurgency, police-led, 117, 131, 143, 217, 265n6
Cowart, B., 133, 135, 140–46, 216
Cox, W. Harold, 179, 207, 208
Cromwell, Oliver, 27
Crosby, Walter C., 198
Current, Gloster, 100

Davis, Angela, 160, 168
Deacons for Defense, 174, 184
Deanes, Elton Franklin, 94–95, 98, 108, 137–38
death penalty. See capital punishment
Dee, Ruby, 160
de la Beckwith, Byron, 127
Democratic Party, 24, 181
deportation raids, 222. See also immigration
desegregation: and Highway Patrol employment, 198–99; of interstate bus facilities, 12, 117; of law enforcement in Mississippi, 200–201; Little Rock Central High School and, 131; of Mississippi colleges, 181;of public schools, 185; and University of Alabama, 127; and University of Mississippi, 119–22; white resistance to, 9–10, 13, 95–98
Dittmer, John, 176
Doar, John, 120, *121*
Douglas, William O., 68
driver licensure, 7, 72
drugs, wars on, 199–200
Du Bois, W. E. B., 11, 151
due process violations, 68, 222

Eastland, James O., 64, 83, 97, 181, 189
El Indio Ranch, 36
Ellington, Kate, 45
Ellington, Yank, 44–46
enslavement: plantation economies, 29; slave patrols, 9, 21–23
Evers, Medgar, 58, 103, 127, 177
Evers, Myrlie, 177
executions. See capital punishment

Fairly, Kenneth W., 132, 192
Farmer, James, 117–18
Farmers Home Administration (FmHA), 86, 138–39
fascism, 53; racial, 232n30
Faubus, Orville, 128, 131
Faulkner, Tobe, 75–76, 88, 215
Featherston, Winfield Scott, 19–20, 21–23, 24, 28, 89; law enforcement reform, 26–27; Militia Committee, 29
Federal Bureau of Investigation (FBI), 143; and Highway Patrol training, 50; impact of on law enforcement, 3; Mississippi as "Most Law-Abiding State," 157; National Training Academy (Quantico, VA), 185, 220
Federal Housing Administration (FHA), 86
Ferguson, James E., 33–35
Finch, Cliff, 207–8
Finch, James, 207
fishing, illegal, 91
Floyd, George, 218
Freedom of Information Act (1967), 208
Freedom Rides, 117–18
Freedom Summer (1964), 6, 15–16, 117, 129–30; arrests during, 135–36, 136; and organized self-defense, 152–53; murders (see Neshoba County, Mississippi murders)
Freedom Vote campaign (1963), 128
Freeman, Rosemary, 124, 126

gardening and subsistence, 85
Gibbs, Phillip Lafayette, 193–95, 213

Gold Coast (Rankin County, MS), 48
Goodman, Andrew, 149–50, 153. See also COFO v. Rainey
"Goon Squad," 219–20
Gordon, Maggie Lee, 177–78
Gray, Victoria J., 181
Great Depression, 42, 53–54
Green, James Earl, 195–96, 213
Griffith, Virgil Alexis, 38, 44–45
Grupper, Ira, 177
Guyot, Lawrence, 126, 256n44

Hamer, Fannie Lou: activism of, 15, 168, 179, 216; COFO v. Rainey, 154, 156–57; Mississippi Black Paper, 165; in Montgomery County Jail, 12, 123–28; sharecropping and family heritage of, 84–85, 123–24; television appearance of in 1964, 2, 5
Hammond, B. A. "Buff," 202–3
Harbour, Arnold, 59–61, 64
Harpole, Bill, 108–9, 186, 189, 190
Harvey, James "Jimmy," 196
Hayden, Casey, 153
Henry, Aaron E., 95–96, 165, 198
Highway Patrol, 12, 186–87; after Emmett Till's murder, 108–9; biometric data gathered by, 142; budget for policing, 190; Bureau of Identification, 109; civil rights activism, policing of, 116–23, 135–36, 142; collaboration of with Cattlemen's Association, 86–88; and discriminatory hiring, 195–97; expansion of, 69–70, 129–30; investigative functions of, 71; and Jim Crow enforcement, 52; Johnson's ideals of police supremacy, 130–32; KKK surveillance, 143–145; Livestock Theft Bureau, 133; local settings, role in, 69–74; militarization of, 136; Mississippi Burning crisis, 162–63; and Montgomery County Jail, 125–28; and pageantry and spectacle, 50–51; paramilitary police reform,

304 Index

7; rural policing, 137–48; and state highway construction, 47–48; on strict enforcement, 52–54; surveillance and counterintelligence, 136–37, 141–42, 207–8, 258n19; traffic enforcement, 50; training of, 50
Hinds County, MS, 48; Hinds County Jail, 41, 42, 65, 118
Hoover, J. Edgar, 10, 131, 157, *163*, 163–64, 185, 186
Horton, Dolph, 27
Howard, Theodore Roosevelt Mason, 72, 105
Hurley, Ruby, 58, 74, 102

immigration: deportation raids, 222; enforcement of, 218; New South support for, 20, 27; and xenophobia, 25
imperialism, US, 7, 11
incarceration. *See* mass incarceration; prison systems
Indian Removal, 21–22, 29
industrialization, 46
infrastructure, 7, 70; state highways, 47–48. *See also* automobility

Jackson, George, 168
Jackson, MS: Capitol Complex Improvement District, 221; fairgrounds as stockade, 176–79; Freedom Rides in, 118; police brutality in, 177–78
Jackson State College: desegregation of, 193–95; protests at, *194*; shooting (1970), 5, 11, 191, 193, 195, 197, 200, 217
Jim Crow social order: and need for militarized police, 29; overview of, 1–4, 229n3; and police power, 8
Johnson, Bessie, 62–64, *63*
Johnson, Buford, 57, 62–64, *63*
Johnson, June, 124, 126, 165
Johnson, Lyndon B., 162; appointment of James Coleman, 179–81, 217; Civil Rights Act, 150; Commission on Law Enforcement and Administration of Justice, 188; and Fannie Lou Hamer's 1964 TV appearance, 5; Great Society liberalism, 2, 167, 174; Law Enforcement Assistance Administration (LEAA), 10; Office of Law Enforcement Assistance (OLEA), 188; on race riots, 183; Voting Rights Act, 146
Johnson, Paul B., Jr.: "anti-hatred vow" of, 128–29; archived papers of, 135; and "color-blindness," 115–16; on desegregation, 120–21, *121*; gubernatorial campaign (1963) of, 128; Highway Patrol expansion, 129–30, 205, 216; on law and order, 11, 118–19; Mississippi Crime Commission, 182–91; and police supremacy ideals, 130–32, 175, 182; and state police reforms, 163–64
Jones, Lloyd Silas, 191, 209
Judeo-Christian traditions, 187–88

Kappa Alpha fraternity, 185
Katzenbach, Nicholas, 181–82
Kennard, Clyde, 110, 181, 185
Kennedy, John F., 121, 127, 151, 181; Justice Department, 123
Kerner Commission, 188
Killen, Edgar Ray, 150
King, Annie Mae, 177
King, Clennon, 181
King, Martin Luther, Jr., 5, 97, 117, 124, 127, 151, 168, 189, 215
King, Maynard, 164
King, R. Edwin "Ed," 155, 176–77
Kinoy, Arthur, 154–56, 161, 162, 169, 179
Ku Klux Klan, 11, 21, 97, 132, 153–54; alliances with law enforcement, 203; *COFO v. Rainey*, 155; cross burnings, 143–44; police surveillance of, 143–45
Kunstler, William "Bill," 154

labor disputes, 7, 46–47
Lake Erie Chemical Company, 42
land ownership, 79; Black farmers and beef industry, 84–85; Black loss of, 77, 110–12, 247n37

"law-and-order liberalism," 9, 11, 129
Law Enforcement Assistance Administration (LEAA), 10, 175, 189, 197–98, 199–200, 203, 217
lawlessness: affirmation of by federal courts, 11–12; Jim Crow law enforcement as, 6, 11–12, 16, 233n41; white civilian, 31–32, 118, 129, 151
Lawrence, Ken, 207
Lawyers' Committee for Civil Rights under Law, 195, 197–99
Lee, George W., 87, 105
Leflore massacre, 27–28
Leroy Miller v. Marvin Wiggins (1949), 57, 67, 68
Lewis, John, 150–51, 181
liquor sales, 47–48. *See also* prohibition, alcohol
literacy tests for voting, 124, 146. *See also* voting rights and voter intimidation
Little Rock Central High School, 131
livestock investigators, 86–87. *See also* Livestock Theft Bureau
livestock pens, 176. *See also* cattle equipment, used on detainees
Livestock Theft Bureau, 12–13, 86–93, 215; arrest and conviction records, 108
Lost Cause mythology, 29, 185
Lowndes County, MS, 71, 98–99, 125; incarceration trends in, 103–4
lynching: and Ida B. Wells' activism, 20–21; "lynch law," 20, 238n7; legal reform, 39–43; prevention and thwarted attempts, 28; threats of, 1
Lyon, Danny, 122–23, *123*

Mangum, Jerome, 192–93, 196–97, 198, 210, 217
March on Washington for Jobs and Freedom (1963), 150–51, 154
marijuana, 48–49, 200
Marshall, Thurgood, 12, 67, 98
Marx, Charles Alvin, 88–89

mass incarceration, 3–4, 233n43; labor regimes, 26; statewide statistics, 3, 217–18. *See also* prison systems
McGee, Willie, 106–7
McGhee, Ernest, 38–39, 42–43
McLean, George, 78–80
McWilliams, Matt, 57–58, 60–64, 215, 242n14
McWilliams, Nettie, 57–58, 60–64
Melton, Clinton, 87
Meredith, James, 119–22, *121*, 185
Metropolitan AME Church (Harlem), 159–60
Mexico: Mexican Revolution, 33, 35; US-Mexico border, 30–37
Milam, J. W., 105–6
Mileston, MS, 135, *136*
militarized police power, 2, 136. *See also* policing
militia, New South, 19–37; background and overview of, 19–21; Black militiamen, 20–21, 27–28; centralization of militia, 28; 1890 constitution, 24–30; funding structures, 23; militias in early America, 22; as Mississippi National Guard, 23; rangers and slave patrols, 21–23; Texas Rangers at borderlands, 30–37
Miller, Leroy, Jr., 1, 2, 4, 7, 9, 12–13, 65–69, 213
Miller v. Wiggins, 57, 67, 68
Minor, Wilson F. "Bill," 206, 208
Misseduc Foundation, Inc., 165
Mississippi: agricultural statistics, 79; Bureau of Drug Enforcement, 199–200; Bureau of Narcotics, 200; coat of arms, 29–30, *30*; demographics, 4; Department of Public Safety, 8, 26; 1890 constitution of, 8, 24–30; incarceration rates, 217–18; Mississippi Supreme Court, 44; police funding, 221–22; race-neutral politics, failure of, 115–16; state budget for policing, 3, 190–91; state flag, 29; state police force, history of,

10; US Supreme Court, 57; Uniform Controlled Substances Act, 199–200
Mississippi Black Paper, 165–68
Mississippi Burning crisis: impact of, 152–53; overview of murders during, 149–52. *See also* Neshoba County, MS murders
Mississippi Cattlemen's Association, 83–86, 215
Mississippi Committee for Human Relations (MCHR), 200–201
Mississippi Crime Commission, 173, 174–75, 182–91; African American commissioners, 185; Clegg as chairman of, 184–85; educational outreach, 188; ethical and moral foundation of, 187–88; Judeo-Christian traditions, promotion of, 187–88
Mississippi Division of Law Enforcement Assistance (DLEA), 190, 202–3
Mississippi Freedom Democratic Party (MFDP), 133–34, 139, 173; lawsuit, 179; *Newsletter*, 173
Mississippi Highway Safety Patrol. *See* Highway Patrol
Mississippi Law Enforcement Training Academy, 186, 193, 220–21
Mississippi Livestock Theft Bureau. *See* Livestock Theft Bureau
Mississippi Plan (1875), 19–20, 24
"Mississippi Squeeze," 100, 103
Mississippi State College, 78, 80; segregation at Cattlemen's Association Field Day, 83
Mississippi State Fairgrounds: arrest of demonstrators (1965), 173–74
Mississippi State Hospital, Whitfield, 81, 192
Mississippi State Penitentiary, Parchman. *See* Parchman Penitentiary
Mississippi State Sovereignty Commission (MSSC), 16, 109–10, 133, 136, 185, 204–5; lawsuits against, 207; surveillance records, 206–9

Mississippi Surveillance Project (AFSC), 207
Mize, Sidney, 157
mob violence: Mississippi Plan (1875), 19–20; in US-Mexico borderlands, 35. *See also* lynching
Moore, Amzie, 116
Moore, Roy K., 186, 190
Morrow, Willie L. "Huckie," 196–97
Morrow v. Crisler, 197–99
Moses, Robert Parris "Bob," 116–17, 122, 153–55, 165, 167, 254n7
Mulholland, Joan Trumpauer, 118–19
Murphree, Dennis, 40–41, 43

NAACP (National Association for the Advancement of Colored People): activism for police reform, 14; and armed Black self-defense, 184; Atlanta Declaration, 99–100; and banking and financial institutions, 100–101; *Brown v. Mississippi*, 44; classism within, 74; *The Crisis*, 45; in Kemper County, MS, 57, 62; Legal Defense Fund, 12, 98; in Lowndes County, MS, 99–104; in Monroe County, MS, 65; in Noxubee County, MS, 102; rural organizing (1950s), 98–104; underground networks, 74; vulnerability of to intimidation, 101–2
National Advisory Commission on Civil Disorders (Kerner Commission), 188
National Council of Churches, 178, 207
National Guard, 11, 23; and chemical weapons, 42; and executions, 38–43; funding for, 28–29; and Ku Klux Klan violence, 183–84; Riot Division, 49; and US-Mexico borderlands, 33
National Sheriff's Association, 189
National Welfare Rights Organization, 165
Nazi Germany, 176

Neshoba County, MS, murders, 2, 6, 149–50, 153, 216; anniversary march, 170, 173; cover-up of, 164–65. See also *COFO v. Rainey*
New South, 9, 232n33
Nixon, Richard, 183; Scranton Commission, 195, 197; Watergate scandal, 205–6
Nixon, Walter J., Jr., 198
non-reformist police reform, 152, 169
Norse, Glen, 38–39, 237n1

O'Dell, Jack, 160
Office of Law Enforcement Assistance (OLEA), 175, 188, 189
Omnibus Crime Control and Safe Streets Act (1968), 162, 188–89
Operation Wet Blanket, 183–84
Oxford, USA (film), 128

paramilitary policing: capital punishment replacing lynching, 39–40; Highway Safety Patrol, 7; race riots as rationale for expansion of, 183–84; as reform, 2, 230n5. See also policing
Parchman Penitentiary, 1, 26, 66, 80, 118–19; cattle prods in, 175; labor unrest in, 47; Parchman Farm, 4, 31; racial statistics, 89, 90, 103; and beef production, 80–81
pardons for law enforcement, 131–32
Park, Robert W., 174, 177, 219
Parks, Rosa, 97, 106
Partridge, Earle Wayne, 125, 126
Patterson, Joe T., 186
Patterson, Robert Boyd "Tut," 95–98, 100, 106
Peoples, John A., Jr., 185, 188, 195
Percy, Walker, 168
Philippines, US occupation of, 7
Pierce, Elijah, 211–13
Pigee, Vera Mae, 165, 168
plantation economies, 29
Plessy v. Ferguson, 96, 98

poaching, 88–89, 91
police brutality, 72; author's criticism of historiographic framework of, 5; Kemper County, 60–61; and law-and-order liberalism, 9; Leroy Miller's abuse, 65–66; and torture, 11, 44–46, 125, 178–79, 215–16, 219. See also police violence
police expansionism: and accountability, 170; as basis of reform, 3, 7, 8–9, 175, 222; limits of, 14; rejection of, 201–2
police reform: "law and order liberalism," 9; non-reformist reform, 152, 169; paramilitary, 2; veiling, 4–5; white criticism of, 52–54. See also police expansionism
The Police Threat to Political Liberty (AFSC), 209
police violence: concealment of, 5–6; Jackson State College shooting (1970), 5; *Mississippi Black Paper* (COFO), 165–68; Mississippi State Fairgrounds (1965), 173–74; and police brutality, 5. See also police brutality
policing: and autocracy, 10–13; as brutality, 111; centralization of power in, 42, 182; equipment for, 202–3; as Jim Crow enforcement, 152; local police role, 65–69; "police-led counterinsurgency," 117, 131, 143, 217, 265n6; reliance on martial force, 184–85; Riotsville training, 186; and secrecy, 6, 204–10; sheriffs vs. state police power, 186–87; state police, 6, 7, 12. See also paramilitary policing
Ponder, Annell, 12, 124, 125, 126, 153, 165
Porvenir, TX, massacre, 36–37
Price, Cecil Ray, 149–50, 160, 162, 164, 170
prison systems: brutality and torture within, 118–19, 125–26; carceral infrastructure and Freedom Riders,

118; and cattle industry, 77–83; Central Mississippi Correctional Facility, 193; farms in, 108–9; labor unrest, 47; penal farms, 32, 66, 69, 78; prisoner transport, 40–41; prison reform, 8; sexual abuse within, 125–26; shift from cotton to beef production, 80–83; women in, 103–4
prohibition, alcohol, 25, 41–42, 47–48; enforcement of, 52
"public safety," 25–26; as euphemism, 8
Pulliam, John West, 106

Quin, Anthony, 179, *180*

race-blind language, 87–88, 115–16, 128–29, 182
racism: bank loans, 94–95; employment, 46–47; institutional level, 138; racial capitalism, 2, 53–54, 59; racial profiling, 11; racial terrorism, 144; rural land ownership, 139–40; structural, in United States, 4; systemic vs. personal, 64
Rainey, Lawrence A., 153–58
Rancher, Lucinda, 173–74, 264n1
Randolph, A. Philip, 151, 154
Random House (publishing company), 165, 167
Rankin County, MS, 48, 192–93, 218–19; Rankin County Auditorium, 48; Rankin County penal farm, 32
rape accusations against Black men, 1, 31, 40, 42, 45, 65–67
Reader's Digest (magazine), 183
Reconstruction era: analogies to, 151–52; Civil Rights Act (1866), 156, 216; multiracial democracy during, 19, 21
Reddix, Jacob L., 190
Redeemers (Southern Democrats), 29
Red Shirts, 19, 21
Reese, Floyd, 143
refugee camps of evicted Black farmers, 42

Regional Council of Negro Leadership (RCNL), 72
rent, 161
Republican Party, 24, 181
Republic of New Afrika, 204–5
Reuss, Henry S., 146, 147
Reuss, Michael, 145–46
Revolutionary Action Movement, 204
road systems. *See* infrastructure
Roberts, Alton Wayne, 150
Robertson, Rubye, 71–72
Roosevelt, Eleanor, 78
Rosenberg, Ethel, 154
Ross, Jim Buck, 92
rurality: activist farmers and livestock sales, 133–35; agriculture balanced with industry, 46, 54, 70, 176; Black land ownership, 12, 79, 84–85; land-based violence, 57–58; livestock theft, 12–13; local police, role of, 65–69; Mississippi agricultural statistics, 79; NAACP organizing (1950s), 98–104; and paved roads, 70; and policing, overview, 3; prohibition enforcement, 52; racism and land ownership, 139–40; rural policing, 4–6, 69–74, 137–48; sheriffs' role in, 58–64. *See also* agriculture; sharecropping
Rustin, Bayard, 154

Scarbrough, Tom, *107*, 107–8, 133–34, 191
Schulke, Flip, 120, 128
Schwerner, Michael, 149–50, 153, 165. See also *COFO v. Rainey*
Scottsboro, AL, rape case, 45
Scranton Commission (Commission on Campus Unrest), 195, 197
Second Creek War (1836), 21
Second Mississippi Plan (1890), 25
secrecy: declassification of police records, 209; in policing, 204–10
segregation: among beef farmers, 83–84; in landownership, 91–92. *See also* desegregation; racism

self-defense, Black, 21, 27–28, 75–76, 152–53, 174, 178, 184, 214, 265n5
sharecropping, 5, 79, 101, 192, 211; and cattle ranching, 76–77, 81–85; and Fannie Lou Hamer family, 123–24
Shelby County Penal Farm (TN), 77
sheriff, role of, 47–48, 58–64; corruption, 59–60; and LEAA, 202–3
Shumate, John Lloyd, 51
Shumate, Louis Lloyd, 61
Sillers, Walter, Jr., 130
Simone, Nina, 4
Simpson, Euvester, 124, 126
Slaughter, Constance Iona, 191, 193, 195–96, 197–99, 202, 217
slave patrols, 9, 21–23
Smith, Charles, 178
Smith, Lamar, 87, 105
Smith, Lynn P., 147
Smith, Ruby, 201
Southern Christian Leadership Conference (SCLC), 12, 119; Citizenship Schools, 124; Montgomery County Jail incidents (1963), 125–28
Southern Democrats, 29
Southern Regional Council, 200
Southern states: Lost Cause mythology of, 29, 185; New South, 9, 232n33; plantation economies in, 29. *See also* Reconstruction era
Southern Tenant Farmers' Union (STFU), 47
Spanish-American War, 7, 32
Spingarn, Arthur B., 67
Stamps, Billie O., 48–49
states' rights, 29, 68, 130, 146
Steel City Lumber Company, 60, 61
Stennis, John Cornelius, 44, 45, 64, 71, 91, 143
sterilization, forced, 124
Strickland, Joe Ed, 133–34, 143, 146, 147
Stringer, Emmett James, 99, 101–3, 104
Stringer, Flora Ghist, 99, 101, 102

Student Nonviolent Coordinating Committee (SNCC), 15, 116–17, 122–23; March on Washington, 150–51. *See also* Freedom Summer (1964)
Summer, Albioun Fernando, 207–8, 210
Supreme Court. *See* US Supreme Court
surveillance: audio eavesdropping, 143. by Highway Patrol, 131, 136–37, 205. *See also* Citizens' Councils; Mississippi State Sovereignty Commission
Swoope, Walter Ashby, *82*, 82–83

Taylor, Frances, 71
tear gas, 42
tenant farming, 76–77, 79, 85
terror, 72; campaigns against Black activists, 100–101; church and home burnings, 144–45, 147, 148; climate of, 35; in *COFO v. Rainey*, 155; and Jackson police department, 177; racial, 144; sexual terror against women, 118–19
Texas Cattle Raisers Association, 35, 36
Texas Highway Patrol, 36
Texas Rangers, 30–37
Thomas, Anthony, 40
Thompson, Allen, 176
Thompson, Bennie G., 191
Till, Emmett Louis, 2, 15, 69, 87, 95, 133; death of, 105; local responses to death of, 105–11
Tobis, David, 133–34
Tombigbee River Valley, 58, 94, 98, 140
Toole, Cornelius, Sr., 85
torture, 11, 44–46, 125, 178–79, 215–16, 219
Tougaloo College, 176–77, 195
traffic tickets, 5, 52–54
Tri-State Bank (Memphis, TN), 100–101, 102
Trump, Donald, 222

310   Index

Ture, Kwame, 175. *See also* Carmichael, Stokely
Turner, Sally, 73
Twenty-First Amendment, 47–48
287(g) program, 222

United League, 201–2
University of Mississippi: desegregation of, 185; James Meredith's attempts to register in, 119–22; police administration degree program, 189; Supreme Court order to desegregate, 119–20
University of Southern Mississippi, 110, 185
US Department of Agriculture (USDA), 137, 246n15; and farm loans, 139
US-Mexico borderlands, 32–37
US Supreme Court: *Brown v. Board of Education* (1954), 15, 91, 95, 96, 98, 181; *Brown v. Mississippi* (1935), 38, 44, 46, 60, 64; desegregation orders, 119; Leroy Miller case, 68; and police lawlessness, 11–12

vagrancy laws, 23, 66, 103
Valentine, Charlotte, 110, 139, 147–48
Vardaman, James K., 31
Villa, Francisco "Pancho," 33, 36
violence against women: in Montgomery County Jail, 125–26; sexual terror, 118–19; at state fairgrounds, 177
Vivian, C. T., 119
Vollmer, August, 7
Voting Rights Act, 146; Mississippi's efforts to resist, 173
voting rights and voter intimidation, 24, 101, 124, 179; Freedom Summer, 129–30; voter registration drives, 116–17

wage labor, 94
Wallace, George C., 127, 128
Waller, William "Bill," 206
War on Crime, 162, 217
war on drugs, 199–200
Washington, Walter, 185, 188
Watts rebellion, 182–83
We Charge Genocide (Civil Rights Congress), 75
Wells-Barnett, Ida B., 5, 14–15, 19, 20–21, 151, 160, 214
West, James, 124, 125
White, Hugh Lawson: "Balance Agriculture with Industry," 54, 70; and capital punishment, 109; and desegregation, 99; first governorship of, 46–47; and Mississippi Highway Patrol, 50–51, *51*; and Mississippi State Fair, 176; and National Guard Riot Division, 49; white criticism of, 52
whitecapping, 28, 32
White Citizens' Councils. *See* Citizens' Councils
white populations: desegregation, resistance to, 9–10, 13; elite control, 8–9; protection of, 8; and segregated beef farmers, 83–84; social stratification among, 8; on state police power, 52–54; weaponization of whiteness by, 94–95
white supremacy, 185–86; Featherston's defense of, 21–22; legislative protection of, 64; in Mississippi state government, 25; Texas Rangers and autocratic policing as tools of, 35; use of "law and order" to maintain, 9. *See also* Citizens' Councils
Whitfield, Henry, 40
Wilkins, Roy, 102–3, 177, 181
Williams, Franklin H., 67, 69–70, 100
Williams, John Bell, 178, 190, 205–6, 217
Williams, Richard O., 198
Wilson, Woodrow, 9, 33, 35
Winona, MS, 12; Staley's Cafe incident, 125. *See also* Montgomery County Jail

women: miscarriage after police brutality, 177; in prison system, 103–4; organizing for justice, 58, 66–67, 73–74; and self-defense, 21, 174, 178; sexual harassment of, 177, 256n47; violence against, 118–19, 125–26
Woodward, C. Vann, 8

Works Progress Administration (WPA), 78
World War I, 33, 35
Wright, Malcolm, Sr., 69

Younger, Lewis T., Jr., 198

Zinn, Howard, 151, 178, 216

www.ingramcontent.com/pod-product-compliance
Lightning Source LLC
Chambersburg PA
CBHW030128240426
43672CB00005B/71